JUDICIAL AUTHORITY IN EU INTERNAL MARKET LAW

This book examines the role of the European Court of Justice in the regulation of the internal market from a competence perspective. However, rather than focusing on the Court's role in enforcing the limits of EU competence in the EU's political decision making, it explores a related, albeit understudied, question: to what extent does the Court observe the constitutional limits of EU competence and its own institutional powers in the interpretation of EU internal market law laid down in the Treaties? The book provides an answer to this question through the analysis of EU free movement case law in light of the constitutional principles that govern the allocation of competences and powers in the EU: conferral, subsidiarity and proportionality, on the vertical level, and institutional balance, on the horizontal level. Why should the Court be bound by these principles? What do they mean when applied to judicial practice? To what extent are they observed in the free movement case law? The book argues that the Court's observance of the four principles has been inconsistent, thereby creating substantive and constitutional tensions in the EU's relationship with the Member States and upsetting the institutional balance of powers between the EU legislature and judiciary.

Volume 113 in the Series Modern Studies in European Law

Modern Studies in European Law

Recent titles in this series:

Framing Convergence with the Global Legal Order: The EU and the World
Edited by Elaine Fahey

EU Citizenship at the Edges of Freedom of Movement
Katarina Hyltén-Cavallius

The Internal Market 2.0
Edited by Sacha Garben and Inge Govaere

New Directions in European Private Law
Edited by Mateja Durovic and Takis Tridimas

Standing to Enforce European Union Law before National Courts
Hilde Ellingsen

The Relative Authority of Judicial and Extra-Judicial Review: The EU Courts, the Boards of Appeal and the Ombudsman
Michal Krajewski

Responsive Human Rights: Vulnerability and the ECtHR
Corina Heri

The Architecture of Fundamental Rights in the European Union
Šejla Imamovic

The EU and its Member States' Joint Participation in International Agreements
Edited by Nicolas Levrat, Yuliya Kaspiarovich, Christine Kaddous and Ramses A Wessel

The UN Convention on the Rights of Persons with Disabilities and the European Union: The Impact on Law and Governance
Carmine Conte

EU Criminal Law, Second Edition
Valsamis Mitsilegas

The EU as a Global Digital Actor: Institutionalising Global Data Protection, Trade, and Cybersecurity
Elaine Fahey

Exporting the European Convention on Human Rights
Maria-Louiza Deftou

Judicial Authority in EU Internal Market Law: Implications for the Balance of Competences and Powers
Vilija Vėlyvytė

For the complete list of titles in this series
see www.bloomsbury.com/uk/series/modern-studies-in-european-law/

Judicial Authority in EU Internal Market Law

Implications for the Balance of Competences and Powers

Vilija Vėlyvytė

•HART•

OXFORD • LONDON • NEW YORK • NEW DELHI • SYDNEY

HART PUBLISHING

Bloomsbury Publishing Plc

Kemp House, Chawley Park, Cumnor Hill, Oxford, OX2 9PH, UK

1385 Broadway, New York, NY 10018, USA

29 Earlsfort Terrace, Dublin 2, Ireland

HART PUBLISHING, the Hart/Stag logo, BLOOMSBURY and the Diana logo are trademarks of Bloomsbury Publishing Plc

First published in Great Britain 2022

A catalogue record for this book is available from the British Library.

A catalogue record for this book is available from the Library of Congress.

Library of Congress Control Number: 2022941390

ISBN: HB: 978-1-50993-899-5
ePDF: 978-1-50993-901-5
ePub: 978-1-50993-900-8

Typeset by Compuscript Ltd, Shannon

Mamai, kurios meilės dėka esu, kas esu.

ACKNOWLEDGEMENTS

The journey of this book began with my doctoral thesis and ultimately took years of thinking, writing and rewriting, many times over. This would not have been possible without the support of so many people – mentors, colleagues, friends and family – to whom I owe a great deal of gratitude.

I want to thank especially Steve Weatherill for supervising me during my doctorate and later mentoring me throughout the British Academy Postdoctoral Fellowship at the University of Oxford. Thank you, Steve, for your kindness and generosity, as well as your constant support, guidance and patience. Thank you for giving me space to make mistakes and learn from them. Thank you for helping me to find my voice as a scholar.

And thank you to Anne Davies, my very first supervisor and academic mentor at Oxford. Anne, you have taught me key lessons in academic research and writing. Your contribution to my success is invaluable. I am also very grateful to Joseph Weiler for his mentorship during and after my time at NYU. Joseph, thank you for your insights and thoughtful criticism of my work, and, most importantly, for challenging and supporting me in equal measure. Thank you to Vicky Kosta, Tom Adams and Stefan Enchelmaier for valuable feedback on different chapters of the manuscript. Thank you to Catherine Barnard and Derrick Wyatt for examining the thesis that was the basis for this book.

I would also like to thank Weidenfeld Scholarships Programme, Oxford Law Faculty and British Academy for financial backing that enabled me to undertake this project and develop it into a monograph. And thank you to my editor, Sinead Moloney, and her team at Hart Publishing for their hard work during the publication process.

Thank you to Marija, Petra and Lisa for their friendship, humour and support during the writing process. I am also deeply grateful to my husband Ben for his love and support, for creating space for me to write and for taking care of Sofia and me while I was finishing this book pregnant with Elena.

Finally, I want to thank my parents for their unconditional love, for supporting me in the pursuit of my dreams and for instilling in me the values of humility and kindness that continue to guide me in everything I do.

CONTENTS

TABLE OF CASES

Court of Justice of the European Union

General Court

European Court of Human Rights

ILO Committee of Experts

National Courts and Administrative Authorities

TABLE OF NATIONAL CONSTITUTIONS

TABLE OF EU MATERIAL

Treaties

Political Declarations

Legislation

Non-Legislative Acts

TABLE OF INTERNATIONAL TREATIES

Introduction

'There simply is no nucleus of sovereignty that the Member States can invoke, as such, against the Community'.[1]

Koen Lenaerts

The question of EU competence and its limits is central to the functioning of the EU. This book is concerned with whether the Court of Justice of the European Union (CJEU) observes the limits of EU competence in the exercise of EU judicial authority. It focuses on the judicial exercise of the EU's internal market competences, specifically, the interpretation by the Court of the free movement rules laid down in the Treaties. It examines the Court's interpretative practice in light of the principles that govern the allocation of competences and powers in the EU: conferral, subsidiarity and proportionality, on the vertical level; and institutional balance, on the horizontal level. The aim of this book is to determine the extent to which the Court's interpretation of free movement rules has shaped the division of competences between the EU and Member States and the balance of powers between the EU's legislature and judiciary.

This book is part of a larger project, which examines the judicial interpretation of both the free movement and competition rules, as the two major components of EU internal market law, in light of EU competence constraints. The scope of this book does not, however, allow a comprehensive analysis of the legitimacy of EU competition case law to be conducted: this topic deserves a separate volume.

If this book is able to show that the Court's interpretative practice has modified the balance of competences and powers in the EU in contravention of the Treaties, this will affect not only the legitimacy of the Court itself as an institution but also the legitimacy of the EU legal order as a whole. For decades, there has been a growing sense of anxiety in the Member States about the activities of the EU creeping into the domain of national competence. This anxiety has fuelled populist, Euro-sceptic narratives, calling, most famously, to 'take back control' from the bureaucrats of the EU and bring it home to national parliaments. Recent years have also witnessed an increasing tendency among national constitutional judiciaries to challenge and in some cases even reject the authority of EU law on the basis that EU institutions, including the CJEU, are acting *ultra vires*.[2]

[1] K Lenaerts, 'Constitutionalism and the Many Faces of Federalism' (1990) 38 *The American Journal of Comparative Law* 205, 220. On the point that Lenaerts is making, see text to n 4. Koen Lenaerts is the President of the Court of Justice of the European Union and was a Judge of the Court of First Instance of the European Communities when the cited article was published.

[2] See, eg, Danish Supreme Court, Case no 15/2014 *Dansk Industri (DI) acting for Ajos A/S v The estate of A*, Judgment of 6 December 2016, which was a response to the Court's judgment in Case C-441/14 *Danske*

We are at a time in European history when the legitimacy of the EU is, as never before, being constantly questioned and its integrity threatened.

Measures taken by the EU in the regulation of the internal market, as poignantly put by Davies, 'continue to be among the most impactful, politically inflammatory and contentious of all its actions'.[3] As one of the EU's central institutions, the Court plays and important role in the regulation of the internal market. Yet the extent of this role remains not fully understood, particularly as regards its implications for Member State autonomy and EU legitimacy. This book addresses that gap in knowledge by investigating the observance by the Court of EU competence constraints in the interpretation of free movement rules. It thus uncovers the scale of the problem of the EU's creeping competence, demonstrating that it extends way beyond the EU's legislative domain, and offers a more nuanced view of its root causes, implications and potential solutions.

Much has been written about the EU's 'competence creep' in the regulation of the internal market, criticising the extension of EU internal market competences into the areas in which the EU has not been granted explicit competence to act.[4] This problem is most often associated with an expansive use by the EU legislature of Art 114 TFEU – the functionally broad legal basis allowing the adoption of harmonising legislation aimed at 'the establishment and functioning of the internal market'.[5] The Court has on many occasions reviewed the validity of EU action taken on the basis of Art 114 in light of the principles governing the limits of EU competence. It is, however, almost universally agreed that the Court has been far from rigorous in doing so. It has construed Art 114 as providing the EU with a close to general competence to regulate the internal market, despite the judicial rhetoric asserting the contrary.[6] On the premise that EU institutions are entitled to a wide measure of discretion in making complex political, economic and social judgements about the regulation of the internal market, the Court

Industri (CJEU, 19 April 2016), analysed in U Šadl and S Mair, 'Mutual Disempowerment: Case C-441/14 *Dansk Industri, acting on behalf of Ajos A/S v Estate of Karsten Eigil Rasmussen* and Case no. 15/2014 *Dansk Industri (DI) acting for Ajos A/S v The estate left by A*' (2017) 13 *European Constitutional Law Review* 347. See also in chronological order the dialogue between the CJEU and the Italian Constitutional Court: Case C-105/14 *Taricco and Others* EU:C:2015:555 (CJEU, 8 September 2015); Corte Costituzionale, Order 24/2017, 26 January 2017, www.cortecostituzionale.it/documenti/download/doc/recent_judgments/O_24_2017.pdf; Case C-42/17 *Criminal proceedings against M.A.S. and M.B.* EU:C:2017:936 (CJEU, 5 December 2017) (*Taricco II*). More recently, see Case C-493/17 *Weiss and Others* EU:C:2018:1000 (CJEU, 11 December 2018) and a response by the German Federal Constitutional Court in BVerfG, Judgment of 5 May 2020, 2 BvR 859/15.

[3] G Davies, 'The Competence to Create an Internal Market: Conceptual Poverty and Unbalanced Interests' in S Garben and I Govaere (eds), *The Division of Competences between the EU and the Member States: Reflections on the Past, the Present and the Future* (Oxford, Hart Publishing, 2017) 74.

[4] The term 'competence creep' was coined by M Pollack in M Pollack, 'Creeping Competence: The Expanding Agenda of the European Community' (1994) 14 *Journal of Public Policy* 95 and popularised by S Weatherill in S Weatherill, 'Competence Creep and Competence Control' (2004) 23 *Yearbook of European Law* 1. See also S Prechal, 'Competence Creep and General Principles of Law' (2010) 3 *Review of European Administrative Law* 5; S Garben, 'Competence Creep Revisited' (2019) 57 *Journal of Common Market Studies* 205.

[5] Consolidated version of the Treaty on the Functioning of the European Union [2008] OJ C115/47 (TFEU), Art 114.

[6] Case C-376/98 *Germany v Parliament and Council* EU:C:2000:544, [2000] ECR I-8419 (*Tobacco Advertising*), paras 83–84, discussed in D Wyatt, 'Community Competence to Regulate the Internal Market' in M Dougan and S Currie, *Fifty Years of the European Treaties: Looking Back and Thinking Forward* (Oxford, Hart Publishing, 2009).

has taken a highly deferential approach to the review of EU action in this context. As long as the measure in question contributes to the functioning of the internal market, regardless that the main purpose of such measure may be unrelated to the internal market, the EU legislature is deemed to have competence to act.[7] Arguments based on subsidiarity hardly push against this conclusion because the subsidiarity review as such displays a centralisation bias: if EU institutions can show the need for the adoption of an EU-wide standard, subsidiarity is complied with. Proportionality review is equally weak, requiring that EU action be not 'manifestly inappropriate' for achieving the objectives pursued. Considering the generosity of the judicial interpretation of Art 114, it is not at all surprising that the EU's internal market competence has allowed the EU to do many things that, arguably, were not envisaged by the authors of this provision.

The focus of this book is not, however, the (lack of) compliance with the limits of competence in the regulation of the internal market by the EU legislative institutions; nor is it the Court's role in policing those limits. Both questions have already benefited from a fair amount of academic commentary. What has been far less researched, described and analysed is whether the Court itself observes the limits of EU competence and its own institutional powers in the interpretation of the substantive rules of the internal market laid down in the Treaties. That is the question that this book is concerned with. It is an important question to address for two reasons. First, it is because the contours of the EU's internal market are shaped by the judicial interpretation of the rules of the internal market just as much, if not more, as they are by the legislative harmonisation undertaken in the name of the functioning of the internal market. Second, the judicial interpretation of the EU internal market rules has significant implications for the constitutional balance of competences and powers in the EU: both the division of competences between the EU and Member States and the distribution of powers between the EU legislature and judiciary.[8] These implications might be less obvious, or less visible at the outset, than in cases concerning competence disputes directly, yet they are nonetheless significant.

Context and Aims

> The Union shall encourage cooperation between the Member States … and, if necessary, lend support to their action. … Union action shall respect the responsibilities of the Member States for the definition of their health policy and for the organisation and delivery of health services and medical care.[9]

[7] Case C-380/03 *Germany v Parliament* EU:C:2006:772, [2006] ECR I-11573 (*Tobacco Advertising II*), para 39. In that connection, see also ch 2, ss I and VI, demonstrating that a wide interpretation of the scope of Art 114 TFEU and other functionally broad legal bases stems from the Court's wide interpretation of the scope of the fundamental freedoms.

[8] Note that the term 'competences' is used in this book predominantly to refer to the powers conferred upon the EU and those retained by Member States. Accordingly, the term 'powers' is used to describe the respective remits of the EU's institutions, in particular, the legislature and judiciary; however, both terms may be used interchangeably if such use appears suitable in the context concerned.

[9] Art 168(1) and (7) TFEU.

The above is an excerpt from Art 168 TFEU – the Treaty legal basis for EU action in the area of public health. Similar stipulations appear in a number of other sector-specific legal bases of the TFEU. The purpose of these clauses is to protect the autonomy of the Member States to regulate independently certain policy areas that are deemed unsuited, mainly due to their political sensitivity, to be subjected to EU-wide legislation. In practice, however, no policy area can be completely insulated from the EU's influence, for the reach of EU law is wider than its legislative competence. Member States must ensure compliance with EU primary law – internal market law forming its core – even in policy areas that in principle fall outside the EU's legislative competence. This obligation is overseen by the CJEU, which is conferred the exclusive authority to 'ensure that in the interpretation and application of the Treaties the law is observed'.[10]

This situation presupposes a constitutional asymmetry of powers between the EU legislature and judiciary and thereby puts a lot of weight on the Court in driving the process of EU integration.[11] Depending on how broadly the Court interprets the scope of the provisions of the Treaties and, hence, the scope of its own powers, its judgments may have serious implications for the substantive law and policy of the Member States, especially where they interfere with distinctive national preferences and traditions. Moreover, the impact of the Court's judgments often cannot be remedied by EU-level legislative solutions due to, on the one hand, the lack of competence deriving from the EU's legislative institutions (Commission, Council and the Parliament acting together) and, on the other hand, political blockages, even where legislative competence may in principle exist under the functionally broad Treaty bases.[12] The case law thus affects both vertical and horizontal relationships in the EU, involving, respectively, the EU's relationship with the Member States and the Court's relationship with the EU legislature.[13]

This, then, raises an important question. To what extent does and should the Court limit the regulatory autonomy of the Member States in order to ensure the effective operation of the internal market? This book provides an answer to this question through a two-fold inquiry: a comparative analysis of four areas of free movement case law which are generally regarded as sensitive from a national point of view; and the assessment of the legitimacy of that case law in light of the constitutional principles which govern the allocation of competences and powers in the EU and, as the book argues, bind the exercise of EU judicial authority. The said principles are conferral, subsidiarity, proportionality and institutional balance.

Ultimately, the aim of this book is to determine the extent to which the Court's interpretation of free movement rules has shaped the division of competences between the EU and Member States (expressed through the principles of conferral, subsidiarity and proportionality) and the distribution of powers between the EU's legislature and

[10] Consolidated version of the Treaty on European Union [2008] OJ C115/13 (TEU), Art 19(1).

[11] On the asymmetry of powers in the EU, see, eg, J Weiler, 'The Dual Character of Supranationalism' (1981) 1 *Yearbook of European Law* 267; E Stein, 'Lawyers, Judges and the Making of a Transnational Constitution' (1981) 75 *The American Journal of International Law* 1; FW Scharpf, 'Negative and Positive Integration in the Political Economy of European Welfare States' in G Marks et al (eds), *Governance in the European Union* (London, SAGE Publications, 1996).

[12] The specific set-up of EU legislative competences is explained in ch 2, s I.

[13] See, eg, J Snell, 'Who's Got the Power? Free Movement and Allocation of Competences in EC Law' (2003) 22 *Yearbook of European Law* 323.

judiciary (expressed through the principle of institutional balance). In light of this analysis, the book proposes certain interpretative solutions on the part of the Court which would rectify inconsistencies in its case law and the constitutional and institutional imbalances which have resulted therefrom.

In order to fully appreciate the aim of this book, it has to be seen in its wider context. The allocation of competences and powers in the EU, being central to the EU's constitutional architecture, defines the very nature of the EU's legal order, characterised by federal power sharing between the EU and Member States.[14] The principles of conferral, subsidiarity, proportionality and, indirectly, institutional balance represent the criteria on whose basis that power is shared. These principles maintain the balance between the values of unity and diversity in the EU, or, in concrete terms, EU supranationalism, necessary for the achievement of common goals, and respect for the regulatory autonomy of the Member States.[15] If EU decision making was not constrained by these principles, there would be nothing to prevent the EU, as a matter of law, from eroding the autonomy of the Member States.

As the EU's constitutional judiciary, the Court has a key role in preserving the federal balance of competences in the EU. It does so both through exercising competence review of the actions of EU institutions and through the judicial interpretation of the substantive provisions of the Treaties, most notably the rules of the internal market. Therefore, when the judicial interpretation of EU internal market rules overstretches the principles that govern the limits of EU competences and institutional powers, it does not simply compromise the credibility of the Court as the guardian of the rule of law in the EU. It implicates the federal foundations of the EU's legal order. In that respect, the inquiry into the Court's interpretation of free movement law in light of the principles of conferral, subsidiarity, proportionality and institutional balance also illuminates broader questions about the role of the judiciary in shaping the federal nature of the EU's legal order and the legitimacy of such practice.

Methodological Approach

The argument advanced in this book builds on a comparative analysis of the Court's reasoning in cases involving conflicts between, on the one hand, the free movement rules and, on the other hand, domestic regulatory measures and practices underpinned by various social policy considerations. The policy areas selected as case studies for the inquiry are healthcare, education, collective labour law and gambling. Two main reasons justify this choice.

First of all, all of these areas are characterised by a particular *social* sensitivity. They are highly regulated at the national level and have been for a long time in order to ensure

[14] See, eg, DJ Elazar, *Exploring Federalism* (Tuscaloosa, University of Alabama Press, 1987) 12, defining federalism as a system combining self-rule and shared rule.

[15] P Pescatore, 'Foreword' in T Sandalow and E Stein (eds), *Courts and Free Markets: Perspectives from the United States and Europe* (Oxford, Clarendon Press, 1982, vol 1) ix–x, describing the search for unity and respect for the autonomy of the participating entities as the two main prerequisites of federalism.

adequate access to public services (in the healthcare and education sectors) and protect vulnerable societal groups (consumers and employees in the case of gambling and collective labour law, respectively). The social sensitivity of the issues involved presupposes only a limited application of market principles. Whilst the modes and exact levels of regulation differ from one Member State to another, governments generally exercise firm control over the behaviour of market actors operating in these areas. It is, therefore, almost inevitable that subjecting them to the application of internal market rules is likely to create tensions between national governments and the EU.

Second, from the point of view of EU law, the four policy areas are considered as areas of particular *political* and *constitutional* sensitivity. None of them has been harmonised at the EU level, save for the legislation essentially codifying the Court's case law – an issue that is discussed at length in chapter four.[16] In the case of healthcare, education and collective labour law, harmonisation is lacking due predominantly to the absence of an explicit legislative competence conferred upon the EU.[17] In the case of gambling, it is due to political blockages to the exercise of competence, since, unlike in the first three areas under study, the Treaties impose no constraints on the EU's action in the gambling sector.[18] In the absence of any meaningful EU legislative action, the four policy areas come within the purview of EU law mainly through the Court, in the form of a case-by-case review of domestic regulatory measures for compatibility with EU internal market rules.

As shall be demonstrated throughout this book, especially in chapters two and three, the particular political and social sensitivities surrounding selected policy areas also manifest themselves in the governments' submissions to the Court. The arguments that governments put forward to justify regulatory action in these areas typically stem from considerations of social protection and solidarity; tend to emphasise the sensitivity of the sector concerned (be it healthcare, education, labour law or gambling); and highlight the need to protect vulnerable groups. In that connection, one of the objectives of this book is to determine to what extent the Court accommodates the various concerns advanced by national governments and, accordingly, how much space it leaves for domestic regulatory action aimed at addressing those concerns. This requires a two-stage inquiry: a comparative analysis of the Court's reasoning in cases involving the areas under study; and an analysis of the impacts of the case law on the scope of national regulatory autonomy in each of those areas. Ultimately, the comparative analysis of the case law is used as a basis to assess the constitutional legitimacy of the interpretation by the Court of free movement rules in light of the principles that govern the allocation of competences and powers in the EU.

Notably, none of those principles – conferral, subsidiarity, proportionality and institutional balance – is formulated as a hard rule and none provides a straightforward

[16] See, eg, Council Directive 2011/24/EU on the application of patients' rights in cross-border healthcare [2011] OJ L88/45, discussed in this regard in ch 4.

[17] Arts 153(1), 165(1) and 168 TFEU.

[18] See, eg, European Parliament, 'Resolution on online gambling in the internal market' 2011/2084(INI), recitals 11–12, and 'Resolution on online gambling in the internal market' 2012/2322(INI), Preamble. See also P Runner, 'EU Parliament Opposes Creation of Online Gambling Market' (*EUobserver*, 10 March 2009) www.euobserver.com/?aid=27752.

answer as to whether a particular interpretation of free movement law by the Court is legitimate.[19] These principles are typically open-textured and offer room for different interpretations. Considering that, this book critically examines the Court's interpretation of the four principles and proposes how they should be construed in light of their functions and objectives, as laid down in the Treaties, in order to guide the judicial interpretation of free movement law. The normative framework developed in the book can be employed to assess the constitutional legitimacy of the Court's case law in any constitutionally and/or politically sensitive area of EU competence.

The comparative analysis of the case law under study in light of the four constitutional principles helps to expose inconsistencies in the judicial interpretation of free movement law, displaying varying degrees of observance by the Court of the limits of EU competences and institutional powers. The analysis reveals that case law involving the areas of healthcare, education and collective labour law, but not gambling, sits in tension with the principles of conferral, subsidiarity and proportionality – the cornerstones of the vertical division of competences in the EU. Similarly, this case law creates and imbalance in the horizontal distribution of powers between the EU legislature and judiciary, thereby upsetting the principle of institutional balance.

In light of this analysis, this book proposes reform of the Court's interpretative methodology in order to achieve coherence in the case law and rectify the constitutional and institutional imbalances which have resulted from that case law. The proposed reform is based on the reinforcement of the principles of subsidiarity and proportionality into EU-level judicial practice involving the areas of national policy that are in principle excluded by the Treaties from the legislative competence of the EU.

Contribution

This book cuts across three controversial themes in EU law and policy: the role of the Court in the process of European integration; EU competence and its limits; and the problematic intersection between internal market law and national social policy.

The Court has been the centre of both academic praise and criticism since the creation of what was then the European Economic Community. There exists a considerable amount of legal and political science literature that explores questions concerning the place of the Court in the EU's legal order and its role in European integration.[20]

[19] For differences between rules and principles, see RM Dworkin, 'The Model of Rules' (1967) 35 *University of Chicago Law Review* 14.

[20] See, eg, H Rasmussen, *On Law and Policy in the European Court of Justice: A Comparative Study in Judicial Policymaking* (Leiden, Martinus Nijhoff Publishers, 1986); A-M Burley and W Mattli, 'Europe before the Court: A Political Theory of Legal Integration' (1993) 47 *International Organization* 41; Scharpf (n 11); G de Búrca and J Weiler, *The European Court's Political Power* (Oxford, OUP, 2001); A Stone Sweet, *The Judicial Construction of Europe* (Oxford, OUP, 2004); A Arnull, *The European Union and its Court of Justice*, 2nd edn (Oxford, OUP, 2006); K Alter, *The European Court's Political Power: Selected Essays* (Oxford, OUP, 2010); D Sindbjerg Martinsen, *An Ever More Powerful Court? The Political Constraints of Legal Integration in the European Union* (Oxford, OUP, 2015).

On the one hand, the Court has been widely acclaimed for its progressiveness and critical contribution to the process of European integration, especially in developing a number of general principles of EU law,[21] which provided the necessary impetus for further integration at both the judicial and legislative levels.[22] On the other hand, on numerous occasions it has been accused of overstepping the limits of judicial propriety and unduly interfering with the sovereign powers of the Member States.[23] Some of the Court's judgments continue to be labelled as activist,[24] thus suggesting their lack of legitimacy.[25] The debate on the Court remains unsettled. However, for the most part, the persisting academic divide can be explained by the fact that the existing strands of inquiry into the Court are either largely theoretical or based on a selective analysis of the case law.[26]

Questions concerning EU competence and its limits have probably attracted an equal amount of academic attention – the main theme in the literature being the EU's

[21] See especially Case C-26/62 *Van Gend & Loos* EU:C:1963:1, [1963] ECR 1; Case C-6/64 *Costa v ENEL* EU:C:1964:66, [1964] ECR 585; Case C-120/78 *Cassis de Dijon* EU:C:1979:42, [1979] ECR 649; Case C-43/75 *Defrenne* EU:C:1976:56, [1976] ECR 455; Case C-4/73 *Nold* EU:C:1974:51, [1974] ECR 491.

[22] For literature discussing these developments, see T Tridimas, 'The Court of Justice and Judicial Activism' (1996) 21 *European Law Review* 199; A Stone Sweet and JA Caporaso, 'From Free Trade to Supranational Polity: The European Court and Integration' in W Sandholtz and A Stone Sweet, *European Integration and Supranational Governance* (Oxford, OUP, 1998) 64–71; S Weatherill, 'Activism and Restraint in the European Court of Justice' in P Capps, M Evans and S Konstadinidis (eds), *Asserting Jurisdiction: International and European Legal Perspectives* (Oxford, Hart Publishing, 2003); H de Waele and A van der Vleuten, 'Judicial Activism in the European Court of Justice – the Case of LGBT Rights' (2011) 19 *Michigan State International Law Review* 639.

[23] See, eg, Rasmussen (n 20); P Neill, *The European Court of Justice: A Case Study in Judicial Activism* (European Policy Forum 1995); FW Scharpf, 'Community and Autonomy: Multi-Level Policy-Making in the European Union' (1994) 1 *Journal of European Public Policy* 219.

[24] For a valuable collection of contributions unpacking the concept of judicial activism in various contexts, see B de Witte, E Muir and M Dawson (eds), *Judicial Activism at the European Court of Justice* (Cheltenham, Edward Elgar Publishing, 2013).

[25] For early examples, see, eg, *Van Gend & Loos* (n 21); *Cosa v ENEL* (n 21); Case C-11/70 *Internationale Handelsgesellschaft* EU:C:1970:114, [1970] ECR 1125; Joined Cases C-6/90 and C-9/90 *Francovich* EU:C:1991:428, [1991] ECR I-5357. For some recent examples in addition to the case law analysed in this book, see Case C-144/04 *Mangold* EU:C:2005:709, [2005] ECR I-09981; Joined cases C-402/07 and C-432/07 *Sturgeon v Air France SA* EU:C:2009:716, [2009] ECR I-10923; Case C-34/09 *Zambrano* EU:C:2011:124, [2011] ECR I-1177; Case C-399/11 *Melloni* EU:C:2013:107 (ECJ, 26 February 2013); Case C-140/12 *Brey* EU:C:2013:565 (CJEU, 19 September 2013). For a multi-faceted discussion of the legitimacy of CJEU case law, see M Adams et al (eds), *Judging Europe's Judges: The Legitimacy of the Case Law of the European Court of Justice* (Oxford, Hart Publishing, 2013).

[26] For directly opposing accounts, see: Rasmussen (n 20) versus M Cappelletti, 'Is the European Court of Justice "Running Wild"?' (1987) 12 *European Law Review* 3, and J Weiler, 'The Court of Justice on Trial – A Review of Hjalte Rasmussen: On Law and Policy in the European Court of Justice' (1987) 24 *CML Rev* 555; Neill (n 23) versus Tridimas (n 22) and J Temple Lang, 'Has the European Court of Justice Been Involved in "Judicial Legislation"?' (2011) 96 *SvJT* 299 svjt.se/svjt/2011/299; T Hartley, 'The European Court, Judicial Objectivity and the Constitution of the European Union' (1996) 12 *Law Quarterly Review* 95 versus A Arnull, 'The European Court and Judicial Objectivity: A Reply to Professor Hartley' (1996) 112 *Law Quarterly Review* 411; FW Scharpf, 'The European Social Model: Coping with the Challenges of Diversity' (2002) 40 *Journal of Common Market Studies* 645 versus J Baquero Cruz, 'The Socioeconomic Model of the European Union: Stuck with the Status Quo' in G Amato et al (eds), *Génèse et Destinée de la Constitution Européenne – Genesis and Destiny of the European Constitution* (Brussels, Bruylant, 2007), and, more generally, HW Micklitz and B de Witte (eds) *The European Court of Justice and the Autonomy of the Member States* (Cambridge, Intersentia, 2012).

'competence creep'.[27] Whilst the academic commentary on the subject is rich, in so far as it concerns the Court, it focuses, by and large, on its role in enforcing the limits of EU competence in the actions of the EU's political institutions.[28] It rarely questions the observance of competence limits by the Court itself in the exercise of its authority to interpret the Treaties.[29]

This book connects the above two streams of inquiry. It analyses questions of competence, but rather than looking at the Court as a guardian of the limits of EU competence, it views it as an institution that is itself subject to those limits. Specifically, it examines the extent to which the interpretation by the Court of free movement law observes the principles of conferral, subsidiarity and proportionality, which govern the scope and exercise of EU competences, and the principle of institutional balance, which governs the limits of the powers of EU institutions. Whilst the free movement case law, and the judicial exercise of EU internal market competences more generally, has been subject to academic criticism before, this book represents the first comprehensive study that examines that case law from a competence point of view.[30] Doing so challenges the prevailing perception of the Court as a guardian of the rule of law in the EU and demonstrates that in the exercise of its authority to interpret the Treaties the Court strains the principles which underlie the constitutional balance of

[27] On competence creep, see literature in n 4. For books on competence, see R Schütze, *From Dual to Cooperative Federalism: The Changing Structure of European Law* (Oxford, OUP, 2009); L Azoulai (ed), *The Question of Competence in the European Union* (Oxford, OUP, 2014); J Öberg, *Limits to EU Powers: A Case Study of EU Regulatory Criminal Law* (Oxford, Hart Publishing, 2017); Garben and Govaere (n 3).

[28] See, eg, P Craig, '"Competence": Clarity, Conferral, Containment and Consideration' (2004) 29 *European Law Review* 323; G Davies, 'Subsidiarity: the Wrong Idea, in the Wrong Place, at the Wrong Time' (2006) 43 *CML Rev* 6; Wyatt (n 6); S Weatherill, 'The Limits of Legislative Harmonisation Ten Years after *Tobacco Advertising*: How the Court's Case Law Has Become a "Drafting Guide"' (2011) 12 *German Law Journal* 827; P Craig, 'Competence and Member State Autonomy: Causality, Consequence and Legitimacy', in H-W Micklitz and B De Witte (eds), *The European Court of Justice and the Autonomy of the Member States* (Cambridge, Intersentia, 2012); S Garben, 'Confronting the Competence Conundrum: Democratizing the European Union through an Expansion of its Legislative Powers' (2015) 35 *Oxford Journal of Legal Studies* 55; J Öberg, 'The Rise of the Procedural Paradigm: Judicial Review of EU Legislation in Vertical Competence Disputes' (2017) 13 *European Constitutional Law Review* 248; A Woodhouse, 'Process Review as Panacea: A Critique of Process Review Advocacy in the European Union' (2020) 45 *European Law Review* 373. See also the volumes mentioned in note 27.

[29] There are notable exceptions, in particular: T Schilling, 'Subsidiarity as a Rule and a Principle' (1994) 14 *Yearbook of European Law Review* 203; GA Bermann, 'Taking Subsidiarity Seriously: Federalism in the European Community and the United States' (1994) 94 *Columbia Law Review* 331; G de Búrca, 'The Principle of Subsidiarity and the Court of Justice as an Institutional Actor' (1998) 36 *Journal of Common Market Studies* 217; ET Swaine, 'Subsidiarity and Self-Interest: Federalism at the European Court of Justice' (2000) 41 *Harvard International Law Journal* 1; T Horsley, 'Subsidiarity and the European Court of Justice: Missing Pieces in the Subsidiarity Jigsaw?' (2012) 50 *Journal of Common Market Studies* 267; D Wyatt, 'If the Court of Justice Ignores the Principle of Conferral Simply Because It Can, How Do We Fix the Problem?' (14th Jean Monnet Seminar in EU Law, Dubrovnik, 17–23 April 2016) www.biicl.org/event/1124; F de Witte, 'The Constitutional Quality of the Free Movement Provisions: Looking for Context in the Case Law on Article 56 TFEU' (2017) 42 *European Law Review* 313; T Horsley, *The Court of Justice of the European Union as an Institutional Actor: Judicial Lawmaking and its Limits* (Cambridge, CUP, 2018).

[30] For critical accounts on EU internal market case law, see J Mulder, *Social Legitimacy in the Internal Market: A Dialogue of Mutual Responsiveness* (Oxford, Hart Publishing, 2018), discussing the social legitimacy of EU internal market case law; J Zglinski, *Europe's Passive Virtues: Deference to National Authorities in EU Free Movement Law* (Oxford, OUP, 2020), examining the use of margin of appreciation in free movement case law. For a thoughtful study that is thematically closest to the present inquiry, see Horsley (n 29), examining, broadly, the 'internal constitutionality' of EU judicial lawmaking in light of the framework of the Treaties.

competences and powers in the EU. The analysis of the implications of the case law for the balance of competences and powers in the EU demonstrates the extent to which the Court has shaped the federal foundations of the EU's legal order through negative integration. This provides a new and original perspective on the role of the Court in the process of European integration. Moreover, the inquiry helps to uncover the scale of the problem of the EU's creeping competence, showing that this extends way beyond the EU's legislative domain, and contributes to a more nuanced understanding of its root causes, implications and potential solutions.

Certainly, it is an ambitious inquiry. It measures the case law against four constitutional principles – conferral, subsidiarity, proportionality and institutional balance – involving both the vertical division of competences and the horizontal distribution of powers in the EU. This methodological choice is, however, dictated by the central aim of the project, which is to understand fully the implications of the free movement case law for the balance of competences and powers in the EU. As will be demonstrated in this book, especially chapter one, the principles which underpin that balance are interconnected in their respective functions and theoretical underpinnings. Therefore, the assessment of the Court's case law in light of either of these principles individually, without taking into account the wider constitutional context, would tell only an incomplete story.

Similar considerations apply to the case law selected for the analysis. A distinctive feature of this book is that it takes the case law seriously and studies it comprehensively rather than for illustrative purposes. It conducts a systematic, cross-cutting analysis of the judgments involving situations where the free movement rules come into conflict with national social policy. The analysis covers main developments in the case law from the earliest to most recent judgments. This approach makes it possible to capture the evolution of the case law and assess the consistency of the Court's reasoning throughout time and across policy areas of comparable political and social sensitivity. The breadth and detail of the inquiry allows it to expose and consider problems of a constitutional nature, described above, that transcend issues specific to social policy. Accordingly, the findings and propositions advanced in this book are suited to guide the Court's interpretative choices in any constitutionally and/or politically sensitive area of EU action.

The importance of this book lies in that it showcases the unspoken, constitutional implications of the Court's exclusive authority to interpret EU internal market law. Having placed the Court at the centre of supranational decision making involving questions of particular political and social sensitivity, this authority has allowed the Court to shape the balance of competences and powers in the EU. The book demonstrates that the Court has shaped that balance by overstretching the principles of conferral, subsidiarity and proportionality. Doing so has undermined the autonomy of the Member States protected by the vertical division of competences enshrined in the Treaties and has upset the institutional balance of powers between the EU legislature and judiciary, depriving the former of the core of its constitutional prerogatives. This practice not only compromises the legitimacy of the Court as the guardian of the rule of law in the EU, but also implicates the legitimacy of the EU as a supranational polity and threatens to jeopardise the integrity of its legal order.

Structure

The book is organised into five chapters.

Following this Introduction, chapter one, 'An Unfree Court: Constitutional Constraints on the Exercise of EU Judicial Authority', examines the principles governing the allocation of competences and powers in the EU – conferral, subsidiarity, proportionality and institutional balance – in light of a broader discussion of the constitutional constraints that ought to guide the exercise of EU judicial authority. It focuses on three questions the answers to which form the theoretical background for the inquiry conducted in this book. The first question discusses the significance of the four constitutional principles for the EU's federal balance of competences and examines the role of the Court in preserving that balance. The second question considers substantive, or value, constraints that bind the exercise of EU judicial authority. The chapter rejects the idea that non-market, social values are mainly to be protected through the division of competences between the EU and Member States. It argues that the protection of social values is ingrained in the very fabric of the Treaties and, therefore, binds the Court in the interpretation of internal market law independently of its duty to respect national regulatory autonomy. The third, and final, question challenges the conventional perception whereby the principles of conferral, subsidiarity and proportionality apply exclusively to the EU legislative and executive practices, as opposed to its judicial practice. The chapter develops an argument for why these principles should govern the judicial exercise of EU internal market competences – in particular, the interpretation by the Court of free movement law.

Chapter two, 'Free Movement Case Law in Light of the Principle of Conferral', examines the case law under study in light of the principle of conferral. After considering the gap between the theory and practice of the principle of conferral, it proposes how this principle should be construed to guide the judicial interpretation of EU internal market law. Then, it turns to the analysis of the main developments in the case law. It focuses on those aspects of judicial reasoning that have a bearing on the observance by the Court of the principle of conferral, namely, the judicial interpretation of the scope of free movement rules. A comparative analysis of the Court's reasoning reveals that the Court has adopted an expansive reading of the scope of free movement rules, giving little to no consideration to circumstances that would suggest a more conservative interpretation of their scope in the constitutionally sensitive areas of EU competence. This goes to show that the Court has systematically disregarded the requirements of the principle of conferral in the interpretation of EU free movement law.

Chapter three, 'Free Movement Case Law in Light of the Principles of Subsidiarity and Proportionality', examines the case law under study in light of the principles of subsidiarity and proportionality. The chapter begins by considering the meaning and place of the principles of subsidiarity and proportionality in the EU's constitutional structure, focusing on how these principles inform, or should inform, the judicial interpretation of internal market law. Then, it moves to the case law analysis. It examines main developments in the case law, both from a chronological and thematic perspective, involving each of the policy areas under study. The analysis is centred around the Court's approach to national derogations from the free movement rules. This stage of judicial inquiry is what determines the scope of national regulatory autonomy left to the Member States in the area concerned, thereby revealing the extent to which the Court takes account of the principles of subsidiarity and proportionality in the interpretation of free movement rules. A comparative analysis of the Court's reasoning reveals varying degrees of respect for the two principles. Whilst the language of the Court, especially the standard of judicial review, demonstrates a strong and, at times, express commitment to the principles of subsidiarity and proportionality in the context of the regulation of gambling, it does no such thing in the context of the other areas under study. The chapter argues that the discrepancies in the judicial observance of the two principles cannot be justified considering the comparable political and social sensitivity of these areas.

Chapter four, 'The Horizontal Balance of Powers: The Implications of Free Movement Case Law for the Principle of Institutional Balance', examines case law developments in light of the principle of institutional balance, which governs the relationship between the EU legislature and judiciary. The analysis begins with a discussion of the meaning and normative content of this principle, including its relationship with the principle of conferral. This discussion serves as a basis to determine the extent to which the principle of institutional balance allows for judicial lawmaking at the EU level as a legitimate expression of the interpretative authority conferred upon the Court. Against this background, the chapter argues that the case law under study has undermined the institutional balance of powers between the EU legislature and judiciary. It did so by creating an interinstitutional dynamic, best described as 'the judicial trap', which has effectively deprived the EU legislature of its constitutional lawmaking prerogative, thereby minimising its role to the 'legislative legitimisation' of the case law. To illustrate this dynamic, the chapter identifies three models of interaction which have developed between the Court and EU legislature in light of the case law and which have determined the scope of EU-level legislative action in the areas regulated by that case law.

In light of the findings of this book, chapter five, 'Rebalancing the Court, Rebalancing the EU', advances a proposition aimed at reforming the Court's interpretative methodology employed in the free movement case law in order to ameliorate the tensions created by the case law and restore the balance of competences and powers within the EU. It proposes that the principles of subsidiarity and proportionality should be reinforced into EU-level judicial practice concerning the areas of national policy which are in principle excluded by the Treaties from the legislative competence of the EU. In practice, this would require the Court to employ, in relation to those areas, a set of techniques of judicial interpretation – already to be found in the Court's wider case law – that are aimed at relaxing the standard of judicial review. The proposed techniques are the margin of appreciation, the 'fair balance' approach and exemption from the scope of EU law.

The Conclusion summarises the main arguments that have been advanced in this book and discusses the implications of those findings for the integrity of the EU legal order and the future of European integration.

1

An Unfree Court: Constitutional Constraints on the Exercise of EU Judicial Authority

The CJEU does not operate in a vacuum. It derives its powers from the treaties constituting the EU and exercises those powers within the legal framework provided by those treaties. The powers of the Court are laid down in Art 19(1) TEU, which stipulates that the Court 'shall ensure that in the interpretation and application of the Treaties the law is observed'.[1] This provision accords the Court an exclusive authority to interpret EU law – both primary law, including inter alia the rules of the internal market, and secondary law, composed of EU legislative and binding non-legislative measures. Since the Court's authority to interpret EU law includes the interpretation of the Treaties themselves, the Court enjoys a substantial degree of discretion in the exercise of this authority.[2] The discretion it enjoys is not, however, unlimited. The parameters of the Court's authority of interpretation are determined by the wider constitutional framework of the Treaties. This constitutional framework comprises: the values and objectives of the EU;[3] the general principles of EU law developed through the case law, such as supremacy, direct effect and the protection of fundamental rights;[4] and the constitutional principles enshrined in the Treaties which govern the allocation of competences and powers in the EU. The latter category forms the focus of this book.

The principles that govern EU competences and powers are best considered in two dimensions. The vertical dimension, expressed predominantly through the principles of conferral, subsidiarity and proportionality, concerns the division of competences between the EU and Member States. The horizontal dimension, embodied in the principle of institutional balance, governs the distribution of powers among the EU's principal institutions – the legislature, executive and judiciary. Given their central role

[1] Consolidated version of the Treaty on European Union [2008] OJ C115/13 (TEU), Art 19(1).

[2] Exploring this topic, see, eg, K Lenaerts, 'The Court's Outer and Inner Selves: Exploring the External and Internal Legitimacy of the European Court of Justice' in M Adams et al (eds), *Judging Europe's Judges: The Legitimacy of the Case Law of the European Court of Justice* (Oxford, Hart Publishing, 2013) 13–18.

[3] Arts 2 and 3 TEU, accordingly.

[4] Notably, EU fundamental rights are now codified in the Charter of Fundamental Rights of the European Union [2000] OJ C364/1 (CFR).

in structuring the scope and exercise of EU competences and powers, these principles form part of the category of what Von Bogdandy describes as the founding, or structuring, principles of EU law. These are the principles that express 'an overarching normative frame of reference' for all primary law and the whole of the EU's legal order.[5] They are constitutional by nature and, as such, determine the legitimatory basis for the exercise of public authority on behalf of the EU.[6]

This book analyses the said constitutional principles – conferral, subsidiarity, proportionality and institutional balance – for three interrelated purposes. First, it aims to determine how these principles inform, or should inform, the judicial interpretation of EU free movement law. Second, it employs these principles to assess the constitutional legitimacy of the Court's free movement case law in four areas of national policy. Third, it utilises them as a conceptual and legal basis for the proposition to reform the Court's methodology of legal reasoning in cases involving the intersection between the free movement law and areas of national policy that are constitutionally sensitive from an EU law point of view.

This chapter is a background chapter. It focuses on the importance of the four principles in the EU's legal order and reasons why these principles should apply to EU judicial practice. More generally, it considers the meaning of the allocation of competences and powers in the EU in the broader context of the constitutional constraints that bind, or ought to bind, the exercise of EU judicial authority. The chapter thus provides a theoretical basis for the overall analysis conducted in this book. It follows in four sections.

Section I, concerned with the structural constraints on EU judicial authority, opens with a discussion of the significance of the principles of conferral, subsidiarity, proportionality and institutional balance for the EU's constitutional structure – specifically, the EU's federal balance of competences – and examines the Court's role in preserving that structure. Section II considers the substantive, or value, constraints that are meant to guide the exercise of EU judicial authority. It rejects the view that the protection of non-economic values is secondary to the economic objectives of the internal market and should be mainly achieved through the division of competences between the EU and Member States. It argues that the protection of those values is ingrained in the very fabric of the Treaties and, therefore, binds the judicial interpretation of internal market law independently of the Court's duty to respect national regulatory autonomy. Section III challenges the conventional perception whereby the principles that govern the vertical division of competences in the EU – conferral, subsidiarity and proportionality – apply exclusively to the EU's legislative and executive practices, as opposed to its judicial practices. It presents an argument for why these principles should bind the judicial exercise of EU internal market competences – in particular, the interpretation by the Court of the free movement rules enshrined in the Treaties. Section IV concludes.

[5] A von Bogdandy, 'Founding Principles' in A von Bogdandy and J Bast (eds), *Principles of European Constitutional Law* (2nd edn, Oxford, Hart Publishing, 2009) 21.

[6] See Von Bogdandy (n 5) ch 1, describing the legitimising function of the founding principles of EU law, including, inter alia, democracy, rule of law and fundamental rights.

I. Structural Constraints: The Allocation of Competences and Powers in the EU

As set out in the Introduction, the central theme of this book is the assessment of the exercise of EU judicial authority in the area of the internal market – in particular, the free movement law – for compliance with EU competence constraints; that is, in light of the constitutional principles that govern the allocation of competences and powers in the EU. Does the Court observe these principles in the judicial exercise of EU internal market competences? Specifically, does it engage with them in the interpretation of free movement law? Should it? If so, how and to what extent? These questions will be examined at various places throughout the book. However, two important points need to be addressed at the outset: why these principles and why apply them to the Court? Accordingly, the first step is to explain the focus on the four principles – conferral, subsidiarity, proportionality and institutional balance – as a benchmark to measure the legitimacy of the exercise of judicial authority at the EU level. This is dealt with in the following discussion, which considers the significance of these principles for the EU's constitutional structure, specifically, the EU's federal balance of competences, and examines the role of the Court in preserving that structure. The second step, then, is to challenge the conventional wisdom whereby the principles governing the division of competences between the EU and Member States apply exclusively to the exercise of the EU's legislative and executive powers, as opposed to its judicial powers. This point is addressed in the last section of this chapter.

A. The Federal Nature of the EU's Legal Order, and the Balance of Competences and Powers in the EU

The use of the term 'federation' is highly contested in the context of the EU, for a federation is normally associated with the quality of having a statehood.[7] Yet few would disagree that the EU is in principle structured as a federal system, where power is shared among different levels of government.[8] The reason behind such power sharing in federal systems, including the EU, lies in the double telos, or dual raison d'être, of such systems: the desire to achieve certain common goals whilst at the same time maintaining the autonomy of the constituent States.[9] Accordingly, the exact criteria on whose basis power is shared – or, in Elazar's terms, the balance between 'self-rule' and 'shared rule' – form the central question of federal governance.[10] If the power balance shifts to the

[7] For an overview of the debate on the matter, see SR Larsen, *The Constitutional Theory of the Federation and the European Union* (Oxford, OUP, 2021) 11–14, in her book defending the view that the EU is a federation. See also R Schütze, *From Dual to Cooperative Federalism: The Changing Structure of European Law* (Oxford, OUP, 2009) 14–74.

[8] On this point, see M Stuart, 'Problems of the European Community: Transatlantic Parallels' (1987) 36 *The International and Comparative Law Quarterly* 183, 185.

[9] Larsen (n 7) 105, referring to a 'double telos' behind federal constitutions: the wish to live together without being one.

[10] DJ Elazar, *Exploring Federalism* (Tuscaloosa, University of Alabama Press, 1987) 12, defining federalism as a system combining self-rule and shared rule.

side of self-rule by the constituent States, the ability of the central authority to achieve common goals may be hindered. By the same token, if the balance shifts towards shared rule, or the centre, the autonomy of the constituent States will be eroded.

The balance between the central authority of the EU and the autonomy of the Member States is the cornerstone of the EU's constitutional structure. The EU possesses significant supranational power, which allows it to achieve the aims it was created for – in the broadest terms, 'to promote peace, its values and the well-being of its peoples' through the means of economic and political integration.[11] However, that power sits in tension with the desire of the Member States to maintain their independence and autonomous self-regulation. The balance between the two – supranationalism and autonomy, or unity and diversity[12] – is preserved by the principles that govern the allocation of competences and powers in the EU. On the vertical level, these are the principles of conferral, subsidiarity and proportionality; on the horizontal level, this is the principle of institutional balance.[13]

The principle of conferral delineates the outer boundaries of EU competence and could, therefore, be considered the central principle underlying the federal balance of competences in the EU. Spelled out in Art 5(2) TEU, conferral requires that the Union act only within the limits of the competences conferred upon it by the Member States and 'competences not conferred upon the Union in the Treaties remain with the Member States'. Arts 2–6 TFEU list the areas of competence conferred upon the EU, dividing them into three categories: the EU's exclusive competences, which preclude any action by the Member States; competences shared with the Member States; and the EU's supplementary competences. Whilst in relation to competences that are shared between the EU and Member States the EU has the power to adopt measures that pre-empt and supersede Member State legislation, the EU's powers in relation to the areas falling within its supplementary competences exclude any harmonisation of national laws and are limited to carrying out actions to 'support, coordinate or supplement the actions of the Member States, without thereby superseding their competence in these areas'.[14] This suggests that the prohibition embodied in the principle of conferral precluding interference by the EU with the competences reserved to the Member States effectively extends to the areas falling within the category of the EU's supplementary competences.

The formulation of the principle of conferral in the Treaties resembles the American constitutional doctrine of enumerated powers, which maintains that the federal government has no general powers and possesses only those powers that are granted to it by the constitution.[15] The doctrine of enumerated powers – and, seemingly, the principle of

[11] Art 3 TEU.

[12] P Pescatore, 'Foreword' in T Sandalow and E Stein (eds), *Courts and Free Markets: Perspectives from the United States and Europe* (Oxford, Clarendon Press, 1982, vol 1) ix–x, describing the search for unity and respect for the autonomy of the participating entities as the two main prerequisites of federalism.

[13] There exist other principles which affect but are not central to the distribution of competences in the EU, most notably, the principle of sincere cooperation (Art 4(3) TEU) and respect for national identities (Art 4(2) TEU). The former principle is beyond the scope of this book and the latter will be briefly discussed in s II of this chapter and later in ch 5.

[14] For a more detailed discussion of the categories of EU competences, see ch 2, s I.

[15] CH Johnson, 'The Dubious Enumerated Power Doctrine' (2005) 22 *Constitutional Commentary* 25, scholarship.law.umn.edu/concomm/104.

conferral – appear to embody the ideals of dual, or 'layer cake', federalism, whereby the central authority and the constituent units are considered co-equals, their powers are clearly separated, and interference by one level with the powers of the other is excluded. Even in the context of competences that are, technically, shared between the EU and Member States, Member States can exercise those competences only to the extent that the EU has chosen not to do so. Any action at the level of the EU automatically pre-empts corresponding action at the level of the Member States. In that sense, the competences of the Member States and the EU remain separated.

However, just like the doctrines of enumerated powers and dual federalism, the principle of conferral is much more elastic than constitutional theory might suggest.[16] In practice, it allows an overlap between competences conferred upon the EU and those reserved to the Member States. The elasticity associated with the principle of conferral can be attributed to two factors. On the one hand, it seems to be mandated by the language of the Treaties. The Treaties phrase very broadly both the substantive rules of the internal market and the functionally broad legal bases allowing EU legislative action in the area of the internal market – Art 114 TFEU being a prominent example.[17] This makes it difficult to identify the exact boundaries of the EU's internal market competence. On the other hand, conferral's elasticity stems from the judicial interpretation of this principle in light of the conception of the EU as a functional entity.[18] As will be discussed in detail in chapter two, the Court takes the view whereby the EU can legitimately interfere with competences that are in principle reserved to the Member States, such as healthcare, education and collective labour law, which are under study here, provided that such interference results from the exercise – legislative or judicial – of the competences which have been conferred upon the EU.[19] This suggests a very broad interpretation of the scope of the EU's exclusive and shared competences and presupposes a wide reach of EU action undertaken in the pursuit of the objectives of the internal market.

The conception of the principle of conferral advanced by the Court and in part supported by the language of the Treaties brings the EU's federal structure closer to what has come to be known as cooperative, or 'marble cake', federalism in the US federal constitutional practice. The main characteristic of cooperative federalism is the absence of a rigid delineation of authority among the federal and State levels of government, grounded in the conviction that interaction between the two levels is both inevitable and necessary in order to achieve common objectives.[20] The elasticity inherent in the

[16] On the inadequacy of the doctrine of enumerated powers and the theory of dual federalism to explain the American constitutional practice, see, eg, ES Corwin, 'The Passing of Dual Federalism' (1950) 36 *Virginia Law Review* 1.

[17] Consolidated version of the Treaty on the Functioning of the European Union [2008] OJ C115/47 (TFEU), Art 114, briefly discussed further in this section. See also Art 352 TFEU, discussed in detail together with other functionally broad legal bases in ch 2, s I.

[18] On the EU as a functional entity, see L Azoulai, 'Introduction' in L Azoulai (ed), *The Question of Competence in the European Union* (Oxford, OUP, 2014) 6–7. For a landmark judgment rejecting the enumerated powers doctrine in the context of Community foreign affairs, see Case C-22/70 *Commission v Council (ERTA)* [1971] ECR 263.

[19] See ch 2, s I for a detailed discussion.

[20] JD Donahue, *Disunited States* (New York, Basic Books, 1997) 27. The concept of 'cooperative federalism' was developed by Daniel Elazar in his PhD thesis, published in D Elazar, *The American Partnership: Intergovernmental Co-operation in the Nineteenth-Century United States* (Chicago, University of Chicago Press, 1962).

EU's principle of conferral is indeed desirable from the perspective of an effective resolution of common problems at the EU level. However, the same elasticity also threatens to undermine conferral's ability to protect the autonomy of the Member States from being eroded by EU action, thus putting into question the constitutional raison d'être of this principle. In light of these concerns, this book argues that if the principle of conferral is to have a meaningful normative function, there needs to be a limit to how far the exercise of the EU's internal market competences can legitimately encroach into the areas of national competence that would otherwise be exempted from any binding interference on behalf of the EU. This question is dealt with in chapter two, which examines the existing gap between the theory and practice of the principle of conferral in the EU's constitutional doctrine and demonstrates through a comparative case law analysis the substantive and constitutional tensions that the judicial interpretation of the principle of conferral creates in the context of EU free movement law.

The principle of subsidiarity, enshrined in Art 5(3) TEU, preserves the EU's federal balance through structuring the exercise of competences that are conferred upon the EU. It concerns those EU competences that are shared with the Member States, covering policy areas whose regulation constitutes a common responsibility of the EU and national authorities.[21] As in this context 'both levels, the national and the supranational, have equal possibilities of action',[22] subsidiarity determines under what conditions and to what extent the competence concerned should be exercised by the EU rather than the Member States. It authorises intervention by the EU 'only if and insofar as' the objectives of an action cannot be sufficiently achieved by the Member States but can be better achieved at Union level, 'by reason of the scale and effects of the proposed action'.[23] In that sense, subsidiarity prioritises policy decisions to be taken at the level of the Member States, or 'as closely as possible to the citizen',[24] unless efficiency considerations suggest otherwise.[25] Subsidiarity's preference for decentralised decision making is grounded in the values of democracy and diversity. Such decision making increases the opportunities for individual participation and is subject to greater democratic control.[26] Accordingly, it is more likely to produce rules that are tailored to local needs and preferences and better reflect the interests of the different national *demoi*. However, if decentralised decision making hinders the EU's ability to address collective problems, it has to give way to centralised action at the level of the EU.

From this we can infer both a centralising and decentralising function of the principle of subsidiarity. Subsidiarity encourages the EU to act in the name of all the Member States where they need help, yet it also discourages the EU from taking over those

[21] Donahue (n 20) 248, referring to Commission, *Towards Sustainability: A European Community Programme of Policy and Action in Relation to the Environment and Sustainable Development* [1993] OJ C138/5, ch 8, linking the principle of subsidiarity with the idea of 'shared responsibility'.

[22] S Cassese, 'Ruling Indirectly: Judicial Subsidiarity in the ECtHR' (Seminar 'Subsidiarity: A Double Sided Coin?', Strasbourg, 30 January 2015) 6, 10 www.echr.coe.int/Documents/Speech_20150130_Seminar_Cassese_ENG.pdf.

[23] Art 5(3) TEU.

[24] Preamble to TEU and Arts 1 and 10(3) TEU.

[25] To that effect, see Preamble to TEU, containing a reference to subsidiarity requiring decisions to be taken 'as closely as possible to the citizen'.

[26] ET Swaine, 'Subsidiarity and Self-Interest: Federalism at the European Court of Justice' (2000) 41 *Harvard International Law Journal* 1, 54, discussing the democratic qualities of subsidiarity.

tasks which can be appropriately carried out at the local level.[27] As such, subsidiarity embodies and attempts to reconcile the two ideals of federalism that are in constant tension with one another: the search for unity, on the one hand, and the respect for the autonomy of the participating States, on the other. The real question – one that is key to understanding the role of subsidiarity in the EU's constitutional order – is whether, and if so to what extent, subsidiarity can effectively reconcile the competing ideals of federalism in practice. This question is examined in chapter three, which argues that the reading of the principle of subsidiarity employed by the Court in the context of EU internal market law displays a centralisation bias, thereby compromising the very rationale and objectives of this principle.

Unlike subsidiarity, the principle of proportionality applies to the exercise of all of the EU's competences, including the exclusive ones, and controls the intensity of EU action. A principle of constitutional and administrative law, proportionality is generally designed to protect the individual from an excessive use of public authority. Whilst not associated with federalism specifically, proportionality has been accorded by the Treaties an important role in safeguarding the EU's balance of competences. Laid down in Art 5(4) TEU, it stipulates that the content and form of Union action must not go beyond what is necessary to achieve the objectives of the Treaty.[28] Viewed in relation to subsidiarity, it offers an additional assurance to the Member States that centralisation at the Union level, where it is mandated by the Treaties, will be limited to what is necessary in light of the objectives underlying EU policies. Proportionality's ability to achieve this goal is a separate question and depends on how seriously EU institutions are prepared to consider the impact of EU action – whether legislative, administrative or judicial – on the various (non-market) interests protected by national regulatory policies. Proportionality would require that the EU balance the pursuit of the objectives of the internal market against the protection of these various interests. The extent to which the Court does so in the interpretation of EU free movement law is discussed in chapter three.

Unlike the principles of conferral, subsidiarity and proportionality, the principle of institutional balance is not per se concerned with the division of competences between the EU and Member States. Its purpose is slightly different. Institutional balance governs the horizontal distribution of powers among the institutions of the EU. Enshrined in Art 13 TEU, it requires that EU institutions act within the scope of the powers conferred upon them by the Treaties and not encroach on the powers assigned to other institutions.

As will be discussed in chapter four, the principle of institutional balance in essence embodies the precepts of the principle of separation of powers, applicable in national legal orders.[29] However, unlike in the national systems of the separation of powers, the requirement for powers to be distributed at the EU level is not as such aimed at the

[27] Schütze (n 7) 246, describing the positive and negative aspect of subsidiarity. See also V Constantinesco, 'Who's Afraid of Subsidiarity?' (1991) 11 *Yearbook of European Law* 33, 35, describing the 'Janus-like' character of subsidiarity.

[28] Art 5(4) TEU.

[29] J-P Jacqué, 'The Principle of Institutional Balance' (2004) 21 *CML Rev* 383, 384; G Conway, 'Recovering a Separation of Powers in the European Union' (2011) 17 *European Law Journal* 304.

protection of individuals against the abuse of power by the governing institutions.[30] Rather, its specific and primary purpose is to ensure that the balance among the powers of EU institutions established in the Treaties is maintained.[31] Thus, in a real sense, institutional balance protects the limits of the conferral of powers upon the EU institutions. This is an important aspect because if the institutions of the EU do not observe the limits of their powers, the whole of the EU is implicated. In other words, an *ultra vires* act by an institution of the EU will often mean that the EU, as an organisation, is also in *ultra vires* of its competences.[32] In that respect, the principle of institutional balance serves, ultimately, as an indirect safeguard against the EU overstepping its competences and could thus be viewed as a manifestation of the principle of conferral in the horizontal context.

Institutional balance is predominantly discussed in relation to the distribution of powers among the institutions that are involved in the EU's legislative process – the Commission, Council and Parliament. However, this principle also governs the relationship between the EU's legislature (the Commission, Council and Parliament acting together) and judiciary. The latter relationship is what this book is specifically concerned with. In that connection, chapter four examines how the Court's interpretation of free movement law affects the scope of the EU's legislative activity and assesses the legitimacy of those effects in light of the principle of institutional balance.

Taken together, the principles that govern the allocation of competences and powers in the EU – conferral, subsidiarity, proportionality and institutional balance – serve, or at least are meant to serve, as a guarantee for the Member States that they are entitled to a degree of autonomy of action that the EU cannot infringe upon. In that sphere of autonomy, the doctrines of supremacy and direct effect of EU law do not apply, allowing Member States to take whatever action they deem necessary in the pursuit of domestic policies, choose the form and course of such action, or decide not to take any action at all. In the absence of the protection that the four constitutional principles provide for national autonomy, the EU's federalism, as we know it, would collapse. There would be nothing to prevent the EU, as a matter of law, from undermining the right of the Member States to self-rule, at least in some areas, without external interference.[33]

B. The Role of the Court in Preserving the EU's Federal Balance of Competences

As the highest judiciary of the EU, the Court has a central role in preserving the EU's federal balance of competences. It does so in two main ways. On the one hand, it ensures

[30] For the traditional rationale behind the separation of powers, see, eg, J Madison, 'No. 47' in J Madison, A Hamilton and J Jay, *The Federalist Papers* (I Kramnick ed, London, Penguin Books, 1987).

[31] Jacqué (n 29). See also Case C-282/90 *Industrie-en Handelsonderneming Vreugdenhil BV v Commission* [1992] ECR I-1937, paras 20–21. On the link between separation of powers and liberty, see especially Montesquieu, *The Spirit of the Laws* 157 (AM Cohler et al, eds and trans, Cambridge, CUP, 1989).

[32] As illustrated by Case C-70/88 *Parliament v Council* [1990] ECR I-2041, discussed in ch 4, s I. Also see, most recently, BVerfG, Judgment of 5 May 2020, 2 BvR 859/15 (BVerfG, *Weiss*), challenging Case C-493/17 *Weiss and Others* (CJEU, 11 December 2018).

[33] See, eg, Elazar (n 10) 12; EE Osaghae, 'A Reassessment of Federalism as a Degree of Decentralization' (1990) 20 *Publius: The Journal of Federalism* 83, emphasising the importance to federalism of local autonomy.

that the aims of the EU are not compromised by a lack of observance of EU law within and by the Member States. On the other hand, it protects the autonomous self-regulation of the Member States from unwarranted interference by the EU. This dual responsibility resembles the constitutional function of federal supreme courts, which are charged with the responsibility to maintain the supremacy and uniformity of federal law whilst at the same time protecting the constituent units against encroachment by the central authority. However, various studies observe that the jurisprudence of federal supreme courts tends to have a centralisation bias, which leads to a gradual erosion of the autonomy of the constituent units.[34] The centralist bias has also been observed in the case law of the CJEU.[35] Its presence appears evident in cases involving EU competence review, where the Court is asked to assess whether EU institutions, legislative or administrative, have acted in accordance with the principles of conferral, subsidiarity and proportionality.

The Court has faced particular criticism for failing to control the use by the EU legislature of Art 114 TFEU – the internal market legal basis. It has been argued that the Court's interpretation of Art 114 TFEU has endowed the EU with a nearly general competence to regulate the internal market.[36] Indeed, it has allowed the EU to legislate on any issue – health, consumer protection, worker protection, maintenance of public security, amongst others[37] – as long as the legislation in question contributes to the functioning of the internal market.[38] Case law to date suggests that the threshold for what constitutes an adequate contribution to the internal market is low and easily met.[39] In other words, the criteria that determine a measure's compliance with the principle of conferral are easily met. Furthermore, the inquiry into a measure's subsidiarity does not seem to add much to its assessment for compliance with conferral: if EU institutions can show the need for the adoption of an EU-wide standard with reference to the goals

[34] A Bzdera, 'Comparative Analysis of Federal High Courts: A Political Theory of Judicial Review' (1993) 26 *Canadian Journal of Political Science* 3. Identifying similar trends in the European context, M Claes and M de Visser, 'The Court of Justice as a Federal Constitutional Court: A Comparative Perspective' in E Cloots, G De Baere and S Sottiaux (eds), *Federalism in the European Union* (Oxford, Hart Publishing, 2012).

[35] Bzdera (n 34) 13–17. For seminal accounts, see E Stein, 'Lawyers, Judges and the Making of a Transnational Constitution' (1981) 75 *American Journal of International Law* 1; H Rasmussen, *On Law and Policy in the European Court of Justice. A Comparative Study in Judicial Policymaking* (Leiden, Martinus Nijhoff Publishers, 1986).

[36] See, eg, D Wyatt, 'Community Competence to Regulate the Internal Market' in M Dougan and S Currie, *Fifty Years of the European Treaties: Looking Back and Thinking Forward* (Oxford, Hart Publishing, 2009); S Weatherill, 'The Limits of Legislative Harmonisation Ten Years after *Tobacco Advertising*: How the Court's Case Law Has Become a "Drafting Guide"' (2011) 12 *German Law Journal* 827. For a critical analysis of the Court's standard of review of EU actions in light of the principles of conferral, subsidiarity and proportionality, see chs 2 and 3.

[37] See, eg, on public health, Case C-210/03 *Swedish Match* EU:C:2004:802, [2004] ECR I-11893, para 31; on public security, see Case C-482/17 *Czech Republic v Parliament and Council* EU:C:2019:1035 (CJEU, 3 December 2019), para 37. For academic commentary, see B de Witte, 'A Competence to Protect: The Pursuit of Non-Market Aims through Internal Market Legislation' in P Syrpis (ed), *The Judiciary, the Legislature and the EU Internal Market* (Cambridge, CUP, 2011).

[38] Case C-376/98 *Germany v Parliament* EU:C:2000:544, [2000] ECR I-8419 paras 83–84. See also ch 2, ss I and VI, demonstrating that a wide interpretation of the scope of Art 114 TFEU and other functionally broad legal bases stems from the Court's wide interpretation of the scope of the fundamental freedoms.

[39] For a recent analysis, see S Weatherill, 'The Function and Limits of Legislative Harmonization in Making the Internal Market' in R Schütze and T Tridimas (eds), *Oxford Principles of European Law: Volume II* (forthcoming, Oxford, OUP). See also Weatherill (n 36). For an example of a case where sufficient contribution to the functioning of the internal market was not found, see *Germany v Parliament* (n 38).

of the internal market, subsidiarity is complied with. Proportionality review is equally weak, requiring that EU action be not 'manifestly inappropriate' for achieving the objectives pursued.[40] The Court's overall approach to the scope of Art 114 TFEU effectively sanctions the extension of EU internal market competences into the areas in which the EU has not been granted explicit competence to act, thus contributing to the EU's legislative competence creep.[41]

The focus of this book is not, however, the Court's failure to control competence creep in the EU's legislative decision making. This question has already benefited from a fair amount of academic commentary. This book focuses on a related albeit much less researched and analysed question: whether competence creep can also be observed in the judicial interpretation of the Treaties, as opposed to the review of EU legislation in light of those Treaties. Specifically, it seeks to determine whether the interpretation by the Court of the free movement rules laid down in the Treaties overstretches the constitutional principles that govern the limits of EU competences and institutional powers. This is an important question to address for two reasons. First, because the contours of the EU's internal market are shaped by the judicial interpretation of the substantive rules of the internal market just as much, if not more, as they are by the legislative harmonisation undertaken in the name of the functioning of the internal market. Second, the judicial interpretation of these rules has significant implications for the EU's federal balance. These implications might be less obvious, or less visible at the outset, than in cases which concern competence disputes directly, yet they are nonetheless significant.

Admittedly, the assessment of the case law in light of EU competence constraints is not a straightforward task. Showing that one or another judgment departs from one or another principle governing the scope or exercise of the EU's competences is not enough to demonstrate that the Court's interpretation of free movement law does not respect the limits of EU competence. For instance, a judgment may sit in tension with the principle of conferral but show a strong commitment to the principles of subsidiarity and proportionality, thus ultimately ensuring an effective protection of national autonomy. Therefore, in order to determine the extent to which the case law respects the limits of EU competence, that case law has to be assessed in light of all of the three principles. Furthermore, the selection of the case law has to be sufficiently comprehensive to display the existence of a systematic pattern of interpretation that strains said principles. Finally, in order to understand the broader implications of the Court's practice for the overall balance of competences and powers in the EU, which is the ultimate aim of this book, the case law also needs to be examined in light of the principle of institutional balance, which governs the relationship between the Court and EU legislature.

It is also noteworthy that none of the principles governing the allocation of competences and powers in the EU – conferral, subsidiarity, proportionality and institutional

[40] The meaning and judicial interpretation of the principles of conferral, subsidiarity and proportionality are examined in chs 2 and 3.

[41] The term 'competence creep' was coined by M Pollack in M Pollack, 'Creeping Competence: The Expanding Agenda of the European Community' (1994) 14 *Journal of Public Policy* 95, popularised by S Weatherill in S Weatherill, 'Competence Creep and Competence Control' (2004) 23 *Yearbook of European Law* 1. See also S Prechal, 'Competence Creep and General Principles of Law' (2010) 3 *Review of European Administrative Law* 5; S Garben, 'Competence Creep Revisited' (2019) 57 *Journal of Common Market Studies* 205.

balance – is formulated as a hard rule and none provides a straightforward answer as to whether a particular interpretation of free movement law by the Court is legitimate or not.[42] These principles are classically open-textured and offer room for different interpretations, as demonstrated to an extent in the preceding discussion. Considering this, one of the objectives of chapters two to four is to critically examine the interpretation of the four principles adopted by the Court and propose how these principles should be construed in light of their functions and objectives in order to guide the judicial interpretation of free movement law.

This book argues that the way in which the Court has interpreted the principles of conferral, subsidiarity and proportionality displays a centralisation bias and shows insufficient consideration of the concerns relating to the protection of national competence and regulatory autonomy.[43] Moreover, this interpretative position has informed the Court's understanding of the extent to which EU internal market law can legitimately shape the regulatory landscapes of the Member States, which, in turn, has had implications for the balance of competences and powers in the EU. In that connection, chapters two to three demonstrate that the interpretation by the Court of EU free movement rules in all of the areas under study but one has pushed the limits of the EU's internal market to the point of creating tensions in the vertical division of competences between the EU and Member States. Chapter four argues that the case law has created similar tensions in the horizontal distribution of powers between the Court and EU legislature, extending the powers of EU judiciary to the detriment of the EU's legislative prerogative to regulate the internal market. In light of these findings, chapter five proposes certain interpretative solutions on behalf of the Court that would address the constitutional tensions created by the case law and rectify the ensuing imbalances in the distribution of competences and powers in the EU.

C. The Consequences of the Federal Imbalance of Competences

When the Court's interpretation of the Treaties overstretches the constitutional principles which underpin the EU's federal balance of competences, this does not simply compromise the legitimacy of the Court as an institution. It has consequences for the whole of the EU.

First, there are democratic consequences. In the case of EU legislative competence creep, these consequences stem from the fact that a non-democratic legislature of the EU encroaches on democratic decision making in the Member States in the absence of a sophisticated constitutional mandate. In other words, since the EU legislature does not have the democratic credentials comparable to those of national legislatures, a competence creep on its part becomes not only a constitutional problem, but also a democratic problem.[44] By contrast, when competence creep is attributed to the judicial

[42] For differences between rules and principles, see RM Dworkin, 'The Model of Rules' (1967) 35 *University of Chicago Law Review* 14, describing principles as standards which must be taken into account, where relevant, as a consideration inclining in a certain direction, as opposed to rules, which apply in all-or-nothing fashion.

[43] See especially ch 2, ss I and VI, and ch 3, ss I and VI.

[44] See s III of this chapter for a discussion of the 'democratic deficit' of the EU.

interpretation of the Treaties, namely the substantive rules of the internal market, the concern is not simply about the Court being undemocratic – after all, courts are not expected to be democratic. Rather, it is about the capacity of the Court's judgments to penetrate the domain of democratic decision making at the level of the Member States. This can be explained as follows. The mandate of the Court to interpret the rules of the internal market, both free movement and competition rules, allows it to regulate a broad range of economic and social relations, arguably stretching beyond the relationships that are normally subject to constitutional interpretation in a State setting.[45] Accordingly, the Court's interpretative practice in the area of the internal market is bound to have regulatory and policy implications in the Member States, shaping the contours of public regulatory systems.[46] By the same token, it is also bound to narrow down the space for political decision making at the national level, as the rules developed in the case law replace national rules adopted through democratic decision-making processes.[47]

In principle, the implications of the case law for democratic decision making are a legitimate consequence of the judicial interpretation of the Treaties and not in themselves a problem for democracy. However, they become a problem if the Court's interpretation of free movement pushes the limits of EU internal market competence to the point of creating tensions with the constitutional principles that govern the scope and exercise of that competence. In that situation, the Court's interference with national regulatory autonomy reaches further than is justified by the Treaties, and so does its interference with decision making via national democratic processes. By overstretching the scope of EU internal market competence, the Court places itself in a position which allows it to influence – at times, even determine – government decisions on highly sensitive, socio-economic issues at the core of national public policy, such as, in the context of this study, the financing of public healthcare systems, access to higher education and collective regulation of labour and employment.[48] This judicial practice creates problems for democracy not only at the level of the Member States but also at the level of the EU. It deprives the EU legislature of the opportunity to address the issues concerned through the EU's political decision-making process. This process may not be perfectly democratic, but it nonetheless involves the participation of national governments (through the Council) and EU citizens (through the Parliament), thereby ensuring the representation and deliberation of different interests.[49] By foreclosing opportunities for political deliberation both at the EU and Member State level, the Court threatens to compromise the already fragile democratic legitimacy of the EU.

Furthermore, the failure on behalf of the Court to preserve the limits of EU competence – in fact, even a perception of such failure – threatens the supremacy and integrity of EU law. The past several decades have witnessed a growing tendency among national constitutional courts to question the authority of EU law and institutions – the Court

[45] On this point, see FW Scharpf, 'Legitimacy in the Multilevel European Polity' (2009) 1 *European Political Science Review* 173, 186–87; D Grimm, 'The Democratic Costs of Constitutionalisation: The European Case' (2015) 21 *European Law Journal* 460, 470. This issue is further discussed in s III of this chapter.

[46] See s III of this chapter for a discussion of the regulatory capacity of the CJEU. See also ch 3 for an analysis of the regulatory implications of the case law under study.

[47] Grimm (n 45).

[48] See ch 3, ss II–V for a comparative analysis of the regulatory implications of the case law in four areas of national social policy.

[49] See ch 4 for a comprehensive analysis of the impact of the case law on EU legislative decision making.

in particular. National constitutional courts seem to have become more assertive and, at times, even aggressive in defending the constitutional primacy of domestic constitutional orders over the legal order of the EU. They also seem to have been emboldened by one another to challenge the validity of what they consider as *ultra vires* acts by EU institutions, including the judgments of the Court that uphold such allegedly *ultra vires* acts. From the preliminary references by the Spanish Constitutional Tribunal in *Melloni*[50] and the German Federal Constitutional Court in *Gauweiler*,[51] to the rulings of the Danish Supreme Court in *Dansk Industri/Ajos*[52] and the Italian Constitutional Court in *Taricco*,[53] to, most recently, the judgment of, again, the German Federal Constitutional Court in *Weiss*[54] and decision *K 3/21* of the Polish Constitutional Tribunal[55] – national constitutional courts are sending a clear signal to the CJEU that they are prepared to disobey both its rulings and the rules of EU law which in their view overstep the limits of EU competence. Not only does this undermine the authority of the CJEU as the guardian of the rule of law in the EU, but it also threatens to compromise the supremacy of EU law, which relies on national courts' acceptance of that law as interpreted by the CJEU. Without this acceptance, both the supremacy and integrity of the EU legal order risk being jeopardised.

Finally, tensions over the allocation of competences have political consequences. The EU's competence problem, as it is often perceived,[56] fuels populist, Eurosceptic narratives which might endanger the future of European integration. Recent years have seen the rise of political movements that demonstrate open defiance to the authority of the EU and its core values, such as democracy and the rule of law. Poland and Hungary are the most prominent but not isolated examples. Populist parties have gained election victories or significant increases in the share of votes in a number of other European

[50] Spanish Constitutional Court, Order of 9 June 2011, ATC 86/2011, addressed in Case C-399/11 *Melloni* EU:C:2013:107 (CJEU, 26 February 2013), discussed in A Pliakos and G Anagnostaras, 'Fundamental Rights and the New Battle over Legal and Judicial Supremacy: Lessons from *Melloni*' (2015) 34 *Yearbook of European Law* 97.

[51] BVerfG, judgment of 14 January 2014, 2 BvR 2728/13 (*OMT*), addressed in Case C-62/14 *Gauweiler* (CJEU, 16 June 2015).

[52] Danish Supreme Court, Case no 15/2014 *Dansk Industri (DI) acting for Ajos A/S v The estate of A*, Judgment of 6 December 2016, which was a response to the Court's judgment in Case C-441/14 *Danske Industri*, Judgment of 19 April 2016, analysed in U Šadl and S Mair, 'Mutual Disempowerment: Case C-441/14 *Dansk Industri, acting on behalf of Ajos A/S v Estate of Karsten Eigil Rasmussen and Case no. 15/2014 Dansk Industri (DI) acting for Ajos A/S v The estate left by A*' (2017) 13 *European Constitutional Law Review* 347.

[53] In chronological order, see the dialogue between the CJEU and the Italian Constitutional Court: Case C-105/14 *Taricco and Others* EU:C:2015:555 (CJEU, 8 September 2015); Corte Costituzionale, Order 24/2017, 26 January 2017 www.cortecostituzionale.it/documenti/download/doc/recent_judgments/O_24_2017.pdf; Case C-42/17 *Criminal proceedings against M.A.S. and M.B.* EU:C:2017:936 (CJEU, 5 December 2017) (*Taricco II*).

[54] BVerfG, *Weiss* (n 32). For a discussion of the judgment, see, eg, T Flynn, 'Constitutional Pluralism and Loyal Opposition' (2021) 19 *International Journal of Constitutional Law* 241.

[55] Polish Constitutional Tribunal, Decision No K 3/21, 7 October 2021. Notably, this judgment has been adopted by what can no longer be considered an independent court. As such, it is an example of how legitimate concerns about the reach of EU competence can be exploited for political ends. On the question of the independence of the Tribunal, see 'Statement of Retired Judges of the Polish Constitutional Tribunal' (*VerfBlog*, 11 October 2021) verfassungsblog.de/statement-of-retired-judges-of-the-polish-constitutional-tribunal.

[56] The term 'competence problem' is borrowed from L Azoulai, *The Question of Competence in the European Union* (Oxford, OUP, 2014).

countries, including the original members of the EU.[57] Whilst in some Member States support for membership in the EU has increased since the UK's withdrawal from the EU, it has decreased in others. The calls to leave the EU have been gaining traction, backed by emotionally charged slogans to 'take back control' from the unaccountable bureaucrats of the EU. It is true that the described political developments cannot be attributed solely to the EU's competence problem. The reasons are complex and include economic impacts of globalisation, the neo-liberal policies at the national and EU level, pressures on the welfare State, and the rise in immigration from third countries.[58] However, it is undeniable that a widespread sense of loss of control over national affairs has long percolated the societies of the Member States and has been effectively used by populist movements as a tool to incite anti-European nationalist sentiments. The current political climate threatens, in the long run, to compromise the success of European integration and puts into question the future of the European project as such.

The above developments demonstrate the salience of competence concerns surrounding the governance of the EU. The exercise of EU judicial authority that strains the principles governing the scope and exercise of EU competence aggravates those concerns, thereby risking undermining the legitimacy and integrity of the EU legal order. It is, therefore, crucial that the Court, as the guardian of the rule of law in the EU, duly observes the limits of EU competence and limits of its own institutional powers in the interpretation of the Treaties. Yet, as will be demonstrated in this book, the Court has systematically failed to do so in its free movement case law involving the constitutionally sensitive areas of healthcare, education and collective labour law.

D. Conclusion

This section discussed the constitutional importance of the principles governing the allocation of competences and powers in the EU – conferral, subsidiarity, proportionality and institutional balance. These principles define the very nature of the EU's legal order, which is characterised by federal power sharing between the EU and Member States. They maintain the balance between the values of unity and diversity in the EU, or, in concrete terms, between EU supranationalism and respect for the autonomy of the Member States. As the EU's constitutional judiciary, the Court has a key role in preserving this balance. It does so not only through controlling the constitutionality of the actions of the EU's political institutions, but also through the judicial interpretation of the substantive provisions of the Treaties, most notably the rules of the internal market. Therefore, when the judicial interpretation of those rules overstretches the principles that underpin the EU's federal balance, it implicates the very foundations of the EU's legal order. This practice undermines the credibility of the Court as a guardian of the rule of law in the EU and challenges the legitimacy and integrity of the EU as a supranational polity.

[57] P Sandrin, 'The Rise of Right-Wing Populism in Europe: A Psychoanalytical Contribution' in B de Souza Guilherme et al (eds), *Financial Crisis Management and Democracy: Lessons from Europe and Latin America* (New York, Springer, 2021) 227–28.

[58] ibid.

II. Substantive Constraints: The EU's Constitutional Value Framework

The federal balance of competences in the EU and, in particular, respect for national autonomy as a concept central to that balance are often discussed as a proxy for the protection of the various non-market values and interests in the EU. This section considers the relationship between respect for national regulatory autonomy and the protection of non-market values, most notably the social ones, in EU law.[59] It rejects the view that the protection of social values is secondary to the economic objectives of the internal market and should thus be mainly achieved through the division of competences between the EU and Member States. It argues that the protection of these values is, and has ever been, ingrained in the fabric of the Treaties and, therefore, binds the judicial interpretation of internal market law independently of the Court's duty to protect national regulatory autonomy.

Whilst not the main focus of this study, the theme concerning the interplay between the economic (or market) and social (or non-market) dimensions in EU law – in particular, at the EU's constitutional level – features throughout the book because it offers an important context behind the Court's judicial choices in the area of the internal market, thereby enhancing our understanding of the broader constitutional framework in which the Court operates.

A. Values Associated with the Division of Competences between the EU and Member States

Section I discussed the regulatory autonomy of the Member States as a value which in various ways is protected by the principles of conferral, subsidiarity, proportionality and indirectly by the principle of institutional balance. However, national regulatory autonomy also serves as a proxy concept for a range of other, substantive values, most notably those of a social character, protected through domestic regulatory policies. As a result of the close relationship between national regulatory autonomy and the pursuit of social policy, the vertical division of competences between the EU and Member States has gradually come to be associated with the dichotomy between the economic and social dimensions of EU law. According to this line of thinking, EU law, and internal market law in particular, is primarily concerned with the protection of values of free market and others of a predominantly economic and individual nature, whereas values associated with the non-market goals, such as social protection and solidarity, are mainly to be protected through domestic regulatory policies.[60] Thus, the logic goes, the

[59] The broader substantive constraints on the exercise of EU judicial authority can be derived from the so-called 'horizontal' provisions of the Treaty, to be discussed in this section, but first and foremost Art 2 TEU, which lists the values the EU is founded on, including, inter alia, respect for human dignity, democracy, equality, rule of law, and the protection of fundamental rights.

[60] For a recent account, see G Davies, 'The Competence to Create an Internal Market: Conceptual Poverty and Unbalanced Interests' in S Garben and I Govaere (eds) *The Division of Competences between the EU and the Member States* (Oxford, Hart Publishing, 2017) 82–83. For landmark accounts, see J Weiler, 'The

protection of national regulatory autonomy via the principles of conferral, subsidiarity and proportionality also ensures the protection of the social values that might otherwise be neglected in EU law.

The conception of the internal market and its objectives has evolved over the years, as the EU's non-economic values and interests have found a more prominent place in the Treaties.[61] The EU's internal market competence has been successfully used by the EU legislature to adopt measures aimed at the protection of such values and interests.[62] The same shift has not, however, taken place in the EU's internal market case law. The Court's interpretation of free movement rules remains biased towards economic and individual interests and tends to neglect social and collective interests, as will be demonstrated in this book through a comparative analysis of the case law involving four socially sensitive areas of national policy. Yet it is generally considered that the market bias percolating the case law, whilst regrettable in some instances, is in principle justified by the language of the Treaties. It is said to be grounded in the substantive provisions of the Treaties, which articulate the Court's jurisdiction for the most part in terms of primary economic rights.[63] This, in turn, means that negative law, which is prone to dominate the process of European integration,[64] is bound to contribute to the deregulation of national social policies.

The following discussion challenges the above logic. It argues that the protection of non-economic values via the judicial interpretation of EU internal market law is required by the value system embedded in the broader constitutional framework of the Treaties. This means that the Court must protect non-economic values in its case law not only because, as argued in section I, it has a constitutional duty to respect national regulatory autonomy but also because the protection of non-economic values is embedded in EU law. This argument is based on the analysis of the historical development of EU treaties, focusing on the relationship between the economic and social dimensions embedded in them. The analysis demonstrates that none of the treaties constituting the EU and its predecessors seem to have intended to establish a constitutional hierarchy between the two dimensions, favouring the economic one. Rather, whilst promoted in

Transformation of Europe' (1991) 100 *Yale Law Journal* 2403, 2476–78, referring to R Bieber et al, 'Back to the Future: Policy, Strategy and Tactics of the White Paper on the Creation of a Single European Market' in R Bieber et al (eds), *1992: One European Market?* (Baden, Nomos Verlagsgesellschaft, 1998) 18–20; FW Scharpf, 'The European Social Model: Coping with the Challenges of Diversity' (2002) 40 *Journal of Common Market Studies* 645, 646–67; P Craig, 'Competence and Member State Autonomy: Causality, Consequence and Legitimacy' in HW Micklitz and B de Witte (eds), *The European Court of Justice and the Autonomy of the Member States* (Cambridge, Intersentia, 2012); S Reynolds, 'Explaining the Constitutional Drivers behind a Perceived Judicial Preference for Free Movement over Fundamental Rights' (2016) 53 *CML Rev* 643.

[61] As discussed below.

[62] Although this practice raises its own constitutional issues, specifically, concerning the boundaries of Art 114, as briefly discussed in s I of this chapter and further examined in ch 2, s I and ch 3, s I. On the protection of non-economic interests in EU legislation, see, eg, De Witte (n 37).

[63] N Walker, 'The Philosophy of European Union Law' in D Chalmers and A Arnull (eds), *Oxford Handbook of European Union Law* (Oxford, OUP, 2015) 21–22. For a defence of the Court's methods of interpretation of the Treaties, see, eg, A Arnull, 'The European Court and Judicial Objectivity: A Reply to Professor Hartley' (1996) 112 *Law Quarterly Review* 411; T Tridimas, 'The Court of Justice and Judicial Activism' (1996) 21 *European Law Review* 199.

[64] See s III of this chapter for the discussion of the relationship between positive and negative integration.

different ways, both value dimensions have served the same mission throughout the history of the EU – that of the advancement of the welfare of the European people. The project of market integration was seen as a central instrument for achieving that mission. The framework of the Treaties thus suggests that the Court is required to interpret the provisions of the internal market in light of the EU's non-economic values.

B. The EEC: The Origins of the EU's Social Dimension

The EU's commitment to social values has been enshrined in the Treaties since the creation of the European Economic Community. The preamble of the Treaty of Rome (the EEC Treaty) had ambitiously set out: 'to lay the foundations of an ever closer union among the peoples of Europe' and 'ensure the economic and social progress of their countries' by eliminating the barriers which divided Europe, and to work for 'the constant improvements of the living and working conditions of their peoples'.[65] Art 2 stipulated that the objectives of the Community were to be attained by means of establishing a common market and progressively approximating the economic policies of the Member States. To that end, the Treaty laid down rules prohibiting a range of measures that could restrict trade or distort competition in the common market.[66] So, from the early years of the EEC, the establishment of a common market was seen as a means for achieving the broader objectives of the Community rather than an objective in and of itself.

An important component of the common market introduced by the EEC Treaty was the freedom of movement of workers. Art 48 EEC granted workers the right to move freely within the EU for the purposes of employment and guaranteed them equal treatment in comparison to nationals of the host Member States with regard to employment, remuneration and other conditions of work and employment. The Community was also given a competence to coordinate Member States' social insurance systems[67] and legislate to facilitate the free movement of workers.[68] Moreover, Art 119 EEC (now Art 157 TFEU) enshrined the principle that men and women should receive equal pay for equal work. The grant of equal treatment for workers and the principle of equal pay were intended to prevent regulatory competition in labour standards (at least on certain grounds) that could lead to 'social dumping' (ie foreign workers being used as cheap labour).[69]

The Treaty also contained a separate Chapter on Social Policy. Art 117 of the chapter asserted the Community's commitment to promoting 'improved working conditions

[65] Treaty Establishing the European Economic Community (adopted 25 March 1957, entered into force 1 January 1958) (EEC), Preamble.

[66] Arts 16, 30, 34, 52, 59, 85–86, 92, 95 EEC, corresponding to Arts 28, 34, 35, 49, 56, 101–102, 107, 110 TFEU.

[67] Note that this excludes any binding measures aimed at harmonisation of national laws.

[68] Art 51 EEC.

[69] D Schiek et al, 'EU Social and Labour Rights and EU Internal Market Law' (European Parliament DG for Internal Policies 2015) 22 www.europarl.europa.eu/RegData/etudes/STUD/2015/563457/IPOL_STU(2015)563457_EN.pdf; C Barnard, 'The Economic Objectives of Art 119' in T Hervey and D O'Keeffe (eds), *Sex Equality Law in the European Union* (Hoboken, Wiley, 1996) 321–34.

and an improved standard of living for workers'. However, despite aspirational rhetoric, the concrete competences of the Community in the area of social policy were confined to the adoption of incentive and co-operation measures in matters including, inter alia, employment, social security and vocational training. The weakness of the Community's competence in social policy manifested an unwillingness on the part of the Member States to transfer to the Community any sovereign powers in this area.[70] At the same time, such transfer of powers was not considered necessary. Art 117 EEC expressly stipulated that the anticipated social advantages of the Community were expected to ensue from the establishment of the common market and approximation of national laws.

Overall, the language of the EEC Treaty suggests that social welfare in general has been seen as a desired and natural consequence of market integration since the very origins of what is now the EU.[71]

C. Treaty Reforms: A Gradual Expansion of the Social Dimension

With market integration taking its course, Member States felt the need to expand Community competences in the social policy domain. This was done through successive Treaty reforms. In order to address the issue of social dumping, the Single European Act (SEA) brought health and safety at work into the scope of the Treaty, allowing the Council to adopt, by qualified majority, directives aimed at improving occupational health and safety.[72] It also introduced a horizontal clause requiring that measures adopted in the process of harmonisation of the single market would take as a base a high level of health protection.[73] With regard to the collective aspects of labour law, the SEA entrusted the Commission with the task of developing dialogue between management and labour at European level and, to that end, provided for the possibility of the adoption of EC-wide collective agreements by the social partners.[74] Most significantly, in 1989, the Community adopted the Social Charter, which stipulated that 'the same importance must be attached to the social aspects as to the economic aspects' of the single market.[75] Although the Charter was and remains not legally binding, it has informed a number of EU policies and legislation, being frequently referred to in EU legal instruments and the Court's judgments.[76]

[70] See Art 118 EEC. See also J Kenner, *EU Employment Law: From Rome to Amsterdam and Beyond* (Oxford, Hart Publishing, 2003) 1–6, 10; Schiek et al (n 69).

[71] For support of this view, see also International Labour Organization, Group of Experts, 'Social Aspects of European Economic Co-operation' (1956) 74 *International Labour Review* 99 (Ohlin Report); PH Spaak, *Rapport des chefs de delegation aux Ministres des Affaires Etrangères* (1956 Intergovernmental Committee on European Integration) 19–20, 60–61 (Spaak Report); P Davies, 'The Emergence of European Labour Law' in W McCarthy (ed), *Legal Intervention in Industrial Relations: Gains and Losses* (Hoboken, Blackwell, 1993) 313–59, 322–23; Kenner (n 70) 2–6; D Schiek, 'A Constitution of Social Governance for the European Union' in D Kostakopoulou and N Ferreira (eds), *The Human Face of the European Union: Are EU Law and Policy Humane Enough?* (Cambridge, CUP, 2016) 17–47.

[72] Art 118a EEC, added by Single European Act [1987] OJ L169/1, Art 21.

[73] Art 100a EEC, added by Art 18 SEA.

[74] Art 118b EEC, added by Art 22 SEA.

[75] Community Charter of Fundamental Social Rights of Workers [1989] OJ C323/44, Preamble.

[76] B Ryan, 'The Charter and Collective Labour Law' in TK Hervey and J Kenner (eds), *Economic and Social Rights Under the EU Charter of Fundamental Rights – A Legal Perspective* (Oxford, Hart Publishing, 2003)

The Treaty of Maastricht took a step further in deepening the social dimension of the EU. It created Union citizenship and introduced legal bases for higher education and public health policies, albeit limited to the adoption of non-binding measures and also subject to the principle of subsidiarity.[77] Notably, some of these reforms, such as the creation of a legal basis for education, have been driven by the Court's case law, which will be discussed in the next chapter. The Maastricht Treaty also modified the list of the objectives of the EU, which now included the pursuit of a high level of social protection.

Furthermore, 11 Member States (excluding the UK) signed an Agreement on Social Policy, which was annexed to the Protocol on Social Policy of the Treaty of Maastricht. One of the objectives of the Agreement was to strengthen the role of the social partners in the Community legislative process. To that end, the Agreement imposed a legal obligation on the Commission to facilitate social dialogue and consult social partners on the possible direction of Community action and on the content of proposals in the social policy field.[78] In addition, it stipulated that the agreements negotiated by the social partners at the Community level could be adopted as binding legislation.[79] The Agreement also extended Community competences to a wider range of social policy matters, including working conditions, information and consultation of workers, social inclusion, and equality between men and women in the workplace. With respect to some of the new competences, the Agreement allowed for qualified majority voting, on the basis of which several important social policy measures were adopted in the following years.[80] After the 1997 UK general election, the newly elected government decided to terminate its 'opt-out', and the Social Policy Agreement was incorporated into the revised Chapter on Social Policy of the Treaty of Amsterdam.

The historical overview of the Treaties seems to suggest that the initial thinness of the social policy provisions in the Treaty of Rome was premised on a consensus that the creation of a single market would not require a comprehensive harmonisation of national social policies.[81] This, in turn, determined the nature of the EU's social policy. It developed incrementally and deepened progressively as market integration intensified.

D. The Court's Contribution

The Court has long recognised the importance of the social dimension of EU law and in an important way proved to be instrumental in advancing the EU's social policy beyond the seemingly narrow Treaty framework.

10, referring to L Betten, 'The EU Charter of Fundamental Rights: A Trojan Horse or a Mouse?' (2001) 17 *International Journal of Comparative Labour Law & Industrial Relations* 151.

[77] Consolidated version of the Treaty Establishing the European Community [1992] OJ C224/6 (EC Treaty), Arts 8, 126 and 129, respectively.

[78] Protocol on Social Policy to Treaty on European Union [1992] OJ C191/91, Agreement on Social Policy, Art 3.

[79] ibid, Arts 3, 4.

[80] See, eg, Council Directive 94/45/EC on the establishment of a European Works Council or a procedure in Community-scale undertakings and Community-scale groups of undertakings for the purposes of informing and consulting [1994] OJ L254/64; Council Directive 96/34/EC on the framework agreement on parental leave concluded by UNICE, CEEP and the ETUC [1996] OJ L145/4; Council Directive 97/81/EC concerning the Framework Agreement on part-time work concluded by UNICE, CEEP and the ETUC – Annex: Framework agreement on part-time work [1997] OJ L14/9.

[81] In support of this view, see, eg, D Ashiagbor, 'Unravelling the Embedded Liberal Bargain: Labour and Social Welfare Law in the Context of EU Market Integration' (2013) 19 *European Law Journal* 303.

A particular mention ought to be given to the *Defrenne* case of 1975,[82] in which the Court was asked to give a preliminary ruling on the interpretation of the principle of equal pay, enshrined in Art 119 EEC (now Art 141 TFEU). This provision had not been implemented by any of the Member States apart from France (which had paved the way for its introduction into the Treaties in the first place) and was widely considered to be of an aspirational nature. Mrs Defrenne was a Belgian air hostess who sued her employer on the ground that she was being paid less than her male colleagues. The Court found this to be a breach of Art 119 EEC.

The Court held that Art 119 had a double aim. On the one hand, it sought to prevent a situation in which undertakings established in States which had implemented the principle of equal pay would suffer a competitive disadvantage in intra-Community competition as compared with undertakings established elsewhere. On the other hand, it formed part of the social objectives of the Community, which was not merely an economic union, but was at the same time intended to ensure social progress and seek the constant development of the living and working conditions.[83] This double aim, at once economic and social, showed that the principle of equal pay formed 'part of the foundations of the Community'.[84]

Moreover, the Court ruled that Art 119 was directly applicable and had horizontal direct effect,[85] which meant that the obligation of equal pay, in addition to binding public authorities, extended to all agreements intended to regulate paid labour collectively and to contracts between individuals.[86] This finding was remarkable because Art 119 was, and remains, explicitly addressed only to Member States. Notably, *Defrenne* was the first judgment where the Court pronounced on the horizontal dimension of direct effect in relation to social policy (it had already done so for competition law).

The value of *Defrenne* lies in that the Court for the first time in its jurisprudence acknowledged the salience of the social dimension of the Treaty. The judgment became the driving force for some major legislative developments in EU anti-discrimination law.[87] Moreover, the principle of equal treatment was further expanded beyond the confines of equal pay and gender equality. The new Art 13 EC of the Treaty of Amsterdam conferred on the Community the competence to 'take appropriate action to combat discrimination based on sex, racial or ethnic origin, religion or belief, disability, age or sexual orientation'.[88]

The upshot of *Defrenne* was, however, that indirectly it also strengthened the economic dimension of Community law because it opened up the possibility that some of the free movement rules would be granted horizontal direct effect. Moreover, in the relative absence of concrete, enforceable social policy rules in the Treaty, rights of a social nature could not benefit from the direct effect in the way that the economic freedoms did. EU social policy was for the most part developed in secondary legislation and so depended on achieving political consensus. The principal counterweight to the rules

[82] Case C-43/75 *Defrenne* [1976] ECR 455.

[83] ibid, paras 8–10.

[84] ibid, para 12.

[85] JA Winter, 'Direct Applicability and Direct Effect Two Distinct and Different Concepts in Community Law' (1972) 9 *CML Rev* 425.

[86] *Defrenne* (n 82), paras 24, 39.

[87] For a detailed account, see D Sindbjerg Martinsen, *An Ever More Powerful Court? The Political Constraints of Legal Integration in the European Union* (Oxford, OUP, 2015) 67–71.

[88] Consolidated version of the Treaty Establishing the European Community [1997] OJ C340/173 (EC), Art 13.

of the internal market, therefore, stemmed from the protections embedded in national social models, which served to justify Member State derogations from those rules.

E. The Treaty of Lisbon: The Social Dimension Reinvigorated

The social dimension of the internal market has been reinforced by the Treaty of Lisbon, which strengthened the EU's commitment to strive for a Union whose quest for economic growth is balanced against the maintenance of social progress. Art 2 TEU (originally, Art 2 EEC), which lists the objectives of the EU, encompasses a wide range of social objectives: ranging from, generally, the pursuit of a social market economy, through to concrete commitments to full employment, social justice and solidarity, amongst others.[89] Furthermore, the reference to undistorted competition, previously contained in Art 3(1)(g) EC,[90] has been moved to Protocol No 27 on the internal market and competition and thus no longer appears in the main text of the Treaty.

The Lisbon Treaty has also introduced a number of new provisions of primary social law that are aimed at informing the framework of EU law and policy. The horizontal social clause laid down in Art 9 TFEU requires that the objectives of social protection and employment, education and training, and human health be mainstreamed into EU policies. Similarly, Arts 11 and 12, respectively, assert that requirements of environmental and consumer protection shall be integrated into the definition and implementation of EU policies and activities.[91] Equivalent stipulations appear in the Charter of Fundamental Rights, which has been granted the status of primary law by Art 6 TEU. Art 35 CFR reaffirms the EU's commitment to a high level of health protection and Arts 37 and 38 do so in relation to environmental and consumer protection. The cross-cutting provisions enshrined in the Treaties and the Charter suggest that the various non-economic values and objectives apply across the whole sweep of EU activity, including the internal market. Notably, the Court has relied on these various provisions in the past to soften the deregulatory edge of free movement law.[92]

Moreover, the integration of the Charter into the Treaties elevates a number of social rights to the same normative level as the rules of the internal market. Art 14 of the Charter guarantees to everyone the right to education; Art 35 protects the right to healthcare; and the whole of title IV, entitled 'Solidarity', is dedicated to social protection and the protection of workers. As important as these developments are, the power of the Charter alone should not be overestimated, since the Court tends to interpret it in a way that either adds nothing to the existing protection of EU social rights[93] or,

[89] Art 2(3) TEU.

[90] Consolidated version of the Treaty Establishing the European Community [2002] OJ C325/33 (EC), Art 3(1)(g).

[91] Note that some of these commitments are not new. See, eg, Arts 6 and 152(1) EC (Nice consolidated version) on environmental protection, Art 153(2) EC on consumer protection. See also Art 167(4) TFEU (formerly Art 151(4) EC) requiring that cultural aspects be streamlined into EU activities with the view to respecting and promoting the diversity of cultures.

[92] See, eg, C-28/09 *Commission v Austria* EU:C:2011:854, [2011] ECR I-13525, paras 120–22.

[93] Case C-438/05 *Viking* EU:C:2007:772, [2007] ECR I-10779, paras 43–44; Case C-341/05 *Laval* EU:C:2007:809, [2007] ECR I-11767, para 91; Case C-271/08 *Commission v Germany* EU:C:2010:426, [2010] ECR I-7091, paras 38–44; Case C-390/12 *Pfleger* EU:C:2014:281 (CJEU, 30 April 2014), paras 59–60.

in extreme cases, even favours commercial rights over the social ones.[94] The Treaty also imposes an obligation on the EU to accede to the ECHR.[95] Although the prospect of an imminent accession seems to have become less realistic in light of the Court's *Opinion 2/13*,[96] a delay in expected accession, in turn, has increased the relevance of the Charter as the main instrument of fundamental rights protection in the EU. Notably, the Charter incorporates a number of Convention rights, whose interpretation in EU law must not fall short of the standard of protection accorded to them by the ECHR.[97] As a consequence, the Court now appears to be under pressure from both national courts and the European Court of Human Rights (ECtHR) to ensure the EU's compliance with fundamental rights.[98]

Finally, the Treaty strengthens the role of the principle of conferral in the EU's constitutional framework, which has relevance for the protection of social interests in EU law. Art 6 TFEU clarifies the delimitation of the EU's competences by classifying them into exclusive, shared and supplementary. This makes more explicit the areas of national competence, including a number of social policy areas, protected by the principle of conferral.[99] Art 4(2) TEU stipulates that the Union shall respect the essential State functions of the Member States and their national identities, which are inherent in their fundamental political and constitutional structures. Phrased more generally in the Treaty of Maastricht, this provision used to refer to the EU's duty to respect 'the national identities of its Member States'.[100] It is hard to draw any general conclusions about the exact parameters of Art 4(2) since the Court has taken a piecemeal approach in interpreting this provision, deciding on a case-by-case basis whether the national measures in question fall within the concept of national identity.[101] National constitutional courts, on their part, have generally interpreted Art 4(2) as imposing an additional limit on

[94] Case C-426/11 *Alemo-Herron* EU:C:2013:521 (CJEU, 18 July 2013), paras 30–35, analysed in this respect in ch 3, s IV.

[95] Art 6(2) TEU.

[96] Case C-2/13 *Accession of the European Union to the European Convention for the Protection of Human Rights and Fundamental Freedoms* EU:C:2014:2454 (CJEU, 18 December 2014).

[97] Art 52(3) CFR.

[98] To this effect, see BVerfG, judgment of 29 May 1974, 37 BvR 271 (*Solange I*) and BVerfG, judgment of 22 October 1986, 73 BvR 339 (*Solange II*). For some recent signs that the CJEU is taking seriously the protection of fundamental rights, at least the civil and political ones, see Joined Cases C-293/12 and C-594/12 *Digital Rights Ireland Ltd* EU:C:2014:238 (CJEU, 8 April 2014); Case C-131/12 *Google Spain SL* EU:C:2014:317 (CJEU, 13 May 2014); Joined Cases C-511/18 *La Quadrature Du Net*, C-512/18 *French Data Network* and C-520/18 *Ordre des Barreaux Francophones et Germanophone* EU:C:2020:791 (CJEU, 6 October 2020) (*La Quadrature Du Net*); Case C-623/17 *Privacy International* EU:C:2020:790 (CJEU, 6 October 2020).

[99] On this point, see s I of this chapter and ch 2, s I.

[100] Treaty on European Union [1992] OJ C191/1, Art F(1).

[101] See, eg, Case C-208/09 *Sayn-Wittgenstein* EU:C:2010:806, [2010] ECR I-13693, concerning national constitutional identity; Case C-391/09 *Runevič-Vardyn* EU:C:2011:291, [2011] ECR I-3787, concerning national linguistic identity; Case C-156/13 *Digibet* EU:C:2014:1756 (CJEU, 2 June 2014) and Case C-51/15 *Remondis v Region Hannover* EU:C:2016:985 (CJEU, 21 December 2016), both concerning the division of competences within the State; *La Quadrature du Net* (n 98), concerning national security. For academic discussion on Art 4(2), see M Dobbs, 'Sovereignty, Article 4(2) TEU and the Respect of National Identities: Swinging the Balance of Power in Favour of the Member States?' (2014) 33 *Yearbook of European Law* 298; T Konstadinides, 'Dealing with Parallel Universes: Antinomies of Sovereignty and the Protection of National Identity in European Judicial Discourse' (2015) 34 *Yearbook of European Law* 127; G van der Schyff, 'Exploring Member State and European Union Constitutional Identity' (2016) 22 *European Public Law* 227.

the reach of EU competences; one that is rooted in the value of national constitutional diversity.[102] This suggests that the scope of the national identity clause and its role in EU law remain to be determined. This question will be returned to in chapter five, which argues that Art 4(2) should be construed to protect national social identities.

F. Conclusion

The framework of the EU Treaties, past and present, suggests that despite an unequal distribution of EU competences across the economic and social domains, the EU is obliged to regulate the internal market in a way that would not undermine the pursuit of its social objectives, which are placed on constitutional parity with the economic freedoms, at least since the reforms introduced by the Treaty of Lisbon.[103] This obligation has concrete implications for the judicial interpretation of internal market law. It requires the Court to read the rules of the internal market in light of the non-economic values of EU law.[104] In other words, the Court has a responsibility to protect the non-economic values of the EU not only as part of respect for the regulatory autonomy of the Member States, but also because the protection of such values is enshrined in the substantive provisions of the Treaties.

The case law analysis conducted in the remainder of this book demonstrates that the protection of social values through the judicial interpretation of EU free movement law remains an exception rather than a rule. Whilst the Court has on multiple occasions recognised the importance of these values in the framework of the Treaties, it has failed to protect them in a consistent and systematic way.

III. Justification for Constraining the Court

Section I discussed the importance of the role of the Court in preserving the federal balance of competences in the EU. Most would agree that this judicial role involves ensuring that the institutions of the EU, most notably its legislature, observe the limits governing the scope and exercise of EU competences in EU political decision making. Equally, most would object to the assertion that such competence limits also apply to the judicial interpretation of the Treaties. This section addresses that objection. It challenges the conventional view whereby the principles that govern the vertical division

[102] For academic discussion of the jurisprudence of national constitutional courts, see, eg, M Wendel, 'Lisbon before the Courts: Comparative Perspectives' (2011) 7 *European Constitutional Law Review* 96; G Martinico and O Pollicino, 'Use and Abuse of a Promising Concept: What Has Happened to National Constitutional Identity?' (2020) 39 *Yearbook of European Law* 228. See also *OMT* (n 51), para 29, suggesting that the scope of Art 4(2) reaches 'far beyond' the constitutional identity enshrined in the German constitution. For academic commentary, see M Claes and J-H Reestman, 'The Protection of National Constitutional Identity and the Limits of European Integration at the Occasion of the *Gauweiler* Case' (2015) 16 *German Law Journal* 917.

[103] See, eg, Schiek et al (n 69) 78.

[104] See also D Damjanovic, 'The EU Market Rules as Social Market Rules: Why the EU Can Be a Social Market Economy' (2013) 50 *CML Rev* 1685, 1716–17.

of competences in the EU – conferral, subsidiarity and proportionality – are meant to apply exclusively to EU political decision making and argues that these principles also bind the Court in the judicial interpretation of the Treaties, most notably the rules of the internal market.

The principles of conferral, subsidiarity and proportionality have been widely discussed in the legal literature in relation to questions concerning the constitutional legitimacy of the exercise of EU competences. That discussion is typically focused on the application of these principles to the EU legislative practices and, in particular, the Commission as an institution, given its exclusive power to initiate legislation.[105] The three principles have also been on multiple occasions invoked before the Court, individually or altogether, in order to challenge the validity of EU legislation. Some of that case law will be discussed in the following chapters. Remarkably, there has been very little academic discussion concerning the applicability of these principles to the Court itself with the view to assessing the legitimacy of the exercise of EU judicial authority.[106]

Several reasons explain why the Court has been seemingly overlooked in the academic debate. First and foremost, it is the conventional perception that the principles of conferral, subsidiarity and proportionality are not meant to apply to the Court. As principles directed at Union *action*,[107] they are intended to govern, primarily, the EU lawmaking powers, that is, action taken by EU legislative institutions – the Commission, Council and Parliament acting together – in the pursuit of EU policies. These principles also govern the actions of institutions charged with the execution, or administration, of EU policies as long as this power entails making binding decisions on behalf of the EU. It would thus follow that the principles limiting the scope and exercise of EU competences are meant to control the practices of EU policy making and execution. Now, contrast those practices with the role of the judiciary, or the Court, in the EU's legal order. The argument behind the conventional view is that the Court has little to do with policy making or its execution.[108] Quite the opposite, it is predominantly seen as an apolitical, independent and autonomous institution, concerned exclusively with the rules of law, not policy. After all, its responsibility is to protect the rule of law in the EU through the resolution of legal disputes arising from EU law. Accordingly, it is believed that the principles that govern the limits of EU competences and their exercise should concern the Court only in its role as the central guardian, or enforcer, of those principles through the judicial review of EU action. A further objection against the application of these principles to the Court lies in the difficulty to determine their normative content in relation

[105] As briefly discussed in s I of this chapter and further discussed in ch 2, s I and ch 3, s I.

[106] There are notable exceptions: T Schilling, 'A New Dimension of Subsidiarity: Subsidiarity as a Rule and a Principle' (1994) 14 *Yearbook of European Law* 203; GA Bermann, 'Taking Subsidiarity Seriously: Federalism in the European Community and the United States' (1994) 94 *Columbia Law Review* 331; G de Búrca, 'The Principle of Subsidiarity and the Court of Justice as an Institutional Actor' (1998) 36 *Journal of Common Market Studies* 217; Swaine (n 26); T Horsley, 'Subsidiarity and the European Court of Justice: Missing Pieces in the Subsidiarity Jigsaw?' (2012) 50 *Journal of Common Market Studies* 267; D Wyatt, 'If the Court of Justice Ignores the Principle of Conferral Simply Because It Can, How Do We Fix the Problem?' (14th Jean Monnet Seminar in EU Law, Dubrovnik, 17–23 April 2016) www.biicl.org/event/1124.

[107] Art 5 TEU.

[108] This view is hard to defend though, considering that even CJEU judges themselves admit that the Court makes policy choices in its jurisprudence. See, eg, K Lenaerts, 'Some Thoughts About the Interaction Between Judges and Politicians in the European Community' (1992) 12 *Yearbook of European Law* 1.

to the exercise of EU judicial rather than legislative or executive power. Even those who argue in favour of the application of at least some of these principles to the Court have struggled to define in concrete terms, first, what requirements these principles should impose on the exercise of EU judicial powers, and, second, how to operationalise those requirements in practice.[109] In the relative absence of concrete proposals, the subject has failed to attract widespread support.

While the considerations discussed above are valid, they represent an unduly narrow understanding of the Court's role and institutional place in the EU's legal order. As De Búrca points out writing in the context of subsidiarity, just because the Court's primary function is to interpret the Treaties rather than make policy does not necessarily mean that its interpretative practice cannot be subject to the principles governing EU legislative action. This is especially true considering that the Court is de facto involved in both lawmaking and policy making through its judgments.[110] Drawing on De Búrca's work, Horsley argues, more generally, that the EU Treaty framework should function as the source of normative restraint on all of the EU's institutional activity, including the work of the Court as an institution of the EU.[111] I find these propositions compelling and in this section I build on them when arguing that the Court should be subject to the constraints on competence that bind EU political action. I offer a systemic explanation for why that should be the case. My argument considers two important characteristics which underpin much of EU law and yet often appear to be in tension with one another: the conception of the EU as an organisation of conferred, and thus limited, powers, on the one hand, and the unusually powerful institutional position of the CJEU in that organisation, on the other hand. I begin with the latter and then move to the former.

Ultimately, I argue that the Court's institutional position in the EU endows it with a regulatory capacity characteristic of that possessed by bodies which exercise political authority on behalf of the State. This regulatory capacity is what makes a situation where the Court is exempt from competence constraints that apply to the rest of the EU's institutions constitutionally unacceptable.

A. The Institutional Power of the Court

The scope of the powers that the Court exercises on behalf of the EU is extremely broad. This is due to several factors, both legal and political institutional, discussed in turn below.

i. Treaty Mandate

Key to the assessment of the scope of the Court's powers is the fact that the boundaries of the EU's judicial mandate are difficult to define. The principal constraint on the Court's

[109] See, eg, De Búrca (n 106) and Horsley (n 106), attempting to address these issues in the context of the principle of subsidiarity. See also Bermann (n 106) 402–03.

[110] De Búrca (n 106). For a ground-breaking critique of the CJEU as a policymaker, see Rasmussen (n 35).

[111] T Horsley, *The Court of Justice of the European Union as an Institutional Actor: Judicial Lawmaking and its Limits* (Cambridge, CUP, 2018) 23–32.

powers stems from the jurisdictional boundaries. The Court does not have general jurisdiction. It is authorised by the Treaties to rule in three main types of proceedings: actions for annulment, entailing the review of the legality of acts of EU institutions; infringement proceedings against a Member State failing to comply with its obligations under EU law; and the preliminary reference procedure, whereby the Court delivers an interpretation of EU law at the request of a national court.[112] Cases involving questions of the lawfulness of Member State action, like the majority of those analysed in this book, arise either out of the preliminary reference procedure or infringement proceedings. While the former route is more common, both require that the Court deliver an interpretation of EU law, either in order to enable the national court to resolve the dispute at hand or directly to rule on the rights and obligations of a Member State in light of the relevant provisions of EU law.

The authority to deliver an interpretation of EU law is what makes the Court the powerful institution that it is. Art 19 TEU, which bestows upon the Court the responsibility to ensure the observance of EU law, is framed in very broad terms. As a consequence, the Court enjoys a high degree of discretion in the exercise of its interpretative authority.[113] The Court's interpretative choices are essentially limited only by the wording of the substantive Treaty provisions that it interprets. Yet the wording of those provisions appears to be broad, abstract and at times vague, thus leaving ample space for interpretation, such as with regard to the scope of application or policy orientation of the rule in question.[114]

The problem is compounded by the fact that the scope of relationships governed by the Treaties is very wide. The Treaties are not limited to those provisions that, as Grimm puts it, reflect the core functions of a constitution.[115] They contain a wide range of provisions that are more suited for political determination than constitutional interpretation and, as such, would constitute ordinary law in State legal systems.[116] This refers, most notably, to the EU's fundamental freedoms and competition rules, which have extensive application and govern the rights and obligations of not only Member States but also EU citizens and businesses operating in the EU. Moreover, according to the long-standing case law of the Court,[117] these rules have a constitutional (rather than international law) character: they enjoy primacy over all legislation, national and EU, and are directly judicially enforceable.[118] This means that the Court's power of interpretation includes the power to determine the content of a vast body of rules of general application, which,

[112] Arts 258–260, 263, 269 TFEU. See also Arts 265 and 268 TFEU. The less frequent proceedings include actions for failure to act, brought against an EU institution, and appeals on points of law from decisions adopted by the General Court.

[113] See, eg, Lenaerts (n 2) 13–18.

[114] The various concrete provisions are analysed in the following chapters.

[115] Grimm (n 45) 470.

[116] Scharpf (n 45) 186. See also SK Schmidt, 'Governing by Judicial Fiat? Over-Constitutionalisation and its Constraints on EU Legislation' (EUSA International Biennial Conference, Denver, May 2019), arguing that the Treaties are 'rich in policy content'.

[117] See Case C-26/62 *Van Gend & Loos* EU:C:1963:1, [1963] ECR 1 and Case C-6/64 *Costa v ENEL* EU:C:1964:66, [1964] ECR 585, both analysed in the context of 'constitutionalisation' of the Treaties in Weiler (n 60).

[118] In that respect, the Treaties can be contrasted with the constitutions of federal states with internal markets, whose internal market provisions make up just a small feature of the constitution, and the details of their implementation are usually left for the legislature. See, eg, Constitution of the United States of America:

as a matter of law, cannot be challenged or otherwise changed except by a unanimous agreement by all the Member States.[119] This significantly enhances the position of the Court vis-à-vis both national and EU legislatures.

ii. Political Institutional Context

In order to fully appreciate the strength of the Court's institutional position, one also needs to look beyond the rules of the Treaties into the political institutional context in which the Court operates. Whilst in theory of no direct concern to the judiciary, the EU's political institutional context may in practice enhance or diminish the Court's powers. In particular, there are two interrelated factors pertaining to this context that merit a discussion: the relative weakness of the EU's legislative institutions and the persisting democratic deficit associated with the EU's legislative process.

a. The Weakness of the EU Legislature

The position of the Court vis-à-vis the EU legislature has to be assessed in the context of the interaction between negative and positive integration, as a defining feature of the process of European integration.[120] 'Negative integration' describes a process, driven by the Court, of setting aside national laws and practices which pose obstacles to free movement and competition within the EU. The term 'negative law' refers to the rules developed by the Court in the process of negative integration. 'Positive integration' refers to EU-level policy making, whose outcomes determine the conditions under which national markets operate.[121] This form of integration is grounded in the provisions of the Treaties that are not, normally, directly enforceable in themselves but provide the legal bases for the adoption of EU legislation. 'Positive law' encompasses a range of measures, such as regulations and directives, that are adopted using those legal bases.[122]

In principle, negative and positive law are meant to complement each other. Where the Court finds market restrictions stemming from national measures justified, hence compatible with EU law, the EU's legislature is invited to replace those measures with a common legislative standard.[123] If the legislature decides to do so, the sector will then

September 17, 1787 (as amended to 7 May 1992), Art 1, S 8; Commonwealth of Australia Constitution Act: July 9, 1900 (as amended to 31 October 1986), Arts 51, 92; Basic Law for the Federal Republic of Germany: 23 May 1949 (as amended to 11 July 2012), Art 73.

[119] This problem is returned to in ch 4.

[120] For a landmark account on positive and negative integration in the context of integrated economic areas, see J Tinbergen, *International Economic Integration* (Amsterdam, Brussels, Elsevier, 1954). In the context of European integration, see J Pinder, 'Positive Integration and Negative Integration: Some Problems of Economic Union in the EEC' (1968) 24 *The World Today* 88.

[121] FW Scharpf, 'Negative and Positive Integration in the Political Economy of European Welfare States' in G Marks et al (eds), *Governance in the European Union* (London, SAGE Publications, 1996).

[122] Positive law includes both legislative acts, such as regulations and directives, and non-legislative acts, such as Commission decisions.

[123] For accounts analysing the dynamic between the Court and EU legislature, see A Easson, 'Legal Approaches to European Integration: The Role of Court and Legislator in the Completion of the European Common Market' (1989) 12 *Journal of European Integration* 101, 114 ff; L Gormley, 'Free Movement of Goods and EU Legislation in the Court of Justice' in P Syrpis (ed), *The Judiciary, the Legislature and the EU Internal Market* (Cambridge, CUP, 2012) 48; A Stone Sweet, 'The European Court of Justice' in P Craig and G de Búrca (eds), *Evolution of EU law*, 2nd edn (Oxford, OUP, 2011) 121, 147–48. For a critical account on EU consumer

be harmonised, usually, through directives. So, national measures that are considered compatible with EU law stay that way until the EU takes legislative steps to regulate the matter at the European level.[124] If a national measure is found incompatible with EU law, it will no longer apply in respect of foreign actors or products, so, normally, there is no need for EU-wide harmonisation of the matter.[125] However, the EU legislature retains the right to re-regulate the area that has been deregulated as a result of the Court's case law and might choose to do so if there is pressure from commercial interests for a more reliable set of rules than is delivered by conditional mutual recognition[126] or, more generally, the need for transparency and uniformity in the area concerned.[127] When either of the branches in this dynamic process of interaction between the judiciary and legislature is not functioning properly, asymmetries may occur, making one branch more powerful than the other.

The EU's integration process has been characterised as inherently asymmetric since the early years of the EEC, owing to the dualism between supranational Community law, epitomised by judicial lawmaking, and intergovernmental European policy making.[128] The said dualism, a term coined by Weiler, describes in particular the period of integration when the asymmetry between negative and positive law was most pronounced as a result of the unanimity requirement that governed the process of adoption of EU legislation. Even today, when most EU legislation is passed by the majority vote, the EU's legal order remains biased towards negative integration. That is so because although qualified majority vote is easier to assemble than unanimity, it still requires a high degree of consensus among the political actors involved,[129] whereas negative law does not require, nor depend on, political will or agreement at the EU level. It stems directly from the rules contained in the Treaties and is directly judicially enforceable. For those reasons, it is prone to dominate the process of legal integration, making the Court the key actor shaping the contours of EU law.

The history of the EU suggests that the Court's own understanding of its judicial role in the EU is impacted by the dynamics of European integration. Recall the periods of EU political stagnation in the 1960s and 1970s. At that time, unanimous voting in Council was the norm for adopting legislative measures and consensus on the European political arena was lacking.[130] The Court used that situation as an opportunity to develop a

law *acquis*, see S Weatherill, 'The Consumer Rights Directive: How and Why a Quest for "Coherence" Has (Largely) Failed' (2012) 49 *CML Rev* 1279.

[124] Gormley (n 123) 51.

[125] Easson (n 123) 112–14. In the context of free movement of goods, see Commission, 'Communication from the Commission concerning the Consequences of the Judgment Given by the Court of Justice on 20 February 1979 in Case 120/78 ("*Cassis de Dijon*")' (Communication) COM (1980) OJ C256/2.

[126] S Weatherill, 'Did Cassis de Dijon Make a Difference?' in A Albors-Llorens, C Barnard and B Leucht (eds), *Cassis de Dijon: 40 Years On* (Cambridge, CUP, 2021), providing the example of regulation of blackcurrant liqueur and crème de cassis by EU legislation.

[127] Gormley (n 123) 55. See also M Van Empel, 'The 1992 Programme: Interaction between Legislator and Judiciary' (1992) 19 *Legal Issues of European Integration* 1.

[128] J Weiler, 'The Dual Character of Supranationalism' (1981) 1 *Yearbook of European Law* 267; Stein (n 35); Weiler (n 60); Scharpf (n 121) 15; FW Scharpf, 'Community and Autonomy: Multi-Level Policy-Making in the European Union' (1994) 1 *Journal of European Public Policy* 219, 219–20.

[129] These problems are examined in detail in ch 4.

[130] See, eg, Arts 100, 101, 235 EEC.

number of general principles of EU law, most notably supremacy and direct effect,[131] (conditional) mutual recognition,[132] equal treatment,[133] and the protection of fundamental rights,[134] thus providing a necessary impetus for further integration at both the judicial and legislative levels.[135] Judicial activism in the 1960s and 1970s was undoubtedly influenced by the political hurdles stalling collective decision making at the EU level. As such, it demonstrates that the Court is responsive to the EU's political institutional dynamics and may find itself empowered by them.

b. The EU's Democratic Deficit

The institutional position of the Court vis-à-vis the EU legislature is further enhanced by the lack of democratic legitimacy in the EU's political decision-making process. The EU is widely perceived to suffer from a democratic deficit,[136] which is attributed, on the one hand, to an inadequate level of parliamentary control over EU decision making and, on the other hand, an excessive influence of national governments in the EU's legislative process. The EU's democratic deficit has been addressed through a number of successive Treaty reforms: the creation of the European Parliament; giving the right of EU citizens to elect its members; and transforming its role from a consultative chamber into a co-legislative institution, having equal legislative and budgetary powers with the Council of Ministers in most areas.[137] However, notwithstanding these reforms, the EU's decision-making process remains dominated by the executive branch: national ministers in the Council and government appointees in the European Commission.[138] The Commission has control over the EU's policy agenda and holds an exclusive power

[131] *Van Gend & Loos* (n 117); *Costa v ENEL* (n 117).

[132] Case C-120/78 *Cassis de Dijon* EU:C:1979:42, [1979] ECR 649. For subsequent case law, see Case C-261/81 *Walter Rau* EU:C:1982:382, [1982] ECR 3961; Case C-178/84 *Commission v Germany ('Beer Purity')* EU:C:1987:126, [1987] ECR 1227; Case C-198/89 *Commission v Greece* EU:C:1991:79, [1991] ECR I-727; Case C-470/93 *Mars GmbH* EU:C:1995:224, [1995] ECR I-1923.

[133] *Defrenne* (n 82).

[134] See, eg, Case C-4/73 *Nold* EU:C:1974:51, [1974] ECR 491. See also Joined Cases C-402/05 P and C-415/05 P *Kadi v Council* EU:C:2008:461, [2008] ECR I-6351.

[135] The literature discussing these developments is rich. See, eg, Weiler (n 60); FG Mancini, 'The Making of a Constitution for Europe' (1989) 26 *CML Rev* 595, 612; Lenaerts (n 108); H Rasmussen, 'Towards A Normative Theory of Interpretation of Community Law' (1992) *University of Chicago Legal Forum* 135, 137; Tridimas (n 63); A Stone Sweet and JA Caporaso 'From Free Trade to Supranational Polity: The European Court and Integration' in W Sandholtz and A Stone Sweet, *European Integration and Supranational Governance* (Oxford, OUP, 1998) 64–71; S Weatherill, 'Activism and Restraint in the European Court of Justice' in P Capps, M Evans and S Konstadinidis (eds), *Asserting Jurisdiction: International and European Legal Perspectives* (Oxford, Hart Publishing, 2003); H de Waele, 'The Role of the European Court of Justice in the Integration Process: A Contemporary and Normative Assessment' (2010) 12 *Hanse Law Review* 3.

[136] For a comprehensive analysis, see M Avbelj, 'Can the New European Constitution Remedy the EU "Democratic Deficit"' (*Open Society Institute*, 2009) www.opensocietyfoundations.org/uploads/330ac5f8-e247-42e7-b60f-c6d3bde12a01/democratic-deficit-20050310.pdf. For seminal accounts arguing against the existence of a democratic deficit in the EU, see, eg, G Majone, 'Europe's "Democratic Deficit": The Question of Standards' (1998) 4 *European Law Journal* 5; A Moravcsik, 'The Myth of the European Democratic Deficit' (2003) 10 *Raisons Politiques* 87.

[137] Art 14(1) TEU. For a discussion of the reforms concerning the Parliament, see U Box, 'The European Parliament: historical background' (January 2021) www.europarl.europa.eu/factsheets/en/sheet/11/the-european-parliament-historical-background.

[138] For a more detailed analysis, see A Follesdal and S Hix, 'Why There is a Democratic Deficit in the EU: A Response to Majone and Moravcsik' (2006) 44 *Journal of Common Market Studies* 533, 535.

to initiate legislation. The Council, which combines legislative and executive functions, deliberates and adopts that legislation jointly with the Parliament.[139] Neither the Commission nor the Council is directly elected or accountable to the public in a meaningful way.

A more fundamental issue is that the EU is unlikely to ever become genuinely democratic because of the absence of a single European demos, who would act as both the *pouvoir constituent* and the legitimating source of the EU's governmental authority. Whilst, as pointed out above, the European Parliament is elected directly by EU citizens, it does not represent EU citizens as a unified whole. The system for allocating the seats within the Parliament employs the principle of 'degressive proportionality', which favours smaller Member States, with a view to ensuring fair representation of all the Member States (as opposed to all the citizens).[140] This system departs from a central democratic principle of electoral equality. As such, it demonstrates the absence of a European demos and highlights the importance of representing at EU level the individual demoi of the Member States.[141]

The lack of democratic legitimacy in the EU's political decision making highlights the importance of the rule of law in the EU as an alternative source of legitimacy in the absence of genuine democracy. This strengthens the importance of the Court as a guardian of the rule of law against the EU's political institutions.[142] At the same time, it lessens the constraining impact that the doctrine of separation of powers normally exerts on the judiciary in the conditions of democratic governance. Separation of powers has an important role to play in defining the limits of constitutional adjudication. It invites judicial restraint on behalf of constitutional courts in situations where they are faced with questions of interpretation that involve political or policy considerations.[143] The basis for the exercise of such restraint lies, first, in the awareness by the judiciary of the institutional limitations inherent in the exercise of judicial functions and, second, the ensuing willingness to defer to the views of the elected branches of government on questions whose nature requires democratic deliberation. In this respect, the presence of democratic deficiencies in the EU's decision-making process removes an important premise for the exercise of judicial restraint on behalf of the Court in cases whose resolution would involve making a policy choice or have policy implications.

It is clear from the above that the scope of the institutional power of the Court is not only determined by the Treaties but is also shaped by the broader political institutional context in which the Court operates. That power is enhanced by the relative weakness

[139] The powers of the Commission and the Council are stipulated in Arts 16 and 17 TEU, respectively.

[140] Art 14(2) TEU.

[141] See also R Bellamy, '"An Ever Closer Union Among the Peoples of Europe": Republican Intergovernmentalism and Demoicratic Representation within the EU' (2013) 35 *Journal of European Integration* 499, 509 referring to BVerfG, judgment of 30 June 2009, 2 BvE 2/08 (*Lisbon*), paras 280, 286.

[142] See, eg, Case C-550/09 *E and F* [2010] ECR I-6213, para 44.

[143] On the link between separation of powers and judicial restraint, see, eg, G Marshall, *Constitutional Theory* (Clarendon Press 1971) 109–14; PA Talmadge, 'Understanding the Limits of Power: Judicial Restraint in General Jurisdiction Court Systems' (1999) 22 *Seattle University Law Review* 695. For a case against judicial review of legislation, see also J Waldron, 'The Core of the Case Against Judicial Review' (2006) 115 *Yale Law Journal* 1346. See also AC Hutchinson, 'A "Hard Core" Case against Judicial Review' (2008) 121 *Harvard Law Review Forum* 57.

of the EU's legislative institutions and the persisting lack of democratic legitimacy in the EU's legislative process. Both of these circumstances serve – and possibly have always served – as an incentive for the Court to be proactive in its mission of protecting the rule of law in the EU. This involves, as will be demonstrated in this book, making bolder choices both in the interpretation of the Treaties themselves and the interpretation of EU legislation in light of those Treaties.[144]

iii. Regulatory Capacity

Considering the breadth of the EU's judicial mandate and the favourable political institutional context in which the Court operates, it seems almost inherent in the very exercise of the Court's powers that its judgments are prone to have policy implications.[145] But the Court's influence is not limited to producing policy implications – that notion does not capture the full extent of the Court's powers. In this context, it would appear more helpful to speak of the Court's regulatory capacity, that is, the capacity to regulate economic and social relations through its judgments. The concept of a regulatory capacity is intertwined with that of policy-making capacity: the latter is usually a precondition for the presence of the former, and the former is a necessary consequence of the latter. However, the concept of a regulatory capacity captures the depth of penetration of the case law into national legal systems in a way that a discussion of policy implications would not be able to. It highlights the power of the Court to shape the conditions of social and economic life of EU citizens – a power that is normally associated with the exercise of public authority by legislative and executive bodies. The Court's regulatory capacity is entrenched in the structure of the EU. It is a natural product of the legal constitutional and political institutional circumstances discussed above: the broad scope of the EU's judicial mandate; the equally broad framing of the numerous substantive rules of the Treaty, whose interpretation lies in the hands of the judiciary; and, indirectly, the procedural weaknesses and democratic deficiencies pertaining to the EU's political decision making. It is this regulatory capacity which makes the Court amenable to constitutional control.

It is important to distinguish the regulatory capacity of the Court's judgments from their deregulatory capacity. The term 'deregulatory' denotes the character of the judicial interpretation of the Treaties. The deregulatory effects of the case law, especially the internal market case law, have been widely discussed in the literature. The term has been employed to describe, in the first place, the dynamic between negative and positive law: the Court deregulates while the EU legislature re-regulates. Increasingly, however, the term has come to be associated with the damaging consequences of the judicial interpretation of internal market law for national public policy, particularly social policy. This phenomenon has been most famously documented and analysed by Fritz Scharpf, whose work will be referred to at different points in this book. The main

[144] Notably, while it is true that the Court remains largely deferential in the judicial *review* of EU legislation, as will be discussed in chs 2 and 3, the Court's apparent self-restraint in this context may be explained by the general centralist, pro-integration bias in its case law rather than the separation of powers concerns.

[145] Discussed by De Búrca and other authors. See nn 110 and 111.

idea in Scharpf's analysis is that the case law tends to favour the values of free market and individual choice over market-correcting policies and values of social solidarity, thereby threatening to dismantle the socio-economic models of the Member States.[146] Moreover, the deregulatory effects of the case law often remain unremedied due to the constitutional constraints on EU legislative action that stem from the judicial interpretation of EU primary law.[147]

The deregulatory aspect of EU judicial practice is an important issue, which will be discussed at length in this book. However, it should not be confused with the concept of regulatory capacity discussed in this chapter. Regardless of the nature of the Court's regulatory activity (that is, the deregulatory nature), the primary concern of this chapter is that the Court seems to possess, to begin with, the capacity to regulate economic and social relations in a way that resembles legislative or executive activity. The character of the rules it lays down through interpretation is of secondary importance at this point. Put differently, the Court should be subject to constitutional constraints on competence not because it deregulates; it should be subject to competence constraints because it has an unprecedented capacity, comparable to that of the EU's legislature, to reform and transform the regulatory landscapes of domestic legal systems.

Finally, I do not contend that the regulatory capacity exercised by the Court is analogous to that of EU legislative institutions. There are notable differences. Writing about the Court as an institutional actor, De Búrca rightly observes that the Court is not free in the same sense as other institutions to use law as an instrument of policy.[148] By the same token, I would add, the Court is not completely free to use law as an instrument of regulation. The Court does not possess a direct regulatory mandate, which would allow it to take action whenever it deems necessary to do so in order to implement a premeditated policy agenda, address unanticipated policy issues or fill regulatory gaps as they occur. As an institution which is primarily concerned with the resolution of legal disputes, the Court is limited in its decision making by the framework of the cases that come before it, the concrete provisions of the Treaties, which it is bound to interpret, and the standards and methods of legal reasoning it must adopt in its judgments. However, none of these limitations detract from the fact that the Court possesses a broad-scale capacity to regulate economic and social relations and that it engages in regulatory activity through its judgments.

Incrementally but systematically, the judgments of the Court have shaped the regulatory landscape at both the European and Member State level, thus constraining the permissible scope of action by the EU legislature and national governments. The history of European integration offers a multitude of examples that demonstrate this tendency. For instance, the doctrines of supremacy and direct effect of EU law, mentioned earlier, are primarily discussed in the context of the constitutionalisation of EU law, their regulatory significance being somewhat of secondary importance.[149] Yet it is undeniable

[146] To that effect, see, eg, FW Scharpf, 'The Asymmetry of European Integration, or Why the EU Cannot Be a "Social Market Economy"' (2010) 8 *Socio-Economic Review* 211.
[147] This issue will be examined in ch 4.
[148] De Búrca (n 106) 232.
[149] See, eg, Stein (n 35); Weiler (n 60).

that these legal doctrines, along with the principle of (conditional) mutual recognition, have transformed the regulatory landscape of the EU's internal market and induced systemic reforms in the domestic legal systems of the Member States.[150] These are not isolated examples, as will be demonstrated in chapter three through a comprehensive study of the regulatory implications of the case law across four distinct areas of national social policy. Chapter four will further illuminate this issue by examining the implications of the case law for EU legislative outcomes. The book will demonstrate that the breadth of the Court's regulatory capacity, presupposed by its powerful institutional status in the EU, makes it not only desirable, but also essential for the legitimacy of the Court and the EU more generally, that the Court be subject to the same constraints on competence as the rest of the EU institutions.

B. The EU as an Organisation of Limited Powers, or Why the CJEU is an Unfree Court

There is a caveat to the argument advanced above. The regulatory and policy-making capacity associated with judicial practice, and constitutional adjudication in particular, is not an unusual phenomenon. In that sense, it might not seem a sufficient reason in and of itself to subject the Court to the competence constraints that bind EU political institutions.

In that connection, the following discussion contrasts the institutional position of the Court with that of national constitutional courts. It argues that the Court, despite being a judicial institution, is not free from constraints on power in the exercise of its interpretative authority in the same way as national constitutional courts are, because it operates in a polity whose own powers are constrained.

i. The Institutional Position of National Constitutional Courts

National constitutional courts and supreme courts with a constitutional role[151] possess considerable regulatory capacity, yet the decision-making powers of those courts remain largely unconstrained.

The various comparative studies on judicial lawmaking seem to agree that constitutional adjudication has a substantial impact on policy making and legislative activity.[152]

[150] M Maduro, *We the Court: The European* Court *of Justice and the European Economic Constitution* (Oxford, Hart Publishing, 1998) chs 2 and 3, demonstrating the regulatory effects of the case law in the context of the free movement of goods.

[151] See, generally, L Garlicki, 'Constitutional Courts versus Supreme Courts' (2007) 5 *International Journal of Constitutional Law* 44, suggesting that supreme courts with a constitutional role may be more powerful than specialised constitutional courts, which find themselves in competition with supreme courts when their jurisdictions overlap.

[152] On constitutional adjudication and judicial lawmaking, see, eg, A Stone Sweet, *Governing with Judges: Constitutional Politics in Europe* (Oxford, OUP, 2000) chs 2, 3, 7; AR Brewer-Carías, *Constitutional Courts as Positive Legislators. A Comparative Law Study* (Cambridge, CUP, 2017) pt I. On judicial lawmaking, see, eg, M Cappelletti, 'The Law-Making Power of the Judge and Its Limits: A Comparative Analysis' (1981) 8 *Monash University Law Review* 15; M Fichera, 'Constitutional Courts / Supreme Courts as Positive Legislators,'

Contrary to the Kelsenian vision of constitutional adjudication, constitutional courts do not (or no longer) confine themselves to the role of negative legislators, limited to the exclusion from the legal system of a provision declared unconstitutional.[153] Increasingly, they choose to remedy legislative gaps and shortcomings via judicial reasoning rather than leave that task for the democratically elected legislature.[154] Courts do so by drafting their judgments in a manner that provides a detailed interpretation of the law in question or prescribes concrete guidelines to the legislature on the course of legislative action to be taken.[155] As a consequence, even if not directly intended,[156] the decisions of supreme and constitutional courts around the world come to determine regulatory outcomes in key areas of public policy, such as public health, education, equality law, social protection, industrial relations, and many others.[157]

Whether desirable or not, these developments suggest that supreme and constitutional courts possess a significant regulatory capacity and do not shy away from exercising it. Regardless, they are subject to none of the constitutional legal constraints or checks on power that apply to decision making by political institutions. They operate in the conditions of full autonomy and independence and have exclusive authority to decide on the scope of their competence.[158] The decision making of constitutional courts is constrained solely by the text of the constitution, which they are bound to interpret.[159] This, accordingly, means that constitutional judges must transform disputes concerning public policy 'into questions of constitutional interpretation that can be decided by texts, procedures, principles, and rules that are generally accepted as legal and not

Max Planck Encyclopedia of Comparative Constitutional Law (2020) oxcon.ouplaw.com/view/10.1093/law-mpeccol/law-mpeccol-e644#law-mpeccol-e644-div1-5.

[153] For a seminal account on constitutional courts as negative legislators, see H Kelsen, 'La Garantie Juridictionnelle de la Constitution' (1928) 45 *Revue de Droit Public* 197.

[154] See, eg, Stone Sweet (n 152) ch 2; Fichera (n 152).

[155] See, eg, Initial decision, No 3011 of 1997, ILDC 442 (IN 1997) on sexual harassment in the workplace, summarised in 'Vishaka v State of Rajasthan' blogs.lse.ac.uk/vaw/landmark-cases/vishaka-v-state-of-rajasthan; *Minister of Health v Treatment Action Campaign*, 2002 (5) SA 721 (CC), discussed in S Bilchitz, 'South Africa: Right to Health and Access to HIV/AIDS Drug Treatment' (2003) 1 *International Journal of Constitutional Law* 524; *Government of the Republic of South Africa v Grootboom*, 2001 (1) SA 46 (CC), deriving from the Constitution the obligation for the government to provide rudimentary shelter to children and their parents on demand if the parents are unable to shelter their children.

[156] Stone Sweet (n 152) ch 7, esp 200–01, pointing out that constitutional courts seek to demonstrate that the policy consequences of their decisions 'are second order effects that are not of themselves desired by the judges, but rather are required by the law'.

[157] R Hirschl, 'The Judicialization of Mega-Politics and the Rise of Political Courts' (2008) 11 *Annual Review of Political Science* 98. For a study of the jurisprudence of European constitutional courts, see Stone Sweet (n 152) chs 3–4; A Stone Sweet, 'The Politics of Constitutional Review in France and Europe' (2007) 5 *International Journal of Constitutional Law* 79, examining the 'transformative' effects of lawmaking by supreme and constitutional courts. See also LP Claus and RS Kay, 'Constitutional Courts as "Positive Legislators" in the United States' (2010) 58 *American Journal of Comparative Law* 479, discussing the jurisprudence of the US Supreme Court.

[158] Basic Principles on the Independence of the Judiciary (United Nations) UN Doc A/CONF.121/22/Rev.1, 58. For a collection of essays on judicial independence, see S Shetreet and C Forsyth (eds), *The Culture of Judicial Independence: Conceptual Foundations and Practical Challenges* (Leiden, Martinus Nijhoff Publishers, 2012) pts I, II. On the relationship between the rule of law, separation of powers and judicial independence, see, eg, SJ Ervin Jr, 'Separation of Powers: Judicial Independence' (1970) 35 *Law Contemporary Problems* 108.

[159] Notably, the constitution in the broad sense of the word also includes unwritten constitutional principles, which do not appear in the formal text of the constitution but are developed through court practice.

political'.[160] Constraints of this kind are, however, inherent in the very nature of constitutional adjudication. They should not, therefore, be confused with the mechanisms of control placed on the exercise of political power. Whilst constitutional courts routinely rule on the legitimacy of the exercise of political power in light of the constitutional principles which determine the scope of that power, they are not themselves bound by such principles in the exercise of their authority to interpret the constitution.[161] So why should the CJEU be treated any differently?

ii. Why the CJEU is Different

The crucial difference between the institutional position of the CJEU and that of national constitutional courts stems from the fact that the CJEU operates in the constitutional framework of the EU. It is often said that the EU is not a State. This might be stating the obvious, yet the implications of the EU's non-state character for its judiciary are often overlooked in the academic discourse concerning the Court. Arguably, the differences between the *modi operandi* of the EU and national governments are significant enough to place the CJEU in a *sui generis* institutional position that excludes it from some of the constitutional protections enjoyed by national constitutional courts.

National governments are normally entrusted by the people with a general and, by and large, unconditional mandate to govern in the territory of the State. As Schütze points out, in that respect, governments are omnipotent, or omnicompetent: they enjoy the power and authority to act in all matters.[162] Such omnipotence is inherent in the idea of a sovereign State. Certainly, governments do not have absolute freedom, at least not in the conditions of democratic governance. Their powers are constrained by higher constitutional principles, such as the rule of law and the protection of fundamental rights, amongst others. These constraints do not, however, detract from the general competence of the government to rule in the territory of that State and, in that sense, are qualitatively different from the constitutional limits imposed on the powers of a supranational polity such as the EU.

The EU's mandate to govern in the territory of the EU is only indirect. It derives from the governments of the Member States – the masters of the Treaties – rather than the European demos as such. This mandate is confined to the specific areas of competence conferred upon the EU and restricted by the constitutional principles which govern the exercise of those competences. Arguably, the mandate conferred upon either of the EU's governing institutions, through which EU competences are exercised, cannot be broader, at least not legitimately, than the mandate conferred upon the EU itself. In other words, the powers of either the EU's legislature, executive or judiciary cannot

[160] H Schwartz, *The Struggle for Constitutional Justice in Post-Communist Europe* (Chicago, University of Chicago Press, 2000) 5.

[161] For example, the German Federal Constitutional Court has the duty to uphold the principles of subsidiarity and proportionality in the actions of the federal government, but it is not bound by these principles in the interpretation of the Basic Law. For an analysis of these principles in German constitutional law, see, eg, G Taylor, 'Germany: The Subsidiarity Principle' (2006) 4 *International Journal of Constitutional Law* 115; G Nolte, 'General Principles of German and European Administrative Law: A Comparison in Historical Perspective' (1994) 57 *Modern Law Review* 191.

[162] R Schütze, 'EU Competences: Existence and Exercise' in Chalmers and Arnull (n 63) 76.

exceed the scope of powers of the EU as a whole. By the same token, none of the EU institutions should be exempted from the constitutional constraints on power, applicable both to its scope and exercise, that bind the rest of them. This logic is supported by Art 5 TEU, which does not differentiate between the institutions of the EU when referring to competence constraints applicable to Union action, and Art 13 TEU, which lists the Court as one of the EU institutions.[163] The constitutional and institutional framework of the EU thus seems to suggest that the principles governing the scope and exercise of EU competences must be observed by all of the EU institutions, including the judiciary. This is all the more true given that the Court is endowed with a broad regulatory capacity in the judicial exercise of EU competences.

The above considerations are not limited to the EU. The constitutional framework of the Council of Europe offers support for the proposition that supranational courts ought to be subject to the same competence constraints that bind the organisation in which they operate. The ECtHR, the principal judicial organ of the Council of Europe, has long recognised in its jurisprudence that it is bound by the principle of subsidiarity in the interpretation of the ECHR.[164] Remarkably, as Cassese points out, this was a self-imposed restraint.[165] For most of its existence, the Convention did not require the ECtHR to observe the principle of subsidiarity. Subsidiarity did not even appear in the text of the Convention up until 2013, when Protocol 15 introduced a reference to the principle of subsidiarity and its corollary, the doctrine of margin of appreciation, into the Preamble of the Convention.[166] In fact, what Protocol 15 did was effectively to codify the position held by the ECtHR since late 1970s whereby the court declared that the mechanism for the protection of human rights established by the Convention was subsidiary to the national systems safeguarding human rights. The subsidiary nature of the Convention implies that the primary responsibility for the protection of human rights lies with national authorities, which 'by reason of their direct and continuous contact with the vital forces of their countries' are 'in principle in a better position than the international judge' to determine the content of public interest requirements that restrict human rights and the necessity of the restrictions intended to meet such requirements.[167] In consequence, national authorities are given a margin of appreciation when making assessments as regards the balance to be sought between the protection of public interests and individual rights.[168]

The example of the ECtHR does not mean that the constitutional constraints limiting the scope and exercise of EU competences should apply to the judicial interpretation of EU law on the same basis or in the same manner as the requirements of subsidiarity apply to the interpretation of the Convention by the ECtHR. Nor does it mean that

[163] On this point, see Horsley (n 111) 2–9, 23–32.

[164] Convention on the Protection of Human Rights and Fundamental Freedoms (ECHR) (adopted 4 November 1950, entered into force 3 September 1953) ETS 5. The landmark cases were *The Belgian Linguistic case (No 2)* (1968) 1 EHRR 252, paras 10–13 and *Handyside v UK* (1976) 1 EHRR 737, paras 48–50.

[165] Cassese (n 22) 6.

[166] Protocol No 15 amending the Convention for the Protection of Human Rights and Fundamental Freedoms [2013] ETS 213, Art 1.

[167] *Handyside v UK* (n 164), paras 48–50.

[168] See ch 5, s II for a comprehensive analysis of the relationship between the principle of subsidiarity and the doctrine of margin of appreciation.

the constitutional framework in which the CJEU operates is analogous to that of the ECHR.[169] It does, however, mean that there exists no general a priori objection to applying competence constraints to judicial practice at a supranational level.

Moreover, the jurisprudence of the CJEU itself lends support to this conclusion. It demonstrates that the Court already recognises that certain constitutional constraints, in particular, the need to protect fundamental rights, apply to the judicial interpretation of EU law. The language of fundamental rights has entered the jurisprudence of the Court in an attempt to defend the claim to supremacy of, then, Community law over national law.[170] The Court first pronounced on the status of fundamental rights in Community law in the *International Handelsgesellschaft* case,[171] in response to the challenge by the German Federal Constitutional Court to the legitimacy of Community law and case law.[172] The Court then recognised that the protection of fundamental rights formed an integral part of the general principles of Community law. Accordingly, Community institutions were bound by the requirement to act in compliance with fundamental rights. The recognition by the Court of the binding status of fundamental rights in EU law also meant that EU case law would be guided, and thus constrained, by the general principle requiring that the protection of fundamental rights be ensured in cases which had human rights implications.[173] In other words, the Court recognised that it was bound by the duty to protect fundamental rights in the exercise of its authority to interpret EU law. This case law confirms that there exists no principled, conceptual objection against the application to the Court of the constitutional principles that would constrain the exercise of EU judicial authority.

C. Conclusion

This section argued that the Court is bound to abide by the principles of conferral, subsidiarity and proportionality in the judicial interpretation of the Treaties. It demonstrated that there exists no principled objection as to why the Court, as a supranational judicial institution, should be subject to competence constraints applicable to the polity it operates in. Moreover, it argued that the Court's institutional position in the EU endows it with a regulatory capacity, characteristic of that possessed by bodies which exercise political authority on behalf of the State, which makes it constitutionally unacceptable for the Court to be exempt from the constraints on competence that govern the actions of the EU's political institutions.

[169] For an account comparing and contrasting EU subsidiarity and ECHR margin of appreciation, see F Fabbrini, 'The Margin of Appreciation and the Principle of Subsidiarity: A Comparison' (2015) iCourts Working Paper Series 15/2015, papers.ssrn.com/sol3/papers.cfm?abstract_id=2552542.

[170] See, eg, A Coppel and J O'Neill, 'The European Court of Justice: Taking Rights Seriously' (1992) 29 *Common Market Law Review* 669.

[171] Case C-11/70 *Internationale Handelsgesellschaft* EU:C:1970:114, [1970] ECR 1125, paras 3–4. See also *Nold* (n 134). Note that the Court mentions fundamental rights in passing already in Case C-29/69 *Stauder* EU:C:1969:57, [1969] ECR 419, para 7.

[172] *Solange I* (n 98).

[173] T-I Harbo, 'The Function of the Proportionality Principle in EU Law' (2010) 16 *European Law Journal* 158, 164.

IV. Conclusion

This chapter analysed the principles governing the allocation of competences and powers in the EU – conferral, subsidiarity, proportionality and institutional balance – in light of a broader discussion of the constitutional constraints that ought to guide the exercise of EU judicial authority.

Section I discussed the significance of these principles for the EU's constitutional structure – specifically, the EU's federal balance of competences – and examined the role of the Court in preserving that structure. It demonstrated that the principles of conferral, subsidiarity, proportionality and, indirectly, institutional balance maintain the balance between the qualities of supranationalism and uniformity of EU law, on the one hand, and respect for the autonomy and diversity of the Member States, on the other. As the EU's constitutional judiciary, the Court has a duty to uphold this balance through ensuring the observance of these principles both in the decision making by the EU's political institutions and in the judicial interpretation of the Treaties. Failure on behalf of the Court to do so comes with consequences. It leads to undue interference by EU law with the democratic decision making at the Member State level, thus further weakening the EU's democratic legitimacy; creates tensions in the Court's relationship with national constitutional courts, thereby threatening to compromise the authority of the Court and supremacy of EU law; and – on the political level – fuels populist, anti-EU narratives, which may in the long run jeopardise the future of European integration.

Section II considered the relationship between the vertical division of competences in the EU and the protection of non-market, social values in EU law. It rejected the view that the protection of social values is secondary to the economic objectives of the internal market and is to be mainly achieved through the protection of the regulatory autonomy of the Member States. It argued that the protection of these values is and has ever been ingrained in the very fabric of the Treaties. The historical analysis revealed that none of the treaties constituting the EU and its predecessors seem to have intended to establish a constitutional hierarchy between the economic and social domains of EU law. Quite the contrary, social welfare and the pursuit of social objectives have always been an integral part of the internal market project and were seen as a desired and natural consequence of market integration. Therefore, despite an unequal distribution of EU competences across the two domains, the Court remains obligated to interpret the rules of the internal market in light of the EU's social values.

Section III challenged the conventional perception whereby the principles governing the division of competences between the EU and Member States (conferral, subsidiarity and proportionality) apply exclusively to the EU's legislative and executive practices, as opposed to its judicial practices. It presented an argument for why these principles should govern the interpretation by the Court of EU internal market law. It demonstrated that the structure of the EU endows the Court with a regulatory capacity characteristic of that possessed by institutions which exercise political authority on behalf of the State – legislative and executive institutions. This regulatory capacity is presupposed by a set of constitutional and political institutional circumstances: the broad scope of the EU's judicial mandate; the equally broad framing of a wide range of the substantive rules of the Treaty, whose interpretation lies in the hands of the judiciary; and, lastly, the procedural weaknesses and democratic deficiencies pertaining to the EU's political decision making, which indirectly strengthen the role of the judiciary as a guardian of the rule of law in the EU. The regulatory capacity possessed by the Court is what makes a situation where the Court is exempt from competence constraints that apply to the rest of the EU's governing branches constitutionally unacceptable.

2

Free Movement Case Law in Light of the Principle of Conferral

Chapter one discussed the importance of the principles of conferral, subsidiarity and proportionality for preserving the federal balance of competences in the EU and demonstrated why these principles should apply to the exercise of EU judicial authority. The aim of chapters two and three is to determine the legitimacy of the Court's interpretation of free movement law in light of these principles. The analysis of the case law conducted in these chapters also helps to illuminate the constitutional issues raised in chapter one. It exposes the extent of the Court's regulatory capacity, manifesting itself through the judicial interpretation of free movement law, and demonstrates why and how the way in which the Court exercises that capacity sits in tension with the constitutional principles that govern the division of competences between the EU and Member States. Chapter four then examines the implications of the case law for the institutional balance of powers between the Court and EU legislature. Chapter five proposes certain interpretative solutions on the part of the Court which could rectify the constitutional and institutional imbalances resulting from the case law.

This chapter is dedicated to the principle of conferral. It assesses the implications of EU free movement case law under study for the effectiveness of the protections of national competence provided by this principle. The chapter is organised in seven sections. Section I discusses the meaning and place of the principle of conferral in the EU's constitutional structure, highlights the problems inherent in the gap between the theory and practice of this principle, and derives from the Treaties the normative requirements that this principle imposes on the exercise of EU judicial authority. Sections II–V are dedicated to the analysis of the case law involving the policy areas under study. Each section begins with an introduction of the main competence questions surrounding EU regulation of the area concerned and discusses the extent to which that area has been covered by EU law. Then, it moves to the analysis of central developments in the case law involving that policy area, focusing on the Court's interpretation of the scope of free movement rules in the given situation. The judicial interpretation of the scope of free movement rules reveals to what extent the Court considers the requirements of the principle of conferral in the interpretation of free movement law. The discussion is centred around the historically first judgments in each of the areas concerned because the question of whether the situation falls within the scope of EU law normally arises and is resolved early on in the case law. Section VI takes a comparative view of the developments across the four policy areas and examines them against the requirements of the principle of conferral. Section VII concludes.

I. The Principle of Conferral in Application to EU Judiciary

This section examines the EU's relationship with the Member States in light of the principle of conferral with the view to determining the requirements that this principle imposes on the judicial interpretation of the Treaties.

A. The Principle of Conferral in Theory

While having been in operation since the origins of the EEC, the principle of conferral was expressly enshrined in EU primary law in the Maastricht Treaty and later reinforced by the Lisbon reforms.[1] As is well known, it governs the existence, or the scope, of Union competences. Spelled out in Art 5(2) TEU, it requires that the Union act only within the limits of the competences conferred upon it by the Member States, and 'competences not conferred upon the Union in the Treaties remain with the Member States'.

Although the principle of conferral did not gain express Treaty recognition until Maastricht, it did not need to. This principle is, and always has been, foundational to the operation of the EU and its predecessors, reflecting the fact that the Union (and previously, Community) is not omnipotent in a way that the State is towards its subjects.[2] The EU derives its powers from the Member States and only has as many powers as Member States have specifically agreed to confer on it in the founding treaties. Accordingly, the Community, before it became the EU, never possessed competences that were not included in the text of the treaties in force at the time.[3] Every action on behalf of the Community required a legal basis to be found in the specific provisions of the Treaties.[4] So, for example, the Community had no competence to act in the field of higher education up until 1992. Similarly, if a certain competence was granted but its scope was limited by the text of the Treaties, such as in the areas of social policy and public health, that competence existed only to the extent provided by the Treaties. These observations might seem basic, but, as will be demonstrated in the case law analysis below, their salience has too often been neglected by the Court.

As part of the reforms introduced by the Treaty of Lisbon, EU competences are classified into exclusive, shared and supplementary.[5] The prohibition on the EU interfering with the competences reserved to the Member States effectively extends to the areas falling within the category of the EU's supplementary, or complementary, competences.

[1] Consolidated version of the Treaty on European Union [2008] OJ C115/13 (TEU), Arts 4(2) and 5(1); Consolidated version of the Treaty on the Functioning of the European Union [2008] OJ C115/47 (TFEU), Arts 2–6.

[2] R Schütze, 'EU Competences: Existence and Exercise' in D Chalmers and A Arnull (eds), *Oxford Handbook of European Union Law* (Oxford, OUP, 2015) 76.

[3] See Treaty establishing the European Economic Community (adopted 25 March 1957, entered into force 1 January 1958) (EEC), Art 4, establishing what could be regarded as an institutional version of the principle of conferral, stipulating that in order to achieve the tasks entrusted to the Community, each of the Community institutions shall act within the limits of the powers conferred upon them by the Treaty.

[4] Art 3 EEC, stipulating that the activities of the Community should be pursued only 'under the conditions … provided for in this Treaty'.

[5] Arts 2–6 TFEU.

These are the areas in which the Union has been granted competence 'to carry out actions to support, coordinate or supplement' Member State action, excluding the possibility of adopting harmonising legislation.[6] So, whilst the areas falling within the supplementary competences of the EU are not completely exempt from the influence of EU law and policy, they seem to be protected from any substantial interference on the EU's behalf. This means that the principle of conferral in theory should protect the majority of the policy areas under the present study. The list of areas falling within the category of EU supplementary competences includes, *inter alia*, the protection and improvement of human health, education and vocational training, and social policy, except for the aspects of social policy belonging to competences that are shared with the Member States.[7] By contrast, the gambling sector, also under study here, does not benefit from the same protections. As an internal market service, gambling falls within the category of shared competences,[8] giving the EU an unrestricted mandate to supersede Member State action in the regulation of gambling. The Treaties contain no other provision that would limit EU competence to regulate gambling.

The sector-specific legal bases for healthcare, education and collective labour law reiterate and make more concrete the limitations expressed in the principle of conferral. Art 168 TFEU provides the EU with complementary competences in the area of public health, excluding the possibility of harmonisation, and obliges the EU to 'respect the responsibilities of the Member States for the definition of their health policy and the organisation and delivery of health services and medical care'.[9] Art 165(1) TFEU charges the EU with a duty to 'contribute to the development of quality education by encouraging cooperation between Member States and, if necessary, by supporting and supplementing their action'. However, any EU action must be taken while fully respecting the responsibilities of the Member States in the field and therefore excludes any harmonisation of national laws or regulations.[10] Similarly, Art 153(1) TFEU stipulates that the EU shall support and complement the activities of the Member States in, inter alia, the representation and collective defence of the interests of workers and employers. This provision is subject to para (5) of the same article, which expressly excludes the right to strike and the right of association from EU-level harmonisation. The right to collective bargaining is not explicitly listed among the exclusions, but the Treaty provides no clear legislative basis for it.[11] In addition, Art 156 suggests that collective bargaining is not subject to binding legislation by stipulating that in matters relating to collective bargaining the Commission shall encourage cooperation between Member States and facilitate the coordination of their action. Also, collective bargaining may well fall within the definition of the 'right of association',[12] which, together with the right to strike, is excluded from harmonisation.

[6] Arts 2(5) and 6 TFEU.

[7] Art 4(b) TFEU.

[8] Art 4 TFEU.

[9] Art 168(7) TFEU.

[10] Art 6 TEU; Art 165(4) TFEU.

[11] B Ryan, 'The Charter and Collective Labour Law' in TK Hervey and J Kenner (eds), *Economic and Social Rights Under the EU Charter of Fundamental Rights – A Legal Perspective* (Oxford, Hart Publishing, 2003) 67–68, 84–85.

[12] See, eg, *Demir and Baykara v Turkey* (2009) 48 EHRR 54, holding that collective bargaining is an integral part of freedom of association.

The general and sector-specific definitions of the principle of conferral thus seem to preclude the kind of interference by the EU into the areas of healthcare, education and collective labour law that would go beyond non-binding incentive measures.[13]

B. The Principle of Conferral in Practice: The Scope of EU Law, Competence and Legal Basis

The way that the principle of conferral operates in practice, rather than in theory, is less straightforward because, owing to the asymmetry between negative and positive law,[14] Member States must comply with EU primary rules, including the internal market law, even in the areas that in principle fall outside the EU's regulatory competence. In that respect, the Court holds a position whereby the lack of legislative competence on behalf of the EU does not remove the matter from the *scope of EU law* – a legal category that is broader than competence and encompasses the substantive rules of EU primary law. This line of reasoning has by now become the standard opening line of judgments that concern constitutionally sensitive areas of EU law and policy. Labelled as the 'retained powers formula' by Azoulai, it reiterates that in the absence of EU-level harmonisation, Member States retain the competence to regulate the area concerned, but when exercising that competence, they nevertheless need to comply with the rules laid down in the Treaties.[15] In the context of the present inquiry, this means that national laws and practices, regardless of whether they concern matters that fall within the scope of the EU's legislative competence, must in any event comply with EU internal market law, including the free movement rules laid down in the Treaties and interpreted by the CJEU. This, in turn, suggests that the limits placed on EU action in sectoral legal bases, discussed previously, do not apply to the directly enforceable EU internal market rules and that the principal of conferral is limited to legislative conferral.

Yet that conclusion is not entirely correct either because the logic underlying the judicial interpretation of the scope of internal market law also extends to EU legislative action. Here, a distinction should be made between the existence of EU competence and the *legal basis* behind the exercise of a particular competence. For example, a competence has not been conferred on the EU to issue binding legislation in either of the areas of healthcare, education or collective labour rights. However, in practice that does not preclude the EU's legislative intervention in those areas. The Treaties contain a number of functionally broad, or horizontal, legal bases that are not confined to a specific policy area and, therefore, can be used to regulate any matter that falls within the framework of the internal market, provided that certain conditions are satisfied.[16]

Art 114 TFEU, the internal market legal basis, has attracted a great amount of academic commentary, so its discussion here will be brief and tailored to the inquiry.

[13] To that effect, see Arts 165(4) and 168(5) TFEU, referring to the power of the EU to adopt incentive measures.

[14] On this point, see ch 1, s III.

[15] L Azoulai, '"Retained Powers" Formula in the Case Law of the European Court of Justice: EU Law as Total Law?' (2011) 4 *European Journal of Legal Studies* 192.

[16] See, in particular, Arts 21, 50, 59, 114 and 352 TFEU.

Art 114 authorises the adoption of harmonising measures that have the objective of improving the conditions for the establishment and functioning of the internal market where no other specific legal basis applies. The internal market is, in turn, defined in Art 26(2) TFEU as 'an area without internal frontiers in which the free movement of goods, persons, services and capital is ensured in accordance with the provisions of the Treaties'. Accordingly, the Court holds that the conditions for the recourse to Art 114 are met if the measures in question contribute to the elimination of existing or likely obstacles to the exercise of fundamental freedoms or to the removal of appreciable distortions of competition likely to arise from the diverse national rules.[17] EU judicial practice to date suggests that these conditions are easily met and that the threshold for what constitutes an adequate contribution to the internal market is low.[18] Where that threshold is met, the EU legislature can rely on Art 114 even if the decisive factor for the legislative intervention is a policy concern not related to the functioning of the internal market per se.[19] Moreover, the latter rule applies to situations where the EU has not been accorded competence to regulate the matter in question in a binding way, such as in the areas under study. This makes the scope of Art 114 extremely broad in practice.[20]

Arts 50 and 59 TFEU are also concerned with measures aimed at the functioning of the internal market, but their material scope is narrower than that of Art 114. Art 50 authorises the adoption of directives in order to attain the 'freedom of establishment as regards a particular activity' and Art 59 is aimed at the liberalisation of a specific service. Notably, since there exists an overlap in the scope of the three provisions, EU legislation will at times refer to Arts 50 and 59 together with Art 114.[21] By contrast, Art 21 TFEU is concerned with the movement of people rather than goods and services. It can be relied on in order to adopt measures aimed at facilitating the exercise of the right of EU citizens to move and reside freely within the territory of the EU.[22] However, just like Art 114, it can be invoked only where the Treaties have not otherwise provided the EU legislature with the necessary powers to act on the matter concerned.

[17] Case C-376/98 *Germany v Parliament* EU:C:2000:544, [2000] ECR I-8419, paras 83–84, 95, 106; Case C-491/01 *British American Tobacco* EU:C:2002:741, [2002] ECR I-11543, paras 60–61; Case C-380/03 *Germany v Parliament* EU:C:2006:772, [2006] ECR I-11573 (*Tobacco Advertising II*), paras 37–38, 41; Case C-210/03 *Swedish Match* EU:C:2004:802, [2004] ECR I-11893, paras 29–30.

[18] For a recent analysis, see S Weatherill, 'The Function and Limits of Legislative Harmonization in Making the Internal Market' in R Schütze and T Tridimas (eds), *Oxford Principles of European Law: Volume II* (forthcoming, Oxford, OUP).

[19] See, eg, *Tobacco Advertising II* (n 17), para 39. For academic commentary, see, eg, B de Witte, 'A Competence to Protect: The Pursuit of Non-Market Aims through Internal Market Legislation' in P Syrpis (ed), *The Judiciary, the Legislature and the EU Internal Market* (Cambridge, CUP, 2011).

[20] For a comprehensive analysis of the judicial interpretation of Art 114, see D Wyatt, 'Community Competence to Regulate the Internal Market' in M Dougan and S Currie, *Fifty Years of the European Treaties: Looking Back and Thinking Forward* (Oxford, Hart Publishing, 2009); S Weatherill, 'The Limits of Legislative Harmonisation Ten Years after *Tobacco Advertising*: How the Court's Case Law Has Become a "Drafting Guide"' (2011) 12 *German Law Journal* 827. Most recently, see Weatherill (n 18).

[21] See, eg, Council Directive 2003/33/EC of 26 May 2003 on the approximation of the laws, regulations and administrative provisions of the Member States relating to the advertising and sponsorship of tobacco products [2003] OJ L152/16, Preamble.

[22] For the interpretation of this provision by the CJEU, see Case C-413/99 *Baumbast* EU:C:2002:493, [2002] ECR I-7091, paras 85–86, 91. For academic commentary, see, eg, P Craig and G de Búrca, *EU Law: Text, Cases, and Materials*, 6th edn (Oxford, OUP 2015) ch 23.

Recourse to Art 352 TFEU may be had as a last resort. This provision lays down a 'flexibility clause' that empowers the EU to take action in situations where no other Treaty article provides the necessary powers, but Union action is necessary, in the context of Union policies, to attain one of its objectives. This phrasing implies two possible uses of Art 352: first, where the Union is granted competence to regulate the area in question, but the available legal bases do not provide sufficient powers to adopt the envisaged legislative measure;[23] and, second, where the Treaties contain no legal basis that would authorise the EU to take action in the area concerned. The latter option seems to codify the federal doctrine of implied powers, construed in a wide sense, whereby 'the existence of a given objective implies the existence of power reasonably necessary to attain it'.[24] Such possible use of Art 352 is why some consider this provision to be dangerous. It is said to give the EU a broad, essentially unlimited, legislative mandate, allowing it to enter into policy areas that lie outside the scope of the Treaties.[25] Yet the potential of Art 352 should not be overestimated. There are strict limitations attached to its use.[26] First of all, unlike in the context of Art 114 TFEU, the envisaged EU action must not entail harmonisation measures where the Treaties exclude such harmonisation. Second, it must not lead to the EU's competences being extended beyond those provided for by the Treaties, thus circumventing the procedures for amending the Treaties.[27] Third, on the procedural level, the Commission must inform national parliaments of proposals adopted under Art 352, in accordance with the procedure for monitoring subsidiarity.[28] Finally, any such proposals will require a unanimous vote in the Council.[29]

Questions surrounding the use of the functionally broad legal bases will be returned to in chapter four in the discussion of the institutional power dynamic between the EU legislature and judiciary. For the purposes of this chapter, what matters is that the existence of these legal bases in the Treaties suggest that the permissible scope of EU action is much broader in practice than what could be inferred from the wording of the principle of conferral and its detailing through the list of areas of EU competence laid down in Arts 3–6 TFEU. There is a gap between the theory and practice of the principle of conferral. In part, this gap can be attributed to the language of the Treaties – an open-ended phrasing of the concept of the internal market, in the first place, and of the provisions that are dedicated to achieving the objectives of the internal market, including both the substantive rules on free movement and the functionally broad legal bases. However,

[23] Case 45/86 *Commission v Council* EU:C:1987:163, [1987] ECR 1493.

[24] Craig and De Búrca (n 22) 77.

[25] Schütze (n 2) 79.

[26] Notably, the same cannot be said about the predecessor of Art 352 TFEU, Art 308 of the Consolidated version of the Treaty Establishing the European Community [2002] OJ C325/33 (EC), which was formulated more broadly, as discussed in R Schütze, *From Dual to Cooperative Federalism: The Changing Structure of European Law* (Oxford, OUP, 2009) 133–40.

[27] On the latter point, see C-2/94 *Accession by the Community to the European Convention for the Protection of Human Rights and Fundamental Freedoms* EU:C:1996:140, [1996] ECR I-1759, para 30. See also Declaration No 42 on Article 352 of the Treaty on the Functioning of the European Union [2012] OJ C326/353.

[28] See Art 5(3) TEU; Art 352(2) TFEU. See also P Kiiver, *The Early Warning System for the Principle of Subsidiarity: Constitutional Theory and Empirical Reality* (London, Routledge, 2012).

[29] For a detailed analysis of the limitations inherent in Art 352 TFEU, see T Konstadinides, 'Drawing the Line between Circumvention and Gap-Filling: An Exploration of the Conceptual Limits of the Treaty's Flexibility Clause' (2012) 31 *Yearbook of European Law* 227.

the gap also exists because of the way the Court has actively chosen to interpret the interplay between the concepts of competence, legal basis and scope of EU law. It is the judicial interpretation of these concepts that has granted the EU the power to interfere, through both the judicial and legislative routes, into the areas falling outside its explicit regulatory competences to the extent that such interference stems from the exercise of a competence (such as the regulation of the internal market) that the EU does possess. Moreover, the Court's interpretation of the breadth of competences possessed by the EU has been extremely generous. It has authorised EU legislative action under Art 114 in the areas that would otherwise be excluded from the EU's legislative competence based on a tenuous link of such action with the objectives of the internal market. Similarly, as will be demonstrated through case law analysis in the remainder of this chapter, the Court has construed the scope of the free movement rules laid down in the Treaties broadly enough to catch domestic regulatory practices that have little to do with the functioning of the internal market. In fact, it is the generous judicial interpretation of the scope of these rules that has empowered a wide use of Art 114 and other functionally broad legal bases by the EU legislature.[30]

The main justification behind the Court's interpretative approach regarding the principle of conferral comes from the well familiar doctrine of *effet utile*, or effectiveness, of EU law. This doctrine resembles the doctrine of pre-emption developed by the US Supreme Court, whereby state legislation will be pre-empted and consequently set aside where it poses an obstacle to the full and complete achievement of the objectives of federal legislation.[31] Similarly, EU law doctrine of effectiveness, applied in the context of the principle of conferral, means that no measure or policy area should be a priori excluded from the reach of the Treaties – most notably, the rules of the internal market – because doing so would risk compromising the objectives of the internal market and the EU's integration process more generally.[32]

My view is that the Court's broad reading of conferral in light of the doctrine of effectiveness is in principle justified, if apt to create some tensions of a constitutional nature. The existence of an overlap between competences conferred on the EU and those reserved predominantly to the Member States seems to be mandated by the wording of the relevant provisions of the Treaty. As previously mentioned, both the functional legal basis and the substantive provisions of the internal market are framed broadly, allowing for considerable latitude in their interpretation and application.[33] Moreover, the broad framing of these provisions has a practical justification. As Weatherill rightly points out, the EU requires a flexible set of competences and powers in order to be able to address collective problems that could not have been foreseen and addressed through

[30] For a comprehensive analysis of the relationship between deregulation and re-regulation at the EU level, see S Weatherill, *The Internal Market as a Legal Concept* (Oxford, OUP, 2017) ch 13. This point is further discussed in the context of the areas under study in s VI of this chapter.

[31] Azoulai (n 15) 211–14, 215.

[32] For examples of other constitutionally sensitive areas, see Arts 84 (crime prevention), 113 (tax), 147(1) (employment), 165(1) (sport), 166(1) (vocational training), 167(1) (culture), 195(1) (tourism) TFEU.

[33] G Davies, 'The Competence to Create an Internal Market: Conceptual Poverty and Unbalanced Interests' in S Garben and I Govaere (eds) *The Division of Competences between the EU and the Member States* (Oxford, Hart Publishing, 2017) 75–76.

a more narrowly worded principle of conferral.[34] In other words, a flexible interpretation of the principle of conferral is mandated by the need for an effective government at the EU level. This rationale is not confined to the context of the EU. The need for an effective government is exactly why the theory of 'dual federalism', which presupposes a strict division of competences between local and central governments and which was originally used to explain US federalism, has not stood the test of time and practice.[35]

However, the flexibility inherent in the judicial interpretation of the principle of conferral can become problematic if pushed to an excess. It may have serious consequences for the scope of the regulatory autonomy of the Member States as it extends the EU's regulatory mandate into the areas that should in principle be exempted from interference by the EU. By doing so, it risks putting into question the raison d'être of the principle of conferral as a constitutional constraint on EU powers. These concerns, given their constitutional relevance, must be taken into account in the judicial application of the principle of conferral in the individual cases that come before the Court. Accordingly, it is argued here that if the principle of conferral is to have a meaningful normative function, there needs to be a limit to how far the exercise of the EU's internal market competences can legitimately encroach into the areas of competence that would otherwise be exempted from any binding interference on behalf of the EU. The purpose of this inquiry is to determine that limit in the context of the judicial interpretation of EU free movement law. What requirements does the Court need to satisfy in interpreting the free movement rules laid down in the Treaties in order to comply with the principle of conferral?

The answer to this question is simpler than might appear at the outset. The free movement law, just like the law of the internal market more generally, does not have general application. It is triggered when certain conditions are met. There are two such conditions in the context of the freedom of establishment and freedom to provide services: the cross-border activities governed by these freedoms must be of an economic, as opposed to social, character; and the national measure or practice in question must constitute a 'restriction' on those activities. So, there must be a market involved and there must be an effect on the *internal* market. The detailed meaning of these conditions will be examined in the following sections, but two points should be made clear to begin with. First, the principle of conferral does not authorise judicial interference with the constitutionally sensitive areas of national policy in the name of the internal market *unless* the aforementioned conditions regarding the nature of the activity and the presence of a restriction are met. Second, when interpreting the meaning of those conditions in a given case, the Court is expected to adopt a systemic approach, contextualising them in the constitutional requirements of the principle of conferral. In other words, the concepts of an economic activity and restriction of free movement should be interpreted and applied in a way that is cognisant of the fact that both concepts have a constitutional basis in the principle of conferral. This presupposes a judicial interpretation of the two concepts that

[34] S Weatherill, *Law and Values in the European Union* (Oxford, OUP, 2016) 21; Weatherill (n 18).

[35] For a groundbreaking work on the inadequacy of the theory of 'dual federalism', see D Elazar, *The American Partnership, Intergovernmental Cooperation in the Nineteenth-Century United States* (Chicago, University of Chicago Press, 1962). See also Schütze (n 26), exploring the theories of federalism in the context of the EU. For a discussion of the principle of conferral in light of federal theory, see ch 1, s I.

balances the objectives of the internal market inherent in them with the concerns about the protection of national regulatory autonomy in policy areas that are constitutionally sensitive from EU law point of view. Such interpretation could suggest, for example, that activities which have some economic features but are otherwise heavily regulated at the national level in the interests of social policy and solidarity would fall outside the scope of free movement.

The Court should also be guided by the requirements of conferral when the free movement law manifests itself through the principle prohibiting discrimination on the basis of nationality. This principle applies only if the situation at hand falls within the scope of application of the Treaties, which accordingly means that the said situation must be governed by or otherwise connected with a substantive rule of EU law.[36] Conferral would require that the judicial assessment of whether this condition is met in the circumstances of the case take into account potential competence concerns that might arise when establishing a situation's connection with EU law.

The discussion above has demonstrated how the normative requirements of the principle of conferral can, and should, be applied to the judicial interpretation of EU free movement law. A comprehensive analysis of whether the free movement case law in the areas under study is consistent with the principle of conferral will be conducted in section VI in light of the comparative analysis of the case law conducted in sections II–V.

II. Healthcare

This section begins with an introduction of the main competence questions surrounding EU regulation of the healthcare sector and discusses the extent to which this sector has been covered by EU law. Then, it moves to the analysis of central developments in the case law, focusing on the Court's interpretation of the scope of application of free movement rules in relation to the provision of public healthcare.

A. Competence and Legal Framework

The following discussion addresses competence questions relating to EU regulation of healthcare. It analyses the EU legal framework for the regulation of healthcare, provides an overview of EU legislative action concerning access to cross-border healthcare, and explores the constitutional limits of such action. It also discusses certain aspects of the regulatory frameworks of the Member States insofar as such discussion helps to

[36] The conditions governing the application of the principle of non-discrimination on grounds of nationality have been laid down in: Case C-197/86 *Brown* EU:C:1988:323, [1988] ECR 3205, para 18; Case C-186/87 *Cowan* EU:C:1989:47, [1989] ECR 195, paras 14–20; Cases C-92/92 and C-326/92 *Collins* EU:C:1993:847, [1993] ECR I-5145, paras 17–28; Case C-209/03 *Bidar* EU:C:2005:169, [2005] ECR I-2119, paras 28–48. See also Case C-427/06 *Bartsch* EU:C:2008:517, [2008] ECR I-7245, Opinion of AG Sharpston, para 69, discussing the scope of application of general principles of EU law. For an academic discussion, see S Prechal, 'Competence Creep and General Principles of Law' (2010) 3 *Review of European Administrative Law* 5, 8–11.

illuminate the challenges linked to the regulation of healthcare at the EU level. The aim of the analysis is to help the reader understand the specifics of the legal context in which the Court makes determinations about the scope and meaning of free movement rules in situations involving the provision of healthcare as a constitutionally sensitive area of EU competence.

i. Member State Legal Frameworks: Universal Healthcare

The healthcare systems of EU Member States share one central common characteristic: they are organised predominantly on the basis of the principle of social solidarity, whereby access to healthcare is guaranteed to all patients, in accordance with their medical needs and regardless of ability to pay.[37] For that reason, national healthcare sectors in the EU are largely controlled and managed by the State and are characterised by high levels of public funding, cross-subsidisation and rationing, aimed at controlling costs.[38]

The concrete ways in which Member States organise their healthcare systems differ from one Member State to another. However, two basic models of organisation can be distinguished according to the financing and delivery of the healthcare services: the Bismarckian system, or the Social Health Insurance System; and the Beveridgean system, or the National Health Service.[39] Both systems have been adopted by a roughly equal number of European countries.[40] In the Bismarckian system, compulsory social insurance insures the entire population of the State through either the reimbursement or benefits-in-kind system. In the reimbursement systems, the patient is reimbursed for outpatient services. For inpatient, or hospital, services, which are normally more costly, the insurance carrier reimburses the healthcare provider directly. In most cases, the patient remains free to select the healthcare provider of their choice, whether public or private. Benefits-in-kind systems offer direct benefits through specific providers. Specialist procedures are performed on a referral basis. Therefore, patients have a smaller range of choice of healthcare providers in comparison to the reimbursement systems. The Beveridgean system, or the National Health Service, provides universal coverage to all residents through a publicly organised system that is financed from general taxation. Medical services are generally free of charge, but patients must receive their care from providers within or connected to the public health system. Many countries also offer healthcare services funded on the basis of upfront payments and voluntary private insurance schemes. However, the proportion of these services provided in Europe is relatively small and, in principle, does not change the predominantly social character of national healthcare.

[37] See Council, 'Council Conclusions on Common values and principles in European Union Health Systems' [2006] OJ C146/1; Council Directive 2011/24/EU on the application of patients' rights in cross-border healthcare [2011] OJ L88/45 (Patients' Rights Directive), Preamble, Recital 21; E Mossialos et al, 'Health Systems Governance in Europe: The Role of European Union Law and Policy' in E Mossialos et al (eds), *Health Systems Governance in Europe: The Role of European Union Law and Policy* (Cambridge, CUP, 2010) ch 1.

[38] RF Rich and KR Merrick, 'Cross Border Health Care in the European Union: Challenges and Opportunities' (2006) 23 *Journal of Contemporary Health Law and Policy* 64.

[39] Covered in detail in Rich and Merrick (n 38).

[40] M Gaeta et al, 'An Overview of Different Health Indicators used in the European Health Systems' (2017) 58 *Journal of Preventive Medicine and Hygiene* 114.

ii. *EU Legal Framework: From Coordination Measures to EU-Wide Rights for Patients*

The Treaties recognise the prerogative of the Member States to organise and manage their healthcare systems independently from the interference of the EU. As noted earlier, Art 168 TFEU provides the EU only with complementary competences in the area of public health, excluding the possibility of harmonisation of national laws, and obliges the EU to 'respect the responsibilities of the Member States for the definition of their health policy and the organisation and delivery of health services and medical care'.[41] These responsibilities also include the allocation of the resources assigned to the management of healthcare. In addition, Art 9 TFEU requires that the objective of a high level of protection of human health be streamlined into the definition and implementation of EU policies.[42] Furthermore, Art 35 of the European Charter of Fundamental Rights guarantees to everyone the right of access to preventive healthcare and the right to benefit from medical treatment under the conditions established by national laws and practices.[43]

Given the constraints on EU legislative action, the EU's involvement in the healthcare sector has been confined to regulating certain aspects concerning the access of EU citizens to healthcare in other Member States. Central aspects are covered by Regulation 883/2004 on the coordination of national social security systems,[44] which replaced Regulation 1408/71 on the application of social security schemes to employed persons and their families moving within the Community.[45] Regulation 883/2004 allows EU nationals to travel to another Member State for medical goods and services at the expense of their own healthcare system provided that their healthcare authorities give express authorisation beforehand. Like its predecessor, Regulation 883/2004 is limited to the coordination of basic national rules in the field of social and healthcare benefits, thus falling short of achieving any substantial degree of harmonisation.[46] In content not much different from the original version of 1971, Regulation 883/2004 extends its personal scope to cover, in addition to the economically active persons, any individual, irrespective of their economic status, who receives authorisation to obtain medical treatment abroad.[47]

According to Art 20(2) of the Regulation, the competent institutions must grant the authorisation if two conditions are met: the treatment in question is among the benefits provided for by the legislation where the person concerned resides; and a person cannot be given such treatment in their home Member State within a time limit which is medically justifiable, taking into account their current state of health and the probable

[41] See also Art 6(a) TFEU.
[42] See also Arts 114(3) and 168(1) TFEU.
[43] Charter of Fundamental Rights of the European Union [2000] OJ C364/1.
[44] Council Regulation (EC) 883/2004 on the coordination of social security systems [2004] OJ L166/1 (Reg 883/2004).
[45] Council Regulation (EEC) 1408/71 on the application of social security schemes to employed persons and their families moving within the Community [1971] OJ L149/2 (Reg 1408/71).
[46] Parliament, DG Internal Policies of the Union, 'The ECJ Case Law on Cross-Border Aspects of Health Services' (Briefing note) [2006] IP/A/IMCO/FWC/2006-167/C3/SC1.
[47] Cf Reg 883/2004 (n 44), Art 2 and Reg 1408/71 (n 45), Art 2. This amendment has been influenced by Case C-182/78 *Pierik* [1979] ECR 1977.

course of illness. The phrasing of the second condition has been heavily influenced by the Court's case law. It is, therefore, more detailed than the original text of Art 22(2) of Regulation 1408/71, which conditions the grant of authorisation, broadly, upon the impossibility of receiving the treatment in question in the patient's Member State of residence. If the authorisation is provided, the patient's healthcare system covers the costs of treatment by paying directly to the foreign healthcare provider according to the rate and rules applied in the State where the treatment is performed.

The conditions for granting authorisation for reimbursement of medical expenses under Regulation 1408/71 and its amended versions have been interpreted by the Court on multiple occasions, and the Court has at times pronounced on issues that were not directly covered or even intended to be covered by the Regulation.[48] The majority of judicial actions brought before the Court were inspired by restrictive pre-authorisation policies maintained by the Member States, as a result of which patients would be refused permission to obtain treatment abroad. In these situations, claimants would normally challenge the requirement of prior authorisation in light of both Regulation 1408/71 (and later 883/2004) and Treaty free movement rules. In addition, the Court was faced with cases falling outside the scope of the Regulation, where patients received treatment abroad without having applied for prior authorisation from their national health insurance institution. This context allowed the Court to develop a set of rules and principles governing cross-border access to healthcare directly on the basis of what is now Art 56 TFEU. The case law thus created a dual system of access to healthcare in the EU: patients seeking healthcare abroad could rely either on Regulation 883/2004, as interpreted by the Court, or directly on Art 56 TFEU (and its predecessors), again, as interpreted by the Court. The Court has recognised that Art 56 entitles patients residing in the EU to receive medical treatment in any other EU Member State and be reimbursed the costs of such treatment according to their home State's tariff. This was probably the most important development in the EU-level regulation of access to public healthcare. The rules developed in the case law have subsequently been codified in the EU Directive 2011/24/EU on the application of patients' rights in cross-border healthcare.[49] The Directive covers all EU citizens wishing to receive medical treatment in other Member States and aims to clarify the legal framework for reimbursement of their medical expenses under Art 56 TFEU. This directive will be considered in detail in chapter four.

B. Case Law on Cross-Border Access to Healthcare

The following discussion analyses EU case law on cross-border access to healthcare. It focuses on how the Court defines the scope of free movement law in situations where patients seek treatment in other Member States. The circumstances in which such treatment should be reimbursed by the patient's State of affiliation will be discussed in the next chapter concerning the principles of subsidiarity and proportionality. The judicial interpretation of the scope of free movement is what exposes the Court's approach to

[48] This argument is developed in ch 4, s VI.
[49] Patients' Rights Directive (n 37), Preamble, Recital 8.

competence concerns raised by national governments in situations where free movement law intersects with policy areas that in principle fall outside of the EU's regulatory competence. This, in turn, determines the extent to which the Court considers the requirements of the principle of conferral in the interpretation of free movement rules.

The starting point in virtually every judgment of the Court involving cross-border healthcare is the recognition, in accordance with Art 168(7) TFEU, that EU law 'does not detract from the power of the Member States to organise their social security systems' and 'decide the level of resources to be allocated to their operation'.[50] At the same time, the Court holds that Art 168(7) does not exclude the possibility that Member States may be required under other Treaty provisions, such as the free movement rules, or measures adopted on their basis, such as Regulation 883/2004, to make adjustments to national social security systems.[51] The Court here employs its 'retained powers' formula, which reflects the broader judicial understanding of the relationship between the categories of EU competence and the scope of EU law in light of the principle of conferral.[52] Despite the fact that healthcare is in principle reserved by the Treaties to the competence of the Member States, while organising and managing their healthcare systems Member States remain obligated to comply with other provisions of the Treaties, such as the free movement rules. However, such obligation only arises if the situation in question falls within the scope of free movement. In that connection, the case law analysis below seeks to determine to what extent the provision of public healthcare falls within the scope of free movement law.

i. Decker *and* Kohll: *Outpatient Medical Care as a Service*

The foundations of the judicial regulation of cross-border access to healthcare were laid down in the *Decker*[53] and *Kohll*[54] judgments, delivered on the same day. Both disputes concerned Luxembourg citizens who had been denied reimbursement for medical goods and services purchased abroad. Mr Decker was refused reimbursement of the cost of spectacles purchased in Belgium. Mr Kohll was denied authorisation for his daughter to travel to Germany for dental treatment. The Court was asked to decide whether national rules, making the reimbursement of medical expenses incurred abroad subject to prior authorisation, were compatible with EU free movement rules. The judgments delivered by the Court in the two cases were almost identical and will thus be considered together.

The Luxembourg government contended that any ruling by the Court on the validity of the national rules in question would also determine the validity of Art 22(1) of Regulation 1408/71. As mentioned earlier, Art 22(1) of the Regulation allowed an insured person to receive sickness benefits in kind in another Member State only on the condition that the person had been authorised to do so by their home State. Accordingly,

[50] Case C-158/96 *Kohll* EU:C:1998:171, [1998] ECR I-1931, para 17; Case C-157/99 *Smits and Peerbooms* EU:C:2001:404, [2001] ECR I-5473, para 44; Case C-372/04 *Watts* EU:C:2006:325, [2006] ECR I-4325, para 121.

[51] See, eg, *Watts* (n 50), para 121.

[52] See text to n 15.

[53] Case C-120/95 *Decker* [1998] ECR I-1831.

[54] *Kohll* (n 50).

it was argued that should the Court rule on the question of prior authorisation, it would inadvertently assess the validity of the Regulation.[55] The Court managed to avoid doing so. First, it pointed out that the fact that a national measure 'may be consistent' with Regulation 1408/71 did not remove that measure from the scope of the provisions of the Treaty.[56] Second, it took the view that Art 22(1) was not intended to regulate, and hence did not in any way prevent, the reimbursement by the patient's State of insurance, at its own tariff, of the cost of medical products and services purchased abroad in the absence of prior authorisation.[57] It should be recalled that the Regulation required the cost of treatment obtained abroad be reimbursed according to the tariff of the Member State which provided the treatment. So, the Court effectively distinguished the scope of application of the free movement rules from that of the Regulation on the basis of the method of calculation of the amount of reimbursement.

Against this background, the Court went on to assess whether the requirement of prior authorisation was compatible with the rules of the Treaty on the free movement of goods (*Decker*) and services (*Kohll*). The Court made it clear at the outset that the free movement rules applied to health services even where the services were provided in the context of a social security scheme: 'the special nature of certain services does not remove them from the ambit of the fundamental principle of freedom of movement'.[58] Accordingly, the Court held that the requirement of prior authorisation that was applicable to the reimbursement of the costs of medical care provided in another Member State but not for the costs incurred in the State of insurance constituted a restriction on free movement.[59] Thus designed, the requirement of prior authorisation encouraged insured persons to purchase medical products at home rather than abroad (*Decker*)[60] and deterred them from approaching providers of medical services established in other Member States (*Kohll*).[61] The Court went on to hold that the restrictions concerned could not be justified by the public interest objectives advanced by governments in the circumstances of the two cases.

From the point of view of the principle of conferral, the importance of the *Decker* and *Kohll* judgments lies in establishing that EU free movement rules applied to healthcare provided under social security schemes. This was so irrespective of the fact that matters of social security, apart from those relating to the free movement of workers, fell within the ambit of Member State competence. Competence sensitivities were also reflected in the wording of Art 22(1) of Regulation 1408/71, which accorded national authorities a wide degree of discretion in making decisions about the grant of prior authorisation.[62] However, *Decker* and *Kohll* made clear that the scope of EU law was broader than the scope of the Regulation and the scope of EU competence more generally. This meant

[55] This question was later addressed in Case C-56/01 *Inizan* EU:C:2003:578, [2003] ECR I-12403 and *Watts* (n 50), discussed in this respect in ch 3, s II.
[56] *Decker* (n 53), para 27; *Kohll* (n 50), para 25.
[57] *Decker*, para 29; *Kohll*, para 27.
[58] *Kohll*, para 20.
[59] *Decker*, paras 34–36; *Kohll*, paras 33–35.
[60] *Decker*, para 36.
[61] *Kohll*, para 35.
[62] See ch 4, s VI for a comprehensive analysis of Reg 1408/71.

that national rules requiring prior authorisation for medical treatment abroad were caught by the free movement law.

At the point when the two cases were decided, it was still unclear whether, and if so, how the free movement rules applied in relation to inpatient medical care or to health-care systems other than those based on the principle of reimbursement for insured services, such as benefits-in-kind and NHS systems. Thus, the potential impact of *Decker* and *Kohll* on national healthcare systems and their budgets remained uncertain. The questions left unanswered by these judgments led to a number of further references to the Court, giving it the opportunity to clarify the scope of application of free movement rules to cross-border healthcare.

ii. Smits and Peerbooms *and* Watts: *Hospital Care as a Service*

Smits and Peerbooms concerned the freedom to provide services in relation to hospital, or inpatient, care and in the benefits-in-kind system. The Dutch social healthcare system provided insured patients with free medical care (benefits in kind) so long as it was obtained from service providers that had contracts with the Dutch sickness funds. If an insured person wished to obtain treatment from a different provider, regardless of whether the provider was established in the Netherlands or elsewhere, they had to obtain authorisation. In this connection, the Court had to consider two issues: first, whether the rules developed in *Decker* and *Kohll* applied to systems of benefits-in-kind or were confined to systems based on reimbursement; second, whether those rules applied to hospital care rather than exclusively outpatient care.

The Dutch government as well as a number of other governments which had submitted written observations to the Court argued that hospital care provided in kind, free of charge and on a non-profit-making basis should not be considered a service within the meaning of Art 50 EC (now Art 57 TFEU).[63] There was a clear competence concern here: was the EU authorised to interfere, through the free movement rules, with the national regulation of the provision of social healthcare? The Court answered in the affirmative. It explained briefly that a service provided in one Member State and paid for by the patient did not cease to fall within the scope of Art 49 EC merely because the patient was later reimbursed under the sickness insurance legislation of a type which provided benefits in kind.[64] What mattered was that contracted hospitals ultimately received consideration from the sickness insurance funds for the treatment they had provided. This consideration represented remuneration for the hospitals receiving it, suggesting that they were engaged in an activity of an economic character within the meaning of Art 50.[65]

The Court went on to rule that the prior authorisation procedure employed by the Dutch sickness funds constituted a restriction on the freedom to provide (and receive) services. Since authorisation was not required for treatment received in contracted hospitals, the majority of which were located in the Netherlands, it prevented, or at least deterred, insured persons from using healthcare services offered in other Member

[63] See Consolidated version of the Treaty Establishing the European Community [1997] OJ C340/173 (EC), Art 50.

[64] *Smits and Peerbooms* (n 50), paras 55–57.

[65] ibid, para 58.

States.[66] This meant that the Dutch system had to be justified by public interest objectives and proportionate in light of free movement rules in order to be considered lawful in EU law.

The scope of application of the free movement rules was further clarified in the *Watts* case,[67] concerning a refusal to grant an authorisation for a British citizen to have surgery in France. In *Watts*, the Court was faced for the first time in its case law with the application of Art 49 EC in relation to an NHS system. As previously discussed, NHS systems are funded through general taxation and medical care is free of charge. This makes it far from obvious whether healthcare provided in the framework of an NHS would qualify as a service for the purposes of free movement law. The Court held that it did, reiterating the by then established principle that Art 49 EC applied to situations where a person went to another Member State and received treatment there for consideration. Although it was questionable whether the provision of hospital care in the context of the British NHS, from which Mrs Watts sought reimbursement, in itself constituted a service within the meaning of Art 50 EC, the Court did not find the need to determine that. It took the view that the way in which the healthcare system to which the patient was affiliated, and from which they sought the reimbursement of the costs of treatment received abroad, operated had no bearing on the classification of medical treatment received abroad as an economic activity.[68]

C. Conclusion

The main take away from the case law on cross-border healthcare is that healthcare services provided in the framework of social security are subject to EU free movement rules. The Court holds that medical services fall within the scope of Art 56 TFEU as long as, first, the patient pays the foreign service provider for the treatment received and, second, healthcare providers, including public hospitals, in the patient's State of affiliation receive consideration for the treatment they provide from the sickness funds or other managing bodies. Both transactions represent remuneration and qualify the healthcare service as an activity of an economic character within the meaning of Art 57 TFEU. This accordingly means that the rules regulating access to cross-border healthcare within the EU apply to all kinds of healthcare systems, irrespective of whether they operate on a reimbursement, benefits-in-kind or NHS basis. There is a difference in the application of these rules depending on whether they concern outpatient or inpatient care, but that difference becomes relevant only at the stage of justification of national measures.

Furthermore, national rules conditioning the reimbursement of the costs of treatment received abroad on the grant of prior authorisation constitute a restriction on the freedom to provide and receive services because such rules have the effect of making the receipt of cross-border healthcare services more difficult than the domestic ones. As a

[66] *Smits and Peerbooms* (n 50), paras 67–69.
[67] *Watts* (n 50).
[68] ibid, paras 89, 91.

result, the Court acquires the exclusive power to decide whether the reasons advanced by national governments to justify the refusal to reimburse the costs of medical treatment received abroad are lawful in light of Art 56 TFEU.

The above judicial developments suggest that that the Court adopts a very generous interpretation of the scope of free movement rules in the context of cross-border access to healthcare. This is particularly noticeable in the way the Court defines the provision of public healthcare as an economic activity. It takes a very broad view of what counts as remuneration for the purposes of Art 57 TFEU. Whether, and if so to what extent, this approach is compatible with the requirements of the principle of conferral will be discussed in section VI in light of the comparative analysis of the case law across all the areas under study.

III. Education

This section begins with a discussion of EU competences in the education sector and then moves to the analysis of central developments in the case law, focusing on the Court's interpretation of the scope of application of free movement law in relation to cross-border access to higher education.

A. EU Competence and Legal Framework

The EU's competences in the field of education have always been modest and remain so to this day. The original competences of the then EEC were limited to regulating certain cross-border aspects of vocational training. According to Art 128 EEC (now Art 166 TFEU), the EC had the power to 'lay down general principles for implementing a common vocational training policy capable of contributing' to the economic goals of the Community. The common vocational training policy was intended to contribute to the advancement of the European labour market by dealing with the issues of worker mobility and the transnational transfer of vocational qualifications.[69] The Treaty of Maastricht introduced a specific legal basis for EU action in the field of general education, thus extending its competences beyond vocational training. The new competence, laid down in Art 126 of the EC Treaty, was, however, complementary in nature, confined to promoting cooperation between Member States' educational establishments and encouraging the mobility of students and teachers.[70] The Treaty of Maastricht also introduced the concept of European citizenship in Art 8 of the EC Treaty (now Art 20 TFEU), which granted nationals of EU Member States, including students, the right to 'move and reside freely' within the territory of the EU, subject to the conditions laid down in the Treaty and secondary legislation.[71] As will be demonstrated in this book,

[69] P Cort, 'The EC Discourse on Vocational Training: How a "Common Vocational Training Policy" Turned into a Lifelong Learning Strategy' (2009) 2 *Vocations and Learning* 87, 91, link.springer.com/article/10.1007%2Fs12186-008-9019-9#page-1.

[70] Consolidated version of the Treaty Establishing the European Community [1992] OJ C224/6 (EC Treaty), Art 126.

[71] See Arts 8 and 8a of the EC Treaty (now Arts 20 and 21 TFEU).

the introduction of Union citizenship later proved to be instrumental in facilitating the access of EU citizens to cross-border education in the territory of the EU.

In the Lisbon Treaty framework, the competence to regulate matters of general education in principle remains with the Member States, whilst the EU is accorded a complementary role to support Member State action.[72] Art 165(1) TFEU stipulates that the EU has the duty to 'contribute to the development of quality education by encouraging cooperation between Member States and, if necessary, by supporting and supplementing their action'. However, any action taken by the EU must fully respect 'the responsibility of the Member States for the content of teaching and the organisation of education systems and their cultural and linguistic diversity'.[73] Accordingly, the EU is only authorised to adopt incentive measures, 'excluding any harmonisation' of national laws and regulations.[74]

The central element of the EU's education policy is the mobility of students.[75] The European Commission has adopted a range of initiatives aimed at facilitating the practical aspects of student mobility. Commission recommendations generally seek to ensure that information about an individual's academic qualifications is easily accessible and comprehensive throughout the EU and that the procedure of academic recognition is speedy, open and transparent.[76] Action aimed at facilitating student mobility has also been taken outside the EU's institutional framework, that is, at the intergovernmental level. In 1998, European governments adopted the Bologna Declaration, which established the Bologna Process. This is a project currently involving 48 European countries, with 27 EU Member States among them, aimed at policy convergence towards a common structure of higher education.[77] The objective underlying the Bologna Process is to enable students and graduates to move more easily from one country to another, which is to be achieved through, inter alia, establishing a three-tier (Bachelor-Master-Doctorate) higher education system as a uniform standard and facilitating the recognition of foreign academic degrees and qualifications. This framework is intended to ensure structural compatibility and comparability of national education systems. It does not, however, entail any substantive harmonisation of the content of education or create binding obligations for the participating governments.[78] An example of voluntary inter-governmental cooperation, the Bologna Process has been described as an attempt to reduce the EU's involvement in the field of higher education.[79]

[72] Arts 6 and 165 TFEU.

[73] Art 165(1) TFEU.

[74] Art 165(4) TFEU.

[75] Commission, 'Communication on an agenda for the modernisation of Europe's higher education system' COM (2011) 567 final. See also ec.europa.eu/education/policies/higher-education/mobility-and-cooperation_en.

[76] For a recent initiative, see Commission, 'Proposal for a Council Recommendation on promoting automatic mutual recognition of higher education and upper secondary education diplomas and the outcomes of learning periods abroad' (2018) 270 final. For an overview of EU measures, see Commission, 'A guide to the rights of mobile students in the European Union' (Staff Working Document) COM (2010) 477 final, 13. See also M Dougan, 'Fees, Grants, Loans and Dole Cheques: Who Covers the Costs of Migrant Education Within the EU?' (2007) 1 *Journal of Contemporary European Research* 4, 7.

[77] See official website at www.ehea.info/pid34250/members.html. See also S Garben, 'The Bologna Process: From a European Law Perspective' (2010) 16 *European Law Journal* 186.

[78] Garben (n 77) 190.

[79] ibid 187, 209–10; S Garben, 'The Future of Higher Education in Europe: the Case for a Stronger Base in EU Law' (2012) LSE 'Europe in Question' Discussion Paper 50/2012, 9–10 http://eprints.lse.ac.uk/53202/1/LEQSPaper50.pdf.

B. Case Law on Cross-Border Access to Education

The following analysis discusses the political context of EU case law in the field of education and examines the reasons why, according to the Court, access to public education falls within the scope of EU law.

i. Political Background

The number of students moving in the territory of the EU has been steadily increasing in the last two decades. In 2018, there were more than half a million of students enrolled in tertiary education in an EU Member State different from the one in which they completed their secondary education, which marks an increase in student mobility levels of about 50 per cent since 2000.[80] Student mobility is, however, not balanced across the region, with some Member States being net-exporters of students and others net-importers.[81] The Court's case law on access to education concerns exactly the latter group of countries, which experience an inflow of foreign students significantly exceeding the outflow of local students. Countries facing this problem are typically those that have low threshold, open access or low tuition fee policies and/or teach in a language also spoken in other Member States. The net-importers of students in the EU are Austria, Belgium and, to a lesser extent, the Czech Republic, Denmark and the Netherlands.[82]

ii. Cross-Border Access to Education

a. *Gravier*: The Prohibition of Discrimination in Relation to Access to Education

The main principle underlying EU case law on access to cross-border education is the prohibition of discrimination on the basis of nationality. *Gravier* was a landmark case in which the Court applied this principle in relation to access to higher education.[83] The case concerned a rule introduced by Belgium in 1970s requiring that foreign students pay an additional enrolment fee ('minerval') as a condition of access to university. The fee resembled the out-of-State tuition that American State universities demand from non-resident students.[84] It was aimed at offsetting the fact that foreign students (or their parents) do not contribute to the financing of education to the same extent as residents

[80] For most recent data, see Eurostat, 'Learning Mobility Statistics' (*Eurostat*, October 2020) ec.europa.eu/eurostat/statistics-explained/index.php/Learning_mobility_statistics. For earlier data, see Commission, 'Progress towards the common European objectives in education and training (2010/2011): Indicators and benchmarks' (Staff Working Document) COM (2011) 526 final, 33–40.

[81] ibid. For a comprehensive study of imbalances in student mobility across the EU, see A Grabher et al, 'Student Mobility in the EHEA: Underrepresentation in Student Credit Mobility and Imbalances in Degree Mobility' (Research Report, Institute for Advanced Studies, Vienna, January 2014) esp 34–45 www.eurostudent.eu/download_files/documents/Student_mobility_in_EHEA.pdf.

[82] C Chevalier and M Gerard, 'Financing Higher Education and Student Mobility across Europe' (2008) ARPEGE Research Paper; JP Myklebus, 'Facing a Rising Imbalance of Mobile Students' (*University World News*, 31 January 2014) www.universityworldnews.com/article.php?story=20140130145446403; Grabher et al (n 81).

[83] Case C-293/83 *Gravier* EU:C:1985:69, [1985] ECR 593.

[84] AP van der Mei, 'Free Movement of Students and the Protection of National Educational Interests: Reflections on *Bressol and Chaverot*' (2011) 13 *European Journal of Migration and Law* 123, 125.

do by paying income taxes.[85] The fee was challenged by Miss Gravier, a student of French nationality who was required to pay the 'minerval' upon her enrolment in the university. On a preliminary reference, the Court was asked to consider the compatibility of the Belgian rule with the principle of non-discrimination on the grounds of nationality.

The prohibition of discrimination laid down in Art 18 TFEU (then Art 7 EEC) only applies in situations that fall within the scope of application of the Treaties. Accordingly, the Court had to decide, first, whether access to education fell within the scope of Community law. It started with an observation that 'although educational organisation and policy [we]re not as such included in the spheres which the Treaty ha[d] entrusted to the Community institutions', access to vocational training, on the other hand, was 'not unconnected' with Community law.[86] It was enshrined in Art 128 EEC and was subject to several soft law measures adopted by the Council concerning vocational training in the context of worker mobility. This led the Court to declare that a 'common vocational training policy' of the Community was being gradually established.[87] Furthermore, vocational training constituted 'an indispensable element of the activities of the Community' because it promoted the free movement of persons by enabling them to obtain the necessary training and qualifications in the Member State where they intended to work and 'develop their particular talents' in Member States whose vocational training programmes included 'the special subject desired'.[88] For all of the above reasons, the conditions of access to vocational training fell within the scope of the Treaty and thus were subject to the prohibition of discrimination under Art 7 EEC.

Since the EEC Treaty did not contain any legal basis specific to education, vocational training being the only link to general education existing in the Treaty, the Court turned to consider whether university education fell under the definition of vocational training. The Court adopted a broad interpretation of the term 'vocational training', describing it as 'any form of education which prepares for a qualification for a particular profession, trade or employment or which provides the necessary training and skills for such a profession, trade or employment, … even if the training programme includes an element of general education'.[89] This meant that, in principle, courses provided by a higher education institution constituted vocational training for the purposes of Art 128 EEC. Consequently, the Court ruled that the imposition on foreign students of an additional enrolment fee as a condition of access to university, which was directly discriminatory against non-nationals, breached Art 7 EEC.

The Court's legal reasoning in *Gravier* is remarkable. On the one hand, we see the already familiar pattern of interaction between the categories of EU competence and scope of EU law: the fact that access to education was deemed to fall within the scope of Community law meant that its cross-border aspects were subject to the principle prohibiting discrimination on grounds of nationality. This was so notwithstanding the fact that the Community's legislative competence with regard to education – vocational training, to be exact – was, and remains, limited to non-binding initiatives. On the other

[85] *Gravier* (n 83), para 12.
[86] ibid, para 19.
[87] ibid, paras 20–23.
[88] ibid, paras 23–24.
[89] ibid, paras 30–31.

hand, *Gravier* displays a high degree of judicial creativity. In real terms, what the Court did in *Gravier* was to derive individual rights for mobile students in the absence of a Treaty basis for a specific competence in the field of education and on the basis of an expansive interpretation of the concept of vocational training. Notably, vocational training itself had been included in the Treaty primarily for reasons relating to the training of migrant workers. Thus, following the Court's logic, access to education fell within the scope of Community law because of its indirect link to the European labour market.[90] Moreover, that indirect link was deemed to be enough to lay down the legal foundations for the free movement of students in the EU.

Notably, *Gravier* remains the only case where the Court dealt with direct discrimination. In subsequent cases, the judicial analysis shifted to assessing to what extent Member States could justify indirectly discriminatory treatment of foreign students.

b. *Commission v Belgium* and *Bressol*: Taking into Account Treaty Reforms

The Court's judgment in *Commission v Belgium*,[91] delivered almost 20 years after *Gravier*, is notable for the way the Court's reasoning changed in light of the reforms brought about by the Treaty of Maastricht. The case arose out of the infringement proceedings brought by the Commission against Belgium, concerning legislation adopted by the French Community of Belgium on the recognition of foreign qualifications and diplomas. The legislation in question stipulated that foreign applicants who were not able to prove that they qualified for admission to university in their own country of origin had to pass an 'aptitude test' to enrol into a Belgian university.[92] Effectively, this requirement ensured that the French students who due to *numerus clausus* (minimum grade requirement) had not been admitted to the French universities were also barred from entering the Belgian schools. The Commission claimed that Belgian legislation was in breach of Art 12 EC (formerly Art 7 EEC, now Art 18 TFEU) read in conjunction with Arts 149 and 150 EC (now Arts 165 and 166 TFEU).

In its judgment, the Court took note of the changes introduced to the EU constitutional framework since *Gravier*. In particular, it pointed out that the Treaty of Maastricht had introduced a legal basis for education in Art 149(2) EC. This provision covered all levels and types of education and expressly provided that Community action shall encourage the mobility of students and teachers by, inter alia, encouraging the academic recognition of diplomas and periods of study. Similarly, Art 150(2) EC provided that Community action shall facilitate access to vocational training and encourage the mobility of instructors and trainees. Consequently, there was no doubt, in the Court's view, that the prohibition of discrimination on grounds of nationality applied to the conditions of access to higher education set by the Member States.[93]

The Court observed that Belgian legislation placed students holding secondary education diplomas awarded in other Member States at a disadvantage, since they could

[90] FG Jacobs, 'Citizenship of the European Union – A Legal Analysis' (2007) 13 *European Law Journal* 591, 602.

[91] Case C-65/03 *Commission v Belgium* EU:C:2004:402, [2004] ECR I-6427.

[92] ibid, paras 5, 13.

[93] ibid, paras 26–27.

not gain access to higher education under the same conditions as the holders of Belgian diplomas. The criterion of differentiation thus worked primarily to the detriment of the nationals of other Member States and for that reason had to be regarded as indirectly discriminatory against them.[94] As Belgium did not advance any grounds of justification for the differential treatment, the Court concluded that it failed to fulfil its obligations under Art 12 EC.

The Court had another opportunity to pronounce on the Belgian rules in the *Bressol* case, which concerned a Belgian quota on the admission of non-resident students to oversubscribed medical courses.[95] The judgment, delivered after the entry into force of the Lisbon Treaty, will be discussed in detail in the next chapter, but it deserves a mention here for some broader observations that the Court made about the distribution of competences between the EU and Member States in the field of education. The Court recognised that whilst EU law did not detract from the power of the Member States as regards the organisation of their education systems, pursuant to Art 165(1) TFEU, when exercising that power, Member States had to comply with the provisions on the freedom to move and reside within the territory of the EU, in accordance with Arts 18 and 21 TFEU.[96] Moreover, the freedom of movement conferred by the introduction of EU citizenship (Art 21 TFEU) was a sufficient basis alone to establish that the situation fell within the scope of the Treaty for the purposes of applying the prohibition of discrimination enshrined in Art 18 TFEU.[97]

In *Bressol*, the Court seemed to solidify the broad interpretation of the scope of free movement rules adopted in *Gravier*, first, by grounding it in the by then well-familiar explanation of a constitutional relationship between EU competence and scope of EU law and, second, by employing the concept of EU citizenship introduced by the Maastricht Treaty to support its conclusions. If in *Gravier* the ruling that access to education fell within the scope of EU law was based on a tenuous link between education policy and the free movement of workers, in *Bressol*, this ruling was backed by a number of Treaty provisions read together: the legal basis for education; the principle prohibiting discrimination on the basis of nationality; and the concept of EU citizenship.

iii. Access to Financial Assistance

In addition to access to education, the Court has also developed rules concerning foreign students' access to financial assistance. Questions concerning financial assistance were raised before the Court as early as in 1988.[98] The Court then distinguished between, on the one hand, financial assistance intended to cover registration and other fees charged for access to education, so, for example, tuition fee loans and grants, and, on the other

[94] *Commission v Belgium* (n 91), para 30. For a similar approach in subsequent cases, see Case C-147/03 *Commission v Austria* EU:C:2005:427, [2005] ECR I-5969, paras 41–47, with further references to Case C-184/99 *Grzelczyk* EU:C:2001:458, [2001] ECR I-6193, para 31 and Case C-224/98 *D'Hoop* EU:C:2002:432, [2002] ECR I-6191, para 28.

[95] Case C-73/08 *Bressol* EU:C:2010:181, [2010] ECR I-2735.

[96] ibid, para 28.

[97] ibid, para 31, with further references to, inter alia, *Bidar* (n 36), paras 32–33 and Case C-158/07 *Förster* [2008] ECR I-8507, paras 36–37.

[98] Case C-39/86 *Lair* EU:C:1988:322, [1988] ECR 3161, paras 23–24; *Brown* (n 36), para 25.

hand, maintenance and training grants. The principle of non-discrimination applied with regard to the former, as forming part of the conditions of access to education, but maintenance assistance fell outside the scope of the EEC Treaty and could not trigger the application of Art 7. The Court took the position that at that stage of the development of Community law, such assistance was both a matter of educational policy, which was not explicitly included 'in the spheres entrusted to the Community institutions', and a matter of social policy, which fell within the competence of the Member States insofar as it was not covered by specific provisions of the Treaty.[99] Essentially, what the Court did in this line of case law was contextualise its interpretation of the scope of EU law in the constitutional requirements of the principle of conferral.

The Court's position changed with the introduction of EU citizenship in 1992, guaranteeing EU citizens the right to move freely in the territory of the EU. From the perspective of the Court, this meant that it no longer had to differentiate between assistance covering tuition fees and that provided for maintenance purposes. In the landmark *Grzelczyk* judgment of 2001, the Court relied on EU citizenship provisions and Arts 149 and 150 EC to find that foreign students could not be refused a social security benefit in the form of a minimum 'subsistence allowance' if the nationals of the Member State in question were entitled to it.[100] EU citizenship required that Member States show a certain degree of financial solidarity with other Member States 'in the organisation and application of their social assistance systems'.[101]

Several years later, in the *Bidar* case, the Court explicitly stated that maintenance grants and loans came within the scope of the Treaty, hence, EU citizens could not be discriminated against in this area.[102] This ruling was not unqualified. The Court recognised that the degree of financial solidarity expected from the Member States did not prevent the application of restrictive measures aimed at avoiding an 'unreasonable burden' on their finances, which could arise if governments were obliged to cover the maintenance costs of students who had no link with the country of studies other than having decided to move there for study purposes.[103] Accordingly, it was legitimate for a Member State to limit granting of financial assistance to students who had demonstrated 'a certain degree of integration into the society of that State'.[104] The judicial interpretation of what qualifies as an appropriate degree of integration into the society of the host Member State will be discussed in the next chapter.

C. Conclusion

It would not be incorrect to conclude that the case law of the Court has created rights for mobile students that were not envisaged by the Treaty, at least not until the amendments introduced by the Maastricht Treaty in 1992. Art 128 EEC, which was initially

[99] *Lair* (n 98), para 15; *Brown* (n 36), para 18.
[100] *Grzelczyk* (n 94), para 31.
[101] ibid, para 44.
[102] *Bidar* (n 36), para 42.
[103] ibid, para 56.
[104] ibid, para 57.

used by the Court to derive the right of access to education in other Member States, authorised the Community to lay down general principles for implementing a common vocational training policy. On that basis, the Court ruled that vocational training was covered by Community action, hence, the prohibition of discrimination applied with regard to access to such training. More importantly, by interpreting the term vocational training broadly enough to include higher education, the Court opened the doors for EU students to study in other Member States on equal conditions with local students. It is noteworthy that the Court's position also paved the way for a wider Community policy within the field of education, leading to the adoption of the Erasmus programme in 1987, which gave students the opportunity to benefit from a period of study in an EU Member State.[105] After the Treaty of Maastricht introduced EU citizenship and a specific legal basis for education, the Court's rationale for granting rights to mobile students has changed. Students were now entitled to pursue studies in other Member States solely by virtue of being EU citizens, regardless of whether they applied for courses that were linked to their later practice of trade or profession.

Similarly to the case law on access to cross-border healthcare, the Court's interpretation of the scope of free movement – expressed through the prohibition of discrimination on the basis of nationality – has been extremely generous since the first cases concerning cross-border access to education. It relied on a broad judicial understanding of the concept of vocational training and its connection with the European labour market. This position was later solidified by reference to subsequent Treaty reforms. The extent to which the described judicial developments are consistent with the principle of conferral will be discussed in section VI in light of the comparative analysis of the Court's reasoning across the areas under study.

IV. Collective Labour Law

This section begins with a discussion of questions of EU competence in the area of social policy and collective labour rights in particular. Then, it moves to the analysis of central developments in the case law, focusing on the Court's interpretation of the scope of free movement in situations involving the exercise of collective labour rights.

A. EU Competence and Legal Framework

i. The Development of EU Social Policy

As discussed in chapter one, the underlying logic of the Treaty of Rome was that a well-functioning market would bring about social progress and improve working

[105] Cort (n 69) 97; AP van der Mei, *Free Movement of Persons Within the European Community: Cross-Border Access to Public Benefits* (Oxford, Hart Publishing, 2003) 343. On the legal basis for the adoption of the programme, see Case C-242/87 *Commission v Council (ERASMUS)* EU:C:1989:217, [1989] ECR 1425. See also Regulation 1288/2013/EU establishing 'Erasmus+': the Union programme for education, training, youth and sport and repealing Decisions No 1719/2006/EC, No 1720/2006/EC and No 1298/2008/EC [2013] OJ L347/50.

conditions.[106] Accordingly, initially the only area of social policy in which the Community was granted competence to enact binding legislation was the free movement of workers.[107] As regards other matters of social policy, such as employment, social security and collective labour law, the Commission was charged with the task of 'promoting close co-operation' between Member States.[108] In theory, Art 100 EEC (now Art 115 TFEU) could be used as a legal basis for harmonising national labour laws to the extent that such harmonisation would 'have a direct incidence on the establishment or functioning of the Common Market'. However, this provision required a unanimous vote in the Council, which made the adoption of any kind of politically sensitive legislation unlikely.[109]

Subsequent Treaty amendments have gradually brought various aspects of social policy within the purview of EU institutions. For instance, the Single European Act introduced a new legal basis for the adoption of legislation by qualified majority voting in the area of health and safety at work.[110] The Community Social Charter, adopted in 1989, recognised rights for workers in areas such as working conditions, employee involvement and health and safety.[111] Although the Charter was and remains not legally binding, it has informed a number of EU policies, being frequently referred to in EU legislation and case law.[112] However, it was not until the Treaty of Maastricht that the EU's powers in relation to social policy were considerably expanded. Eleven Member States, excluding the UK, signed an Agreement on Social Policy, which was annexed to the Treaty of Maastricht. The Agreement gave constitutional recognition to the social partners and institutionalised their role in the Community's legislative process, previously reserved exclusively to EC institutions. At the same time, Community competences in employment and industrial relations were extended, allowing for qualified majority voting with respect to some of the new competences, including, inter alia, working conditions and information and consultation of workers.[113] In 1997, after the newly elected UK Labour Government decided to terminate the UK's 'opt-out' from the Social Policy Agreement, the Agreement was incorporated into a revised Social Chapter of the Treaty of Amsterdam. There have not been any major changes introduced into the Social Chapter since that time.

ii. Treaty Framework for Collective Labour Law

The EU's competences with regard to collective aspects of labour law remain limited. Art 153(1)(f) states that the EU shall 'support and complement' the activities of the

[106] The development of EU social policy is discussed in more detail in ch 1, s II.

[107] Arts 49, 51 EEC.

[108] Art 118 EEC.

[109] But there were some such measures, eg, Council Directive 77/187/EEC on the approximation of the laws of the Member States relating to the safeguarding of employees' rights in the event of transfers of undertakings, businesses or parts of businesses [1977] OJ L61/26.

[110] Art 118a EEC, added by Single European Act [1987] OJ L169/1, Art 21.

[111] Community Charter of Fundamental Social Rights of Workers [1989] OJ C323/44.

[112] Ryan (n 11) 10, referring to L Betten, 'The EU Charter of Fundamental Rights: A Trojan Horse or a Mouse?' (2001) 17 *International Journal of Comparative Labour Law & Industrial Relations* 151.

[113] Protocol on Social Policy to Treaty on European Union [1992] OJ C191/91, Agreement on Social Policy concluded between the Member States of the European Community with the exception of the United Kingdom of Great Britain and Northern Ireland, Art 3.

Member States in the representation and collective defence of the interests of workers and employers. This provision is subject to para (5) of the same article, which expressly excludes the right to strike and the right of association from EU-level harmonisation. The right to collective bargaining is not explicitly listed among the exclusions, but at the same time the Treaty provides no clear legislative basis for it.[114] Furthermore, Art 156 TFEU suggests that collective bargaining is not subject to binding legislation. It stipulates that the Commission shall 'encourage cooperation' between the Member States and 'facilitate the coordination of their action' in matters relating to, inter alia, the right of association and collective bargaining between employers and workers. Besides, collective bargaining may well fall within the scope of the 'right of association', which, together with the right to strike, is excluded from harmonisation by Art 153(5). It is noteworthy that there exists a possibility to adopt EU-level legislation on collective labour rights through the process of Social Dialogue.[115] However, the likelihood of such legislation is small, given the lack of incentives for the social partners to establish an EU-wide standard on collective labour rights.[116]

B. Case Law on Collective Labour Rights

Collective labour rights mainly come within the purview of EU law through the case law of the Court as potential restrictions on the free movement of businesses wishing to establish or provide services across national borders. The landmark judgments in which the Court defined the relationship between collective labour rights and EU economic freedoms are *Viking*[117] and *Laval.*[118] The principles formulated in *Viking* and *Laval* were further elaborated in subsequent cases[119] and ultimately extended to legal situations concerning, more generally, conflicts between commercial interests and those of worker protection.[120] This chapter discusses only those judgments which address the questions whether and why collective labour rights fall within the scope of free movement.

i. Viking: *The Right to Strike*

One of the best known and most discussed cases in EU law, *Viking* concerned a collective action aimed at preventing a Finnish ferry operating company, Viking, from taking advantage of a 'flag of convenience', which would have allowed the company to undercut

[114] Ryan (n 11) 67–68, 84–85; ACL Davies, 'Should the EU Have the Power to Set Minimum Standards for Collective Labour Rights in the Member States?' in P Alston (ed), *Labour Rights as Human Rights* (Oxford, OUP, 2005) 193–95.

[115] Art 155 TFEU.

[116] Davies (n 114) 196, 206–07.

[117] Case C-438/05 *Viking* EU:C:2007:772, [2007] ECR I-10779.

[118] Case C-341/05 *Laval* EU:C:2007:809, [2007] ECR I-11767.

[119] See Case C-346/06 *Rüffert* EU:C:2008:189, [2008] ECR I-1989. See also Case C-319/06 *Commission v Luxembourg* EU:C:2008:350, [2008] ECR I-4323 and Case C-271/08 *Commission v Germany* EU:C:2010:426, [2010] ECR I-7091, both analysed in detail in ch 3, s IV.

[120] Case C-515/08 *Santos Palhota* EU:C:2010:589, [2010] ECR I-9133, analysed in ch 5, s III; Case C-426/11 *Alemo-Herron* EU:C:2013:521 (CJEU, 18 July 2013), analysed in ch 3, s IV.

the minimum wage requirement set out in the applicable collective agreement. Viking challenged trade union actions alleging infringement of its freedom of establishment under Art 43 EC (now Art 49 TFEU).

The first question that the Court had to address was whether collective action fell within the scope of EU law. Trade unions as well as a number of intervening governments submitted that, by analogy to the *Albany* case,[121] the right to strike should be excluded from the application of (then) Arts 43 and 49 EC. In *Albany*, the Court had held that restrictions of competition were 'inherent' in collective agreements concluded between management and labour. Accordingly, collective agreements had to be regarded as falling outside the scope of Art 81 EC (now Art 101 TFEU) since otherwise social policy objectives pursued by such agreements would be seriously undermined.[122] It was argued in *Viking* that the same logic should apply in the context of free movement rules: 'certain restrictions on freedom of establishment and freedom to provide services [we]re inherent in collective action taken in the context of collective negotiations'.[123] The Court disagreed. Without going into much detail, it held that, unlike in the relationship between collective bargaining and competition law, it was 'not inherent in the very exercise of trade union rights and the right to take collective action' that the fundamental freedoms would be prejudiced.[124] This question will be returned to in section VI.

The Danish and Swedish governments further suggested that the right to strike should be exempted from the scope of free movement law by virtue of being a fundamental right. The Court accepted that fundamental rights, being an integral part of the general principles of Community law, constituted a legitimate interest which could justify a derogation from free movement rules; however, this did not remove them from the ambit of EU law.[125] Fundamental rights had to be exercised within the limits of EU law and in accordance with the principle of proportionality. This was reaffirmed by Art 28 of the Charter, which required that the right to collective bargaining and the right to strike be exercised 'in accordance with Community law and national laws and practices'.[126]

Finally, referring to its previous case law, the Court noted that Arts 43 and 49 EC applied not only to the actions of public authorities, but to 'rules of any other nature aimed at regulating in a collective manner gainful employment, self-employment and the provision of services'.[127] Therefore, a strike action aimed at concluding a collective agreement, which constituted a means of collective regulation, fell within the scope of Art 43.[128] This meant that Art 43 could be invoked directly against trade unions. The

[121] Case C-67/96 *Albany* EU:C:1999:430, [1999] ECR I-5751, discussed in ch 5, s IV.
[122] ibid, paras 59–60.
[123] *Viking* (n 117), para 48.
[124] ibid, para 52.
[125] ibid, paras 45–46, with further references to Case C-112/00 *Schmidberger* EU:C:2003:333, [2003] ECR I-5659, para 74 and Case C-36/02 *Omega* EU:C:2004:614, [2004] ECR I-9609, para 35, analysed in detail in ch 5, ss III and II, respectively.
[126] ibid, paras 43–44, affd in *Laval* (n 118), para 91.
[127] *Viking*, para 33, with further references to: Case C-36/74 *Walrave and Koch* EU:C:1974:140, [1974] ECR 1405, para 17; Case C-415/93 *Bosman* EU:C:1995:463, [1995] ECR I-4921, para 82; Case C-281/98 *Angonese* EU:C:2000:296, [2000] ECR I-4139, para 31.
[128] ibid, paras 35–37.

Court's position was grounded in the doctrine of effectiveness of EU law. In this case, the effectiveness of the fundamental freedoms would have been compromised if the abolition of State barriers were to be neutralised by obstacles resulting from the exercise of legal autonomy by trade unions, as organisations not governed by public law.[129] This conclusion could not be altered by the fact that the Community had no competence to regulate the right of association and right to strike. According to by then well-established judicial logic, Member States were 'free, in principle, to lay down the conditions governing the existence and exercise of the rights in question', but when exercising that competence, they remained under an obligation to comply with Community law.[130]

The Court went on to hold that the exercise by trade unions of the right to strike constituted a restriction on Viking's freedom of establishment because it was liable to make 'less attractive, or even pointless', for Viking to reflag its ship.[131] The Court took an essentially identical approach in the *Laval* case, decided a week after *Viking*, where it held that collective action aimed at forcing foreign undertakings to sign the collective agreement applicable to the building sector constituted a restriction on the freedom to provide services because it was 'liable to make it less attractive, or more difficult' for such undertakings to carry out construction work.[132]

ii. Rüffert *and* Commission v Germany: *The Right to Collective Bargaining*

The Court's approach to collective bargaining as a potential restriction of free movement is virtually the same as its approach to the right to strike, as illustrated by judgments in *Rüffert* and *Commission v Germany*, both involving the exercise of the right to collective bargaining in the context of public procurement.

Rüffert concerned a German law that confined the right to contract for public works to undertakings committed to pay the wages laid down in a sectoral collective agreement. The Court found that the obligation to abide by the minimum wage requirement laid down in the collective agreement constituted a restriction on the freedom to provide services within the meaning of Art 49 EC because it imposed on the service providers established in Member States where minimum rates of pay were lower, 'an additional economic burden' that was liable to prohibit, impede or render less attractive the provision of their services in the host Member State'.[133] In other words, the exercise of the right to collective bargaining in the context of public procurement posed an obstacle to the freedom of businesses to operate across borders.

The judgment of the Grand Chamber in *Commission v Germany* arose out of infringement proceedings against Germany and concerned the practice of local authority employers to award contracts for pension services to bodies specified in collective agreements, without a call for tenders in accordance with EU Public Procurement Directives.[134] The Court was asked to consider whether the involvement of the social

[129] *Viking* (n 117), paras 57–61, with further references to judgments mentioned in n 127.

[130] ibid, para 40, with further references to, inter alia: *Decker* (n 53), paras 22–23; *Kohll* (n 50), paras 18–19.

[131] ibid, paras 72–73.

[132] *Laval* (n 118), para 99.

[133] *Rüffert* (n 119), para 37.

[134] Council Directive 92/50/EEC relating to the coordination of procedures for the award of public service contracts [1992] OJ L209/1; Council Directive 2004/18/EC on the coordination of procedures for the award

partners in the award of contracts for pension services placed the issue outside the scope of EU public procurement rules, by analogy to *Albany*. The Court rejected this proposition, reiterating the line of reasoning employed in *Viking*.

First of all, the Court recognised that the right to collective bargaining was a fundamental right which formed an integral part of the general principles of EU law. As such, it was not excluded from the scope of free movement rules and had to be exercised in accordance with those rules.[135] Then, the Court turned to consider the analogy with *Albany*. Citing *Viking*, it held that it was not inherent in the very exercise of collective bargaining that the rules which implemented EU economic freedoms in the field of public procurement would be prejudiced.[136] Conversely, the Court added, unlike the obligation to comply with competition rules, the obligation to designate pension providers consistently with EU free movement rules did not affect the essence of the right to bargain collectively or undermine the objectives pursued by the social partners.[137] Local authority employers remained free to specify in the call for tenders the social policy conditions they wanted tenderers to comply with in the provision of occupational pension services.

C. Conclusion

The Court's position concerning the scope of EU free movement rules in relation to the exercise of collective labour rights in a transnational context is somewhat in line with its case law on cross-border healthcare and education. It is guided by the judicial understanding of the relationship between the existence of EU competence and the scope of EU law, whereby an obligation to comply with EU law applies also in the areas which essentially fall outside the scope of EU competence. In that respect, the Court recognises that EU law does not preclude the territorial application of national legislation or collective agreements that lay down the terms and conditions of employment.[138] Member States also remain free, in principle, to define the conditions governing the exercise of the right to collective bargaining and the right to strike. However, in exercising those competences, they have to comply with EU free movement rules.[139] Moreover, the responsibility to comply with the free movement rules in these situations falls not only on the governments but also trade unions, owing to their capacity to regulate the conditions of work and employment collectively.

The case law also establishes a clear hierarchy between EU economic freedoms and collective labour rights. The latter are viewed as barriers to, or restrictions of, the free movement, capable of dissuading businesses operating in the internal market from exercising their freedoms of establishment and provision of services.

of public works contracts, public supply contracts and public service contracts [2004] OJ L134/114, Art 26, now replaced by Council Directive 2014/24/EU on public procurement and repealing Directive 2004/18/EC [2014] OJ L94/65.

[135] *Commission v Germany* (n 119), paras 37–43.

[136] ibid, para 47, with a further reference to *Viking* (n 117), para 52.

[137] ibid, para 49.

[138] *Laval* (n 118), para 57.

[139] *Viking*, para 40.

The extent to which the Court's position is compatible with the requirements of the principle of conferral is discussed in section VI.

V. Gambling

This section discusses EU competence in the gambling sector and the extent to which this sector has been regulated by EU law. It also considers key aspects of the regulatory frameworks of the Member States as this helps to illuminate the challenges linked to the regulation of gambling at the EU level. Then, it turns to the analysis of the *Schindler* judgment, in which the Court addressed the question regarding the economic nature of gambling for the purposes of application of free movement law.

A. Competence and Legal Framework

i. Member State Legal Frameworks: Reasons behind Regulatory Intervention

The term 'gambling' typically refers to activities that involve wagering a stake with monetary value on something involving chance, usually a game or event, with the purpose of increasing the initial stake. Gambling activities include games of chance, games of skill, and betting on competitive sport and special events. The role played by the element of chance may differ significantly between these various forms of gambling. While in the games of chance, such as bingo, lottery or slot machines, success is random and depends predominantly on coincidence or an unknown future event; in sports betting and in the games of skill, which include most card games, the elements of strategy and skill – be it mental or physical – generally play a greater role than mere chance in determining the outcome.[140]

The gambling sector is different from many other sectors of the economy in that it is highly regulated and, hence, is subject to market forces only to a limited extent. Gambling is generally seen as a morally controversial form of entertainment, which, if unregulated, also carries considerable social costs.[141] Most notably, it is considered to be highly addictive – especially among minors, poorer segments of society and other vulnerable groups[142] – and is often linked to various criminal activities and

[140] Swiss Institute of Comparative Law, 'Study of Gambling Services in the Internal Market of the European Union' (Swiss Institute of Comparative Law 2006) 6 www.e-collection.isdc.ch/zoom/4362/view?page=6&p=separate&tool=info (Swiss Institute, Study of Gambling Services).

[141] For an analysis of the concept of social costs in the context of gambling, see DM Walker and AH Barnett, 'Social Costs of Gambling: An Economic Perspective' (1999) 15 *Journal of Gambling Studies* 181. See also HJ Wynne and HJ Shaffer, 'The Socioeconomic Impact of Gambling: The Whistler Symposium' (2003) 10 *Journal of Gambling Studies* 111; MS Kearney, 'The Economic Winners and Losers of Legalized Gambling' (2005) 58 *National Tax Journal* 281.

[142] Commission Recommendation 2014/478/EU on principles for the protection of consumers and players of online gambling services and for the prevention of minors from gambling online [2014] OJ L214/38 (Commission, Recommendation 2014/478). See also EI Grinols, 'The Hidden Social Costs of Gambling' (Center for Christian Ethics at Baylor University 2011) www.baylor.edu/content/services/document.php/144584.pdf.

illicit operations, such as fraud, money laundering and clandestine gambling.[143] The social costs associated with gambling are believed to have become even greater with an increase of online gambling platforms,[144] which have made the industry more accessible and attractive.[145] A prevalent regulatory response to these issues, at least in Europe, seems to limit gambling operators' access to the market, either partially (by awarding a certain number of licences and thus allowing limited competition in the sector[146]) or entirely (by monopolising the sector[147]). Some countries have also chosen to ban gambling on the Internet or prohibit certain types of online games that are more difficult to monitor, such as poker and casino games.[148]

However, from a purely economic point of view, governments have an abnormal financial interest in the profitability of the gambling industry because it generates significant revenues, derived from tax and State operation of the games of chance.[149] Annual revenues of the EU gambling market reached €98.6bn in 2019, with online gambling accounting for €24.5bn of the total revenue. Online gambling represents one of the fastest growing service activities in the EU, with annual growth rates of almost 15 per cent.[150] Europe's online gambling revenue increased by 7 per cent in 2020 – from €24.5bn to €26.3bn – despite a significant drop in revenue as a result of the cancellation of major European sporting events during the Covid pandemic.[151] The revenues from online gambling are forecasted to reach 33.6 per cent of Europe's total gambling revenue by 2025.

The above data suggests that governments' interest in regulating gambling may stem not so much from a genuine concern about the harmful effects of gambling, but rather, or equally so, from the need to counteract public perceptions about those effects in order to gain more widespread support for the industry among the general, non-gambling public.[152] This explanation seems plausible considering that the various scientific studies on gambling conducted thus far are lacking empirical data to support any conclusive claims about the scale of the negative social effects associated with gambling.[153] This is

[143] J Banks, *Online Gambling and Crime: Causes, Controls and Controversies* (Farnham, Ashgate Publishing, 2014).

[144] Kearney (n 141) 28.

[145] For a comprehensive account, see J Banks, 'Online Gambling and Crime: A Sure Bet?' (2012) *The Ethicomp Journal* shura.shu.ac.uk/6903/1/Banks_online_gambling.pdf.

[146] Commission, 'Towards a comprehensive European framework on online gambling' (Communication) COM (2012) 596 final (Commission, Communication 596/2012); Swiss Institute, Study of Gambling Services (n 140); European Parliament, 'Online Gambling, Focusing on Integrity and a Code of Conduct for Gambling' (Policy Department Economic and Scientific Policy 2008) 19–20 www.europarl.europa.eu/document/activities/cont/200811/20081119ATT42611/20081119ATT42611EN.pdf (EP Study on Gambling).

[147] Swiss Institute, Study of Gambling Services (n 140) xv–xvi.

[148] EP Study on Gambling (n 146).

[149] P Collins, *Gambling and the Public Interest* (Westport, Praeger Publishers, 2003) 66.

[150] F Zibold, 'Online Gambling in the EU' (Library of the European Parliament, 2013) www.europarl.europa.eu/RegData/bibliotheque/briefing/2013/130509/LDM_BRI%282013%29130509_REV1_EN.pdf.

[151] European Gaming & Betting Association, 'European Online Gambling Key Figures 2020 Edition' (2020) www.egba.eu/uploads/2020/12/European-Online-Gambling-Key-Figures-2020-Edition.pdf.

[152] Collins (n 149) 66.

[153] For a comprehensive overview of existing studies, see F Calado and MD Griffiths, 'Problem Gambling Worldwide: An Update and Systematic Review of Empirical Research (2000–2015)' (2016) 5 *Journal of Behavioral Addictions* 592. See also M Griffiths, 'Crime and Gambling: A Brief Overview of Gambling Fraud on the Internet (2010)' *Internet Journal of Criminology* irep.ntu.ac.uk/id/eprint/23349/1/200840_7000%20Griffiths%20Publisher.pdf.

especially true in relation to sports betting and games involving elements of strategy and skill rather than mere chance. Admittedly, the social effects of gambling may often be hard to measure. Against this background, one of the central aims of State controls imposed on gambling operators is to communicate to the public that this extremely profitable industry is, however, tightly controlled and socially responsible.[154] To that end, national laws that regulate gambling activities typically stipulate that their objective is to protect consumers and that the profits derived from gambling will be devoted to various social causes and public interest projects, such as sport, culture, social works or charity.[155] Yet, in practice, it often remains unclear what fraction of the total profits actually goes to social causes and to what extent these social causes benefit the disadvantaged segments of society, and also, more generally, whether the increase in public revenue compensates for the associated social costs.[156]

ii. EU Legal Framework: Subsidiarity-Guided Approach

The EU is conferred an unrestricted mandate to regulate gambling as an internal market service. It can choose to adopt directives in order to achieve the liberalisation of the gambling sector on the basis of Arts 50 and 59 TFEU; or, alternatively, it could use Art 114 TFEU, which authorises harmonisation of national laws for the achievement of the objectives of the internal market. Apart from these functionally broad legal bases dedicated, respectively, to freedom of establishment, freedom to provide services, and the functioning of the internal market, the Treaty contains no other provision that would detail or limit Union powers with respect to the regulation of gambling. Therefore, in contrast to the rest of the policy areas under study (healthcare, education and collective labour law), there exists no controversy in the Treaties as to whether the EU has competence to regulate.

Notwithstanding this unrestricted competence, gambling services are not subject to sector-specific legislation at EU level, and the Commission has not proposed any so far. Quite the contrary, gambling services have been explicitly excluded from the scope of the Services Directive, Consumer Rights Directive and the Directive on Electronic Commerce.[157] These exclusions seem to reflect the general lack of political appetite among the Member States for EU-level regulation of gambling. One reason behind this may be the persisting diversity in the regulatory approaches adopted by Member States, reflecting the variety of attitudes of their respective populations towards the social and cultural acceptability of the gambling industry.[158] On the other hand, reluctance

[154] Collins (n 149) 66. See also S Planzer, *Empirical Views on European Gambling Law and Addiction* (New York, Springer, 2014) 73–81.

[155] Planzer (n 154) 73–81; Swiss Institute, Study of Gambling Services (n 140) xiv.

[156] Collins (n 149) 85–129, esp 124; Kearney (n 141); D Miedema, 'Government – Gambling's Biggest Addict. Profligate Spending Feeds Government Gambling Addiction' (*Institute of Marriage and Family Canada*, March 2012) https://www.imfcanada.org/sites/default/files/Goverment_gambling_addiction_March_2012.pdf.

[157] Council Directive 2006/123/EC on services in the internal market [2006] OJ L376/36, Art 2(2); Council Directive 2000/31/EC on electronic commerce in the internal market [2000] OJ L178/1, Art 1(5); Council Directive 2011/83/EU on consumer rights, amending Council Directive 93/13/EEC and Directive 1999/44/EC of the European Parliament and of the Council and repealing Council Directive 85/577/EEC and Directive 97/7/EC of the European Parliament and of the Council [2011] OJ L304/64, Art 3(3).

[158] Commission, Communication 596/2012 (n 146), 5. For a comprehensive analysis on the issue of regulatory diversity, see J Hörnle, 'Social Policy and Regulatory Models' in J Hörnle and B Zammit, *Cross-Border Online Gambling Law and Policy* (Cheltenham, Edward Elgar Publishing, 2010) 10–30.

towards EU-wide legislation may be motivated by a desire to keep this highly profitable industry within national borders. Either way, this is regrettable. EU-wide action in the area of gambling could potentially be valuable, especially in light of the challenges to national regulatory capacity posed by Internet gambling, which by definition crosses national borders.[159]

The European Parliament, on its part, has expressly rejected 'any European legislative act uniformly regulating the entire gambling sector' other than a coordinated European approach that would complement national regulation.[160] The reasons behind the Parliament's position relate to the social and political sensitivity of the sector. First, gambling should be considered an economic activity of a special nature because of its (potential) negative health and social impacts.[161] Secondly, competition in the gambling sector does not lead to a better allocation of resources, therefore, a pure internal market approach is not appropriate.[162] Thirdly, given the differences in national traditions and cultures among the Member States, any regulation of the gambling sector is subject to, and must be underpinned by, the principle of subsidiarity.[163] The above reasons given by the Parliament seem to reiterate, to a greater or lesser extent, the position taken by the Court in its case law on gambling, to be discussed in this chapter and at length in the next chapter.

Against the apparent resistance on behalf of the political actors to harmonise the gambling sector, the initiatives taken by the Commission have been limited to the adoption of incentive measures, which focus on cooperation among national regulatory authorities and the sharing of good practices for tackling common problems, such as consumer protection, prevention of fraud and money laundering, and preservation of the integrity of sports.[164] In the absence of binding measures at the EU level, national gambling regulations come within the purview of EU law mainly through the case law of the CJEU, just like national measures in the areas of healthcare, education and collective labour law.

B. Gambling as an Economic Activity in the Case Law

Unlike the case law in the constitutionally sensitive areas under study, EU case law on gambling does not present competence concerns. However, it nevertheless involves a politically sensitive area of national policy. In that respect, the Court's treatment of domestic regulatory frameworks for gambling provides a valuable insight into the

[159] A Nair, 'Online Gambling: Gambling with Regulation' (2012) 3 *European Journal of Law and Technology* ejlt.org/index.php/ejlt/article/view/165/265.

[160] European Parliament, 'Resolution on online gambling in the internal market' 2011/2084(INI) (EP Resolution 2011/2084), para 11.

[161] European Parliament, Committee on the Internal Market and Consumer Protection, 'Motion for a European Parliament Resolution on the integrity of online gambling' 2008/2215(INI), para 2 (Motion on Integrity of Gambling); EP Resolution 2011/2084 (n 160), Recital 12; European Parliament, 'Resolution on online gambling in the internal market' 2012/2322(INI), Preamble (EP Resolution 2012/2322).

[162] Motion on Integrity of Gambling (n 161), Recital 2.

[163] EP Resolution 2011/2084 (n 160), Recital 7; EP Resolution 2012/2322 (n 161), Recital 29.

[164] Commission, Communication 596/2012 (n 146); Commission, Recommendation 2014/478 (n 142).

Court's approach to the collision between internal market law and domestic regulatory activity in politically sensitive areas. Most of the case law on gambling will be examined in the next chapter, concerning the principles of subsidiarity and proportionality. This section is limited to the analysis of the judicial reasoning concerning gambling as an economic activity for the purposes of application of free movement law. This question was addressed by the Court in the first EU case involving gambling: *Schindler.*

Decided in 1994, *Schindler* concerned a prohibition on the operation of large-scale lotteries laid down in the British legislation.[165] Mr Schindler was an independent lottery agent who was not permitted to market in the UK a lottery that was organised in Germany. The Court was asked, in the first place, to consider whether lotteries fell within the scope of the Treaty, namely whether the provision of lottery services was an economic activity within the meaning of Art 60 EEC (now Art 57 TFEU). The governments that submitted observations noted that due to their morally controversial nature, lotteries were either prohibited or subject to 'particularly strict regulation and close control by the public authorities', and were operated solely in the public interest.[166] The Court found that this was not sufficient to exclude lotteries from the scope of EU law. Even if the morality of lotteries was questionable, they were not comparable to activities involving illegal products, whose harmful nature would entail a complete prohibition under (then) Community law.[167] Lotteries were 'commonplace' and practised legally in a number of Member States, and it was not for the Court to substitute its assessment for that of the legislatures and declare otherwise.[168]

Two factors were decisive for lotteries to qualify as economic activities within the meaning of EU law: first, the fact that the player paid consideration hoping to receive a prize or winning in return; and, second, that lotteries were operated with a view to profit, as not all the money staked was redistributed as prizes or winnings.[169] Neither the element of chance inherent in a lottery transaction, nor the recreational aspect of lotteries, nor the use of profits thereof in the public interest could, in the Court's view, alter the nature of the transaction itself or deprive it of its economic character.[170] Notably, subsequent case law made clear that this reasoning applied to all games of chance and other forms of gambling, such as games of skill.[171]

The Court ruled that the British prohibition on the operation of lotteries posed an obstacle to free movement, as it was liable to impede the activities of foreign service providers.[172] This restriction was, however, lawful in the context of the public aims pursued by national authorities. The reasons that justified the restriction will be discussed in the next chapter.

[165] Case C-275/92 *Schindler* EU:C:1994:119, [1994] ECR I-1039.

[166] ibid, para 31.

[167] ibid, para 32.

[168] ibid, paras 31–32. See also Case C-159/90 *Grogan* EU:C:1991:378, [1991] ECR I-4685, paras 19–21, holding that medical termination of pregnancy is a service regardless of its questionable morality.

[169] *Schindler* (n 165), paras 33–35.

[170] ibid, paras 34–35.

[171] See, eg, Case C-124/97 *Läärä* EU:C:1999:435, [1999] ECR I-6067, paras 17–18; Case C-67/98 *Zenatti* EU:C:1999:514, [1999] ECR I-7289, paras 24–25.

[172] *Schindler*, para 43.

The conclusions arrived at by the Court in *Schindler* are not surprising. Gambling has long been operated as a commercial activity, at least in the Western societies. Considering this, there appears to be little scope for arguing that it should not be regarded as a service for the purposes of EU law. What is, however, interesting in the Court's reasoning is the expression of judicial deference towards national legislatures in the qualification of gambling as an economic activity. One of the reasons why the Court considers gambling a service in *Schindler* is the fact that gambling activities (lotteries in this case) are practised legally in a number of Member States. This leads the Court to conclude that gambling is a service despite its morally controversial nature. This point will be returned to in the next section.

VI. The Implications of the Case Law for the Principle of Conferral

This section takes a comparative view of case law developments in the areas under study and examines them in light of the principle of conferral.

A. Conferral in Judicial Reasoning

It was discussed in section I of this chapter that there is an inherent flexibility in the application of the principle of conferral to the activities of the EU, according to the interpretation of this principle by the Court. Specifically, conferral does not preclude EU interference into the areas of competence predominantly reserved to the Member States in as much as such interference stems from the exercise – legislative or judicial – of competences that the EU does possess. Accordingly, it does not make it unlawful for the EU internal market law to be enforced across an unlimited range of policy areas, including those under study here, regardless of whether they fall within the EU's exclusive, shared or supplementary competences, or are not at all included in the list of EU competences.

It was also argued that the flexibility associated with the principle of conferral as well as the overlap between competences conferred upon the EU and those reserved to the Member States can become problematic if pushed to an excess. Such situation would have serious consequences for the scope of national regulatory autonomy, thereby putting into question the raison d'être of the principle of conferral as a constitutional constraint on EU powers. Accordingly, if the principle of conferral is to have a meaningful normative function, there needs to be a limit to how far the judicial exercise of EU internal market competences can legitimately encroach into the areas of competence that would otherwise be exempted from any substantial interference on behalf of the EU.

That limit lies in the interpretation by the Court of the conditions that trigger the application of EU internal market law, free movement law in particular in the context of the present study. As discussed earlier, the free movement rules – expressed either in the form of the economic freedoms or the principle of non-discrimination, or the concept of EU citizenship, or sometimes a combination of the above – do not have general application. For any of those rules to apply, the situation in question has to fall within the scope of EU law. For instance, the prohibition of discrimination on grounds of nationality only applies in situations that are connected to EU law through some specific substantive rule of EU law, which governs the situation in question.[173] EU citizenship rights are generally triggered when there is a movement from one Member State to another. For the economic freedoms to apply, two cumulative conditions must be met: first, the cross-border activities governed by these freedoms have to be of an economic, as opposed to social, character; second, the national measure or practice that is challenged must constitute a restriction on those activities. So, there must be an effect on the market and also the *internal* market.

The principle of conferral requires that the Court rule on the matter only when it falls within the scope of EU law. Accordingly, it does not authorise judicial interference with the constitutionally sensitive areas of national policy in the name of the internal market unless the conditions that trigger the application of free movement rules are met. Moreover, when interpreting those conditions, the Court is expected to adopt a systemic approach, contextualising them in the constitutional requirements of the principle of conferral. This presupposes a judicial interpretation of the scope of free movement that balances the objectives of the internal market with the concerns about the protection of national regulatory autonomy in the areas of national policy that are constitutionally sensitive from an EU law point of view. This would suggest, for example, that the judicial interpretation (and application) of the concepts of an economic activity and restriction of free movement in individual cases should weigh the economic and market elements pertaining to the situation in question against the regulatory, non-market objectives underlying the adoption of national measures. Similarly, where free movement law manifests itself through the principle prohibiting discrimination on grounds of nationality, the assessment by the Court of whether the situation in question is governed by or otherwise sufficiently connected with a substantive rule of EU law should take into account potential competence concerns that might arise when establishing the situation's connection with EU law.

The following discussion argues that the interpretation by the Court of the conditions underlying the scope of application of free movement law has systematically failed to achieve an appropriate balance between, on the one hand, the objectives of the internal market and, on the other hand, concerns about the protection of national competence and regulatory autonomy in the areas under study. A comparative analysis of the case law reveals one central common pattern in the Court's reasoning: a consistently generous interpretation of the scope of free movement rules. As a consequence, the degree of overlap determined by the Court between the free movement law, on the one hand, and the areas of healthcare, education and labour law, on the other, becomes substantial, thus overstretching the principle of conferral. This situation also creates tensions with the principle of conferral at the EU's legislative level because it unlocks the legislative mandate for the EU to regulate areas that fall outside its explicit sector-specific legislative competence. Moreover, the Court's reasoning that explains why a certain measure

[173] See cases and literature in n 36.

or practice falls within the scope of free movement is often incoherent and goes beyond both the textual and teleological reading of the Treaties.[174]

B. Healthcare as an Economic Activity

i. The Economic Character of Public Healthcare

The entire case law of the Court concerning the rights of patients to cross-border healthcare is premised on the finding that public healthcare constitutes a service within the meaning of Art 57 TFEU. Art 57 provides that the main criterion for a particular activity to qualify as a service under EU law is remuneration. This brings private provision of healthcare under the definition. The Court, however, extends the application of Art 56 TFEU to healthcare provided under national social security schemes. The basis for this approach lies in the pecuniary nature of the transaction between the patient and the foreign healthcare provider, as the patient pays directly for the treatment obtained in another Member State. The fact that the costs of the treatment are subsequently reimbursed by the social security scheme of the patient's Member State of affiliation is immaterial to the judicial assessment of the situation. In the Court's view, it is sufficient that hospitals which function within social security schemes ultimately receive consideration for the treatment they provide from sickness insurance funds or other managing bodies.[175] This money represents remuneration and indicates that the hospital is engaged in an activity of an economic character. This also explains why the economic character of public healthcare does not change depending on the specific type of health service, inpatient or outpatient treatment, or the specific type of statutory cover, be it reimbursement, benefit-in-kind or national health service.

Notably, the Court's conclusions are based primarily on the economic relationship between the service provider and the recipient within the State that provides treatment. The reasoning of the Court completely disregards the social policy relationship between the citizen and the national welfare system in the patient's State of affiliation.[176] This is remarkable given that this relationship is a necessary precondition for receiving any type of medical service abroad. More importantly, this relationship signals the presence of competence sensitivities involved in the situation concerned, which the Court is required to recognise under the principle of conferral in the interpretation of the scope of free movement rules. As a minimum, such recognition would entail giving due consideration to the relationship between the citizen and the national welfare system when deciding whether the provision of public healthcare should be considered an economic activity for the purposes of application of Art 56.

[174] Cf, eg, Case C-26/62 *Van Gend & Loos* EU:C:1963:1, [1963] ECR 1 and Case C-283/81 *CILFIT v Ministry of Health* EU:C:1982:335, [1982] ECR 3415, para 20 against Case C-50/00 *P UPA v Council* EU:C:2002:462, [2002] ECR I-6677, para 44, suggesting that the CJEU alternates between the textual and teleological interpretations of the Treaty, although the latter method is predominant. For a comprehensive discussion, see G Conway, *Limits of Legal Reasoning* (Cambridge, CUP, 2012) ch 1, esp 21–26.

[175] *Smits and Peerbooms* (n 50), para 58.

[176] *Kohll* (n 50), para 21; *Smits and Peerbooms*, paras 53–58; *Watts* (n 50), para 90. For an academic commentary, see Dougan (n 76) 20.

ii. Comparable Contexts

Furthermore, the Court's approach appears inconsistent with that employed in other, comparable contexts. For instance, in the context of cross-border access to education, the social policy relationship between the citizen and the State is a major factor why public education is not considered a service within the meaning of Art 57. The Court holds that the essential characteristic of remuneration, which constitutes consideration for the service in question, is absent in the case of courses provided under the national education system.[177] The Court's explanation here is two-fold. First, when establishing and maintaining its education system, the State is not seeking to engage in a gainful activity but, rather, it is fulfilling duties towards its own population. Second, the social function of the system is reflected in the fact that education is predominantly financed from the public purse. The fact that students contribute to the operating expenses of the system by paying tuition cannot alter this conclusion.[178]

The reasons for excluding education from the scope of Art 56 by and large apply to the healthcare sector. Healthcare provided in the framework of social security is aimed at protecting the public interest. Accordingly, it is heavily subsidised by the State and delivered on the basis of solidarity as opposed to a profit-making basis. The amount of tax or insurance paid by patients does not even remotely reflect the monetary value of healthcare services provided. In light of this, the fact that technically patients pay for the treatment received from a provider established in another Member State (for which they are later reimbursed) should not affect the characterisation of public healthcare as a predominantly social activity.

The Court's approach to public healthcare as an economic activity in the context of free movement also stands in contrast to its approach in competition law. The free movement rules seem to apply to any healthcare activity involving remuneration of some sort and regardless of whether the activity in question is organised on the basis of solidarity at the national level. Competition law, on the other hand, applies only insofar as bodies involved in the management and delivery of public healthcare are considered undertakings. To be classified as undertakings, these bodies have to be engaged in an economic activity, which will not be the case if they operate in accordance with the principle of solidarity.[179] The principle of solidarity thus plays a crucial role in the classification of an activity as economic in light of competition law, but not free movement law.[180] As a result of the divergent approaches that the Court employs in relation to essentially the same issue, the provision of healthcare that is free of charge and financed through social security contributions may be considered as economic (and thus within the scope of EU

[177] Case C-263/86 *Humbel* EU:C:1988:451, [1988] ECR-5365, paras 17–18.

[178] ibid, paras 18–19; Case C-109/92 *Wirth* EU:C:1993:916, [1993] ECR I-6447, para 15.

[179] See, eg, T Hervey, '"Social Solidarity": A Buttress Against Internal Market Law?' in J Shaw (ed), *Social Law and Policy in an Evolving European Union* (London, Hart Publishing, 2005); J Baquero Cruz, 'Beyond Competition: Services of General Interest and European Community Law' in G de Búrca (ed), *EU Law and the Welfare State: In Search of Solidarity* (Oxford, OUP, 2005); T Prosser, 'EU Competition Law and Public Services' in E Mossialos et al (eds), *Health Systems Governance in Europe: The Role of European Union Law and Policy* (Cambridge, CUP, 2010); D Gallo, 'Functional Approach and Economic Activity in EU Competition Law, Today: The Case of Social Security and Healthcare' (2020) 26 *European Public Law* 569.

[180] For situations where competition law does not apply, see, eg, Case C-159/91 and C-160/91 *Poucet and Pistre* EU:C:1993:63, [1993] ECR I-637, paras 8–12; Case C-205/03 *FENIN* EU:C:2006:453, [2006] ECR I-6295, paras 8–26.

law) or social (and thus outside the scope of EU law) depending on whether the question is assessed in light of free movement or competition law.

The Court might have reasons for employing an approach that is more sensitive to social solidarity concerns in the area of competition law, but it does not reveal those reasons.[181] The bottom line is, however, that both competition law and free movement law are dedicated to the protection of the internal market. This does not mean that they are the same in their detailed scope, nor that the legal interests at stake should be interpreted in exactly the same way. It does mean, though, that the two sets of rules should not lead to conflicting outcomes without a convincing justification, as they seem to at the moment in the context of healthcare.

iii. The Legislative Dimension

Viewing public healthcare as an economic activity also has consequences for the effectiveness of the legislative dimension of the principle of conferral. If a matter is considered to fall within the scope of free movement law, it can then be regulated at the EU's legislative level. Specifically, the provision of healthcare, as a service, can be harmonised under Art 114, the internal market legal basis, or Art 59, which provides a legal basis for the liberalisation of a specific service across the EU. The Patients' Rights Directive, to be examined in chapter four, harmonises national rules on patients' access to cross-border healthcare services and is a prominent example of an EU legislative measure whose adoption was inspired by the free movement case law.[182]

The impact of the case law on EU legislative activity showcases the power of the judicial interpretation of the Treaties. An expansive interpretation by the Court of the scope of free movement rules in the context of the provision of public healthcare effectively authorises the EU legislature to disregard the safeguards of non-interference contained in the principle of conferral and made more specific in Arts 6 and 168 TFEU, which explicitly preclude binding legislation in the healthcare sector. As a result, the EU can now legitimately regulate cross-border access to healthcare via both the judicial and legislative routes.[183] This outcome has major implications for national regulatory autonomy in the healthcare sector, which is hard to justify from a constitutional point of view, given that the Court has never provided a convincing explanation for why public healthcare should be considered a service in the first place.

C. Vocational Training, University Education and EU Citizenship

Case law concerning cross-border access to education displays a similar pattern, whereby the Court adopts an expansive reading of the scope of the Treaties and, by doing so, challenges both the judicial and legislative dimensions of the principle of conferral.

[181] For a discussion of the differences and similarities between the free movement and competition law, see ch 5, s II.

[182] Patients' Rights Directive (n 37), Recital 2, referring to Art 114 TFEU as the legal basis for its adoption. The details of this directive, including its adoption history, are discussed in ch 4, s IV.

[183] For a comprehensive analysis of the impact of the case law on EU legislative activity, see ch 4.

i. The Prohibition of Discrimination

The Court has used two Treaty provisions to derive individual rights for mobile students: the prohibition of discrimination on the basis of nationality, and, after the entry into force of the Maastricht Treaty, EU citizenship. As pointed out earlier, for the principle of non-discrimination to apply, the situation in question has to fall within 'the scope of application of the Treaties'. This would suggest, in the broadest sense, that the situation concerned is governed by a substantive rule of EU law, primary or secondary, or is otherwise connected with such a rule.[184] The existence of a legal basis potentially covering the situation is not normally deemed sufficient to establish connection with EU law.[185] In light of this, was the Court right to hold in *Gravier* that cross-border access to education fell within the scope of application of the Treaties?

The EEC Treaty, in force at the time when *Gravier* was delivered, did not foresee any powers for the Community in the field of education, with the exception of vocational training. Art 128 EEC contained a vague stipulation that the Commission would lay down general principles for implementing a common vocational training policy that would contribute to the economic objectives of the Community. The primary economic objective referred to in Art 128 concerned the advancement of the European labour market. A common vocational training policy was meant to contribute to the advancement of the European labour market by addressing issues of worker mobility, such as the transnational transfer of vocational qualifications. On that basis, the Court ruled that vocational training fell within the scope of Community law. Furthermore, it took the view that the concept of vocational training encompassed any form of education which prepared for a qualification for a particular profession, trade or employment, even if the training programme included an element of general education.[186] Essentially, this meant that access to cross-border education fell within the scope of Community law by virtue of its indirect link to the European labour market. Such access was likely to promote the free movement of workers by enabling them to obtain the necessary qualifications in the Member States whose education programmes included their desired subjects.

The Court's reasoning appears strained and unconvincing. It relies on an indirect link between higher education, vocational training and the European labour market. Essentially, what the Court is saying is that since access to higher education, in principle, falls within the scope of vocational training, and the latter contributes to the free movement of workers, higher education also contributes to the free movement of workers and thus falls within the scope of Community law. Needless to say, the link is tenuous.

It has been pointed out above that the Court never considered public education to be a service within the meaning of Art 57 TFEU. However, it did have to consider the strength of the connection between higher education and the internal market (expressed through the free movement of workers in this case) in order to establish whether national practices that posed obstacles to foreign students' access to education fell within the scope of application of the prohibition of discrimination on grounds of nationality. Just like in the case of healthcare, the Court found the existence of such a connection whilst

[184] Discussed in Prechal (n 36) 11. See also cases mentioned in n 36.
[185] Prechal (n 36) 11.
[186] *Gravier* (n 83), paras 30–31.

offering no consideration or even recognition of competence concerns pertaining to the application of free movement law to the education sector. Having adopted a rather one-dimensional interpretation of the role and character of higher education in the EU, the Court effectively moved it from the domain of social and public policy, protected by national regulatory autonomy, into the domain of activities that are instrumental to enabling the free movement of workers.

Ultimately, the fact that the Court employed different legal bases in cases involving healthcare, on the one hand, and education, on the other, did not have much effect on the development of the case law. Mobile patients and mobile students seem to have been granted comparable amplitude of rights to access foreign healthcare and education systems, respectively. This outcome may be an indication that the Court interprets the Treaties in a result-driven way: where bringing a measure directly within the scope of the economic freedoms seems too far-fetched, the Court will arrive at virtually the same conclusion through the principle of non-discrimination or the concept of EU citizenship, both formulated broadly enough in the Treaties to be susceptible to a generous judicial interpretation.

ii. EU Citizenship

The entry into force of the Maastricht Treaty provided the Court with an explicit basis for its student mobility case law by introducing the concept of EU citizenship and a legal basis for EU action in education. The Court thus no longer needed to distinguish between general education and one that prepared for a profession or employment, although in practice this distinction never mattered. More importantly, the Court used the concept of EU citizenship to expand further the EU's interference into national education systems. Pursuant to Art 8(a)(1) of the EC Treaty, EU citizenship granted nationals of EU Member States the right to move and reside freely within the territory of the Union. The Court read this provision as embedding a 'fundamental status of EU citizens', which, interpreted along with the principle of non-discrimination, guaranteed EU citizens equal treatment irrespective of their nationality when they found themselves in the same circumstances as the nationals of the Member State concerned. Such equal treatment extended to situations where students were applying for financial support for education in another Member State. As a result, educational maintenance grants and loans, previously having been outside the scope of the Treaty, were brought within its scope.

The above interpretative choices taken by the Court seem to sit uncomfortably within the wider framework of the Treaties, specifically key amendments introduced into the Treaties in 1992. It is highly significant that the new legal basis for education (Art 126 of the EC Treaty) introduced in Maastricht highlighted the complementary nature of the EU's role in education. This role was limited to encouraging cooperation between Member States. An almost identical stipulation was added to Art 127 of the EC Treaty as regards vocational training. Moreover, the Treaty made explicit the principles of conferral and subsidiarity, which were supposed to clarify the division of competences between the EU and Member States. The Maastricht reforms were widely interpreted as signifying an attempt by the Member States to curtail the EU's ambitions in the area of education, as well as in other politically sensitive policy areas.[187] However, the Court ignored the wider context and focused exclusively on those Treaty amendments, such as the introduction of EU citizenship, which justified broadening the scope of freedom of movement.

iii. The Legislative Dimension

The Court's interpretation of EU citizenship in the context of cross-border access to education has created tensions with the principle of conferral on multiple levels. First, it brought within the scope of the Treaties a question which was considered to be at the core of national sovereignty – that of cross-border access of economically inactive individuals to national social security schemes. Second, in doing so, it went against an explicit EU-wide legislative consensus on the matter enshrined in Community residence directives, which precluded economically inactive individuals residing in other Member States from accessing welfare benefits in the host States and conditioned their right of residence on the possession of sufficient financial resources.[188] Third, it ultimately inspired the adoption of the Citizens' Rights Directive of 2004, to be discussed in chapter four, which by and large transposed the rules laid down in the case law into EU legislation.[189] Thus, the judicial interpretation of the scope of free movement in the area of higher education has effectively neutralised the principle of conferral as a safeguard against legislative encroachment by the EU into several policy areas that in principle lay outside the scope of EU competence.

Overall, the judicial developments concerning cross-border access to education display the already familiar, pro-integration pattern of interpretation. The Court tends to focus on the circumstances which justify the application of EU free movement rules to the situation concerned whilst disregarding, almost completely, the factors that play against such application. In the context of healthcare, there has been a nearly exclusive emphasis by the Court on the economic nature of the transaction between the patient and foreign healthcare system. In the context of education, the importance of EU citizenship and principle of non-discrimination trumped any concerns about the encroachment of EU law into the regulation of national education and social security systems. Such interpretative choices on behalf of the Court are hard to defend both as a matter of the principle of conferral and as a matter of convincing judicial reasoning.

[187] Dougan (n 76) 6.

[188] See Council Directive 90/364/EEC on the right of residence [1990] OJ L180/26, Preamble, Recital 4, Art 3; Council Directive 90/365/EEC on the right of residence for employees and self-employed persons who have ceased their occupational activity [1990] OJ L180/28, Preamble, Recital 4, Art 3; Council Directive 93/96/EEC on the right of residence for students [1993] OJ L317/59, Preamble, Recitals 10 and 11, Art 4. For a comprehensive analysis on this point, see ch 4, s VI.

[189] Council Directive 2004/38/EC on the right of citizens of the Union and their family members to move and reside freely within the territory of the Member States [2004] OJ L158/79, whose adoption is analysed in ch 4, s VI.

D. Collective Labour Rights as Obstacles to the Exercise of the Economic Freedoms

Case law on collective labour rights reveals similar constitutional tensions to those that arise in the first two areas under study. The Court employs an extremely broad judicial interpretation of the scope of free movement rules. There are two particular aspects of the Court's reasoning that deserve a deeper analysis: the fact that the right to collective bargaining and right to strike are regarded as potential restrictions on the exercise of the economic freedoms; and the assertion that those freedoms have horizontal direct effect in the context of collective regulation of labour and employment, and hence can be invoked directly against trade unions in private disputes.

i. The Restriction of Free Movement

The Court had to confront questions about the scope of free movement in relation to collective labour rights in its first judgments involving the exercise of the right to strike in transnational situations. In *Viking* and *Laval*, it was specifically asked to consider whether collective labour rights should be excluded from the scope of free movement law. The question was not framed using the terms of the principle of conferral, but it expressed concerns that lie at the heart of this principle: that the free movement law may creep into the areas of national policy that are supposed to be protected from any substantial interference by the EU. The proposition to exclude collective labour rights from the scope of free movement relied on the analogy with the *Albany* case, where the Court held that collective bargaining fell outside the scope of competition law because the two interests were inherently incompatible: the application of competition rules to collective agreements would have inevitably undermined the social policy objectives pursued by trade unions.[190] The Court, however, considered that the same logic did not apply in the context of free movement. According to the Court, the free movement rules did not affect the essence of trade union rights in a manner equivalent to competition rules.[191] At the same time, it was not inherent in the very exercise of trade union rights that EU fundamental freedoms would be prejudiced.[192]

The former statement has some logic to it. The provision of services on a temporary or permanent basis in another Member State does not in itself undermine the right to collective bargaining or collective action. Trade unions remain free to bargain collectively and take collective action to defend the interests of their members. In that sense, there is no inevitable conflict between the two categories of activities. This can be contrasted with the application to collective agreements of competition rules. Collective agreements eliminate wage competition among workers and employers by fixing the price of labour. From the perspective of competition law, price fixing agreements are unlawful. Collective agreements are thus in direct conflict with competition

[190] The *Albany* judgment (n 121) is further analysed in ch 5, s IV.
[191] *Commission v Germany* (n 119), para 49.
[192] *Viking* (n 117), para 52; *Laval* (n 118), para 86; *Commission v Germany*, paras 45–47.

law. However, the purpose of safeguarding the capacity of such agreements to protect workers justifies their exemption from competition law.

The Court also holds that it is not inherent in the exercise of trade union rights that the fundamental freedoms will be prejudiced. This assumption seems inaccurate. The definition of a restriction adopted by the Court is extremely broad and encompasses any measure or practice liable to make free movement 'less attractive'.[193] It seems to be particularly ill suited to apply to collective labour rights as their exercise will almost inevitably create a 'less attractive' environment for any business. Just like relevant statutory rules, collective regulation of conditions of work and employment is meant to restrict the commercial freedom of the employer. This is done in order to protect the employees, who are the weaker party in the employment relationship. However, from the perspective of an undertaking coming from a Member State with lower standards of worker protection, any such regulation in the host Member State takes away its competitive advantage of using cheaper labour, thus making cross-border movement less attractive.[194] It therefore seems that in these situations, virtually every exercise of collective labour rights will trigger a *prima facie* breach of free movement rules. In other words, a transnational exercise of collective bargaining and right to strike is bound to prejudice the exercise of economic freedoms. This suggests that there exists an 'inherent conflict' between collective labour rights and economic freedoms, which could in turn justify an exclusion of the former from the scope of the latter.

More generally, the case law on collective labour rights showcases the shortcomings of the Court's definition of a restriction. Due to its virtually all-encompassing character, it does not leave much room for accommodating national practices that fall squarely outside the scope of the EU's regulatory competence or are otherwise sensitive. Of course, the Court cannot be expected to predict all the situations where its definition of a restriction may cause problems. At the same time, it can and should be expected to consider competence concerns when applying that definition to constitutionally and politically sensitive contexts. In fact, the Court has demonstrated the capacity to do so in the past. For instance, it decided in *Keck* that non-discriminatory, market-correcting measures that restrict businesses' commercial freedom are not considered as obstacles to free movement even if they make the movement of goods across borders 'less attractive'.[195] The Court thus showed awareness of and sensitivity to the regulatory prerogatives of the Member States, which could have been undermined if the Court had adopted a more aggressive interpretation of the scope of free movement law. Whilst *Keck* did not go as far as to narrow down the scope of the Court's definition of a restriction in relation to all economic freedoms (as opposed to being confined to the free movement of goods), it made clear that this definition was subject to exceptions. There is no reason why the interpretative approach employed in *Keck* could not have been

[193] Case C-55/94 *Gebhard* EU:C:1995:411, [1995] ECR I-4165, para 37; *Laval* (n 118), para 99. For an analysis of non-discriminatory restrictions in the case law, see L Daniele, 'Non-Discriminatory Restrictions to the Free Movement of Persons' (1997) 22 *European Law Review* 191.

[194] J Malmberg and T Sigeman, 'Industrial Actions and EU Economic Freedoms: The Autonomous Collective Bargaining Model Curtailed by the European Court of Justice' (2008) 45 *CML Rev* 1115.

[195] Joined cases C-267/91 and C-268/91 *Keck and Mithouard* EU:C:1993:905, [1993] ECR I-6097.

applied in relation to collective regulation of employment and working conditions in the context of Arts 49 and 56.

ii. *Horizontal Direct Effect*

Furthermore, the Court holds that in order to avoid inequality in the application of free movement rules across the EU, Arts 49 and 56 can be invoked in courts directly against trade unions.[196] In other words, Arts 49 and 56 have horizontal direct effect in the context of collective regulation of labour and employment. This represents a very broad interpretation of the scope of these articles. On the one hand, the Court recognises that trade unions are private actors, whose actions are covered by legal autonomy and governed by private law. On the other hand, it equates them to States in terms of their regulatory role and responsibility in complying with EU free movement rules.[197]

This approach is predominantly driven by the desire to preserve the effectiveness of the free movement rules. However, the focus on effectiveness in these circumstances sits uncomfortably with Art 153 TFEU, which protects trade unions against any substantial interference with their activities on the part of the EU. The principle of conferral would require that in this situation the goal of preserving the effectiveness of free movement law should be weighed against the constitutional importance of the protection of the regulatory autonomy of trade unions. Yet the Court does not engage in any sort of weighing of these competing objectives. Competence considerations, which could suggest a more conservative interpretation of the scope of Arts 49 and 56, do not enter the Court's reasoning, aside a passing mention.[198] Considering that the questions at stake have a direct bearing on the principle of conferral, one would expect the Court to be more rigorous in its reasoning.

iii. *The Legislative Dimension*

Just like in the context of cross-border access to healthcare and education, the Court's interpretation of the scope of free movement in relation to collective labour rights also calls into question the legislative dimension of the principle of conferral. Taking the example of the right to strike, Wyatt observes that by holding that collective action could amount to a restriction on the freedom of establishment, the Court implies that national rules on strike action can be regulated under the Treaty's chapter on establishment, namely Art 50(1) TFEU.[199] This sends a signal to the Commission that it can legitimately disregard the exclusion in Art 153(5) of EU regulation of strike action.[200]

[196] *Viking* (n 117), paras 33–34, 59–61.

[197] Malmberg and Sigeman (n 194) 1130–31; L Azoulai, 'The Court of Justice and the Social Market Economy: The Emergence of an Ideal and the Conditions for its Realisation' (2008) 45 *CML Rev* 1335, 1343–46.

[198] See, eg, *Viking*, paras 40–41.

[199] In this connection, see ch 4, s V for a discussion of Commission, 'Proposal for a Council Regulation on the exercise of the right to take collective action within the context of the freedom of establishment and the freedom to provide services' COM (2012) 130 final (Monti II).

[200] D Wyatt, 'If the Court of Justice Ignores the Principle of Conferral Simply Because It Can, How Do We Fix the Problem?' (14th Jean Monnet Seminar on EU Law, Dubrovnik, 17–23 April 2016) www.biicl.org/event/1124.

The same applies to EU-level regulation of collective bargaining. If collective agreements are apt to restrict the freedom of establishment or the freedom to provide services, it follows that national rules on collective bargaining can be lawfully regulated under the relevant functionally broad legal bases provided in the Treaties. This effectively circumvents the constraints on EU regulatory competence laid down in Arts 153(5) and 156, which both suggest that collective bargaining is not subject to binding legislation.

E. Gambling as an Economic Activity

As pointed out earlier, gambling does not benefit from the protections offered by the principle of conferral because it falls within the category of competences that are shared between the EU and Member States, and the Treaties contain no other provision that would limit EU competence to regulate gambling. However, it is a politically sensitive area of EU policy. In view of that, governments have argued before the Court that gambling activities should be excluded from the scope of application of the free movement rules due to their morally controversial nature.

One aspect in the Court's reasoning is worth a closer look. The Court holds a position that gambling services are not comparable to activities involving illegal products, whose harmful nature would entail a complete prohibition under EU law, thus putting their cross-border movement out of the question. Gambling activities are commonplace and practised legally in many Member States. In that connection, the Court emphasises that it is not for the judiciary to substitute its assessment for that of national legislatures and declare otherwise.[201] This part of the Court's reasoning is important in that it shows deference to the choices of national legislatures in characterising gambling services as legal or illegal. It also throws into sharp relief the Court's approach in the rest of the areas under study whereby national classification of an activity in question is considered, in principle, immaterial to the judicial assessment of the nature of that activity in light of EU free movement rules.[202]

VII. Conclusion

This chapter assessed the legitimacy of the Court's free movement case law under study in light of the principle of conferral. It argued that if the principle of conferral is to have a meaningful normative function, there needs to be a limit to how far the judicial exercise of EU internal market competences can legitimately encroach into the areas of national competence which would otherwise be exempted from interference by the EU. That limit lies in the conditions that trigger the application of free movement law. In the context of the economic freedoms, there are two such conditions: the economic nature of the activity and the presence of a restriction of free movement. In relation to the prohibition of discrimination on grounds of nationality, the activity in question

[201] *Schindler* (n 165), paras 31–32.
[202] See, eg, discussion above regarding healthcare as an economic activity.

must be governed by or otherwise connected with EU law (that is, free movement law for the purposes of this study). The principle of conferral does not authorise judicial interference with the constitutionally sensitive areas of national policy in the name of the internal market unless the above conditions are met. Accordingly, when interpreting those conditions, the Court is expected to adopt a systemic approach, contextualising them in the constitutional requirements of the principle of conferral. This requires that the interpretation by the Court of the scope of free movement be approached in a way that is cognisant of competence concerns that might arise in cases involving the intersection between the free movement law and areas of national policy that are constitutionally sensitive from the point of view of EU law.

The chapter argued that the Court's interpretation of the conditions underlying the application of free movement law does not show adequate consideration of questions of competence pertaining to the areas under study. On the contrary, the judicial reading of the scope of free movement is expansive, giving little to no regard to circumstances which would suggest the exclusion of the matter from the scope of EU law, and often incoherent in light of the wider case law and framework of the Treaties.

To summarise, the Court considers the provision of public healthcare an economic activity despite the social policy relationship between the patient and the healthcare system they are affiliated with. At the same time, it excludes the provision of public education from the classification as an economic activity for reasons that equally apply to the provision of public healthcare. Yet access to cross-border education is deemed to fall within the scope of free movement for other reasons. It is subject to the principle of non-discrimination on grounds of nationality. The connection between access to education and a substantive rule of EU law, required for the principle of non-discrimination to apply, is found on the basis of a tenuous link between higher education, vocational training and the free movement of workers. In more recent case law, that connection is established via the concept of EU citizenship. EU citizenship also serves as a source of rights that facilitate students' access to education abroad, such as the right to financial assistance. Notably, this line of case law largely ignores the amendments introduced into the Treaties in 1992, which seem to caution against a broad interpretation of the concept of EU citizenship in constitutionally sensitive areas of EU competence. Finally, the Court treats collective labour rights as obstacles to free movement. This position misconceives the nature of collective regulation of conditions of work and employment, which is designed specifically to restrict the commercial freedom of the employer. The Court also holds that Arts 49 and 56 TFEU can be invoked directly against trade unions. This approach is justified by the need to preserve the effectiveness of free movement rules. Competence considerations, which could potentially tip the balance in favour of a more conservative interpretation of the scope of those rules, do not enter the Court's reasoning.

The judicial neglect of the principle of conferral has consequences for the effectiveness of the legislative dimension of this principle. Once the free movement or citizenship rules are triggered at the level of the EU judiciary, this opens up the possibility for matters that are reserved to the regulatory prerogative of the Member States to be addressed at the EU's legislative level through the functionally broad legal bases. This means that the prohibitions contained in sectoral legal bases excluding interference by the EU into politically sensitive areas can be legitimately circumvented. The Patients'

Rights Directive and the Citizens' Rights Directive are both examples of this judiciary–legislature dynamic.[203]

The above analysis demonstrates the importance of the judicial observance of the principle of conferral. If the Court fails to recognise and take into account the requirements of the principle of conferral when making decisions about whether a matter falls within the scope of free movement, its interpretation of the Treaties will create severe constitutional tensions on multiple levels. As far as this study is concerned, the Court has systematically failed to engage in any meaningful reflection of competence aspects pertaining to the judicial interpretation of the scope of free movement rules. It has also failed to achieve a satisfactory level of coherence in its reasoning in light of the broader context of the Treaties, whether this meant giving consideration to its wider internal market case law or taking a balanced view of the reforms relating to questions of competence introduced by the Maastricht Treaty. The broad reading of the scope of free movement rules by the Court has not only created tensions with the principle of conferral at the judicial level, but it has also unlocked the legislative mandate for the EU to regulate policy areas that were supposed to be constitutionally protected from any substantial interference through the means of EU law, thereby further diminishing the practical significance of the principle of conferral.

An important consequence of the Court's broad interpretation of the scope of EU free movement rules is that it prompts the need for public authorities (and other regulatory actors) to establish justification for the adopted measures. This empowers the EU, and specifically the Court, to decide what is allowed and what is not allowed across a very wide range of areas of national policy. The constitutional implications of this situation are discussed in the following chapter.

[203] These directives are discussed in detail in ch 4, s VI in the context of the principle of institutional balance.

3

Free Movement Case Law in Light of the Principles of Subsidiarity and Proportionality

Chapter one demonstrated the significance of the principles of conferral, subsidiarity and proportionality in protecting the EU's federal balance of competences. It then presented an argument for why these principles should bind the exercise of EU judicial authority rather than, exclusively, its legislative and executive authority. Against this background, chapter two assessed the interpretation by the Court of EU free movement rules in the areas under study in light of the principle of conferral.

The assessment of the case law for compliance with the principle of conferral forms only one part of the overall assessment of the legitimacy of the Court's interpretative practice in the area of the internal market in light of the constitutional constraints on EU competences and powers. The EU is obliged to exercise competences conferred upon it in line with the principles of subsidiarity and proportionality. This concern becomes particularly acute when the judicial exercise of EU internal market competences involves policy areas that are constitutionally or politically sensitive, such as the areas forming the subject of this study. The relevance of subsidiarity and proportionality further increases if, as seen in relation to the areas under study, the principle of conferral fails to serve as an effective safeguard against the EU's interference within national regulatory autonomy.

Accordingly, this chapter examines the case law under study in light of the principles of subsidiarity and proportionality. This analysis has a dual purpose. First, it serves to illuminate the tensions with the principles of subsidiarity and proportionality created by the case law, thereby in itself demonstrating the need to enforce these principles in EU judicial practice. Second, it contributes to the broader inquiry of this monograph into the constitutional legitimacy of the judicial interpretation of free movement law.

The chapter follows in seven sections. Section I considers the place of the principles of subsidiarity and proportionality in the EU's legal order. It examines the meaning and functions of the two principles in EU constitutional theory and practice and, in light of that analysis, proposes how these principles should inform the judicial interpretation of EU free movement law. Sections II–V are dedicated to the analysis of the case law in the policy areas under study. Each section analyses central developments in the case law in the area concerned from a chronological and thematic perspective. The analysis is focused on the Court's interpretation of the scope of national derogations from the free movement rules, or, in other words, the judicial assessment of Member

State justifications for restrictive measures. The reason why this stage of judicial review forms the focus of the analysis is two-fold. First, the Court's assessment of the validity of national derogations from free movement determines the scope of national regulatory autonomy left to the Member States in the areas concerned. Secondly, and relatedly, it reveals whether and to what extent the Court takes account of the principles of subsidiarity and proportionality in the interpretation and application of free movement rules.[1] Accordingly, sections II–V conduct the analysis not only of the judicial reasoning regarding the validity of national justifications for restrictive measures but also the implications of that reasoning for the scope of national regulatory autonomy, which is meant to be protected by the principles of subsidiarity and proportionality. Section VI takes a comparative view of case law developments across the four policy areas and examines them against the requirements of the principles of subsidiarity and proportionality. Section VII concludes.

I. The Principles of Subsidiarity and Proportionality, and their Application to the EU Judiciary

A. The Principle of Subsidiarity

i. Subsidiarity in the Treaties

Known as 'the word that saved Maastricht',[2] the principle of subsidiarity was introduced into the Treaties in response to the expansion of, then, Community competences. While subsidiarity is usually sourced to the Roman Catholic Church, its essence can nowadays be found in any system of multi-level governance, where it is designed to structure the exercise of competing competences between central and local governments. That is exactly the purpose the principle of subsidiarity serves in EU law and it is, therefore, considered to be definitive of the EU's federal nature.[3]

Pursuant to Art 5(3) TEU, subsidiarity must be observed whenever the EU exercises its non-exclusive competences.[4] This category includes competences that are shared between the EU and Member States, such as internal market law, as well as the EU's supplementary competences, involving, amongst others, the areas of healthcare, education and collective labour law under study here.[5] In reality, subsidiarity has a minor role to play in the context of the EU's supplementary competences because the EU has no explicit power to enact harmonising measures in relation to the areas belonging to those competences. The specific legal bases authorising EU action in those areas tend to

[1] The relationship between the principles of subsidiarity and proportionality and the protection of national regulatory autonomy is explained in ch 1, s I and also s I of this chapter.

[2] Z Cass, 'The Word That Saved Maastricht? The Principle of Subsidiarity and the Division of Powers within the European Community' (1992) 29 *CML Rev* 1107.

[3] On the relationship between the principle of subsidiarity and the federal nature of the EU legal order, see ch 1, s I.

[4] Consolidated version of the Treaty on European Union [2008] OJ C115/13 (TEU), Art 5(3).

[5] Consolidated version of the Treaty on the Functioning of the European Union [2008] OJ C115/17 (TFEU), Arts 4 and 6.

limit such action to the adoption of non-binding, incentive measures.[6] The real value of subsidiarity thus lies in structuring the exercise of competences that are shared between the EU and Member States, where 'both levels, the national and the supranational, have equal possibilities of action'.[7]

Subsidiarity authorises intervention at the Union level 'only if and insofar as' the objectives of an action cannot be sufficiently achieved by the Member States but can be better achieved by the EU 'by reason of the scale and effects of the proposed action'.[8] So, subsidiarity governs the conditions to be fulfilled for the EU to act ('only if') as well as the extent of that action ('insofar as'). Furthermore, it imposes a two-fold test to justify EU-level action: Member States alone must be unable to achieve the objectives of the action in question; and if Member States are capable of acting alone, action by the EU will be justified only if the objectives of the proposed action can be better achieved at Union level by reason of its scale and effects. Therefore, in order to pass the test of subsidiarity, EU-level intervention must carry with it an added value.[9]

Just like in the case of conferral, the TEU is silent on the application of the principle of subsidiarity to the Court. Therefore, some argue that it was never meant to limit the judicial interpretation of the Treaties.[10] A lot has been said in chapter one about the applicability to judicial practice of the principles governing the scope and exercise of EU competences. It should also be noted that there is nothing in the Treaties to suggest that subsidiarity cannot, or should not, guide the exercise of EU judicial authority. Art 5 TEU clearly states that the principles of subsidiarity and proportionality apply when the Union exercises its competences through its institutions. Of course, in the conventional view, this provision is supposedly addressed to the EU's legislative institutions acting together in their lawmaking capacity. That is, however, not what the Treaty language suggests. Art 13 TEU, which sets out the institutional framework of the EU, explicitly lists the Court as one of the EU's institutions.[11] As an EU institution, the Court exercises the competences conferred upon the EU through the interpretation of the Treaties (rather than policy making on the basis of the Treaties) and the adjudication of legal disputes concerning the interpretation and application of those Treaties.[12] Moreover, as discussed in chapter one, due to the autonomy inherent in the institutional position

[6] See ch 2, s I for a detailed discussion in the context of the areas under study here.

[7] S Cassese, 'Ruling Indirectly: Judicial Subsidiarity in the ECtHR' (Seminar 'Subsidiarity: A Double Sided Coin?', Strasbourg, 30 January 2015) 6, 10 www.echr.coe.int/Documents/Speech_20150130_Seminar_Cassese_ENG.pdf.

[8] Art 5(3) TEU.

[9] To that effect, see European Council, 'Conclusions adopted at Edinburgh European Council, Annex 1 to Part A: Overall Approach to the Application by the Council of the Subsidiarity Principle and Article 3b of the Treaty on European Union' Bulletin of the European Communities 12–1992, 11–12 December 1992, 20, requiring that action at Community level produce 'clear benefits' by reason of its scale or effects.

[10] G Davies, 'Subsidiarity: The Wrong Idea, in the Wrong Place, at the Wrong Time' (2006) 43 *CML Rev* 6.

[11] For accounts conceptualising the Court as an institutional actor for the purposes of the application to it of the principle of subsidiarity, see G de Búrca, 'The Principle of Subsidiarity and the Court of Justice as an Institutional Actor' (1998) 36 *Journal of Common Market Studies* 217; T Horsley, 'Subsidiarity and the European Court of Justice: Missing Pieces in the Subsidiarity Jigsaw?' (2012) 50 *Journal of Common Market Studies* 267.

[12] In support of this reading of Arts 5 and 13 TEU, see GA Bermann, 'Taking Subsidiarity Seriously: Federalism in the European Community and the United States' (1994) 94 *Columbia Law Review* 331, 337, 400–02; ET Swaine, 'Subsidiarity and Self-Interest: Federalism at the European Court of Justice' (2000) 41 *Harvard International Law Journal* 1, 54, 62–63.

of the Court, it has a fair amount of latitude in making interpretative choices, which in itself suggests that those choices must be guided by some higher principles, not least for reasons of judicial legitimacy. As a principle that is central to structuring the exercise of EU competences, subsidiarity should without a doubt occupy a place among such higher principles, alongside the principles of *effet utile* of EU law, proportionality, protection of fundamental rights, and others regularly employed in the Court's reasoning.[13]

ii. Subsidiarity in the Case Law

The principle of subsidiarity has been on multiple occasions pronounced on in the case law of the CJEU. However, in the Court's interpretation, subsidiarity, as a legal rather than political principle,[14] means nothing more in practice than a competence review, that is, a review aimed at compliance with the principle of conferral. The case law on Art 114 TFEU suggests that as long as harmonisation of a specific sector is justified by reference to the objectives of the internal market, subsidiarity is complied with.[15] The logic follows that Member States cannot adopt common rules needed for the governance of the internal market by acting alone and, inevitably, the EU is better placed than them to do so. This is circular logic, making subsidiarity virtually impossible to breach once the competence is shown to exist. As Wyatt rightly observes, the objectives, scale and effects of harmonisation as a legislative technique will always be transnational and thus intrinsically pan-European, thereby making it worthwhile to act at the EU level.[16] Accordingly, the existence of a conferred competence for the adoption of a harmonising measure will also determine compliance with subsidiarity.[17]

The reading of the principle of subsidiarity employed by the Court is unduly narrow and displays a centralisation bias. As such, it cannot be justified in light of the Treaties. Not only does this reading depart from the text of Art 5(3) TEU, which seems to be more nuanced than the Court suggests, but, crucially, it fails to achieve the main objective of the principle of subsidiarity: to determine whether action on EU level is more advantageous than no action at all or action by individual Member States. This objective, however, needs to be seen in light of the rationale behind the principle of subsidiarity,

[13] In support of this proposition, see T Schilling, 'A New Dimension of Subsidiarity: Subsidiarity as a Rule and a Principle' (1994) 14 *Yearbook of European Law* 203, conceptualising subsidiarity both as a rule addressed to EU legislative institutions and a general principle of EU law which applies to the interpretation and application of EU law.

[14] On the political dimension of subsidiarity, see I Cooper, 'The Watchdogs of Subsidiarity: National Parliaments and the Logic of Arguing in the EU' (2006) 44 *Journal of Common Market Studies* 281; P Kiiver, *The Early Warning System for the Principle of Subsidiarity: Constitutional Theory and Empirical Reality* (Oxford, Routledge, 2012).

[15] See, eg, Case C-491/01 *British American Tobacco* EU:C:2002:741, [2002] ECR I-11543 (*BAT*), paras 180–83; D Wyatt, 'Subsidiarity: Is It Too Vague to Be Effective as a Legal Principle?' in K Nicolaidis and S Weatherill (eds), *European Studies at Oxford: Whose Europe? National Models and the Constitution of the European Union* (Oxford, OUP, 2003) 92; S Weatherill, 'The Limits of Legislative Harmonisation Ten Years after *Tobacco Advertising*: How the Court's Case Law Has Become a "Drafting Guide"' (2011) 12 *German Law Journal* 827.

[16] Wyatt (n 15) 88.

[17] Weatherill, 'The Function and Limits of Legislative Harmonization in Making the Internal Market' in R Schütze and T Tridimas (eds), *Oxford Principles of European Law: Volume II* (forthcoming, Oxford, OUP).

which is the desire to preserve the distinctive national political, social and cultural identities of the Member States insofar as this is compatible with effective problem solving.[18] One of the main ways in which national identities manifest themselves in real life is through the regulatory policies pursued by the Member States. Such policies are disregarded when the assessment of a measure's compliance with subsidiarity focuses exclusively on its capacity to attain EU-wide advantages. This kind of assessment leaves out a whole array of impacts, including potential disadvantages, that EU action might have on national regulatory policies. Certainly, understanding those impacts should inform the judgement as to whether it is indeed more advantageous to take action at the EU level as opposed to letting Member States act alone or resort to alternative, intergovernmental solutions, if they so deem fit.[19]

In light of the inadequacies of the judicial interpretation of subsidiarity, legal scholars have long argued for a conception of subsidiarity that is more sensitive to national regulatory concerns and preferences. For example, Bermann highlights the need to weigh the gains of economic integration against the Member State's 'loss of freedom to govern subjects that lie squarely within its sphere of competence'.[20] In the same vein but in more detail, Weatherill suggests that subsidiarity at its core requires an inquiry into 'whether even if the EU's objectives are advanced by and best achieved by the proposed measure, it is nevertheless important enough to override objections rooted in the worth of national diversity and autonomy'.[21] Davies goes even further. Arguing that subsidiarity is simply a 'wrong idea' for the EU, he identifies as the central flaw of this principle that it assumes the absolute primacy of EU objectives and thus allows no mechanism for questioning whether it is desirable, in light of the interests of the Member States, to pursue those objectives.[22]

The underlying logic of the above propositions is convincing and in line with the spirit of the conception of subsidiarity that is advanced in this monograph. However, the propositions themselves miss an important aspect of subsidiarity by assuming that there exists a juxtaposition between the interests and objectives of the EU and those of the Member States. In other words, these propositions, as well as most of the criticisms of the EU's principle of subsidiarity,[23] adopt an unduly narrow view of what constitutes the category of the EU's interests and objectives. It seems crucial to recognise that the objectives of EU action taken in the exercise of its internal market competences include

[18] Swaine (n 12) 54–55, referring to European Council in Edinburgh, 'Overall Approach to the Application by the Council of the Subsidiarity Principle and Article 3b of the Treaty on European Union' (1992) Conclusions of the Presidency SN 456/92, Annex 1 to pt A. See also Case C-233/94 *Germany v Parliament and Council* EU:C:1997:231, [1997] ECR I-02405, Opinion of AG Léger, paras 88, 150, 152–53.

[19] See, eg, Member State initiatives taken on the intergovernmental level in the education and gambling sectors, discussed in ch 2, ss III and V respectively.

[20] Bermann (n 12) 337, 390–403.

[21] Weatherill (n 15).

[22] Davies (n 10) 68.

[23] For various conceptions of subsidiarity considered in academic literature, see, eg, Schilling (n 13) 247–55 and Bermann (n 12) 400–03, both arguing that subsidiarity requires to limit the reach of internal market rules to what is necessary. Similarly, see M Kumm, 'Constitutionalising Subsidiarity in Integrated Markets: The Case of Tobacco Regulation in the European Union' (2006) 12 *European Law Journal* 503, 523. See also the argument advanced by Germany in Case C-415/93 *Bosman and Others* EU:C:1995:463, [1995] ECR I-4921, para 72. On conceptualising subsidiarity as federal proportionality, see R Schütze, 'Subsidiarity after Lisbon: Reinforcing the Safeguards of Federalism?' (2009) 68 *Cambridge Law Journal* 525.

much more than simply the removal of obstacles to free movement or distortions of competition in the EU. The Court recognises the EU's competence under Art 114 TFEU to enact regulatory measures aimed at a wide array of policy objectives. In fact, more often than not, the legislative action taken on the basis of Art 114 will be primarily aimed, and overtly so, at finding solutions to problems that lie at the heart of national regulatory policies, such as public health protection,[24] consumer protection[25] and the maintenance of public security,[26] amongst others.[27] Weatherill observes that the Court takes an analogous approach in the regulation of services markets under Arts 53(1) and 62 TFEU, generating common rules which also address fair competition and the protection of workers.[28] There is no way in which the EU's capacity to solve these various problems effectively, as required by the principle of subsidiarity, can be assessed fully without taking into account the capacity of the Member States to do so. In that connection, the inquiry into a measure's subsidiarity should not be as much about the juxtaposition between the EU's objectives and national regulatory objectives, but rather about discerning a range of distinctive objectives that lie behind the exercise of EU internal market competences and assessing the EU's capacity to attain each of them.

However, in order to assess the EU's capacity to attain a regulatory objective, one necessarily has to take into account the relative capacity of the Member States to do so. Admittedly, those sorts of assessments require knowledge, expertise and familiarity with the local context that the EU legislature, let alone the Court, is unlikely to have. This is where the concept of national regulatory autonomy comes into play. The concept of national regulatory autonomy is distinct from that of regulatory capacity in that it does not require an active assessment on behalf of the EU legislature of the capacity of the Member States to resolve the issues concerned. Rather, it requires respect for their right to deal with the relevant issues without external interference. So, an inquiry that is grounded in respect for national regulatory autonomy essentially assesses the extent to which Member States might lose their regulatory capacity as a result of the EU taking action in the area concerned. Such inquiry is far less intrusive than an inquiry based on a comparative assessment of the capacity of the EU and Member States to address the problems at hand. Ultimately, it entails an assessment of the necessity of the particular exercise of EU internal market competences in light of its potential impact on the scope of national regulatory autonomy in the area concerned. In practice, such inquiry requires two things: first, that the EU legislative institutions, specifically the Commission, takes seriously its duty to substantiate the need for EU

[24] See, eg, *BAT* (n 15), para 62; Case C-210/03 *Swedish Match* EU:C:2004:802, [2004] ECR I-11893, para 31.

[25] See, eg, Case C-58/08 *Vodafone* EU:C:2010:321, [2010] ECR I-4999, para 32.

[26] See, eg, Case C-482/17 *Czech Republic v Parliament and Council* EU:C:2019:1035 (CJEU, 3 December 2019), para 37.

[27] See also D Wyatt, 'Could a "Yellow Card" for National Parliaments Strengthen Judicial as well as Political Policing of Subsidiarity?' (2006) *2 Croatian Yearbook of European Law and Policy* 1; B de Witte, 'A Competence to Protect: The Pursuit of Non-Market Aims through Internal Market Legislation' in P Syrpis (ed), *The Judiciary, the Legislature and the EU Internal Market* (Cambridge, CUP, 2011).

[28] Weatherill (n 17), referring to Case C-620/18 *Hungary v Parliament and Council* EU:C:2020:1001 (CJEU, 8 December 2020), affirming the validity of Council Directive 2018/957/EU amending Directive 96/71/EC concerning the posting of workers in the framework of the provision of services [2018] OJ L173/16 (Posted Workers Amendment Directive).

action by 'qualitative or, wherever possible, quantitative' analysis in light of the principle of subsidiarity, as construed here;[29] secondly, that the Court be more vigorous than it is now in examining the Commission's analysis as part of the procedural review of compliance with subsidiarity.[30]

iii. Judicial Subsidiarity

The above considerations concerning the function of subsidiarity as a competence constraint on EU action by and large apply to the *judicial* exercise of EU internal market competences in the form of the interpretation of EU free movement rules. The removal of obstacles to free movement through the judicial interpretation of the Treaties in reality means much more than just the advancement of free movement as such. Like EU legislation, the case law inevitably interferes with and shapes domestic regulatory activity in a number of ways. As will be demonstrated in this book through a comprehensive analysis of the case law under study, the Court's interpretation of free movement law has the capacity to trigger radical reforms in the highly regulated areas of public policy. Take, for example, reforms in the Scandinavian countries concerning the regulation of employment and working conditions, which have resulted from the *Viking* and *Laval* judgments, or the pressures that the student mobility case law has placed on the organisation and financing of higher education in Austria and Belgium. These are but a few examples of the wider phenomenon, discussed in this and other chapters of this book. The bottom line is that the regulatory capacity associated with the Court's judgments should be considered not a mere externality of the judicial interpretation of the free movement rules but, rather, an intended and integral part of the judicial exercise of EU internal market competences.[31] As such, it should be accounted for in light of the requirements of the principle of subsidiarity. The question is how.

One point needs to be made clear at the outset. The assessment by the Court of whether its interpretation of the Treaties – the rules of free movement in the context of this study – is consistent with the requirements of subsidiarity cannot be analogous to the assessment performed by the Commission in preparation of legislative proposals. In particular, it is not suggested here that when interpreting the free movement rules, the Court should premeditate the various regulatory objectives that might be pursued by a particular interpretation of those rules in a given situation. Nor is it suggested that the Court should weigh the potential costs and benefits of its interpretative choices in light of those objectives. This would entail making policy judgements that no court should be expected to make, at least not openly, when delivering a judicial interpretation of the law. However, the Court could, and should, be expected to pursue

[29] Protocol No 2 to TFEU on the application of the principles of subsidiarity and proportionality [2008] OJ C115/206, Art 5.

[30] For criticism of the Court's review in this respect, see Weatherill (n 15) and (n 17). For a recent account arguing for a stronger procedural review in light of subsidiarity, see J Öberg, 'Subsidiarity as a Limit to the Exercise of EU Competences' (2017) 36 *Yearbook of European Law* 391.

[31] See ch 1, s III, discussing the regulatory capacity of the Court as a basis for the application of constitutional constraints to EU judicial practice.

an interpretation of EU law that is sensitive to subsidiarity concerns. This would require that the Court advance the free movement law to a degree that is necessary in light of the impact of that law – or, specifically, the impact of the judicial interpretation of that law – on the scope of national regulatory autonomy.

A subsidiarity-sensitive approach can be illustrated by the landmark judgment in the *Keck* case, which concerned the compatibility with the free movement rules of a French law prohibiting resale at a loss.[32] The two-fold aim of this prohibition was to prevent unfair competition practices and protect the consumers. The Court found the French law compatible with the Treaties. Contrary to the Court's by then already established position, it ruled that non-discriminatory, market-correcting measures that restrict businesses' commercial freedom were not to be considered as restrictions of free movement even if they made the movement of goods across borders 'less attractive'.[33] That type of measure fell outside the scope of free movement rules. So, technically, the *Keck* judgment was about competence – the concern of the principle of conferral – rather than subsidiarity. However, in real terms, it is an example of the application of subsidiarity in a loose sense.[34] It demonstrates a judicially sensitive approach to the regulatory prerogatives of the Member States, which could have been undermined if the Court had adopted a more aggressive interpretation of free movement law.[35] This approach represents the spirit in which the Court ought to interpret the free movement law in light of the requirements of subsidiarity.

An exemption of a certain matter from the reach of EU law, as in *Keck*, is not the only way in which the requirements of subsidiarity can be accounted for in the judicial interpretation of the Treaties. A method of exempting a matter from the scope of free movement addresses the question *whether* action at EU level should be taken at all in a given situation. This question represents only one of the two dimensions of the principle of subsidiarity. The second one focuses on *the extent to which* EU competence should be exercised where it has already been determined that it should indeed be exercised. In these situations, the way in which subsidiarity will manifest itself in the judicial interpretation of the Treaties is through the standard of judicial review employed to assess the lawfulness of national restrictions of free movement. The standard of judicial review employed to assess the validity of Member State justifications for restrictive measures is what determines the scope left for national regulatory action in the area concerned, which, in turn, has a direct bearing on the judicial compliance with the principle of subsidiarity. The case law under study suggests that the Court is more likely to incorporate subsidiarity concerns into its reasoning at this stage of judicial inquiry rather than when deciding whether the situation in question falls within the scope of free movement.[36] The justification stage will thus form the focus of the comparative case law analysis conducted in the remainder of this chapter.

[32] Joined cases C-267/91 and C-268/91 *Keck and Mithouard* EU:C:1993:905, [1993] ECR I-6097.
[33] ibid, paras 16–18. The question of what constitutes a restriction of free movement is examined in ch 2.
[34] Thank you to Stephen Weatherill for making that remark.
[35] In this respect, see Bermann (n 12) 402.
[36] See s VI of this chapter for a detailed analysis.

B. The Principle of Proportionality

i. Competence Proportionality

Proportionality is a general principle of EU law, which was developed in the case law of the CJEU, drawing on the German and French conceptions of this principle.[37] As a principle of constitutional and administrative law, proportionality is designed to protect the individual from an excessive use of public authority. It performs this function in EU law when employed as a ground of judicial review of EU action. Proportionality requires that measures employed by the EU in the pursuit of its policies should be both appropriate and necessary to attain the objectives underlying those policies.[38] Accordingly, the Court holds that 'when there is a choice between several appropriate measures, recourse must be had to the least onerous, and the disadvantages caused must not be disproportionate to the aims pursued'.[39] The notion of disadvantages refers, generally, to the negative impact that EU action, legislative or executive, might have on a wide range of interests protected by the principle of proportionality, including, but not limited to, individual commercial interests, the interests of economic operators, an interest to be free from excessive administrative or financial burdens, and the protection of fundamental rights.[40]

Since Maastricht, the principle of proportionality also enjoys express Treaty recognition as one of the constitutional principles that govern the exercise of EU competences. It is laid down in Art 5(4) TEU, which stipulates that the content and form of Union action must not go beyond what is necessary to achieve the objectives of the Treaty.[41] In structuring the exercise of EU competence, proportionality is inextricably linked to subsidiarity: while subsidiarity generally concerns the propriety of EU-level action (the EU shall act 'only if'), proportionality defines the degree and scope of that action.[42] The two principles also seem to overlap because the subsidiarity inquiry comprises the elements of degree and scope of EU action (the EU shall act 'insofar as'). In essence, both principles are designed to protect national regulatory autonomy but in slightly different ways. If subsidiarity is primarily concerned with the protection of the *scope* of national regulatory autonomy, proportionality ensures that EU regulatory intervention does not intrude excessively into the various *values and interests* protected within the scope of national regulatory autonomy. In light of this, an inquiry into a measure's

[37] N Emiliou, *The Principle of Proportionality in European Law: A Comparative Study* (London, Kluwer Law International, 1996). See also T Tridimas, 'The Principle of Proportionality in Community Law: from the Rule of Law to Market Integration' (1996) 31 *Irish Jurist* 83, referring to Case C-11/70 *Internationale Handelsgesellschaft mbH v Einfuhr- und Vorratsstelle für Getreide und Futtermittel* EU:C:1970:114, [1970] ECR 1125, Opinion of AG De Lamothe.

[38] See, eg, Case C-331/88 *Fedesa* EU:C:1990:391, [1990] ECR 1-4023, paras 13, 41; Case C-84/94 *UK and Northern Ireland v Council* EU:C:1996:431, [1996] ECR I-5755, para 57.

[39] *Fedesa* (n 38), paras 13, 41; Case C-265/87 *Hermann Schräder HS Kraftfutter GmbH* EU:C:1989:303, [1989] ECR 2237, para 21. For an overview of the early case law on proportionality as a ground of judicial review, see, eg, G de Búrca, 'The Principle of Proportionality and its Application in EC Law' (1993) 13 *Yearbook of European Law* 13, 105; Tridimas (n 37).

[40] For a taxonomy of protected interests, see V Kosta, 'The Principle of Proportionality in EU Law: An Interest-Based Taxonomy' in J Mendes, *EU Executive Discretion and the Limits of Law* (Oxford, OUP, 2019).

[41] Art 5(4) TEU.

[42] Swaine (n 12) 1.

proportionality examines whether the regulatory means employed to pursue a particular policy objective at the EU level do not infringe excessively on the interests protected at the national level – whether legal, socioeconomic or cultural. Notably, proportionality becomes of central importance in controlling the exercise of EU competence when matters at hand fall within the areas of the EU's exclusive competence, for example, competition law, where subsidiarity does not apply.[43]

In practice, however, the value of proportionality as a check on the exercise of EU competences is minimal because of the substantial degree of deference that the Court is prepared to give to EU institutions, particularly the legislature, in political decision-making. Judicial review is premised on the recognition that the 'legislature must be allowed a broad discretion in areas in which its action involves political, economic and social choices and in which it is called upon to undertake complex assessments and evaluations'.[44] As a result, the standard of judicial review is low: the Court will not invalidate a measure unless it considers it to be 'manifestly inappropriate' in light of the objective pursued.[45] The low standard of review is potentially justified in light of the principle of separation of powers and concerns relating to the institutional competence of the judiciary: the Court is not willing to substitute its judgment for that of the legislature.[46] That said, the Court's approach has been subject to active criticism – including, most recently, from national constitutional courts – for depriving the principle of proportionality of a meaningful normative function.[47]

ii. Judicial Proportionality

There is no question as to whether proportionality binds the judicial interpretation of the Treaties. It does. According to the long-established practice of the CJEU, proportionality is employed as the central principle guiding the interpretation of internal market law. In this line of case law, the Court uses proportionality to assess the lawfulness of the national regulatory measures in light of their effect on the internal market: the restriction of free movement has to be proportionate to the public objectives pursued by national authorities. The proportionality review in this context normally entails a two-fold inquiry. The first part of the inquiry examines whether the measure in question is appropriate, or suitable, for achieving the given objective. The second part, the test of necessity, focuses on whether national authorities could employ an alternative measure that would be equally effective in achieving the given objective but less restrictive of free movement in the EU. In individual cases, the Court might choose to focus only on one of the parts of the inquiry, either appropriateness or necessity. The circumstances in

[43] T Tridimas, *The General Principles of EU Law*, 2nd edn (Oxford, OUP, 2007) 176.

[44] See, eg, *BAT* (n 15), para 123; Case C-380/03 *Germany v Parliament* EU:C:2006:772, [2006] ECR I-11573 (*Tobacco Advertising II*), para 145.

[45] See, eg, *BAT*, para 123; *Vodafone* (n 25), para 69. For an analysis of the standard of review in light of proportionality, see W Sauter, 'Proportionality in EU Law: A Balancing Act?' (2013) 15 *Cambridge Yearbook of European Legal Studies* 439.

[46] See also K Lenaerts, 'The European Court of Justice and Process-Oriented Review' (2012) 31 *Yearbook of European Law* 3.

[47] See BVerfG, Judgment of 5 May 2020, 2 BvR 859/15 (*Weiss*), analysed in M Höpner, 'Proportionality and Karlsruhe's Ultra Vires Verdict: Ways out of Constitutional Pluralism?' (2021) MPIfG Discussion Paper 21/1 hdl.handle.net/21.11116/0000-0007-EACA-E.

which the Court would do so will be examined in detail in this chapter. In theory, there exists a third part of the proportionality review: proportionality *sensu strictu*, which involves weighing the restrictive effect of the measure in question against the importance of the public objective pursued by that measure.[48] This means that a measure that is suitable and necessary in the context of the aims pursued may nevertheless be deemed disproportionate if it imposes an excessive burden on the individual.[49] In practice, this part of the review is rarely performed. When it is, it will most likely be subsumed into the test of necessity.

Notably, the Court does not normally assess the proportionality of its particular interpretation of free movement rules in light of the interests protected at the national level.[50] One might contend that this sort of application of proportionality has no place in the Court's reasoning, given that the dispute itself arises from a challenge to national laws and practices as alleged restrictions of free movement rather than vice versa. Yet, apart from the broad wording of EU economic freedoms, there is nothing in the Treaties to suggest that the requirements of proportionality should apply in such an asymmetrical manner. Moreover, if proportionality is meant to govern the intensity of EU regulatory interference with the legal interests protected at the national level, then it should not matter that the source of that interference is the judiciary rather than the legislature or executive. Accordingly, the judicial exercise of EU internal market competences should be subject to the principle of proportionality for the same reasons as it should be subject to the principles of conferral and subsidiarity.[51]

Judicial proportionality would require that the Court take into consideration the impact of EU free movement law – or the judicial interpretation thereof – on the various non-market interests protected by national regulatory policies. One way this could be achieved is through employing a balancing approach in situations involving conflicts between the free movement rules and constitutionally or politically sensitive areas of EU competence.[52] However, that is not the only technique of interpretation that ensures judicial compliance with proportionality. The extent to which the Court observes the requirements of proportionality generally translates into the choice of the judicial standard of review and standard of proof employed to assess the lawfulness of national measures which restrict the free movement in the EU. The standard of judicial review and standard of proof are, therefore, the elements of judicial reasoning that this chapter will be looking at in order to assess the Court's interpretation of EU free movement rules for compliance with proportionality.

II. Healthcare

The following four sections, including this one, are concerned with the analysis of EU free movement case law in the areas under study. This section discusses case law

[48] De Búrca (n 39) 117.

[49] T-I Harbo, 'The Function of the Proportionality Principle in EU Law' (2010) 16 *European Law Journal* 158, 165.

[50] There are rare exceptions, which will be discussed in ch 5, s III.

[51] See ch 1, s III for a comprehensive discussion.

[52] Further discussed in ch 5, s III.

involving questions of access to cross-border healthcare. Thematically, it focuses on the rights of mobile patients, whilst also giving an outline of developments concerning the rights of cross-border healthcare providers. The analysis is structured with the view to covering the main developments in the case law and demonstrating its evolutionary character. It is centred around two questions: the scope for justification of national measures that restrict the free movement in the EU; and the implications thereof for national regulatory autonomy in the healthcare sector.

Since the Court's interpretation of the scope of free movement rules is extremely broad and the threshold for a measure to qualify as a restriction on free movement is generally extremely low,[53] any national measure that may potentially discourage a patient or healthcare provider from exercising their freedom to access the healthcare systems of other Member States has to be justified as proportionate in light of the legitimate objectives pursued by such measure. Consequently, the extent to which governments are allowed to maintain regulatory laws and practices that are restrictive of free movement will depend upon the degree to which they can justify them. The justification stage thus often becomes the focal point of the analysis in the free movement case law. It is also the part of the judicial reasoning that has a direct bearing on the observance by the Court of the principles of subsidiarity and proportionality.

A. Cross-Border Access to Outpatient Care

The greater, and most problematic, part of the case law in the area of healthcare concerns the extent of the right of patients to access medical treatment in other Member States. The rules governing access to cross-border healthcare laid down by the Court apply to both outpatient and inpatient, or hospital, care. However, there are differences between how these rules apply in each circumstance. In terms of judicial inquiry, those differences become apparent at the stage of justification of national measures. Essentially, restrictions concerning cross-border access to outpatient medical care cannot be justified. This rule was first established in the *Decker*[54] and *Kohll*[55] cases and confirmed in subsequent case law. The disputes in *Decker* and *Kohll* concerned Luxembourg citizens who had been denied reimbursement for medical goods and services purchased abroad (a pair of spectacles and dental treatment, respectively). The Court had to decide whether national rules, which made the reimbursement of medical expenses incurred abroad subject to prior authorisation, were compatible with EU free movement rules.

The government advanced two grounds to justify the requirement of prior authorisation: the maintenance of financial balance of the social security system and the protection of public health. Having recalled that aims of a purely economic nature could not justify a barrier to a fundamental freedom, the Court suggested that the healthcare sector might be an exception. It agreed that the financial balance of the social security scheme was an acceptable ground of justification if aimed at ensuring a balanced

[53] See ch 2 for a comprehensive analysis.
[54] Case C-120/95 *Decker* EU:C:1998:167, [1998] ECR I-1831.
[55] Case C-158/96 *Kohll* EU:C:1998:171, [1998] ECR I-1931.

medical and hospital service accessible to all patients.[56] Yet, in the circumstances of the two cases before the Court, the government failed to show that the prior authorisation procedure was a necessary measure.[57] In that respect, the Court held that neither the reimbursement of the cost of products at a flat rate nor treatment in accordance with the tariff of the home State were likely to have a significant effect on the 'financing or balance' of Luxembourg's social security system.[58]

With regard to the second ground, the protection of public health, the government submitted, inter alia, that prior authorisation was meant to ensure the quality of medical products and services purchased abroad. The Court was not convinced. It considered that this situation should be governed by the principle of mutual recognition of professional qualifications, which was spelled out in several Community directives applicable to the medical profession.[59] Accordingly, the purchase of medical goods and services from providers established in other Member States was to be considered as affording the same quality standards as those provided at home. In other words, the principle of mutual recognition required a degree of trust to be afforded to healthcare provided in other Member States.

Subsequent case law made clear that a requirement of prior authorisation for outpatient medical care abroad could not, as a matter of principle, be justified by overriding reasons of general interest, irrespective of the circumstances of a given case.[60] The narrow exception to this rule is where medical treatment requires the use of 'major medical equipment', such as an MRI or a PET-SCAN.[61] The Court's rationale behind the rule granting unconditional access to outpatient care provided abroad is mainly financial. The Court considers that patient outflows in the context of outpatient care are likely to stay relatively small, owing to the 'linguistic barriers, geographic distance, the cost of staying abroad and lack of information about the kind of care provided [abroad]'.[62] Therefore, unrestricted access to outpatient care abroad is unlikely to become a burden on public budgets.

B. Cross-Border Access to Inpatient Care

i. Smits and Peerbooms

The question concerning the justification for the prior authorisation requirement in relation to inpatient, or hospital, care[63] was addressed for the first time in the *Smits and Peerbooms* case, certain aspects of which have already been discussed in chapter two.[64] Mrs Smits, a Dutch national, went to Germany to receive a specialised treatment for Parkinson's disease. Mr Peerbooms, also a Dutch citizen, received treatment

[56] *Kohll* (n 55), paras 38–39, 41; *Decker* (n 54), para 39.
[57] *Kohll*, para 52.
[58] *Decker*, para 40; *Kohll*, para 42.
[59] *Decker*, para 43; *Kohll*, para 48.
[60] See, eg, Case C-385/99 *Müller-Fauré* EU:C:2003:270, [2003] ECR I-4509.
[61] Case C-512/08 *Commission v France* EU:C:2010:579, [2010] ECR I-8833, paras 33–42.
[62] *Müller-Fauré* (n 60), paras 95–96.
[63] See *Müller-Fauré*, para 75, defining inpatient treatment narrowly as treatment that cannot be offered except within a hospital setting.
[64] Case C-157/99 *Smits and Peerbooms* EU:C:2001:404, [2001] ECR I-5473.

for a neurological disorder in Austria. Both patients had been denied reimbursement for the services received abroad on the basis that such services were available in the Netherlands and neither patient had obtained prior authorisation.

The Dutch social healthcare system provided insured patients with free medical care (or 'benefits in kind') as long as it was obtained from the service providers that had contracts with the Dutch sickness funds. If an insured person wished to obtain treatment from a different provider, regardless of whether the provider was established in the Netherlands or elsewhere, they had to obtain authorisation. Such authorisation was granted under two conditions: first, the treatment in question fell within the scope of the Dutch sickness insurance scheme, which covered treatments considered as 'normal in the professional circles concerned'; and second, the treatment was medically necessary, meaning that adequate treatment could not be provided in time by a contracted provider.[65]

The Court accepted that the Dutch system of prior authorisation could in principle be justified on two grounds, to some extent already discussed in *Decker* and *Kohll*: the need to ensure the financial stability of the social security system and the protection of public health. The protection of public health involved considerations relating to the maintenance of a 'balanced medical and hospital service open to all' and 'treatment capacity or medical competence' within the territory of a Member State insofar as was 'essential for the public health, and even the survival, of the population'.[66] As these health-related considerations were 'intrinsically linked' to the method of financing of the social security system, the Court decided to consider the two objectives together.

Considering the need for a prior authorisation requirement in light of the aforementioned objectives, the Court found it important to take into account the specificity of the hospital sector in that it generated considerable costs and had to satisfy increasing needs yet with limited financial resources available. Accordingly, the maintenance of the hospital care and infrastructure required adequate planning in order to be able to ensure the supply of hospital services, control costs and prevent wastage of resources.[67] In this context, unlike in the context of outpatient care, a requirement of prior authorisation for treatment received abroad helped to ensure that all the planning that went into the hospital sector was not jeopardised. As such, it was considered to be a necessary and reasonable measure.[68]

That was not, however, the Court's final conclusion. The Court held that the specific conditions attached to the grant of authorisation had to fulfil the requirement of proportionality. In particular, a scheme of prior authorisation had to be designed in a way that would prevent discretionary decisions which could potentially negate the effectiveness of the fundamental freedoms. The scheme had to be based on 'objective, non-discriminatory criteria which are known in advance, in such a way as to circumscribe the exercise of the national authorities' discretion, so that it is not used arbitrarily'.[69] The procedure itself had to be easily accessible, capable of ensuring impartial and timely decision making and subject to judicial or quasi-judicial review. The language of the

[65] *Smits and Peerbooms* (n 64), para 60.
[66] ibid, paras 72–74.
[67] ibid, paras 76, 78–79.
[68] ibid, paras 80–81.
[69] ibid, para 90.

Court seemed to suggest that it was going to perform a procedural proportionality review in relation to the Dutch scheme of prior authorisation.

In that connection, the Court recalled that the Dutch authorities used a two-fold test for granting authorisations: first, the treatment had to be regarded as normal in the professional circles concerned, and second, it could not be obtained in sufficient time from a contracted provider. The Court expressed doubts as to the necessity of the first condition. It considered that what was regarded as normal in professional circles could be interpreted in a number of ways. If the test was confined to the professional opinion within the country, this would effectively restrict patients' access to treatments readily accepted as normal in other Member States. Such system could not be regarded as fair and objective. The required objectivity could only be assured by interpreting 'normal in professional circles' to include international professional circles, thus including treatment 'sufficiently tried and tested by international medical science'.[70]

With regard to the second condition, concerning the medical necessity of the treatment, the Court held that it had to be construed to the effect that authorisation could be refused only if the same or equally effective treatment was available in a contracted hospital without undue delay.[71] In order to determine the availability of such treatment, national authorities were required to have regard to all the circumstances of each specific case and to take due account not only of the patient's medical condition at the time when the authorisation was sought but also of their past record.[72] The Dutch prior authorisation scheme was to be considered justified insofar as the criteria for the grant of authorisations were construed in the way suggested by the Court.

Smits and Peerbooms is remarkable in how the Court applies the test of proportionality in relation to a scheme requiring prior authorisation for receiving medical care abroad. There seems to be a dissonance between the language used by the Court to describe the type of review it is performing and the actual content of that review. Although the language of the Court indicates it will be performing a procedural proportionality review, the judicial inquiry into the proportionality of the Dutch scheme seems to focus on the substantive criteria that the scheme must meet in order to be considered lawful in EU law. The Court makes clear that the decision to grant or refuse prior authorisation for medical treatment abroad must be based on an examination of the circumstances, past and present, of the patient's medical condition. If such examination suggests that 'the same or equally effective' treatment is indeed available in a contracted hospital 'without undue delay', the authorisation for treatment abroad may be lawfully denied.

ii. Watts

The test of proportionality employed in *Smits and Peerbooms* was clarified and further elaborated in the *Watts* case, in which the Court was faced for the first time in its case law with an NHS system.[73] As discussed in chapter two, NHS systems are peculiar in

[70] *Smits and Peerbooms* (n 64), para 94, affd in Case C-173/09 *Elchinov* EU:C:2010:581, [2010] ECR I-8889, paras 62, 70.
[71] ibid, para 103.
[72] ibid, para 104.
[73] Case C-372/04 *Watts* EU:C:2006:325, [2006] ECR I-4325.

that they provide free medical care, which is funded from general taxation, and rely on the use of waiting lists in the organisation and planning of that care. Mrs Watts, a British citizen, applied twice for prior authorisation under (then in force) Regulation 1408/71[74] to go to France for a hip replacement surgery. Both applications were refused on the ground that treatment in a local hospital could have been received 'within the government's NHS Plan targets' and thus 'without undue delay'. Mrs Watts would have had to wait for one year, a waiting period that was upon appeal reduced to three or four months due to the deterioration in her state of health. Instead, she proceeded with the surgery in France and subsequently sued for reimbursement in the UK.

The Court accepted that the UK's scheme of prior authorisation could in principle be justified in light of the overriding reasons of general interest advanced by the government, such as: the risk of seriously undermining the financial balance of the social security system; the objective of maintaining a balanced medical and hospital service open to all; and the maintenance of treatment capacity or medical competence on national territory.[75] However, to be justified on either of these grounds, the scheme had to fulfil the criteria laid down by the Court in *Smits and Peerbooms*. This meant in the circumstances of the case that a refusal to grant prior authorisation could not be based exclusively on the existence of waiting lists, even if they served to enable the planning and management of the supply of hospital care. The system of the waiting lists was unacceptable insofar as it was based on predetermined general clinical priorities, without carrying out 'an objective medical assessment of the patient's medical condition, the history and probable course of his illness, the degree of pain he is in and/or the nature of his disability at the time when the request for authorisation was made or renewed'.[76]

Accordingly, where the delay arising from the waiting lists appeared to be excessive, having regard to an objective medical assessment of all the circumstances of the situation and the clinical needs of the person concerned, none of the following considerations, put forward by the government, could justify a refusal to grant prior authorisation: an alleged distortion of the normal order of priorities linked to the relative urgency of the cases to be treated; the fact that the hospital treatment provided under the national system in question was free of charge; that an NHS system would have to establish a financial mechanism for reimbursement of the cost of treatment provided abroad; or that the costs of treatment may have been lower in the patient's home Member State than abroad.[77]

The Court also made some important comments regarding the calculation of the reimbursement for medical treatment received abroad. The fact that NHS systems are funded through general taxation and medical care is free of charge means that the question of reimbursement does not arise and is not regulated. This did not, however, have any effect on the Court's conclusions. The Court held that when a patient relied on

[74] See Council Regulation (EEC) 1408/71 on the application of social security schemes to employed persons and their families moving within the Community [1971] OJ L149/2 (Reg 1408/71), Art 22, which stipulates that authorisation for medical treatment in other Member States may not be refused where the treatment in question cannot be provided for the person concerned within the territory of the Member State in which that person resides. This regulation and its amendments are discussed in detail in ch 2, s II and ch 4, s VI.

[75] *Watts* (n 73), paras 103–05.

[76] ibid, paras 62, 68, 119.

[77] ibid, paras 113, 119–20, 123.

Regulation 1408/71, they were entitled to receive a full reimbursement for the cost of treatment received in another Member State. If the legislation of the host Member State did not provide for the reimbursement in full of the cost of treatment provided in its territory, the patient was entitled to the reimbursement of the difference between the costs, in order to ensure that they were not placed in a less favourable position when seeking treatment abroad. Where the patient relied on Art 49 EC alone,[78] foregoing the procedure laid down in Regulation 1408/71, the reimbursement could legitimately be limited to the cost of equivalent treatment in the patient's State of affiliation.[79]

In conclusion, the *Watts* judgment concretised the substantive criteria of the test of proportionality laid down in *Smits and Peerbooms*. An acceptable waiting time for medical treatment must be determined on the basis of a detailed, individual examination of the medical situation and clinical needs of the patient concerned. Virtually no other considerations, such as those reflecting general planning and budgeting objectives, are relevant.

In order to comply with the *Watts* judgment, the UK government introduced two reforms into its healthcare system. It established a tariff system for calculating the costs of medical procedures performed in the UK and increased the powers of specialist doctors so that their clinical judgment was given more weight in relation to the decisions of healthcare managers charged with rationing resources.[80]

C. The Free Movement Rights of Healthcare Providers

In addition to case law on patients' access to cross-border healthcare, the Court has also laid down rules governing the right of healthcare providers to establish themselves or provide services in another Member State under Arts 49 and 56 TFEU respectively.[81] The following discussion analyses this line of case law in order to assess how the Court's treatment of Member State derogations from the free movement compares to the approach employed in the context of patient mobility.

There are various ways in which Member States can restrict access to their healthcare markets for foreign operators. A study conducted by Gekiere and others finds that the types of restrictions range from quantitative measures (such as restricting the number of providers according to population size or catchment area, or regulating staff levels, pricing and quality), to more qualitative restrictions (such as rules on professional conduct and qualification, ownership, or legal form).[82] To be justified, restrictive measures must

[78] See ch 2, s II for an explanation of the relationship between, then, Regulation 1408/71 and Consolidated version of the Treaty Establishing the European Community [2002] OJ C325/33 (EC), Art 49.

[79] See also Case C-777/18 *WO* EU:C:2020:745 (CJEU, 23 September 2020), para 48, clarifying that a person is entitled to full reimbursement if 'for reasons relating to his or her state of health or to the need to receive urgent treatment in a hospital, that person was prevented from applying for such authorisation or was not able to wait for the decision of the competent institution on the application for authorisation submitted'.

[80] SL Greer, 'Power Struggle: The Politics and Policy Consequences of Patient Mobility in Europe' (Observatoire Social Européen Policy Paper 2/2008) 2.

[81] W Gekiere, R Baeten and W Palm, 'Free Movement of Services in the EU and Health Care' in Mossialos et al (eds), *Health Systems Governance in Europe: The Role of European Union Law and Policy* (Oxford, CUP, 2010) ch 1.

[82] ibid 506–07.

fulfil four standard conditions developed in the landmark *Gebhard* judgment, itself an adaptation of *Cassis de Dijon*[83] in relation to the mutual recognition of the activities of the self-employed.[84] National measures must be (i) applied in a non-discriminatory manner; (ii) justified by imperative requirements in the general interest, related to the protection of public health or the financial balance of the social security system;[85] (iii) suitable for securing the attainment of the objective that they pursue; and (iv) not go beyond what is necessary in order to attain that objective.[86]

The necessity review is, however, employed rarely.[87] It is confined to cases where national rules seem to be unreasonable, thereby suggesting that their adoption might be motivated by protectionist goals rather than a genuine aim to protect public health. Good examples of such rules are offered by the *Greek Opticians* and *French Laboratories* cases. In the former, qualified opticians were prohibited from operating more than one optician's shop.[88] In the latter, bio-medical laboratories were essentially required to have a place of business in France in order to be allowed to provide services in its territory.[89] In both cases, national measures were struck down as unlawful.

The standard of review adopted by the Court is generally premised on the recognition that EU law does not detract from the powers of the Member States to organise their social security systems and, in particular, health services and medical care. Accordingly, it is in the discretion of the Member States to determine the level of health protection they wish to pursue and employ the means they deem fit to that end.[90] Consequently, the fact that one Member State imposes rules that are more or less strict than those applied in other Member States is immaterial for the assessment of the need for, or the proportionality of, the adopted rules.[91] National rules will be assessed on their own merits, in light of the objectives and the level of protection pursued by the government. The Court will, however, require that these rules be appropriate for the achievement of the objectives in question, that is, the rules must be applied in a consistent and systematic manner.

The seminal judgment delivered in the *Hartlauer* case by the Grand Chamber illustrates how the test of consistency is applied in practice and, in particular, what it takes to fail this test. *Hartlauer* concerned Austrian legislation establishing a prior authorisation scheme for setting up and operating independent outpatient dental clinics, but not for setting up new group practices. The scheme was based on an assessment of the needs of the market and was supposed to help social security institutions to

[83] Case C-120/78 *Cassis de Dijon* EU:C:1979:42, [1979] ECR 649.
[84] Case C-55/94 *Gebhard* EU:C:1995:411, [1995] ECR I-4165, para 37.
[85] Case C-108/96 *Mac Quen* EU:C:2001:67, [2001] ECR I-837, para 26; Case C-294/00 *Deutsche Paracelsus* EU:C:2002:442, [2002] ECR I-6515, para 39; Case C-169/07 *Hartlauer* EU:C:2009:141, [2009] ECR I-1721, para 47.
[86] *Hartlauer* (n 85), para 44.
[87] See, eg, Case C-141/07 *Commission v Germany* EU:C:2008:492, [2008] ECR I-6935, paras 56–57.
[88] Case C-140/03 *Commission v Greece* EU:C:2005:242, [2005] ECR I-3177, paras 34–35.
[89] Case C-496/01 *Commission v France* EU:C:2004:137, [2004] ECR I-2351, paras 98–101.
[90] See, eg, Case C-70/95 *Sodemare* EU:C:1997:301, [1997] ECR I-3395, para 27; *Commission v Germany* (n 87), para 51; *Hartlauer*, paras 29–30; Joined cases C-570/07 and C-571/07 *Pérez and Gómez* EU:C:2010:300, [2010] ECR I-04629, para 44.
[91] *Commission v Germany*, para 51; *Mac Quen* (n 85), paras 33–34.

control expenditure, in order to maintain the financial balance of the social security system and ensure a balanced supply of medical service.[92] The Court agreed that, in principle, a prior authorisation requirement was a necessary and reasonable measure for that purpose. However, the authorisation scheme was to be regarded as appropriate only if it 'genuinely' reflected a concern to attain the objectives pursued 'in a consistent and systematic manner'.[93] Having clarified that group practices generally offered the same medical services and were subject to the same market conditions as outpatient clinics, the Court concluded that the prior authorisation scheme could not have consistently and systematically pursued the public interest objectives concerned.[94]

Moreover, referring to its patient mobility case law, the Court recalled that prior authorisation schemes had to be based on objective, non-discriminatory criteria known in advance, in such a way as to adequately circumscribe the exercise of national authorities' discretion.[95] No pre-existing criteria were in place in the Austrian case, and each of the Austrian provinces involved in the scheme applied different criteria in the assessment of the existence of a need for the services of a new dental clinic. As a result, the scheme lacked procedural fairness and, hence, was not suitable for attaining the objectives pursued by the government.[96]

The above analysis demonstrates that the Court's review of national measures restricting access to the market for foreign operators in the healthcare sector is predominantly procedural. The Court does not question the necessity of each and every rule but instead requires that the regulatory system be internally consistent and offer guarantees of procedural fairness. Unlike in cases concerning patients' access to medical treatment abroad, the Court does not lay down any substantive criteria that the governments must fulfil when making decisions about accepting foreign healthcare providers into their markets.[97] Overall, the Court's approach, especially when compared to that employed in the patient mobility case law, demonstrates judicial awareness of and sensitivity to concerns regarding national regulatory autonomy in the regulation of public healthcare. Notably, the Court has not had the chance to pronounce on the application of the consistency requirement to federal healthcare systems that allow the co-existence of a number of individual regulatory regimes within the country. However, the case law concerning areas other than healthcare suggests that the Court will take into consideration the specific structures of government when applying this test.[98]

[92] *Hartlauer* (n 85), para 41.

[93] ibid, para 55, with a further reference to Case C-500/06 *Corporación Dermoestética* EU:C:2008:421, [2008] ECR I-5785, paras 39–40, concerning the inconsistency of advertising rules. See also, more recently, *Pérez and Gómez* (n 90), paras 94–103, on consistency in relation to the geographical organisation of pharmacies.

[94] *Hartlauer*, paras 57–63.

[95] ibid, para 64.

[96] ibid, paras 66–71.

[97] See ch 5, s II for the analysis of the Court's approach to individuals, on the one hand, and businesses, on the other, across the free movement case law.

[98] See Case C-156/13 *Digibet* EU:C:2014:1756 (CJEU, 2 June 2014), discussed in s V of this chapter.

D. The Implications of Patient Mobility: Less Room for National Regulatory Autonomy, Better Healthcare for EU Citizens?

i. Access to Cross-Border Healthcare in the EU: The Scope for Restrictive Measures

Before turning to a discussion of the implications of the analysed body of case law for the scope of national regulatory autonomy, this section will provide a summary of the Court's approach to government justifications of measures restricting the freedom to receive and provide healthcare services. The judicial approach to justifications is what determines the space left for national regulatory activity regarding the organisation and management of public healthcare, which, in turn, has a direct impact on the observance of the principles of subsidiarity and proportionality by the Court.

First, the Court has made it clear that the requirement of prior authorisation for reimbursement of the costs of outpatient treatment received abroad constitutes a type of restriction which cannot be justified by considerations relating to the financial balance of the social security system. Therefore, if certain medical goods and services provided on an outpatient basis are covered by the patient's national healthcare system, they can be purchased in another Member State and refunded as if they had been delivered in the patient's home State. By contrast, the requirement of prior authorisation in relation to inpatient, or hospital, treatment is not in itself incompatible with the freedom to receive cross-border services because it is considered necessary in order to ensure that the efforts that go into the planning of hospital care are not jeopardised by uncontrollable outflows of patients that must be funded by the national healthcare system.

However, the specific conditions attached to the grant of authorisation must comply with Art 56 TFEU. These conditions have to be justified by overriding reasons of general interest and comply with the test of proportionality. In terms of procedure, the scheme for granting authorisations must be fair, transparent and subject to review. For instance, this would require that the scope of treatment covered by public healthcare system be defined in terms that do not discriminate between national and foreign healthcare providers. From the substantive point of view, authorisation cannot be refused if equally effective treatment in the patient's home country is not available within a medically justifiable time.

The Court's interpretation of what constitutes a medically justifiable time focuses on the individual situation of the patient. National authorities must take into account all the circumstances of each specific case, including the history and probable course of the patient's illness, the degree of pain they are in, and the nature of their disability at the time when the request for authorisation was made and when it was renewed.[99] A refusal to grant prior authorisation cannot be based merely on the existence of government-mandated waiting lists drawn on the basis of predetermined general clinical priorities. Therefore, where the delay arising from the waiting lists appears to be excessive, having regard to 'an objective medical assessment of all the circumstances of the situation and

[99] *Smits and Peerbooms* (n 64), para 53; *Müller-Fauré* (n 60), para 89–90; *Watts* (n 73), paras 59–61.

the clinical needs of the person concerned', virtually no considerations advanced by the government are capable of justifying the refusal to grant prior authorisation.

The Court also reviews all regulatory rules applicable in the Member States that are liable to hinder or make less attractive the *provision* of healthcare in their territory by foreign service providers. However, unlike in situations of patient mobility, restrictive measures are considered justified provided that they are applied in a consistent and systematic manner.

ii. The Regulatory Implications of the Case Law

It was argued in chapter one that an important reason why the Court should be subject to the competence constraints that bind the EU's political institutions is the regulatory capacity of its judgments. The analysis below demonstrates the extent of this regulatory capacity in the context of free movement case law involving healthcare. It shows that the Court's interpretation of the scope of justifications available to governments wanting to restrict the free movement of patients in the EU has a considerable impact on national regulatory autonomy in the healthcare sector, thus raising tensions with the principles of subsidiarity and proportionality. A comprehensive analysis of the case law in light of these principles will be conducted in section VI, taking a comparative view of case law developments across all four areas under study.

The starting point in virtually every judgment of the Court involving cross-border healthcare is the recognition, in accordance with Art 168(7) TFEU, that EU law 'does not detract from the power of the Member States to organise their social security systems' and 'decide the level of resources to be allocated to their operation'.[100] At the same time, Art 168(7) does not exclude the possibility that Member States may be required under other Treaty provisions (such as the free movement rules) or measures adopted on their basis (such as Regulation 883/2004)[101] to make adjustments to national social security systems.[102] These necessary adjustments do not, however, undermine Member States' sovereign powers in the field.[103] This is the well-familiar 'retained powers' formula, which has already been discussed in chapter two in the context of the principle of conferral.

Apart from expressing the relationship between the categories of EU competence and scope of EU law, the retained powers formula also has a bearing on the judicial interpretation of the permissible scope of national derogations from free movement. The Court holds that its interpretation of conditions for the grant of authorisation for treatment abroad is meant to balance EU citizens' right to cross-border healthcare with national concerns relating to the sustainability and financial stability of social security systems.[104] The Court thus recognises that its rulings may have an impact on the

[100] See, eg, *Kohll* (n 55), para 17; *Smits and Peerbooms* (n 64), para 44; *Watts* (n 73), para 121.
[101] Council Regulation (EC) 883/2004 on the coordination of social security systems [2004] OJ L166/1 (Reg 883/2004), discussed in ch 2, s II and ch 4, s VI.
[102] See, eg, *Watts*, para 121.
[103] ibid, para 121.
[104] ibid, para 122.

organisation and management of healthcare in the Member States and that the judicial advancement of patient mobility in the EU has to be weighed against such impact.

However, the substance of the Court's judgments does not live up to the above rhetoric. In this book it will be argued that the case law interferes substantially with the competence of the Member States to organise and manage national public health systems and threatens to jeopardise their financial sustainability, thereby endangering the protection of the most vulnerable groups of patients.

a. The Relationship between Medical Necessity and the Protection of Public Health

The most problematic aspect of the case law is the judicial interpretation of what constitutes an undue delay in receiving medical treatment. The Court holds that the requirements arising from Art 56 TFEU are based on 'the need to balance the objective of the free movement of patients against overriding national objectives relating to the management of available hospital capacity, control of health expenditure and financial balance of social security systems'.[105] This balance is to be achieved by drawing a distinction between, on the one hand, a reasonable waiting time for receiving medical treatment in the home State and, on the other hand, undue delay, or medically unjustifiable, waiting time. If the waiting time is reasonable, the fact that equally effective treatment is available more quickly in another Member State does not suffice to challenge a decision to refuse authorisation (and consequently claim reimbursement of the costs of treatment received abroad). Otherwise, the Court explains, patient migration would be liable to put at risk governments' planning and rationalisation efforts, which could in turn create problems of hospital overcapacity, imbalance in the supply of hospital medical care and logistical and financial wastage.[106] However, where the waiting time for treatment in the home State exceeds the medically justifiable time, according to the interpretation of this concept provided by the Court, the granting of authorisation and subsequent reimbursement of costs cannot be considered as liable to jeopardise the sustainability of hospital care.[107]

The Court's reasoning does not seem to reflect the realities of the operation of the healthcare sector. Its interpretation of medical necessity is solely focused on the examination of the individual situation of the patient, excluding any comparative analysis in a broader context, which would take into account the medical needs of other domestic patients. While this approach is fairly common in adjudication of individual rights, it does not seem suitable for dealing with complex socioeconomic issues, such as the distribution of funds allocated for public healthcare. As Newdick points out, where the inquiry focuses on the individual's personal circumstances, especially when these circumstances relate to serious health issues, 'every human inclination will be to rescue [them] by providing treatment even if its likelihood of success is uncertain'.[108] However, such inquiry leaves aside those whose treatment may be affected as a result, in this way

[105] *Watts* (n 73), para 145.
[106] *Smits and Peerbooms* (n 64), para 106; *Müller-Fauré* (n 60), para 91; *Watts*, para 71.
[107] *Watts*, para 75.
[108] C Newdick, 'Citizenship, Free Movement, and Healthcare: Cementing Individual Rights by Corroding Social Solidarity' (2006) 43 *CML Rev* 1645, 1650.

allowing the vocal minority of patients to gain priority over other patients potentially with more urgent medical needs.[109]

From the systemic perspective, the focus on the individual interferes with the governments' capacity to plan healthcare expenditure. Since the budget allocated to social healthcare is usually not sufficient to allow for a swift provision of treatment to all patients, competent authorities make use of the available resources by planning and setting priorities.[110] Waiting lists, routinely used in the NHS systems, reflect those priorities and are intended to maintain fairness and equality between patients who require hospital treatment.[111] By dispensing with the waiting lists, the test of medical necessity may divert resources from the most vulnerable groups of patients, typically composed of those with disabilities, mental health problems and those who are elderly.[112] As a consequence, the waiting time for those groups of patients will become longer. This is not just a theoretical problem. In many European countries, the waiting times for medical treatment have increased dramatically in recent years due to the Covid-19 pandemic.[113] Backlogs in treatment will take years to clear. This situation creates a condition where patients who are affluent and vocal are able to make full use of their right to access medical treatment in a Member State that is able to provide such treatment without undue delay. The home Member States are under the obligation to cover the costs of such treatment. What then happens to the group of patients who are vulnerable, unable to travel and potentially not even aware of their rights under EU law? They may be left behind. To avoid this outcome and maintain equal access to hospital care, governments would need to either provide additional financing for the healthcare budget or restrict the range of treatments available. Neither of the two options are without consequences and neither may be a choice that governments are prepared to make. Yet these are the choices they may be compelled to consider in light of the case law. This speaks to the magnitude of the potential implications of the case law for national health systems as well as the right of national governments to manage them without interference by the EU.

b. Impact on the Less Developed Member States

The financial pressures created by the case law may exacerbate the existing inequalities among the healthcare systems of EU Member States. The reality is that many of the

[109] *Watts* (n 73), para 42; Newdick (n 108) 1650, 1662.
[110] *Watts*, para 13.
[111] ibid, para 14.
[112] Newdick (n 108) 1646.
[113] See, eg, Vanguard Healthcare Solutions, 'How Do Our Waiting Times Compare?' (*Vanguard Healthcare Solutions*, 27 April 2021) www.vanguardhealthcare.co.uk/news-and-events/how-do-our-waiting-times-compare, comparing waiting times for medical treatment across OECD countries. On the impact of Covid in the UK, which is no longer a member of the EU, but provides a good illustration of the problem of waiting times: T Gardner and C Fraser, 'Elective Care: How Has Covid-19 Affected the Waiting List?' (*The Health Foundation*, 27 September 2021) www.health.org.uk/news-and-comment/charts-and-infographics/elective-care-how-has-covid-19-affected-the-waiting-list; Editorial, 'The Guardian View on NHS Waiting Lists: Blame Cuts as well as Covid' *The Guardian* (London, 7 October 2021) www.theguardian.com/commentisfree/2021/oct/07/the-guardian-view-on-nhs-waiting-lists-blame-cuts-as-well-as-covid. For a pre-Covid analysis of waiting times across the OECD countries, see OECD, *Waiting Times for Health Services: Next in Line* (OECD Health Policy Studies, OECD Publishing, Paris 2020) doi.org/10.1787/242e3c8c-en.

newer, less economically powerful Member States invest into healthcare considerably less than the original Member States, which in turn affects the quality of and access to healthcare that they are able to offer. The patients of these new Member States are therefore likely to be among the most active users of their right to cross-border healthcare, especially since the Directive on Patients' Rights has made cross-border healthcare more accessible to ordinary citizens by clarifying their rights and entitlements.[114] The tendency of increasing patient mobility from the less developed Member States to the more developed ones can be observed in recent case law.[115] For instance, the Court has ruled in the *Petru* case that Romanian authorities should pay for open heart surgery performed on a Romanian citizen in Germany because the treatment available for her in Romania could not be considered as sufficiently effective, owing to the lack of basic medical supplies and healthcare infrastructure in the country.[116] The hospital expenses incurred by Ms Petru amounted to over 17,000 euros. What this ruling means for Romania – or any other economically less developed Member State, for that matter – is that it is obliged to pay for the treatment provided abroad, which may involve complex and expensive procedures, at the rates charged by a more developed Member State (assuming that the patient relies on Regulation 883/2004), whilst at the same time continuing to cover the infrastructural costs of maintaining domestic hospitals.[117] This situation may create serious financial problems for the health systems of the less developed Member States and those problems are only going to get worse in the face of the pressures that the Covid pandemic has put on the management and financing of public healthcare.[118] Therefore, if the frequency of cross-border healthcare were significantly to increase, the additional financial pressure would arguably hurt the less developed Member States much more than the original Member States, possibly further decreasing the level of healthcare protection in their territories.[119] Considering this, it seems plausible to suggest that without an EU-level fund for balancing the extremes of the inequalities between Member States, patient mobility in the EU may sooner or later prove to be unsustainable.[120]

[114] See Council Directive 2011/24/EU on the Application of Patients' Rights in Cross-Border Healthcare [2011] OJ L88/45 (Patients' Rights Directive), discussed from different perspectives in ch 2, s II and ch 4, s IV.

[115] See, eg, Case C-268/13 *Petru* EU:C:2014:2271 (CJEU, 9 October 2014), paras 33–36; *Elchinov* (n 70); *WO* (n 79).

[116] *Petru* (n 115), paras 33–36. See also *Elchinov*.

[117] For an account on financial impacts of cross-border healthcare, see G Davies, 'The Process and Side-Effects of Harmonisation of European Welfare States' (2006) NYU Jean Monnet Program Working Paper 2/2006 jeanmonnetprogram.org/paper/the-process-and-side-effects-of-harmonisation-of-european-welfare-states 125–28.

[118] See, eg, K Gillet, 'Romania's Underfunded Health System Creaks under the Pressure of the Pandemic' *The New York Times* (New York, 3 March 2021) www.nytimes.com/2021/10/01/world/romanias-underfunded-health-system-creaks-under-the-pressure-of-the-pandemic.html.

[119] This problem is further discussed in: A Kaczorowska, 'A Review of the Creation by the European Court of Justice of the Right to Effective and Speedy Medical Treatment and its Outcomes' (2006) 12 *European Law Journal* 345, 366–67. See also Health and Consumer Protection Directorate-General, European Commission, Summary report of the responses to the consultation regarding 'Community action on health services' SEC (2006) 1195/4.

[120] Kaczorowska (n 119); G Davies, (n 117) 125–28; D Schiek, 'The EU Constitution of Social Governance in an Economic Crisis: in Defence of a Transnational Dimension to Social Europe' (2013) 20 *Maastricht Journal of European and Comparative Law* 195.

c. The Unresolved Questions

Last, the case law leaves certain issues unresolved. It offers no guidance for the Member States which receive patients. Are they permitted to decline to treat foreign patients where this would lead to waiting list problems for their own nationals? Would Art 56 apply in this case, and if so, how strictly? The EU Patients' Rights Directive explicitly states in the Preamble that 'nothing in this Directive should oblige healthcare providers to accept for planned treatment patients from other Member States or to prioritise them to the detriment of other patients, for instance by increasing the waiting time for treatment of other patients'.[121] The Directive further explains (not in the clearest of language) that Member States receiving patients should retain the possibility of relying on the grounds of public health to limit the inflows of patients that may create a demand exceeding the capacities for a given treatment in that Member State. However, the existence of EU secondary legislation cannot prevent the Court from relying directly on the Treaty in order to derive rights and obligations for individuals moving across the EU.[122] It is thus not inconceivable that when faced with restrictions imposed on incoming patients by a Member State, the Court might adopt a position whereby States would not be able to refuse treatment of foreign patients whose medical condition necessitates such treatment.[123] Future case law will have to clarify this question, but the mere fact that questions of this sort are decided by a supranational judicial body rather than national healthcare authorities seems problematic, both from a democratic and a competence perspective,[124] in light of the assurances provided in Art 168 TFEU that the EU shall respect the regulatory autonomy of the Member States in the area of public health.

III. Education

Despite questions of student mobility having long been the focus of both EU (and previously Community) and intergovernmental action, up until the 1980s the rights of students wishing to take up studies in other Member States depended solely on the national legislation in the host State. Incoming students could be subjected to special admission criteria and charged higher tuition fees, and they did not have general access to government grant systems for maintenance support. This situation changed when in the landmark *Gravier* judgment, discussed in the previous chapter, the Court brought access to higher education within the framework of the Treaty.[125] Since then, case by case, the Court has gradually developed what has ultimately become a fully fledged right of EU citizens to study in another Member State under equal conditions of access and, to a certain extent, maintenance with the nationals of that State. Notably, the rights associated with student mobility have been derived from the principle of non-discrimination

[121] Patients' Rights Directive (n 114), Preamble, Recital 8.
[122] This issue is further discussed in ch 4, ss IV–VI.
[123] To that effect, see s III of this chapter, discussing thematically similar issues in the case law concerning cross-border access to education.
[124] See ch 1, s I for a discussion of the democratic implications of the judicial interpretation of internal market law.
[125] Case C-293/83 *Gravier* EU:C:1985:69, [1985] ECR 593, discussed in ch 2, s III.

and EU citizenship provisions rather than the economic freedoms, since the Court has never considered the provision of public education to be a service within the meaning of what is now Art 57 TFEU.[126]

The aim of the following analysis is two-fold: to examine the Court's approach to government justifications for restricting the access of foreign students to local universities; and to assess the regulatory implications of this body of case law in light of Art 165 TFEU, which guarantees Member States the right to organise and manage their education systems independently, without interference by the EU.

A. Cross-Border Access to Education

The analysis focuses on the case law concerning two Member States: Austria and Belgium. The two countries share some important common characteristics. Both of them pursue a policy of unrestricted access to higher education, allowing any student with a secondary school degree to register into any BA degree at any university;[127] and they are both bordered by a large Member State with the same or shared official language in which access to certain university programmes is subject to restrictive entrance conditions. As a consequence, every year universities in both Austria and Belgium receive a great number of applications from students who have failed admission in Germany and France, respectively. According to the data produced by the Belgian government, the proportion of study places occupied by foreign (mainly French) students at medical and paramedical schools in the French-speaking part of the country in some years can be as high as 86 per cent.[128] In Austria, universities that are close to the German border often have more than 80 per cent of foreign students in some of the most popular courses.[129] Seeking to reduce the high inflows of foreign students, the authorities in Belgium and Austria have on multiple occasions taken measures limiting foreign students' access to their universities, in particular in relation to medical and paramedical studies. These policies have been repeatedly challenged before the CJEU and, by and large, declared incompatible with the Treaties.

i. Commission v Austria

Commission v Austria, which arose out of infringement proceedings brought against Austria, concerned restrictive conditions for admission to Austrian universities. The

[126] See, eg, Case C-263/86 *Humbel* EU:C:1988:451, [1988] ECR-5365, paras 18–19; Case C-109/92 *Wirth* EU:C:1993:916, [1993] ECR I-6447, para 15. For the analysis of the Court's reasons why education falls outside the scope of free movement, see ch 2, s VI.

[127] There are exceptions to this general rule, but they are few; some will be discussed in this chapter. On the Austrian higher education system, see OECD/European Union, *Supporting Entrepreneurship and Innovation in Higher Education in Austria* (OECD Skills Studies, OECD Publishing, Paris 2019) ch 1 doi.org/10.1787/1c45127b-en. On the Belgian higher education system, see EuroEducation, 'Belgium (Flemish Community) Higher Education System' (*euroeducation.net*) www.euroeducation.net/prof/belco.htm.

[128] Case C-73/08 *Bressol* EU:C:2010:181, [2010] ECR I-2735, Opinion of AG Sharpston, para 20; AP van der Mei, 'Free Movement of Students and the Protection of National Educational Interests: Reflections on *Bressol and Chaverot*' (2011) 13 *European Journal of Migration and Law* 123.

[129] M Mc Govern, 'Vienna Aims to Halt Influx of German Students' (*Presseurop*, 28 May 2013) voxeurop.eu/en/vienna-aims-to-halt-influx-of-german-students.

Austrian Law on University Studies granted students holding a secondary education diploma awarded in Austria unrestricted access to university but laid down special admission criteria for foreign students. This law sought to increase the percentage of Austrian citizens with a higher education qualification, in line with the government's policy seeking to increase the number of university graduates in the country.[130] Foreign applicants had to demonstrate that they met the specific entrance requirements for the relevant course of study within the State which issued their general qualification. For the German applicants, the majority of whom could not follow the study of their choice in Germany due to the *numerus clausus* (minimum grade requirement), this condition meant that they would also not be admitted for the study in question in Austria. The Commission alleged that Austrian measures infringed the right of foreign students to study in another Member State on equal conditions with nationals of that State.

Austria argued that the difference in treatment between Austrian and foreign nationals was justified, as it served to protect the homogeneity of the Austrian higher education system.[131] The concept of homogeneity referred to one of the objectives of Austrian education policy, which aimed to guarantee Austrian citizens unrestricted access to education from primary school to university. The idea behind this policy was that if citizens completed their educational path in Austria, they would most likely establish themselves in its territory. The government pointed out that this was particularly important with regard to medical studies, as it ensured that there would be a sufficient number of qualified graduates in order to maintain a balanced and unrestricted medical service in the country.[132] In that connection, the government submitted that if EU students were granted unrestricted access to education in Austria, its education system would be flooded by foreign (mainly German) students, whose number in medicine courses could then be as high as five times the number of available places. Drawing analogy with the patient mobility case law,[133] the government also argued that the influx of foreign students would entail 'structural, staffing and financial problems' in the education sector, thus posing a risk to the financial equilibrium of the Austrian education system and, consequently, to its very existence.[134]

The Court accepted that the considerations advanced by Austria could in principle justify the difference in treatment between local and foreign students, but only if they were substantiated by 'specific evidence' and 'accompanied by an analysis of the appropriateness and proportionality of the restrictive measure' adopted by the government.[135] In that connection, the Court observed that Austria did not present any figures to support its claim that in the absence of the restriction concerned, 'the existence of the Austrian education system in general and the safeguarding of the homogeneity of higher education in particular would be jeopardised'.[136] Moreover, Austrian authorities had

[130] Case C-147/03 *Commission v Austria* EU:C:2005:427, [2005] ECR I-5969, Opinion of AG Jacobs, para 26.

[131] *Commission v Austria* (n 130), paras 49–59.

[132] C Rieder, 'Case C-147/03, *Commission of the European Communities v. Republic of Austria*, Judgment of the Court (Second Chamber) 7 July 2005' (2006) 43 *CML Rev* 1711 (note), 1718–19.

[133] *Commission v Austria*, para 50, with a further reference to *Kohll* (n 55), para 41.

[134] ibid, paras 50, 64 and Opinion of AG Jacobs, para 26.

[135] *Commission v Austria*, para 63.

[136] ibid, para 66.

accepted that the national legislation in question was 'essentially preventive in nature'.[137] Finally, the Court suggested that excessive demand for access to specific courses could be met by the adoption of non-discriminatory measures, such as the establishment of an entry examination or the requirement of a minimum grade.[138]

For its second ground of justification, Austria argued that restrictive measures prevented abuse of Community law by German students, who would come to Austria to reap the benefits of its education system without contributing to its financing.[139] The Court swiftly dismissed this argument, noting that the right for EU nationals to study in another Member State under equal conditions with nationals of that Member State constituted the 'very essence of the principle of freedom of movement for students guaranteed by the Treaty' and, as such, could not be regarded as an abuse.[140]

ii. The Aftermath

In order to comply with the judgment in *Commission v Austria*, the Austrian government amended its laws so that secondary diplomas from other Member States were to be regarded equal to Austrian diplomas. This caused an influx of German students into the country, who applied to Austrian universities after having been rejected by German ones.[141] In response, in 2006 Austrian authorities introduced a new set of measures restricting access to medical programmes whereby 75 per cent of study places were reserved for students holding an Austrian secondary diploma.[142]

To put the Austrian situation in context, let us recall the *Commission v Belgium* case, discussed in the previous chapter, which concerned Belgian legislation that restricted the right of foreign applicants to study in Belgium unless they could prove that they qualified for admission in their own country of origin. Effectively, this requirement ensured that the French students who due to *numerus clausus* (minimum grade requirement) had not been admitted to the French universities were also barred from entering the Belgian schools. As Belgium had not advanced any reasons to justify the measures in question, the Court found them unlawful. After the measures were abolished, for three years in succession the French Community of Belgium organised an entry exam for those applying to study veterinary science. As a result of the entry exam, a very limited number of Belgian nationals qualified for entry: for example, in 2005, only 34 out of 250 successful candidates were Belgian.[143] To address this situation, in 2006, the French Community of Belgium adopted a decree limiting access to certain medicine programmes for students who were 'non-resident' in Belgium. This decree was challenged in the *Bressol* case, to be discussed below.

After Belgium and Austria introduced the measures discussed above, the Commission sent letters of formal notice to both Member States for the infringement

[137] *Commission v Austria* (n 130), paras 64–65.
[138] ibid, para 61.
[139] ibid, para 67.
[140] ibid, para 70.
[141] For figures, see Rieder (n 132) 1715–16.
[142] ibid 1716.
[143] *Bressol* (n 128), Opinion of AG Sharpston, para 115.

of Community law. On the basis of the replies received, the Commission considered that there was prima facie evidence that without the restrictions, the health systems of Belgium and Austria would experience problems arising from a potential shortage of health professionals.[144] In view of that, the Commission decided to suspend the infringement procedures for five years, a period that was later extended until the end of 2016, in order to give both Member States the opportunity to provide more complete and more detailed data to justify the restrictions. Based on the data provided by the Austrian authorities, the Commission concluded in 2017 that the quota system in place for medical studies could be maintained, as it was justified and proportionate in light of the objective of protecting the Austrian public health system.[145] The Belgian situation had not yet been settled at the time of writing.

However, it is important to understand that the political agreement with the Commission cannot preclude the possibility of private litigation in the future and the consequences that such litigation may have on the ability of national governments to maintain measures restricting foreign students' access to education. This is poignantly demonstrated by the preliminary reference to the Court in the *Bressol* case, decided in 2010 after the Commission had already made the decision to suspend the infringement proceedings against Austria and Belgium. The case was brought against Belgium but in terms of the Court's reasoning is equally applicable to the Austrian situation.

iii. Bressol

The *Bressol* case reached the Court after a group of French students and university lecturers challenged the then newly-introduced Belgian admission rules, setting a quota of 30 per cent for non-resident students enrolling in any of the nine medical and para-medical courses that were over-subscribed. In order to qualify as resident, students were effectively required to have their principal residence in Belgium.

The Belgian government, supported by the Austrian government, advanced three grounds to justify the difference in treatment: the need to avoid excessive burdens on the financing of higher education; the protection of the homogeneity of the higher education system; and the protection of public health. With regard to the first point, Belgium argued that a difference in treatment helped to avoid excessive burdens on the financing of education as it prevented the number of foreign students from becoming excessively high.[146] The Court found this argument unfounded because the financing of education in the French Community was organised through a 'closed envelope' system, where the overall allocation of funds did not vary depending on the total number of students, ie an increase or decrease in student numbers was budget-neutral.[147]

With regard to the second ground of justification, Belgium claimed that the high level of non-resident students in the courses concerned was likely to cause a deterioration in

[144] S Garben, 'The Belgian/Austrian Education Saga' (2008) *Harvard European Law Working Paper* 1/2008, 17.

[145] European Commission, 'Free movement of students: Commission closes infringement case against Austria' (2017) ec.europa.eu/commission/presscorner/detail/en/IP_17_1282.

[146] *Bressol* (n 128), para 49.

[147] ibid, para 50.

the quality of higher education, since there were inherent limits 'in the capacity of the educational establishments to welcome them and in the staff available'.[148] In this respect, restrictions were necessary in order to safeguard the homogeneity of the system and 'to ensure wide and democratic access for the population of the French Community to quality higher education'.[149] The Court accepted that the prevention of a risk to the existence and homogeneity of a national education system could justify a difference in treatment between some students.[150] In the Belgian case, this consideration was in fact linked to the protection of public health, as all the courses concerned fell within the medical field. Accordingly, the Court decided to examine the homogeneity argument in light of Belgium's third ground of justification relating to the protection of public health.

Belgium put forward two reasons to explain why unrestricted numbers of non-resident students could put public health at risk. First, the practical training required for medical programmes could not be provided adequately when a certain number of students was exceeded. Second, non-resident students would return to their home State after completing their studies, which would ultimately cause a shortage of qualified medical personnel in Belgium.

The Court held that the objective of maintaining a balanced high-quality medical service open to all could in principle justify the adoption of restrictive measures. However, the measures taken had to comply with the principle of proportionality. Whilst it was for the national court to determine whether these conditions were met in the circumstances of the case, the Court offered to 'provide guidance' in order to 'enable' the national court to give judgment.[151]

First, the national court had to assess if there were genuine risks for the protection of public health. In that respect, the CJEU observed that it could not be ruled out a priori that a reduction in the quality of training of future health professionals could ultimately impair the quality of healthcare.[152] Also, a decrease in the number of local students in the courses concerned could result in a shortage of health professionals, thus creating problems of healthcare capacity.[153] In assessing the likelihood of those risks materialising, the referring court had to take into consideration that the link between the training of future medical specialists and the objective of protecting public health was only indirect. The assessment would thus be based on 'a number of contingent and uncertain factors', taking into account the 'future development of the health sector'.[154] This meant that Member States had to be allowed to take protective measures without having to wait for the quality of education to deteriorate or the shortage of health professionals to materialise.[155] However, in order to take those measures, national authorities had to provide 'an objective, detailed analysis, supported by figures, … capable of demonstrating, with solid and consistent data' that the risks to public health were 'genuine'.[156]

[148] *Bressol* (n 128), para 52.
[149] ibid, para 52.
[150] ibid, para 53, with a further reference to *Commission v Austria* (n 130), para 66.
[151] ibid, paras 62, 65.
[152] ibid, para 67.
[153] ibid, para 68.
[154] ibid, para 69.
[155] ibid, para 70.
[156] ibid, para 71.

Secondly, national authorities had to provide 'specific evidence' showing that the measures adopted were appropriate and proportionate for attaining the objective of the protection of public health.[157] In particular, it had to be demonstrated that a limitation of the number of non-resident students could 'really bring about an increase in the number of graduates ready to ensure the future availability of public health services within the French Community'.[158] In this respect, Belgium provided data from veterinary studies. Since these studies required clinical practice by each student on a sufficient number of animals, it was not possible to train more than 200 veterinarians a year; however, due to an influx of foreign students, the total number of students spread over the six years of studies rose by nearly 50 per cent, from 1233 in 1995 to 2343 in 2002. The government claimed that the situation was similar with regard to other medical and paramedical courses. In this connection, the Court pointed out that government analysis could not merely refer to figures concerning one or other group of students and infer that all the non-resident students would establish themselves in the State in which they resided before commencing their studies.[159] Belgium was required to provide data for each of the nine courses covered by the restrictive measures which would make it possible to determine: first, the maximum number of students who could be trained at a level which complied with the desired training quality standards; and, second, the number of graduates needed to establish themselves within the territory of the French Community in order to ensure the provision of adequate public health services.[160] Such analysis also had to take into account the possibility that resident students could decide to exercise their profession abroad and, equally, that foreign professionals who had or had not studied within the French Community could establish themselves there later.[161]

Finally, the Court emphasised that access to higher education within the EU constituted the very essence of the principle of freedom of movement for students. Accordingly, restrictions thereof had to be limited to what was necessary in order to obtain the objectives pursued and had to allow 'sufficiently wide' access to higher education.[162] The national court, therefore, had to assess whether the objectives pursued could not be attained by less restrictive means, such as measures aimed at encouraging foreign students to establish in the French Community or attracting medical professionals educated abroad.[163]

Following the guidance of the CJEU, the Belgian Constitutional Court found that the relevant quotas were justified only with respect to three out of nine medical courses in question, there being a lack of evidence for the rest.[164] In 2012, Belgium introduced new quotas for foreign students entering medicine and dentistry programmes.[165]

[157] *Bressol* (n 128), para 71.
[158] ibid, para 76.
[159] ibid, para 73.
[160] ibid, para 72.
[161] ibid, para 73.
[162] ibid, para 79.
[163] ibid, paras 77–78.
[164] A Hoogenboom 'Mobility of Students and the Financial Sustainability of Higher Education Systems in the EU: a Union of Harmony or Irreconcilable Differences?' (2013) 9 *Croatian Yearbook of European Law and Policy* 15, 24, referring to the judgment of Belgian Constitutional Court.
[165] A Benjamin, 'La Belgique Instaure des Quotas D'Étudiants Étrangers en Médecine et Dentaire' *Le Monde* (Paris, 2012 June 29) www.lemonde.fr/europe/article/2012/06/29/la-belgique-instaure-des-quotas-d-etudiants-etrangers-en-medecine-et-dentaire_1726610_3214.html.

B. Cross-Border Access to Financial Assistance

As discussed in the previous chapter, since the *Bidar* case, the Court holds a position whereby EU citizens must also not be discriminated against when applying for educational maintenance grants and loans. The right to access to financial assistance in the context of education is not, however, unqualified. Member States are not prevented from the application of restrictive measures aimed at avoiding an 'unreasonable burden' on their finances, which could arise if governments were obliged to cover the maintenance costs of students who had no link with the country of studies other than having decided to move there for study purposes.[166] Accordingly, it is legitimate for a Member State to limit granting of financial assistance to students who had demonstrated 'a certain degree of integration into the society of that State'.[167] This demonstrates a judicial approach that is sensitive to national regulatory and budgetary concerns in the sector of higher education. The existence of a degree of integration would be established if a student in question had resided in the host State for a certain length of time. For instance, the Court accepted in *Förster*, decided in 2008, that a condition of five years of prior residence is not excessive in that respect.[168] Notably, this decision might have been influenced by the political agreement on the matter at that time. The Citizens' Rights Directive, adopted in 2004, provided that the host Member State only had to provide financial assistance to those individuals who had obtained a right to permanent residence in its territory, which would normally have happened after five years of lawful residence.[169]

The Court has also pronounced on the question of the portability of financial assistance available at the home Member State in situations of nationals leaving to study in another Member State. The seminal judgments in this area are *Morgan and Bucher* and *Prinz and Seeberger*.[170] The *Morgan and Bucher* case concerned a German rule that made financial assistance for studies abroad subject to the condition that the course of study had to represent the continuation of studies pursued for at least one year in Germany. Similarly, the more recent *Prinz and Seeberger* case concerned a German rule conditioning access to grants on the requirement of having a permanent residence in Germany for at least three years prior to commencing studies abroad. The Court held that conditions like those were likely to discourage German citizens from studying abroad, owing to the costs and inconvenience this could create.[171] The Court accepted that, in principle, it was legitimate for the Member States to grant assistance only to students who had demonstrated a sufficient degree of integration into the home society in order for the home Member State to avoid an unreasonable financial burden.[172] However, the proof required to demonstrate the necessary degree of integration could not be 'too exclusive

[166] Case C-209/03 *Bidar* EU:C:2005:169, [2005] ECR I-2119, para 56.

[167] ibid, para 57.

[168] Case C-158/07 *Förster* EU:C:2008:630, [2008] ECR I-8507, para 54.

[169] Council Directive (EC) 2004/38/EC [2004] on the right of citizens of the Union and their family members to move and reside freely within the territory of the Member States OJ L158/79, Arts 16, 24.

[170] Joined Cases C-11/06 and C-12/06 *Morgan and Bucher* EU:C:2007:231, [2007] ECR I-9161, para 28; Joined Cases C-523/11 and C-585/11 *Prinz and Seeberger* EU:C:2013:524 (CJEU, 18 July 2013), para 30.

[171] *Morgan and Bucher* (n 170), para 30; *Prinz and Seeberger* (n 170), para 32.

[172] *Morgan and Bucher*, para 43; *Prinz and Seeberger*, para 36.

in nature or unduly favour one element which is not necessarily representative of the real and effective degree of connection between the claimant and the [Member State concerned], to the exclusion of all other representative elements'.[173] The German rules were considered to be 'too general and exclusive' in both of the aforementioned cases and, accordingly, found unnecessary for achieving the objective pursued.

Since *Prinz and Seeberger* and *Morgan and Bucher*, the Court has expressly ruled that a requirement to prove a genuine link with the society of the home State based solely on periods of residence cannot justify government's refusal to grant financial assistance for studies abroad.[174] Member States are required to take a broad range of elements into consideration, such as the nationality of the student, their schooling, family, employment, language skills, and other social and economic factors.[175]

The Court's reasoning in the *Morgan and Bucher* and subsequent cases resembles its approach in cases concerning the mobility of patients, where the individual circumstances of the patient in question constitute the decisive factor when granting authorisation for treatment abroad. Here, too, the individual circumstances of the student is what determines the presence of a genuine link with the society of their home Member State. This approach may suggest that the judicial scrutiny of national measures restricting access to financial assistance for studies abroad is more intense in relation to grants provided by the *home* Member State as opposed to the *host* Member State because the sufficient degree of integration is already presumed by virtue of possessing the citizenship of the State concerned. On the other hand, the latter approach may put into question the validity of the requirement of five years of prior residence as an appropriate period of time for a non-national to become integrated in the host Member State for the purpose of receiving financial assistance from that State. It cannot be excluded that in the future the Court might bring its position concerning the financial assistance available in the *host* Member State closer to that taken in cases involving the *home* Member State. This would entail a more rigorous application of the test of proportionality in relation to the rules in place in the host Member State, for instance, by making explicit the requirement to take into account the individual circumstances of the student in question as opposed to applying a general rule requiring a certain period of integration into the society of the host State.

C. The Implications of Student Mobility for the Scope of National Regulatory Autonomy

i. Access to Cross-Border Education in the EU: The Scope for Restrictive Measures

The main rule to take from the case law on student mobility is that the principle of equal treatment, which underlies the case law, requires that the conditions of access

[173] *Prinz and Seeberger* (n 170), para 37.

[174] Case C-359/13 *B Martens v Minister van Onderwijs, Cultuur en Wetenschap* EU:C:2014:2240 (CJEU, 26 February 2015), para 39.

[175] ibid, para 41.

to university, including entrance requirements, tuition fees and fee loans, must be the same for all EU students. Differential treatment can in principle be justified by public interest objectives, but the specific measures in place will be subject to strict judicial scrutiny. Governments have thus far advanced three main types of arguments to justify the difference in treatment between local and foreign students: the need to avoid excessive burdens on the financing of higher education; the protection of the homogeneity of the education system; and the protection of public health.

The Court's stance regarding the financial concerns remains unclear because in *Bressol* this argument was dismissed as irrelevant in the circumstances of the case: since Belgium financed education through a 'closed envelope' system, technically, an increase or decrease in student numbers was budget-neutral, hence, it did not entail an additional burden on finances. As is well known, the Court holds a long-established position whereby reasons of a purely economic nature are not generally accepted as a valid justification for measures restrictive of free movement. Future case law will thus have to show how seriously the Court will consider financial concerns in the context of access to education and, more importantly, whether such concerns will be considered from a purely budgetary perspective or assessed in light of the broader objectives of the education system, such as the protection of its homogeneity or its capacity to produce a sufficient number of future specialists.[176] The Court's approach in other areas of case law, such as patient mobility, suggests that it will be the latter.

The concept of the homogeneity of the education system in the Court's understanding typically refers to concerns regarding the quality of and access to education. These concerns are considered to be valid and in principle capable of justifying restrictive measures. However, in practice, they must be substantiated by specific evidence and accompanied by an analysis of the appropriateness and proportionality of restrictive measures.[177] Moreover, the Court takes a view that the homogeneity of higher education can be protected by recourse to non-discriminatory measures designed to counteract excessive demand for specific programmes, such as an entry examination or the requirement of a minimum grade.[178] This suggests that it might be very difficult, if not impossible, for governments to prove the necessity of quotas on foreign students on the basis of the homogeneity argument.

The third ground – protection of public health – seems to offer the strongest argument for justifying differential treatment between local and foreign students in the context of medical and paramedical programmes. The standard of proof required by the Court is, however, high. Member States have to demonstrate – with an objective, detailed analysis, supported by solid and consistent data – that there are real risks to the protection of public health and that the restrictive measures in question are an appropriate and necessary means for counteracting those risks. Such analysis also has to account for the possibility that resident students may decide to exercise their profession abroad and, equally, that foreign students and professionals may establish themselves in the Member State concerned.

[176] In this respect, see *Bressol* (n 128), Opinion of AG Sharpston, paras 92, 94, expressing the view that budgetary concerns should be considered as a justification of a purely financial nature.
[177] *Commission v Austria* (n 130), para 63.
[178] *Commission v Austria*, para 61; *Bressol*, Opinion of AG Sharpston, para 105.

The principle of equal treatment also applies in relation to access to financial assistance for studies abroad. The host Member State is not allowed to discriminate against foreign students when granting financial aid intended to cover the tuition and other costs of access to university.[179] However, it retains the right to restrict foreign students' access to maintenance grants until these students have achieved a required level of integration into the society of the host State. The Court's approach in this context seems to strive for a balance between, on the one hand, ensuring that EU students' right to cross-border education does not become meaningless due to the financial hurdles associated with it and, on the other hand, avoiding the situation where student mobility would place an unreasonable burden on national budgets.

ii. The Regulatory Implications of the Case Law: The Costs of Student Mobility

The case law on student mobility is premised on the principle that while Member States retain the power to organise and manage their education systems, in accordance with Art 165(1) TFEU, when exercising that power they must comply with the rules regarding EU citizens' freedom to move and reside within the territory of the EU.[180] As discussed in chapter two, this principle, also known as the 'retained powers' formula, demonstrates the judicial understanding of the principle of conferral in application to constitutionally sensitive areas of EU competence. However, the retained powers formula also has a bearing on the observance by the Court of the principles of subsidiarity and proportionality. Its interpretation in relation to Member State justifications of restrictions of free movement determines the extent to which the EU can interfere with national regulatory autonomy through the judicial exercise of EU internal market competences.

The language of the Court expresses a recognition that Member States are free to choose an education system based on free and unrestricted access or one that is based on controlled access, in which students go through a selection process, provided that foreign students are not treated less favourably than local students.[181] This approach is meant to balance the interests of mobile students against the prerogative of the Member States to manage their education systems – a concern that lies at the heart of the principle of subsidiarity. It will be argued that this balance has not been achieved in the case law. The Court has advanced the individual rights of students at the expense of the capacity of the Member States to control the financing of public education, maintain the desired quality of teaching, and, more fundamentally, pursue education policies that reflect national preferences and traditions.

a. Financial Implications

The mobility of students of the extent advanced by the Court may have serious financial and structural implications for national education systems because it obliges

[179] For case law analysis on this point, see ch 2, s III.
[180] See, eg, *Bressol* (n 128), para 38; *Morgan and Bucher* (n 170), para 24.
[181] *Bressol*, para 29.

governments, including those with open access, low-threshold education policies, to provide free education to students who do not contribute to its financing.[182] This is a concern for all countries who 'import' foreign students, regardless of the way they finance their higher education – whether this is through a 'closed envelope' system or otherwise. As Hoogenboom observes, even where incoming students have to pay tuition fees, these fees will typically cover only a fraction of the total cost of education, with the rest being subsidised by the government.[183] Ultimately, the overall costs of education enjoyed by foreign students are borne by the taxpayers of the host Member State. The financial burden on the taxpayer becomes even greater when equal treatment is extended into the area of tuition and maintenance grants.[184] Admittedly, students who after their studies enter the employment market of the host State do provide a 'return on investment' for that State, but this does not happen often. For instance, the data provided by Belgium in *Bressol* showed that during the period between 2003 and 2006, nearly one third of the veterinarians establishing themselves in France had obtained their diploma in Belgium.

It could be argued that the Court is justified in requiring a certain degree of financial solidarity among the Member States in order to ensure that the fundamental freedom of free movement of students in the EU does not become nominal.[185] Yet this requirement seems to be quite unfair in cases where foreign students make up more than 80 per cent of the class, as is the case for certain courses in Belgian and Austrian universities. As Dougan rightly points out, this situation raises serious issues of equity between Member States in sharing the financial burdens of cross-border education.[186]

b. Systemic Implications

An uncontrolled influx of foreign students may also cause systemic problems in the education sector, affecting the quality of teaching and the system's overall capacity to produce a sufficient number of professionals ready to establish in the country concerned. The Court seems to show a degree of sensitivity to these concerns in relation to medical courses, possibly because the protection of public health is one of the derogations from free movement expressly authorised by the Treaty. The Court admits that the assessment of the link between the training of future health professionals and the objective of maintaining an adequate medical service on the territory involves 'a number of contingent and uncertain factors'.[187] For that reason, Member States should be allowed to take preventive measures without having to wait for either a shortage of health professionals or a deterioration of the quality of medical education to materialise.[188] However, the standard of proof required by the Court to justify the taking of preventive measures seems to be virtually impossible to meet.

[182] On this point, see *Commission v Austria* (n 130), Opinion of AG Jacobs, para 36.
[183] See data cited in Hoogenboom (n 164) 43.
[184] For a comprehensive analysis of financial pressures, see M Dougan, 'Fees, Grants, Loans and Dole Cheques: Who Covers the Costs of Migrant Education within the EU?' (2007) 1 *Journal of Contemporary European Research* 4, 9.
[185] Case C-184/99 *Grzelczyk* EU:C:2001:458, [2001] ECR I-6193, para 44; *Bidar* (n 166), para 56.
[186] Dougan (n 184) 9.
[187] *Bressol* (n 128), para 69.
[188] ibid, para 70.

National authorities must submit an objective and detailed analysis, supported by figures, capable of demonstrating, with solid and consistent data, that there are genuine risks to public health. Such analysis needs also to account for the fact that after graduation some foreign students may be willing to establish themselves in the host Member State while some local students may decide to pursue professional careers abroad. These are hard estimations to make and even harder to substantiate with detailed and specific evidence. To illustrate, the Court did not find sufficient the estimates provided by the Austrian and Belgian governments that in the absence of restrictions, the number of foreign students in certain courses would exceed the amount of available places by five or ten times.[189]

Moreover, the Court leaves governments with a lot of unanswered questions. What degree of deterioration in the quality of medical training and provision of healthcare services would allow Member States to take restrictive measures without risking infringing students' right to free movement? Would it make a difference if the said deterioration was sudden or gradual? And what is the period of time sufficient to show that a correlation exists between the influx of foreign students and the quality of the provision of education and healthcare in the country? It also remains unclear whether a decline in the quality of medical education alone, without there being a shortage of health specialists, would suffice to justify restrictive measures. The Court's reasoning seems to focus mainly on the shortage of specialists as the ultimate risk to be avoided, which would suggest that the possibility of the quality of medical training decreasing is considered by the Court a risk worth taking for the sake of protecting the students' right to pursue education across the EU.

The standard of proof is equally high when it comes to showing that national measures taken to counteract health risks comply with the proportionality requirement. Governments are required to provide specific evidence showing that discriminatory measures are the least restrictive option available capable of guaranteeing the quality of teaching and the provision of healthcare. In *Bressol*, Belgium provided figures showing that when the French Community organised an entrance exam three years in a row, only a small percentage of locals had passed it. The Court, however, considered these figures not enough to illustrate the problem throughout the whole field of medicine. Austria found itself even in more trouble: it had discriminated against foreign students since becoming a member of the EU in 1995 and thus could not possibly collect such data. Austrian and Belgian cases aside, it is hard to envision how governments could conduct an analysis, other than a hypothetical one, that would provide for a comparative assessment of the effectiveness of the various restrictive measures and be backed by specific evidence.

c. The Space Left for National Policy Preferences

The Court's rigorous position is in part based on the conviction that there exist non-discriminatory alternatives capable of counteracting excessive demand for access to specific courses, such as the establishment of an entry examination or the requirement

[189] *Commission v Austria* (n 130), Opinion of AG Jacobs, para 27; *Bressol* (n 128), para 57.

of a minimum grade. However, there are two serious problems with these alternatives: they do not achieve the same result as discriminatory measures; and, more importantly, they interfere with the autonomous right of the Member States to organise their education systems as they deem fit, thereby raising serious subsidiarity concerns.

Admittedly, the suggested non-discriminatory alternatives can be effective in countering the concerns of inadequate resources and, hence, ensuring that the quality of education remains unaffected by the influx of foreign students. However, these measures also cut to the heart of the systems based on free and open access to education. For instance, the Austrian policy of the 'widest possible public access to higher education' seeks to increase the percentage of Austrians with a higher education qualification, since in Austria this percentage is among the lowest in the EU and the OECD.[190] In Belgium, on the other hand, any suggestion of introducing more stringent entry requirements for universities is usually met with scepticism by the general public because this is perceived as contrary to the social character of the Belgian welfare State.[191] Against this background, if either Belgium or Austria ultimately had no choice but to replace quotas on foreign students with some non-discriminatory alternatives, as proposed by the Court, the Treaty guarantee to preserve the prerogative of the Member States to organise their education systems independently according to national preferences would become meaningless.

Moreover, in practice, no non-discriminatory alternative can ensure that a sufficient number of graduates will establish themselves in the country of study. The French Community of Belgium had already tried a system based on a general entry exam in the area of veterinary science and only a limited number of Belgian nationals qualified for entry. Nearly one third of the veterinarians establishing themselves in France during that period had obtained their diploma in Belgium. The obvious reason behind this situation is that Belgian population is approximately six times smaller than that of the bordering France. The Austrian population is almost ten times smaller than Germany's, for that matter. It seems that it will always be the case that a small country will face an influx of candidates coming from a large neighbouring country in which the same language is spoken and which employs restrictive conditions of access to education.[192] However, there is no basis whatsoever to suggest that foreign students will be willing to remain in the country in which they completed their studies after graduation.

In light of the case law, the costs of having a free, open access higher education system may simply turn out to be too high for some countries. If a government decides that it does not want to limit the number of study places, it is left with a limited set of options. On the one hand, it may accept that the quality of education it provides will inevitably go down. In order to avoid this outcome, it may be forced to give financial injections to its education system, whilst bearing the consequences that this decision may have on the sustainability of the public financing of education.[193] Both of these options entail sacrifices in the pursuit of the desired education policy, which, from the

[190] *Commission v Austria* (n 130), Opinion of AG Jacobs, para 26.

[191] N Cambien, 'Student Mobility in the European Union: Facing New Hurdles?' (2009) 11 Revista Universitaria Europea 77, 86–87.

[192] ibid 86–87, referring to the judgment of the Belgian Constitutional Court.

[193] Van der Mei (n 128) 124.

constitutional point of view, seems to sit uncomfortably with the EU's commitment to respecting national regulatory autonomy in the field of education. Equally problematic is the fact that choices of such high political significance are effectively determined by the judiciary rather than the legislature – national or EU – thus highlighting broader problems with the EU's democratic legitimacy.[194]

IV. Collective Labour Law

This section continues the free movement case law analysis by looking into the main developments in the area of collective labour law. The landmark judgments in which the Court defined the relationship between collective labour rights and EU economic freedoms are the widely known *Viking*[195] and *Laval*[196] judgments. The principles formulated in *Viking* and *Laval* were further elaborated in subsequent cases[197] and ultimately extended to legal situations concerning, more generally, conflicts between commercial interests and those of worker protection.[198]

The analysis below is focused on the part of the Court's reasoning which defines the permissible scope of the exercise of the right to strike and the right to collective bargaining in transnational situations. Ultimately, the analysis aims to determine the implications of this reasoning for the viability of the industrial relations systems of the Member States and the level of worker protection in the EU.

A. The Scope of the Right to Strike

The limits of the lawful exercise of the right to strike in EU law were established in the landmark *Viking* and *Laval* judgments.

i. Viking

Viking, also discussed in the previous chapter, concerned an industrial action aimed at preventing a ferry operating company from taking advantage of a 'flag of convenience'.[199] Viking, a Finnish ferry-operating company, sought to reflag its ship under the Estonian flag, arguably in order to undercut the minimum wage requirement set out in the collective agreement with the Finnish Seamen's Union (FSU). Following

[194] For a comprehensive analysis of the judiciary-legislature dynamic in the EU, see ch 4. For the democratic consequences of judicial lawmaking, see ch 1, s I.

[195] Case C-438/05 *Viking* EU:C:2007:772, [2007] ECR I-10779.

[196] Case C-341/05 *Laval* EU:C:2007:809, [2007] ECR I-11767.

[197] Case C-346/06 *Rüffert* [2008] ECR I-1989; Case C-319/06 *Commission v Luxembourg* EU:C:2008:189, [2008] ECR I-4323; Case C-271/08 *Commission v Germany* EU:C:2010:426, [2010] ECR I-7091.

[198] Case C-515/08 *Santos Palhota EU:C:2010:589*, [2010] ECR I-9133; Case C-426/11 *Alemo-Herron* EU:C:2013:521 (CJEU, 18 July 2013).

[199] *Viking* (n 195), para 8.

Viking's notice about the reflagging, the FSU and the International Transport Workers' Federation (ITF) organised industrial action, with reference to the latter's policy against 'flags of convenience'. Viking brought an action against the ITF and FSU, claiming that its freedom of establishment under Art 43 EC (now Art 49 TFEU) had been infringed.

The Court recognised that as a fundamental right, the right to strike constituted a legitimate interest which could justify a derogation from the free movement rules, but it had to be exercised 'in accordance with Community law and national laws and practices'.[200] Before turning to consider whether the strike action in question could be justified, the Court made some important general observations about the nature of (then) Community law. It pointed out that the Community had not only an economic but also a social purpose. The regulation of the internal market was one of Community activities, but it also had 'a policy in the social sphere', aimed at, inter alia, 'a high level of employment and of social protection'.[201] This meant that the fundamental freedoms had to be 'balanced against the objectives pursued by social policy', which included improved living and working conditions, proper social protection and dialogue between management and labour.[202]

The Court accepted that 'the right to take collective action for the protection of workers' was a legitimate interest, which in principle justified a restriction on Art 43.[203] It also accepted that the protection of workers was one of the overriding reasons of public interest, yet only when invoked in the circumstances where jobs or conditions of employment were 'jeopardised or under serious threat'.[204] The Court observed that it was unclear whether this was the case in the situation at hand because in the course of conciliation proceedings Viking had given an undertaking that the reflagging would not involve any redundancies.[205] The Court also made clear that the 'flags of convenience' policy alone, without evidence of a serious threat to working conditions, was insufficient to justify a restriction on Art 43.[206]

As regards the proportionality of strike action, the Court held that it was for the national court to decide whether the FSU had less restrictive means at its disposal in order to bring negotiations with Viking to a successful conclusion and whether it had exhausted those means before initiating strike action.[207]

The *Viking* judgment laid down the core principles governing the status and exercise of the right to strike in EU law. On the one hand, it recognised that the right to strike was protected as a fundamental right, forming part of the general principles of EU law. It also suggested that a balance had to be sought between the exercise of the fundamental freedoms and the right to strike. However, the judgment did not reflect any sort of balancing between the two legal interests. The exercise of the fundamental right to strike was made subject to a test of proportionality which set a very high threshold to justify

[200] *Viking* (n 195), paras 43–46, referring to Charter of Fundamental Rights of the European Union [2000] OJ C364/1 (CFR), Art 28; affd in *Laval* (n 196), para 91.
[201] *Viking*, para 78, citing Arts 2, 3(1) EC (now Art 3(3) TEU).
[202] ibid, para 79.
[203] ibid, para 77.
[204] ibid, paras 77, 81.
[205] ibid, paras 82–83.
[206] ibid, paras 88–89.
[207] ibid, paras 87–89.

taking collective action. Strike action had to be aimed at protecting the terms and conditions of employment which were 'jeopardised or under serious threat' *and* it had to be taken after all the less extreme means to persuade the employer had been exhausted. Notably, no such justification was required from Viking, which effectively used the fundamental freedoms granted by EU law in order to benefit from social dumping.

ii. Laval

The Court's judgment in *Laval* was delivered a week after the *Viking* judgment. The case concerned a collective action aimed at obliging a Latvian construction company to sign a Swedish collective agreement applicable to the building sector. Laval, a Latvian company with a subsidiary in Sweden, won a public tender to build a school there and posted workers from Latvia to perform the job. The wages paid to Latvian workers were 40 per cent lower than their Swedish equivalent. After negotiations with Laval fell through, the Swedish building workers' trade union took collective action in the form of blockading the construction site. This action was followed by several sympathy actions, boycotting all of Laval's sites in Sweden, which led to the eventual bankruptcy of the company's Swedish subsidiary. Laval sued the Swedish trade unions, alleging that its freedom to provide services in the EU had been violated.

The Court assessed the collective action taken by the Swedish trade unions first in light of the Posted Workers Directive, as it informed the meaning of Art 49 EC (now Art 56 TFEU) in posting situations.[208] The Court observed that the objective of the PWD was to coordinate national laws in order to lay down a 'nucleus of mandatory rules for minimum protection' to be observed in the host Member State by employers who posted workers there to perform temporary work.[209] Regardless of the law applicable to the employment relationship, undertakings had to guarantee posted workers the terms and conditions of employment covering the matters listed in Art 3(1) PWD, such as maximum work periods, minimum paid annual holidays, minimum rates of pay, health and safety at work, and some others. The Court noted that this provision had a two-fold goal. On the one hand, it ensured fair competition between local and foreign undertakings by guaranteeing the minimum level of worker protection that they needed to observe. On the other hand, it allowed posted workers to benefit from the more favourable terms and conditions of employment applicable in the host Member State, if that was the case.[210]

The PWD itself did not define the material content of the rules listed in Art 3(1). It authorised Member States to apply their national rules as long as they were laid down in accordance with one of the means provided for in the Directive. Collective agreements that had been declared universally applicable were listed as one of such means.[211] A universally applicable collective agreement was defined as an agreement that had to be

[208] Council Directive 96/71/EC concerning the posting of workers in the framework of the provision of services [1997] OJ L18/1 (Posted Workers Directive), further analysed in ch 4, s VI. See *Laval* (n 196), Opinion of AG Mengozzi, para 145, referring to the PWD as a 'specific interpretation' of Art 49 EC.
[209] *Laval*, para 59.
[210] ibid, paras 74–75, 76–77, 79.
[211] Posted Workers Directive (n 208), Art 3(1).

observed by all undertakings in the geographical area and in the profession or industry concerned.[212] If Member States did not have a system for declaring collective agreements universally applicable, they were allowed to base themselves on agreements that were 'generally applicable to all similar undertakings in the industry concerned' or those that had been concluded by the most representative employers' and labour organisations at national level and applied throughout the national territory.[213]

Swedish laws made no provision for the universal applicability of collective agreements, and, according to settled practice, the rates of pay in the building sector were normally set by means of collective negotiations on a case-by-case basis. The Court considered that this method of setting wages was unacceptable because it was not provided for by the PWD and, moreover, could not be regarded as establishing the *minimum* rate of pay within the meaning of Art 3(1) PWD.[214] Therefore, Swedish trade unions could not rely on the PWD in order to impose on foreign undertakings the obligation to negotiate wages on a case-by-case basis. Consequently, strike action taken to force Laval to enter into such negotiations could not be justified on the basis of the Directive.

The Court then turned to assess whether collective action could nevertheless be justified directly under Art 49 EC. It held that collective action could, in principle, be justified by the objective of the protection of workers against social dumping, but it was not in the circumstances of the case. The strike action in question could not be considered as appropriate or necessary due to the uncertainties that the Swedish system of wage determination presented to Laval. The system, which was based on autonomous collective bargaining, lacked provisions that would be 'sufficiently precise and accessible' and rendered it 'impossible or excessively difficult in practice' for Laval to determine its minimum pay obligations.[215] Consequently, collective action aimed at enforcing these obligations was unlawful.

The terms of pay aside, the Court also observed that the collective agreement in question contained terms in respect of some matters referred to in Art 3(1) PWD, such as working time and annual leave, that were more favourable than the protections offered to posted workers by Swedish law.[216] In addition, the agreement imposed on the employer certain pecuniary obligations that were not included in the list of matters contained in Art 3(1). The Court held that the application of terms that went above or beyond the hard nucleus of rules for minimum protection laid down in Art 3(1) was not authorised under the PWD and had to be regarded as unlawful under Art 49 EC. It added that obligations relating to matters that went beyond those listed in Art 3(1) could be imposed by the government having had recourse to the public policy exception contained in Art 3(10) PWD. However, trade unions, as bodies governed by private, not public, law could not avail themselves of that exception.[217]

[212] Posted Workers Directive (n 208), Art 3(8).
[213] *Laval* (n 196), para 65, referring to Art 3(8) PWD.
[214] ibid, paras 68, 70–71.
[215] ibid, paras 107–10.
[216] ibid, para 78.
[217] ibid, paras 83–84.

The *Laval* judgment seems to have further narrowed down the scope of exercise of the right to strike in the context of the internal market and, in addition, established the limits of collective bargaining in situations involving the posting of workers. Those limits were defined through the judicial interpretation of the PWD. Strike action taken by Swedish unions was held unlawful because it purported to enforce an unlawful collective agreement. That type of agreement was unlawful because it was not provided for under the PWD and, therefore, made it excessively difficult for Laval to determine its minimum pay obligations. *Laval* has made it clear that in order to be considered lawful in EU law, collective action has to be aimed at defending working conditions that have been laid down in accordance with the terms of the PWD, where it applies. Furthermore, it established that the PWD does not authorise the application to posted workers of working conditions that are not included in the hard nucleus of rules laid down in Art 3(1) PWD or offer greater protection than those rules, unless the application of such conditions is justified under Art 3(10) PWD.

B. The Scope of the Right to Collective Bargaining

Judgments following *Viking* and *Laval* clarified the limits of collective bargaining in situations involving the posting of workers and public procurement.

i. Rüffert *and* Commission v Luxembourg

Rüffert was the first judgment after *Laval* to clarify the limits of collective bargaining in situations involving the posting of workers. The case concerned a German law that confined the right to contract for public works to undertakings committed to pay the wages laid down in a sectoral collective agreement. The law was aimed at counteracting the distortions of competition that could arise through the use of cheap labour. In the circumstances of the case, it was invoked against a German undertaking whose Polish subcontractor was paying Polish workers less than half of the minimum wage provided for in the collective agreement applicable to the construction sector.

Considering whether the law was justified under the terms of the PWD, the Court followed the reasoning employed in *Laval*. First, it observed that the collective agreement in question had not been declared universally applicable, even though Germany had the mechanism for giving collective agreements universal effect. Second, the agreement applied only to public sector contracts falling within the geographical area of the agreement. In other words, it excluded the private sector and had a limited geographical coverage. For that reason, it could not be considered 'generally applicable' within the meaning of Art 3(8) PWD.[218] Equally, the agreement could not be justified on the basis of Art 49 EC, given the absence of evidence that would show that special protection was necessary for construction workers only when employed in connection with a public

[218] *Rüffert* (n 197), paras 26–29. See also Case C-115/14 *RegioPost* EU:C:2015:760 (CJEU, 17 November 2015), suggesting that the condition requiring universal application under Art 3(8) PWD does not apply to statutory pay obligations.

works contract but not private.[219] The judgment thus made clear that sectoral collective agreements, unless they were universally or generally applicable within the meaning of the PWD, were not suitable for regulating the conditions of work and employment of posted workers.

Commission v Luxembourg concerned the implementation by Luxembourg of the PWD, specifically, its Art 3(10), which laid down the public policy exception, previously invoked in *Laval*. Art 3(10) allowed the application to posted workers of the terms and conditions of employment on matters other than those listed in Art 3(1) PWD, provided that the terms and conditions in question constituted provisions of public policy (*ordre public*). Luxembourg law defined public policy provisions as those meeting the imperative requirements of the public interest. This meant that all of its national employment protections, including the obligation to observe collective agreements, were extended to posted workers.

The Court ruled that Member States were in principle free to determine the requirements of public policy. However, when relied on as justification for a derogation from the fundamental principle of the freedom to provide services, the notion of public policy had to be interpreted strictly, hence, its scope could not be determined unilaterally by each Member State.[220] Public policy could be invoked only if there was a 'genuine and sufficiently serious threat to a fundamental interest of society'.[221] This meant that Art 3(10) could not be interpreted as giving governments discretionary power to extend national labour regulations to posted workers. Moreover, the use of this exception in a particular situation had to be substantiated by 'precise' evidence that would enable the Court to determine whether the measures taken by the government were necessary and proportionate.[222]

In light of these observations, the obligation that all undertakings had to abide by 'collective labour agreements', irrespective of whether they were universally or generally applicable, could not be regarded as falling within the scope of the public policy exception.[223] Moreover, the 'actual provisions of such collective agreements themselves' could not fall under the definition of public policy 'in their entirety and for the simple reason that they derive[d] from that type of measure'.[224] The Court here seemed to suggest that certain, but surely not all, provisions of collective agreements, as opposed to the obligation to abide by such agreements, could potentially qualify under the public policy exception, but not if those agreements had not been declared universally applicable. The Court concluded by making it explicit that Art 3(10) could not be read more broadly than relating exclusively to the terms and conditions of employment laid down in collective agreements that had been declared universally applicable.[225]

Commission v Luxembourg made it abundantly clear that governments could not circumvent the narrow judicial reading of Art 3(1) PWD by resorting to Art 3(10) as a

[219] *Rüffert* (n 197), paras 39–40.
[220] *Commission v Luxembourg* (n 197), paras 30–31, 50.
[221] ibid, para 50.
[222] ibid, paras 51–53.
[223] ibid, para 67.
[224] ibid, para 66.
[225] ibid, para 67.

basis to enforce the protections offered by collective agreements applicable in the country to posted workers.

ii. Commission v Germany

The judgment of the Grand Chamber in *Commission v Germany* remains the latest in the line of cases concerning the relationship between economic freedoms and collective labour rights. The case concerned the practice of local authority employers in Germany of awarding contracts for pension services to bodies specified in collective agreements, without a call for tenders in accordance with the EU Public Procurement Directives (PPDs).[226]

The German government argued that the practice of awarding pension contracts to designated bodies had the objective of enhancing the level of retirement pensions and was necessary to preserve the principle of solidarity. In particular, this practice ensured that the selected bodies would not engage in any form of selection of interested applicants based on medical criteria. The Court dismissed the government's argument. It held, firstly, that the right to collective bargaining had to be 'reconciled' with the requirements stemming from the PPDs and comply with the principle of proportionality.[227] In this process of reconciliation, the objective of enhancing the level of retirement pensions had to be fairly balanced against the freedom of businesses to pursue cross-border activities and the value of opening up to EU-wide competition.[228] In that connection, the Court considered that the application of procurement procedures did not preclude the call for tenders from imposing upon interested tenderers conditions reflecting the interests of the workers concerned. Specifically, local authority employers were free to specify the conditions to be complied with by tenderers in order to prevent the selection of workers on the basis of medical grounds.[229] In conclusion, it was possible for Germany to accommodate its social policy objectives without 'completely, and for an indefinite period' disregarding the framework of EU public procurement rules.[230]

The rhetoric of *Commission v Germany* seems to resemble that of the *Viking* and *Laval* judgments. The Court talks about the need to balance, or, in this case, 'fairly' balance, the social objectives with those of the internal market, yet the conclusion it arrives at seems to subordinate the former to the latter. In result, *Commission v Germany* effectively excludes the possibility that social partners operating in the public sector could on their own accord, without a European call for tenders, award service contracts for occupational pensions. The judgment is yet another reminder from the Court that

[226] Council Directive 92/50/EEC relating to the coordination of procedures for the award of public service contracts [1992] OJ L209/1; Council Directive 2004/18/EC on the coordination of procedures for the award of public works contracts, public supply contracts and public service contracts [2004] OJ L134/114, now replaced by Council Directive 2014/24/EU on public procurement and repealing Directive 2004/18/EC [2014] OJ L94/65.

[227] *Commission v Germany* (n 197), paras 43–44.

[228] ibid, para 52, with a further reference to Case C-112/00 *Schmidberger* EU:C:2003:333, [2003] ECR I-5659, paras 81–82.

[229] ibid, paras 57–58.

[230] ibid, paras 53–56.

governments must pursue social policy objectives by means that are least restrictive on the exercise of the economic freedoms.

C. The Scope for the Exercise of Collective Labour Rights in Transnational Situations

Before discussing the regulatory implications of the body of case law analysed above, this section will provide a summary of the main developments concerning the scope for the exercise of collective labour rights in transnational situations.

The case law has established that there is a clear hierarchy between EU economic freedoms and collective labour rights. The latter are viewed as barriers to free movement, capable of dissuading businesses operating in the internal market from exercising their freedoms of establishment and provision of services. Accordingly, in order to be lawful, the exercise of collective labour rights in a transnational context must be justified as appropriate and necessary in light of the objective of the protection of workers.

The exercise of the right to strike has to pass a rigorous review involving three cumulative conditions. First, strike action must be invoked with the objective of securing employment conditions that are under serious jeopardy. Second, those employment conditions must be laid down in accordance with EU directives implementing EU free movement rules, where applicable. Third, the exercise of the right to strike must be necessary, which means that strike action must be taken as a last resort after other, possibly less restrictive means have been exhausted.

As regards the right to collective bargaining, its permissible scope is effectively determined by the terms of the PWD. Member States are only allowed to use collective agreements – for laying down the minimum rules of protection on matters listed in Art 3(1) – that are universally or generally applicable within the meaning of Art 3(8) PWD. Accordingly, collective agreements must be observed by all similar undertakings in the geographical area and in the profession or industry concerned or concluded by the most representative worker and employer organisations and applied throughout the territory. This suggests that ordinary or sectoral collective agreements, unless they are nationwide and representative, cannot be used as a means for regulating the terms and conditions of employment in situations of cross-border provision of services.

The scope of application of collective agreements is also affected by the Court's interpretation of the public policy exception laid down in Art 3(10) PWD. An obligation to observe collective agreements applicable in the territory of a Member State, as such, cannot qualify as a provision of public policy. Neither can certain specific rules laid down in collective agreements, unless those agreements have been declared universally or generally applicable, in line with the Court's reasoning in *Commission v Luxembourg*.

Finally, *Commission v Germany* suggests that public authorities cannot bypass EU public procurement rules by reference to obligations stemming from collective agreements unless they can demonstrate that collective bargaining constitutes the least restrictive means for implementing the social policy objectives pursued in the given situation. In practice, this precludes public authorities from delegating to the social partners the task of awarding contracts for social insurance services.

D. Collective Labour Rights Beyond the Free Movement: *Alemo-Herron*

The principles formulated in the free movement case law were ultimately extended by the Court to legal situations concerning conflicts between collective labour rights and commercial interests more generally. The judgment in *Alemo-Herron* is a prominent example.

Alemo-Herron concerned the validity of the UK's transposition of Directive 2001/23 regulating employees' rights in the event of transfers of undertakings, known as the Acquired Rights Directive (ARD).[231] Art 3 ARD stipulates that the rights and obligations of the transferor arising from a contract of employment or collective agreements will be transferred to the transferee. Under UK law, these obligations included 'dynamic' clauses, which were clauses that referred to the terms negotiated externally, such as collective agreements, and post-transfer. The Court was asked to determine whether this interpretation of Art 3 was compatible with EU law.

In that connection, the Court observed that the purpose of the Directive was not just to protect the rights of the employees in the event of a transfer, but to seek a 'fair balance' between the interests of employees and transferee employers.[232] This balance required that the transferee be in a position allowing it 'to make adjustments and changes necessary to carry on its operations' after the transfer had taken place.[233] In the view of the Court, clauses providing dynamic contractual rights were liable to undermine this balance because they were capable of limiting 'considerably' the transferee's room for manoeuvre necessary to make the relevant adjustments and changes.[234]

This conclusion was supported by the Charter, whose Art 16 protected the freedom to conduct a business, including the freedom to enter into a contract. The Court held that in situations of transfer of undertakings, this freedom required that the transferee were able 'to assert its interests effectively in a contractual process … and to negotiate the aspects determining changes in the working conditions of its employees'.[235] Without the opportunity to participate in the negotiations of the working conditions, the transferee's contractual freedom was 'seriously reduced to the point that such a limitation [was] liable to adversely affect the very essence of its freedom to conduct a business'.[236] Therefore, Art 3 ARD had to be interpreted as precluding the enforceability of dynamic clauses in cases where the transferees were not provided with the possibility of participating in the post-transfer negotiation processes.

The *Alemo-Herron* judgment attracted immediate criticism. First, the Court was criticised for misconstruing the very purpose of the ARD. The ARD was designed as

[231] Council Directive 23/2001/EC on the approximation of the laws of the Member States relating to the safeguarding of employees' rights in the event of transfers of undertakings, businesses or parts of undertakings or businesses [2001] OJ L82/16 (Acquired Rights Directive).
[232] *Alemo-Herron* (n 198), para 25.
[233] ibid, paras 25–27.
[234] ibid, paras 28–29.
[235] ibid, paras 32–33.
[236] ibid, paras 34–35.

a worker-protective measure and, as such, should not presuppose an act of balancing between the interests of employers and employees.[237] This view is supported by the Preamble of the Directive, which stipulates that the Directive is the Community's legislative response to the new 'economic trends' that result in 'changes in the structure of undertakings', necessitating a regime which would safeguard the rights of employees in the event of a change of employer.[238] In line with this logic, Art 8 ARD further explicitly states that that the Directive is a minimum harmonisation measure allowing Member States to apply rules and collective agreements that are more favourable to employees.

Somewhat consistently with the rest of the judgment, the Court's reading of the Charter also seems to be biased towards the protection of business interests. It singles out the freedom to conduct a business protected under Art 16 CFR while completely disregarding the Charter's 'Solidarity' chapter,[239] which almost in its entirety is dedicated to the protection of workers.[240] By doing so, it elevates a commercial freedom to the level of a seemingly absolute fundamental right.[241] This interpretation of Art 16 seems to depart from the previous case law according to which the freedom to conduct a business can be subject to restrictions, provided that those restrictions do not prevent 'a business activity from being carried out as such'.[242] Restrictions that arise from the need to protect the weaker party in the employment relationship should arguably fall within this category.[243]

The conclusions drawn by the Court in *Alemo-Herron* have been somewhat refined in subsequent case law. In *Asklepios Kliniken*, the Court held that dynamic clauses referring to collective agreements could be enforced against the transferee in situations where 'national legislation provides for the possibility, after the transfer, for the transferee to adjust the working conditions existing at the date of the transfer, either consensually or unilaterally'.[244] In other words, dynamic clauses will be enforceable if national legislation provides for a mechanism that allows the transferee to make adjustments to the conditions of work and employment post-transfer. This exception to the general rule does not seem to bring a meaningful change to the protection of workers in the event of transfer of undertakings. The Court's stance remains essentially the same – clearly favouring the freedom to conduct a business over the right to collective bargaining and thus the interests of the transferee over those of the employees.

[237] J Prassl, 'Freedom of Contract as a General Principle of EU Law? Transfers of Undertakings and the Protection of Employer Rights in EU Labour Law: Case C-426/11 *Alemo-Herron and Others v Parkwood Leisure Ltd*' (2013) 42 *Industrial Law Journal* 434. See also *Alemo-Herron* (n 198), Opinion of AG Cruz Villalón, para 20.

[238] Acquired Rights Directive (n 231), Recitals 2–3.

[239] CFR, title IV 'Solidarity'.

[240] See Art 27 CFR on the right of information and consultation and Art 28 CFR on the right to collective bargaining.

[241] S Weatherill, 'Use and Abuse of the EU's Charter of Fundamental Rights: on the Improper Veneration of "Freedom of Contract". Judgment of the Court of 18 July 2013: Case C-426/11, *Mark Alemo-Herron and Others v Parkwood Leisure Ltd*' (2014) 10 *European Review of Contract Law* 167, 177–80.

[242] Prassl (n 237) 442–43, referring to Case C-281/11 *Sky Österreich v Rundfunk* EU:C:2013:855 (CJEU, 22 January 2013), para 49; Weatherill (n 241) 177–180, discussing CJEU consumer case law.

[243] Weatherill (n 241) 172.

[244] Joined Cases C-680/15 and C-681/15 *Asklepios Kliniken* EU:C:2017:317 (CJEU, 27 April 2017).

E. The Regulatory Implications of the Case Law for National Industrial Relations Systems

The Court's position concerning the lawfulness of the exercise of collective labour rights in the context of the commercial freedoms is somewhat in line with its case law on cross-border healthcare and education. The Court recognises that, in principle, EU law does not preclude the territorial application of national legislation or collective agreements laying down the terms and conditions of employment.[245] Member States are also free to define the conditions of the exercise of the right to collective bargaining and the right to strike.[246] However, in doing so, they have to comply with EU free movement rules. The Court's language here displays the familiar tension between, on the one hand, the judicial exercise of EU internal market competences through the interpretation of free movement rules and, on the other hand, the EU's commitment to the protection of national regulatory autonomy in constitutionally sensitive areas.

It will be argued that the judicial interpretation of what compliance with EU free movement rules entails in the context of employment and labour relations significantly narrows down the scope of the exercise of collective labour rights in transnational situations. By doing so, it reduces the scope of application of domestic standards of worker protection to posted workers. This position threatens to undermine the viability of national systems of industrial relations, thereby endangering the level of worker protection in the EU.

i. *The Impact on Trade Union Activity*

The proportionality review employed to assess the legality of strike action considerably weakens the position of trade unions *vis-à-vis* foreign employers. The organisation of collective action by trade unions is normally covered by their legal autonomy, a fact recognised by the Court itself.[247] Yet the case law restricts that autonomy significantly by narrowing down the permissible objectives of strike action to one: securing employment conditions that are under serious jeopardy. Furthermore, it places the right to strike under 'the least restrictive means' test, which simply goes against the nature of the right to strike. As Davies convincingly argues, the point of collective action is precisely to act out of proportion, thereby causing economic harm to the employer, in order to put pressure on them to enter into collective agreement on reasonable terms.[248] The threat of recourse to strike action is often the sole bargaining tool that workers have to offset the imbalance of power inherent in the employment relationship.[249] The requirement that strike action be a necessary last resort thus also risks compromising the effectiveness of collective bargaining.

[245] *Laval* (n 196), para 57.

[246] See, eg, *Viking* (n 195), para 40.

[247] ibid, paras 33, 57–61. See this issue discussed in ch 2, ss IV and VI.

[248] ACL Davies, 'One Step Forward, Two Steps Back? The *Viking* and *Laval* Cases in the ECJ' (2008) 37 *Industrial Law Journal* 126, 143; KD Ewing and J Hendy, 'The Dramatic Implications of *Demir and Baykara*' (2010) 39 *Industrial Law Journal* 2, 13.

[249] T Novitz and P Germanotta, 'Globalisation and the Right to Strike: The Case for European-Level Protection of Secondary Action' (2002) 18 *International Journal of Comparative Labour Law* 67, 68–69.

Moreover, the focus on the necessity of strike action creates a climate of legal uncertainty. Trade unions can no longer rely on national law to secure the legality of collective action, while EU law makes it conditional on a case-by-case assessment of necessity in relation to the economic freedoms.[250] The outcome of such an assessment is extremely difficult to predict. At the same time, due to the horizontal direct effect of Arts 49 and 56 TFEU, employers are handed a strong incentive to sue or threaten to sue trade unions in courts with a promise of pecuniary compensation.[251] In the *Laval* litigation, the Laval company was awarded approximately 55,000 euros in punitive damages. No wonder that this judgment had a 'chilling effect' on collective action.[252] The *BALPA* case is a good example of this effect. *BALPA* concerned a decision by the British Airline Pilots Association (BALPA) to go on strike following the announcement by the British Airways to set up a subsidiary company in another EU State, which would have had an impact on pilots' terms and conditions of employment.[253] To prevent the strike action, the BA requested an injunction in UK courts, on the basis that the action would be illegal under *Viking* and *Laval*. The company also threatened BALPA with a damages claim estimated at 100 million pounds per day should the work stoppage take place. Under those circumstances, BALPA did not follow through with the strike. This case demonstrates that the uncertainty about the risks involved in taking collective action may dissuade trade unions from doing so in the first place, thus impairing their bargaining power and inhibiting their ability to protect workers' interests.

Apart from the impact on the right to strike, the case law also significantly narrows down the scope of collective bargaining as a means of laying down the terms and conditions of employment. In the Court's view, collective agreements – with the narrow exception of those that are universally applicable – seem to create too much uncertainty in the legal framework for transnational provision of services and, hence, make it excessively difficult for employers to determine the obligations with which they need to comply. Therefore, such agreements cannot be justified as lawful, either under the terms of the PWD or the Treaty free movement rules. This situation appears problematic considering the EU's commitment to promoting social dialogue between management and labour. This commitment is grounded in respect for the autonomy of the social partners and the diversity of national industrial relations systems.[254] The case law, which recognises as lawful in EU law only universally applicable collective agreements, seems to undermine this commitment.

[250] C Barnard, 'A Proportionate Response to Proportionality in the Field of Collective Action' (2012) 37 *European Law Review* 117, 120–21; P Syrpis and T Novitz, 'Economic and Social Rights in Conflict: Political and Judicial Approaches to their Reconciliation' (2008) 33 *European Law Review* 411, 418–19.

[251] For the discussion of the horizontal direct effect, see ch 2, ss IV and VI.

[252] Barnard (n 250) 123.

[253] International Labour Conference (99th Session) Report III (Part 1A) of the Committee of Experts 208–209 (Geneva 24 February 2010) www.ilo.org/public/libdoc/ilo/P/09661/09661%282010-99-1A%29.pdf; International Labour Conference (100th Session) Report III (Part 1A) of the Committee of Experts 187 (Geneva 16 June 2011) www.ilo.org/public/libdoc/ilo/P/09661/09661%282011-100-1A%29.pdf. For a discussion of *BALPA*, see Ewing and Hendy (n 248) 37–40; T Novitz and P Syrpis, 'The United Kingdom' in M Freedland and J Adams-Prassl, *Viking, Laval and Beyond* (London, Hart Publishing, 2014).

[254] Arts 151–152 TFEU, formerly Arts 136 and 138 EC. On the relationship between the economic and social dimension of the Treaties, see ch 1, s II.

ii. Implications for Industrial Relations Systems

The negative effects of the case law extend beyond weakening the position of trade unions as such. The case law challenges the viability of European systems of industrial relations, particularly in those Member States that rely on autonomous collective bargaining in the implementation of national social policy, such as the Scandinavian countries.[255] In the Scandinavian model, trade unions have primary responsibility for safeguarding high-average, flexible levels of wages and other employment conditions for all different categories of employees.[256] They are, however, unable to do so effectively in the face of the Court's case law. In these circumstances, governments must choose: they can modify their traditional methods of labour regulation or do nothing and accept the fact that the working conditions negotiated by trade unions will be set aside wherever the situation in question involves foreign labour or employer. Some governments have followed the former route, some have accepted the consequences of taking the latter. For example, Denmark and Sweden both have introduced legislation limiting the powers of the social partners to regulate the working conditions of posted workers.[257] This and similar developments sit uncomfortably with the fact that, in principle, the Treaties exclude matters pertaining to collective labour law from regulatory interference by the EU.

Finally, the Court's position seems to reinforce the idea that social dumping is an acceptable method by which businesses can compete in the European market. As Deakin observes, it suggests that the working conditions of migrant workers will be governed by labour standards of the least regulated Member State relevant to the situation in question, unless higher standards are able to survive the high-threshold necessity review (save for the nucleus of mandatory rules for minimum protection enshrined in the PWD).[258] This position allows businesses operating in the EU to avail themselves from the competitive advantage that follows from lower labour standards.[259] At the same time, though, it drives down the level of worker protection in the region.

[255] C Joerges and F Rödl, 'Informal Politics, Formalised Law and the 'Social Deficit' of European Integration: Reflections after the Judgments of the ECJ in *Viking* and *Laval*' (2009) 15 *European Law Journal* 1.

[256] J Malmberg, 'The Impact of the ECJ Judgments in *Viking*, *Laval*, *Rüffert* and *Luxembourg* on the Practice of Collective Bargaining and the Effectiveness of Social Action' (2010) *European Parliament Directorate General for Internal Policies*, 7 ff www.europarl.europa.eu/document/activities/cont/201107/20110718ATT24274/20110718ATT24274EN.pdf.

[257] For a broader discussion of these developments, see J Malmberg and T Sigeman, 'Industrial Actions and EU Economic Freedoms: The Autonomous Collective Bargaining Model Curtailed by the European Court of Justice' (2008) 45 *CML Rev* 1115; A Bücker and W Warneck (eds), '*Viking – Laval – Rüffert*: Consequences and Policy Perspectives' (2010) *European Trade Union Institute Report* 111; M Blauberger, 'With *Luxembourg* in Mind … The Remaking of National Policies in the Face of ECJ Jurisprudence' (2012) 19 *Journal of European Public Policy* 109, 114–24; K Fric, 'Statutory Minimum Wages in the EU 2016' (*Eurofond*, 29 January 2016) www.eurofound.europa.eu/sites/default/files/statutory_minimum_wages_in_the_eu_2016.pdf, discussing the growing tendency to regulate minimum wages by statutory law.

[258] S Deakin, 'Regulatory Competition after *Laval*' (2008) 10 *Cambridge Yearbook of European Legal Studies* 581. See also N Hös, 'The Principle of Proportionality in the *Viking* and *Laval* Cases: An Appropriate Standard of Judicial Review?' (2009) EUI Department of Law Working Paper 2009/06, 16, 19–20 cadmus.eui.eu/bitstream/handle/1814/11259/LAW_2009_06.pdf.

[259] Malmberg and Sigeman (n 257) 1144.

This problem has been in part remedied by the recent amendments to the PWD. The reference to the minimum rates of pay to be guaranteed to posted workers has been replaced with the obligation to pay them the same remuneration as received by local workers,[260] thus eliminating wage competition between the two categories of workers. However, this rule will not apply if the terms of pay are laid down through collective agreements that are not universally or generally applicable within the meaning of Art 3(8) PWD. Therefore, it does not protect the models of collective bargaining, such as the Scandinavian model, which are not based on universal applicability of collective agreements. The Directive also improves the status of workers in long-term postings, who after 12 months are entitled to almost all mandatory working conditions of the host Member State.[261] Yet the impact of the latter provision should not be overestimated. Considering that the average duration of posting in Europe remains shorter than four months,[262] the majority of posted workers will not be able to avail themselves of the improved conditions.

For the most part, the amended PWD does not, and cannot, alter the approach of the Court to the relationship between the economic freedoms and collective labour rights and, more generally, commercial interests and those of worker protection.[263] This approach governs all situations with a transnational dimension to them, including those falling outside the scope of the PWD. By subordinating the interests of worker protection to the fundamental freedoms, it encourages regulatory competition between governments as well as competition in labour standards among businesses.[264] While encouraging regulatory competition may be a valid economic policy choice, it threatens to override the legitimate policy of governments wishing to maintain their chosen level of worker protection and challenges the capacity of new Member States to build their own social models. Moreover, the legitimacy of judicial decision making is strained when such extremely political choices are embedded within adjudication.

V. Gambling

As discussed in chapter two, the Treaties contain no restrictions that would limit the EU's mandate to regulate the provision of gambling services in the internal market. However, due to the lack of political appetite for uniform standards, the gambling sector has remained untouched by EU legislative action.[265] In the absence of EU-level

[260] Posted Workers Amendment Directive (n 28), Art 1(2)(a), discussed in more detail in ch 4, s VI.

[261] ibid, Art 1(2)(b), also stipulating that the period of 12 months can be extended to 18 months upon the submission of a 'motivated notification' by the service provider.

[262] F De Wispelaere, L De Smedt and J Pacolet, 'Posting of Workers: Report on A1 Portable Documents issued in 2018' (European Commission Directorate-General for Employment, Social Affairs and Inclusion 2019) 11.

[263] See ch 4, s VI for a detailed analysis of this point.

[264] Deakin (n 258) 103–06; Malmberg and Sigeman (n 257) 1116. See also ETUC, '*Rüffert* case: ETUC Warns that ECJ's Judgment is Destructive and Damaging' (*ETUC*, 3 April 2008) www.etuc.org/en/pressrelease/ruffert-case-etuc-warns-ecjs-judgement-destructive-and-damaging.

[265] See ch 2, s V for a discussion of EU-wide initiatives concerning the regulation of gambling.

harmonisation, national gambling regulations come within the purview of EU law mainly through the case law of the CJEU. The Court's treatment of domestic regulatory frameworks for gambling provides a valuable insight into how the Court approaches the relationship between internal market law and national regulatory autonomy in politically (if not also constitutionally) sensitive areas.

Judicial challenges in the gambling sector typically arise from situations where governments impose restrictions on foreign gambling operators to enter their markets and/or impose penalties for unauthorised gambling activities. In addition to the preliminary reference procedure, a number of cases have reached the Court as a result of the infringement proceedings instituted against the Member States by the Commission. However, at the end of 2017, the Commission announced that it was closing all infringement proceedings and treatment of complaints in the area of gambling. This decision was influenced by two circumstances. First, the Commission had acknowledged the broader political legitimacy of the public interest objectives pursued by Member States when regulating gambling services. Second, it considered that the complaints in the gambling sector could be handled more efficiently by national courts in the light of the numerous judgments of the Court on the matter. Indeed, the existing body of EU case law on gambling is rich and complex. This section analyses this body of case law while focusing on the progressive development of the standard of judicial review employed by the Court to assess national derogations from the free movement rules. Ultimately, the analysis seeks to determine the implications of the case law for the scope of national regulatory autonomy in the gambling sector.

A. Early Case Law: In Support of Regulatory Discretion

Since the early cases on gambling, namely *Schindler*, *Läärä* and *Zenatti*, the Court has taken an approach that is deferential towards national regulatory choices in the area of gambling.

i. Schindler

The *Schindler* case concerned a UK prohibition on the operation of large-scale lotteries. This case was discussed in the previous chapter in relation to the Court's interpretation of gambling as an economic activity. The focus of the present analysis is the part of the judicial reasoning that concerns the justification for the prohibition in question.

The UK government put forward a number of grounds of justification expressing concerns of social policy and of the prevention of fraud, in particular: 'consumer protection, prevention of crime, protection of public morality, restriction of demand for gambling, and the financing of public interest activities'.[266] Having considered these various grounds of justification, the Court grouped them in two broad categories: the protection of consumers and the maintenance of order in society.[267] The Commission

[266] Case C-275/92 *Schindler* EU:C:1994:119 [1994] ECR I-1039, paras 46, 54.
[267] ibid, para 58.

argued that the objectives in question could have been achieved by means that were less restrictive of free movement, such as a multi-licence system with strict conditions and supervision. The Court rejected this argument. It held that the choice between alternative systems of regulation fell within the discretion of the Member States. There were several reasons that justified the grant of discretion to national authorities. First of all, the Court considered that 'it was not possible to disregard the moral, religious or cultural aspects of lotteries, like other types of gambling'.[268] This, in the Court's view, explained the general tendency to restrict or even prohibit the practice of gambling and to prevent it from being a source of private profit. Secondly, lotteries involved a high risk of crime or fraud, particularly when they were operated on a large scale, given the size of stakes and winnings. Thirdly, lotteries were an incitement to spend, which could have damaging individual and social consequences. Finally, although this was not in itself to be regarded as an objective justification for restrictive measures, lotteries made a significant contribution to the financing of benevolent or public interest activities, such as social works, charitable works, sport or culture.[269]

The Court took the view that the 'peculiar' nature of lotteries required that national authorities have a 'sufficient degree of latitude' to determine what was necessary to protect the players and maintain order in society in the context of the particular social and cultural features of each Member State.[270] Accordingly, Member States were entitled to choose the manner in which lotteries were operated, and decide on the size of the stakes and the allocation of the profits yielded.[271] As a result, even a complete prohibition of a certain form of lottery was to be considered as a proportionate restriction on a fundamental freedom.

ii. Läärä *and* Zenatti

In *Läärä*, the Court was asked to pronounce on the legality of gambling monopolies.[272] The case concerned the Finnish licensing system whereby only one licence at a time could be issued to cover certain games of chance and only for the purpose of collecting funds for charity or other non-profit purposes provided for by law. Mr Läärä was the head of a company that operated slot machines without a licence. As a result of unauthorised activities, he was facing criminal charges. Decided a month after *Läärä*, *Zenatti* concerned the Italian regulatory framework for gambling, which generally prohibited the taking of bets, but, by way of exception, allowed betting to be licensed where it was essential for the proper conduct of competitive events.[273] Mr Zenatti was an intermediary for a British sports betting company who ran an information exchange for Italian customers in relation to bets on foreign sports events. Zenatti was ordered by the local authorities to cease his activities. In both cases, the Court was asked to assess

[268] *Schindler* (n 266), para 60.
[269] ibid.
[270] ibid, paras 59–61.
[271] ibid, para 61.
[272] Case C-124/97 *Läärä* EU:C:1999:435, [1999] ECR I-6067, para 10.
[273] Case C-67/98 *Zenatti* EU:C:1999:514, [1999] ECR I-7289, para 3 and Opinion of AG Fennelly, paras 4–6.

the compatibility of national legislation with Art 49 EC. Since the Court's reasoning was almost identical in the two judgments, they will be analysed together.

The list of public interest objectives advanced by governments in *Läärä* and *Zenatti* included the prevention of gambling from being a source of private profit, the avoidance of risks of crime and fraud, and protection against the damaging individual and social consequences of the incitement to spend. The Court considered all of the objectives together as generally relating to the protection of consumers and the maintenance of order in society. In both cases, national measures were found to be justified.

Following the approach employed in *Schindler*, the Court held that it was in the discretion of the national authorities to assess whether it was necessary to prohibit certain gambling practices, totally or partially, or merely to restrict them and lay down procedures for controlling them.[274] The fact that a Member State had chosen a system of protection different from systems adopted by other Member States could not affect the assessment of the need for and proportionality of the system.[275] Accordingly, national rules had to be assessed solely by reference to the objectives pursued by the Member State concerned and the degree of protection which it sought to ensure.[276]

In *Zenatti*, the Court instructed the national court that judicial review should focus on the appropriateness, or suitability, of national measures. The task for the national court was to verify that the measures in question reflected 'a concern to bring about a genuine diminution in gambling opportunities'.[277] In this respect, the Court noted that limited authorisation of gambling on the basis of special or exclusive rights was to be considered as an appropriate means to regulate gambling because it had the advantage of confining the desire to gamble and the exploitation of gambling within controlled channels, thus preventing the risk of fraud or crime and ensuring that resulting profits would be used for public-interest purposes.[278]

In *Läärä*, the Court was also asked to consider whether the stated public interest objectives could have been achieved as effectively by means that were 'less restrictive' than a monopoly system, such as by imposing the necessary code of conduct on operators or by taxing their activities.[279] It was submitted that this regime would be suitable for the operation of slot machines, given the modest size of the stakes and prizes in contrast to large-scale lotteries. The Court rejected this argument. It held that, in light of the risk of crime and fraud, the grant of exclusive rights to a single public body and the obligation imposed on it to pay over the proceeds of its operations was 'certainly more effective in ensuring that strict limits [we]re set to the lucrative nature of such activities'.[280]

Läärä and *Zenatti* made clear that the Court's reasoning in *Schindler* as regards the regulation of lotteries was equally applicable to other forms of gambling, including those, such as sports betting, that involve an element of skill as opposed to mere chance.

[274] *Läärä* (n 272), para 35; *Zenatti* (n 273), para 33.
[275] *Läärä*, para 58; *Zenatti*, para 34.
[276] *Läärä*, para 36; *Zenatti*, para 34.
[277] *Zenatti*, para 36.
[278] *Läärä*, para 37; *Zenatti*, para 35.
[279] *Läärä*, paras 11, 39–41.
[280] ibid, para 41.

The Court expressly recognised that Member States were entitled to a broad margin of discretion when regulating their gaming and betting markets. Accordingly, as long as national measures were 'genuinely' directed at realising public interest objectives, they were to be considered lawful regardless of their degree of restrictiveness.

B. Narrowing Down Regulatory Discretion

i. Gambelli

The *Gambelli* case concerned Italian legislation on betting on sporting events, already examined to an extent in *Zenatti*.[281] The question at issue was the lawfulness of the new amendments made to that legislation, instituting criminal penalties of up to one year's imprisonment for unauthorised collection or assistance in collecting of bets. In addition, it was argued that the legislation was incompatible with the freedom of establishment (a question which had not been raised in *Zenatti*) because the conditions for submitting tenders for the award of the required licences excluded listed companies and required applicants to own premises in Italy.[282] These requirements were supposed to ensure the transparency of the share ownership for the purposes of crime prevention.

Mr Gambelli and other agents had been acting as intermediaries for a British betting company, Stanley, by assisting in collecting bets through a data transmission centre. This data transmission centre had been established lawfully, since the original version of the Italian legislation did not expressly restrict the collection of bets on foreign sporting events, leading to a development of a network of operators acting as intermediaries for foreign betting companies. Criminal proceedings were brought against Gambelli and 147 other defendants for unlicensed practices. The national court referred the case to the CJEU, expressing doubts, in particular, about the compatibility of the Italian measures with the principle of proportionality.

The Court ruled that the Italian measures were indeed disproportionate in light of the objectives pursued by the government. Three factors were taken into account in this respect: the severity of the penalties attached to the prohibition on the collection of bets (up to a year's imprisonment); the fact that the intermediaries had been lawfully constituted before the legislative amendments were enacted and reasonably considered that they were permitted to transmit bets on foreign sporting events; and that the foreign service provider in question, Stanley, was already subject to controls and penalties in the UK, where it was established.[283]

As regards the conditions for the award of licences in particular, the Court held that they went beyond what was necessary to combat fraud because they prevented capital companies quoted on regulated markets of other Member States from obtaining licences, whilst there were other means of checking the accounts and activities of such

[281] Case C-243/01 *Gambelli* EU:C:2003:597, [2003] ECR I-13031.
[282] ibid, para 27.
[283] ibid, para 73.

companies.[284] Moreover, these conditions were to be considered discriminatory if in practice they were met more easily by Italian operators than by the foreign ones.[285]

The defendants argued that the Italian measures were also not genuinely aimed at addressing the concerns of consumer protection because Italy was not pursuing a consistent policy of limiting gambling activities. In fact, it was pursuing a policy of liberalisation of the gambling market in order to increase tax revenue. The government was increasing the range of betting and gaming available and inciting people to engage in such activities by facilitating the collection of bets. The Court observed that in order to be justified, restrictions arising from the Italian licensing system had to 'be suitable for achieving [public interest] objectives, inasmuch as they [had to] serve to limit betting activities in a consistent and systematic manner'.[286] Consequently, if a Member State incited and encouraged consumers to participate in gaming and betting to the financial benefit of the public purse, it could not invoke the need to reduce opportunities for betting as one of the justifications for restrictive measures.[287]

Gambelli seemed to narrow down the margin of discretion accorded to national authorities by previous judgments. It did so, first, by elaborating on the content of the test applied in *Zenatti* regarding the suitability of national measures. In order to be deemed suitable, restrictions had to serve to limit betting activities in a consistent and systematic manner. Therefore, where a Member State pursued an expansionist gaming and betting policy, it could not be considered genuinely to have the concern of reducing opportunities for gambling. Second, the Court seemed strongly to suggest that a rigid licensing system, especially if accompanied by criminal penalties, would be considered disproportionate as a means to combat crime and fraud.

While admittedly more principled than the previous decisions, the Court's reasoning in *Gambelli* might have been influenced by the particular context of the case: its extreme factual circumstances, namely the *de facto* discriminatory character of the measures, which were also accompanied by criminal sanctions; the defendants' submissions exposing the hypocrisy of the regulatory system; and the position of the national court, which expressed particular doubts about the proportionality of the Italian policy.

As regards the final outcome of the *Gambelli* case, ultimately, the Italian Supreme Court decided that the measures in question were non-discriminatory and otherwise compatible with EU law. Possibly, albeit not officially, this decision was influenced by the fact that the Italian government had in the meantime removed the provisions barring listed companies' access to the Italian market. The remaining aspects of the regulatory regime were accordingly deemed to be justified in light of the objective of the maintenance of public order, as they contributed to channelling gambling into controllable systems, thus preventing its exploitation for criminal purposes.[288]

[284] *Gambelli* (n 281), para 74.
[285] ibid, para 71. See also *Gambelli*, Opinion of AG Alber, paras 94–96.
[286] *Gambelli*, para 67.
[287] ibid, para 69.
[288] See Joined Cases C-338/04, C-359/04 and C-360/04 *Placanica* EU:C:2007:133, [2007] ECR I-1891, paras 16–17; Corte di Cassazione, Sezione III penale, case no 23273/2004 (*Gesualdi*), judgment of 26 April 2004; M Bassini, 'ECJ Case Law on Gambling: How Technology Thwarts Regulatory Barriers' (*Media Laws*, 14 December 2014) www.medialaws.eu/how-technology-thwarts-regulatory-barriers-the-ecj-case-law-on-gambling-and-internet/.

ii. Placanica

In *Placanica*, the Court was asked to rule on, inter alia, whether the Italian licensing system, challenged in *Gambelli*, could be justified by the need to channel the games of chance into controllable systems.

This time, the Court drew a clear distinction between, on the one hand, the objective of reducing gambling opportunities and, on the other hand, insofar as the games of chance were permitted, the objective of combating criminality, which was to be achieved by channelling the activities of gambling operators into State-controlled systems. In both cases, the restrictions had to be consistent and systematic in nature. Since the Italian legislature was pursuing a policy of expanding activity in the sector, in order to increase tax revenue, the legislation could not be justified by the objectives of protecting consumers and reducing gambling opportunities.[289] However, viewed as a means of combating fraud, the policy of controlled expansion could be justified because it was consistent with the objective of drawing players away from clandestine gambling towards activities that were authorised and regulated.[290] Moreover, since authorised operators needed to represent a reliable yet at the same time attractive alternative to a prohibited activity, it was acceptable that the government offered an extensive range of games, advertised them on a certain scale and used various new distribution techniques.[291]

Placanica seems to suggest that whether the policy of expansion in the gambling sector will be justified depends on the public interest objective it is assessed against. Although such a policy is not consistent with the objective of consumer protection from addiction, it could successfully be defended by the need to combat crime and fraud. This logic, in turn, suggests that as long as governments are clever about how they draft their laws (and their submissions to the Court), they can maintain a generally restrictive regulatory regime for gambling while at the same time expanding the supply of gambling services within the confines of State-controlled systems, thus maximising the revenues received from gambling.

The following two subsections intend to assess to what extent the latter assumption remains true in light of subsequent case law. To that end, it will be discussed, first, how the requirement of consistency laid down in *Gambelli* and *Placanica* has been elaborated in relation to different national frameworks for gambling, and, second, whether this requirement is applied any differently in the context of Internet gambling.

C. Clarifying the Limits of Discretion: The Test of Consistency

i. Stoss *and* Ladbrokes

The *Stoss* case concerned a German policy on gambling whereby different regulatory regimes applied to different types of gambling.[292] Sporting bets and lotteries were

[289] *Placanica* (n 288), paras 52–54.
[290] ibid, para 55.
[291] ibid.
[292] Joined Cases C-316/07, C-358/07 to C-360/07, C-409/07 and C-410/07 *Stoss* EU:C:2010:504, [2010] ECR I-8069.

covered by regional monopolies, while the organisation of bets on horse racing and the operation of gaming machines and casinos were entrusted to authorised private operators. Germany submitted that this regulatory regime was designed to prevent incitement to 'squander money' on gambling and fight addiction to the latter.

The Court held that the fact that some games of chance were subject to a public monopoly whilst others were subject to a licensing system could not, in itself, call into question the consistency of the whole system because different types of games had different characteristics and thus could require different forms of regulation.[293] However, the German system was regarded as inconsistent for reasons relating to the marketing of the games. First, in order to maximise profits, State monopolies carried out intensive advertising campaigns encouraging participation in gambling, thus going beyond what was necessary for the purpose of channelling consumers' desire to gamble into games that were authorised and regulated.[294] Second, with regard to the games that fell outside the public monopoly, such as casino and automated games, the authorities conducted or tolerated policies of expanding supply, despite the fact that these types of games involved a higher risk of addiction than those covered by public monopoly.[295] Therefore, the objective of consumer protection, which underlined the establishment of the monopoly system, could not be pursued effectively.[296]

The *Stoss* judgment clarified that the test of necessity has a role to play in reviewing the consistency of the regulatory system. Where government policies are aimed at protecting consumers from problem gambling, the marketing and advertising of the games have to be limited to the extent necessary to draw consumers away from unauthorised gambling.

This aspect of the test of consistency was further elaborated in the *Ladbrokes* judgment, concerning Dutch legislation which regulated gambling through the system of exclusive licences for each of the games of chance authorised. The monopoly system was aimed at combatting fraud and curbing addiction to gambling. However, it allowed the introduction of new games and their promotion by means of advertising. The Court noted that it was, in principle, difficult to reconcile the objective of protecting consumers from gambling addiction with a policy of expansion in the gambling sector. In this respect, a fair balance had to be drawn between, on the one hand, a demand for a controlled expansion of authorised games in order to make them attractive for the public (for the purposes of combatting fraud) and, on the other hand, the need to reduce as far as possible consumer addiction to such games.[297] The policy of expansion could not be regarded as consistent, unless 'the scale of unlawful activity was significant and the measures adopted were aimed at channelling consumers' propensity to gamble into activities that were lawful'.[298] For instance, this requirement would not be met if advertising campaigns stimulated active participation in gambling by depicting major winnings in glowing colours or by trivialising gambling, or giving it a positive image.[299]

[293] *Stoss* (n 292), paras 94–96.
[294] ibid, paras 100, 103.
[295] ibid, para 100.
[296] ibid, para 106. See also C-46/08 *Carmen Media* EU:C:2010:505, [2010] ECR I-8149, paras 53, 67–68.
[297] Case C-258/08 *Ladbrokes* EU:C:2010:308, [2010] ECR I-4757, paras 32, 37.
[298] ibid, paras 29–30.
[299] ibid, paras 29–32.

The Court concluded that the Dutch policy was internally consistent, as clandestine gambling in the Netherlands had been increasing and the advertising policy adopted by the authorities was 'sensible and balanced in content'.[300]

The *Ladbrokes* judgment brought some important clarifications regarding the Court's position on the application of the consistency requirement. Where the governments set out to pursue both the objective of preventing gambling addiction and the fight against crime, national courts will have to determine whether the policy of expansion in the sector can be reconciled with the need to curb addiction to gambling. Such reconciliation is possible if the scale of unlawful activity is significant and the measures adopted are designed to channel consumers' 'propensity' to gamble into activities that are lawful.

ii. Pfleger

The *Pfleger* case[301] concerned a challenge to Austrian monopoly on the operation of gaming machines. The referring court expressed the view that the monopoly system was inconsistent. In particular, the court considered that the national authorities had not shown that crime and/or addiction to gambling actually constituted a significant problem during the period at issue and it, therefore, seemed that the real purpose of the legislation was 'a mere increase of State tax revenue'.[302] The latter was apparent from the 'aggressive' commercial policy carried out by the holders of the monopoly, which was characterised by excessive advertising and, hence, could not be considered as a policy of 'controlled expansion'.[303]

The CJEU held that it was the prerogative of the national court to assess whether the legislation genuinely met the public interest objectives pursued by the government in a consistent and systematic manner.[304] At the same time, however, it emphasised that inability on the part of the national authorities to produce 'studies serving as the basis for the adoption of the legislation at issue' was not a sufficient reason to question its proportionality.[305]

The Court was also asked to assess the Austrian laws for compliance with the EU Charter of Fundamental Rights. This was something new. It was argued that the enforcement aspects of the relevant laws, involving administrative and criminal sanctions, were incompatible with the freedom to conduct an occupation, the freedom to conduct a business and the right to property.[306] AG Sharpston had suggested in her Opinion that even if the national rules were substantively in compliance with both the internal market law and the Charter, the details of enforcement could be tested separately for compliance with the Charter alone.[307] The Court, however, did not find the need to conduct a separate examination. It held that a measure that was found incompatible with

[300] *Ladbrokes* (n 297), paras 31, 34–35.
[301] Case C-390/12 *Pfleger* EU:C:2014:281 (CJEU, 30 April 2014).
[302] ibid, paras 43, 47, 53, 55.
[303] ibid, paras 16–17.
[304] ibid, para 49.
[305] ibid, para 51, with a further reference to *Stoss* (n 292), paras 70–72.
[306] Arts 15–17 CFR.
[307] *Pfleger* (n 301), Opinion of AG Sharpston, paras 74, 86.

Art 56 TFEU would also be incompatible with the economic rights protected under the Charter.[308]

This part of the Court's reasoning is important for understanding the role of the Charter in the context of gambling and free movement law more generally. The Charter appears to have no added value in the examination of the validity of national measures. If the measures in question are considered incompatible with Art 56 TFEU, they will also be incompatible with the Charter. By the same token, if they are compatible with Art 56, they seem to be protected from a separate challenge under the Charter.

iii. Stanleybet

In *Stanleybet*, the Court was asked to examine the legality of the Greek gambling monopoly, which was entrusted to one company, OPAP, formerly owned by the State.[309] The Court used this opportunity to elaborate on some of the criteria applicable to the management of public monopolies in light of the consistency requirement.

The government claimed that the monopoly system was justified by, inter alia, the need to combat gambling-related crime. The Court expressed doubts as to the system's capacity to do so effectively. It ruled that 'a measure as restrictive as a monopoly must, inter alia, be subject to strict control by the public authorities'.[310] In this respect, it referred to the view expressed by the referring court that the government's supervision of OPAP was merely superficial: it was confined to approving the regulations governing the activities of OPAP and monitoring the procedure of the organisation of games.[311] Accordingly, the system could not be considered as genuinely aimed at fighting crime and fraud.

Having suggested that the Greek policy was incompatible with EU law, the Court went on to advise the government on two possible courses of action. First, Greece could choose to preserve the monopoly system, while undertaking reforms that would subject it to 'effective and strict controls by the public authorities'.[312] It was in the government's discretion to do so because, as the Court observed, the presence of free and undistorted competition in 'the very specific market of games of chance' could have 'detrimental effects' on consumers: it could lead the operators to compete with each other in making their offers more attractive, thus encouraging consumers' expenditure on gaming and increasing their risks of addiction.[313] Accordingly, a government seeking to ensure 'a particularly high level of protection' was entitled to take the view that it could tackle the risks linked to gambling with 'sufficient' effectiveness 'only by granting exclusive rights to a single entity'.[314] Alternatively, the government could, although it was not obliged to, liberalise the gambling sector by establishing a non-exclusive system of licences,

[308] *Pfleger* (n 301), paras 59–60, affd in *Digibet* (n 98), paras 24, 31–32 and Case C-98/14 *Berlington Hungary and Others* EU:C:2015:386 (CJEU, 11 June 2015), paras 62, 90–91.
[309] Joined Cases C-186/11 and C-209/11 *Stanleybet* EU:C:2013:33, [2013] OJ C71/3.
[310] ibid, para 34.
[311] ibid, para 13.
[312] ibid, para 46.
[313] ibid, paras 44–45.
[314] ibid, paras 28–29.

provided that such reform would not hinder the level of consumer protection sought by the government (which was, again, a question that fell within the government's discretion). In the latter case, the principles of equal treatment and transparency would have to be observed. The licensing scheme had to be based on 'objective, non-discriminatory criteria which are known in advance, in such a way as to circumscribe the national authorities' discretion so that it is not used arbitrarily'.[315]

The *Stanleybet* judgment showcases the regulatory ambition of the Court's judgments. In addition to offering an interpretation of EU law in the given situation, the Court seems comfortable with presenting the government with concrete policy propositions whose implementation would bring the Greek measures into compliance with EU law. Moreover, the content of the Court's propositions makes clear that EU free movement law in no way obliges governments to liberalise their gambling sectors. Governments are allowed to maintain their preferred methods of regulation as long as they are consistent with the public interest objectives pursued.[316]

iv. Digibet

The relatively recent *Digibet* judgment demonstrates to what extent the assessment of the system's consistency is affected by the co-existence of different regional regulatory regimes in the territory of a Member State. The case concerned the German Interstate Treaty on Gambling of 2012, which prohibited the organisation and facilitation of online games of chance, save for exceptional circumstances in the case of lotteries and sporting bets. The issue in the case was, however, not the substantive content of the Treaty,[317] but the fact that one Land, Schleswig-Holstein, had not adhered to it and retained a different regulatory regime. In Schleswig-Holstein, the organisation of online games of chance was authorised provided that operators fulfilled certain conditions required by law. In 2013, Schleswig-Holstein decided to join the Interstate Treaty, but the licences that had already been granted remained valid for their entire duration of six years with the possibility of extension for another four years.

The CJEU held that 'even assuming that the more liberal legislation in Schleswig-Holstein may have undermined the consistency of the policy prohibiting games of chance in the other Länder, such damage to consistency was limited *ratione temporis* and *ratione loci* to a single Land'. Therefore, the legal regime in one Land could not be considered 'seriously' to affect the appropriateness of the restrictions applicable in all the other *Länder*. The Court's phrasing seems to indicate that if not for the temporal and geographical limitations, the German system would have been considered inconsistent.[318] However, this inference is far from definite, given that the Court used quite opaque language ('even assuming', 'may have') in its reasoning. More importantly, it emphasised that it was not calling into question the division of competences between

[315] *Stanleybet* (n 309), para 47.
[316] Affd, more recently, in C-336/14 *Sebat Ince* EU:C:2016:72 (CJEU, 4 February 2016), paras 54–55.
[317] The substantive aspects of the regime were considered in *Sebat Ince* (n 316).
[318] *Digibet* (n 98), para 36.

the *Länder*, which was protected under Art 4(2) TEU, obliging the EU to respect the national identities of the Member States inherent in their fundamental structures, including regional and local self-government.[319]

Digibet seems to suggest that the Court is prepared to take into account Member States' domestic constitutional arrangements when assessing the compatibility of their regulatory regimes with EU law. It will turn to the amendments introduced by the Lisbon Treaty, specifically Art 4(2) TEU, for support of this position.

D. The Special Case of Internet Gambling

The final category of the Court's decisions examines the specifics of the regulation of gambling on the Internet. The judicial review of national measures in this area seems to be premised on the perception that Internet gambling is more dangerous and more difficult to control than offline gambling. Accordingly, the Court is prepared to tolerate virtually any domestic regulatory measure in place unless it constitutes outright discrimination.

The case that best illustrates this approach is *Liga Portuguesa*. It was not the first case involving gambling on the Internet – *Gambelli* preceded it by almost six years – however, it produced the first judgment that focused on the specific nature of online gambling. The case concerned Portuguese legislation that reserved the right to operate online games of chance to a public company holding a monopoly on gambling since 1783.

It was argued that the monopoly system was not necessary because there were less restrictive means to ensure that operators would not engage in fraud and other criminal practices. The Court rejected this argument by agreeing with the government, which claimed that it did not have the means to control foreign online operators as effectively as an internal operator.[320] Referring to the specific features associated with gambling via the Internet, namely the lack of direct contact between consumer and operator, the Court observed that online gambling involved 'different and more substantial' risks of fraud compared with the traditional markets for games of chance.[321] Accordingly, the mere fact that a foreign operator was already subject to the controls of another Member State could not be regarded as amounting to 'sufficient assurance' that national consumers would be protected against the risks of fraud and crime.[322] Such conclusion was based on the fact that the authorities of the Member States of establishment of foreign operators were liable to encounter 'difficulties' 'in assessing the professional qualities and integrity of operators'.[323]

Liga Portuguesa stands in marked contrast with the *Gambelli* judgment. While in *Gambelli* the Court's conclusions about the (lack of) necessity of the Italian restrictions on foreign operators' access to the market were largely based on the fact that those

[319] *Digibet* (n 98), para 34.
[320] Case C-42/07 *Liga Portuguesa* EU:C:2009:519, [2009] ECR I-7633, para 68.
[321] ibid, para 70.
[322] ibid, para 69.
[323] ibid.

operators were already subject to statutory conditions and controls in their States of establishment,[324] this argument seems to be irrelevant in *Liga Portuguesa*. Quite the contrary, the Court takes the view that, at least in the context of online gambling, Member States may not have the general capacity to assess the professional qualities and integrity of operators established in their territories, hence, other Member States are entitled to subject them to their own regulatory regimes, even if that means simply the exclusion of the operator concerned from the market.[325]

A way to explain the difference between the two judgments is by looking at the nature of the regulatory system in question. In *Gambelli*, Italy organised its gaming and betting market through a licensing system, whereas the system challenged in *Liga Portuguesa* was a monopoly system, giving exclusive rights to operate games of chance to one body under the supervision of the State. This would suggest that the procedural requirements of proportionality that apply to non-exclusive licensing systems do not apply to public monopolies. The Court has recently confirmed this to be the case in the *Sporting Odds* judgment, which concerned the Hungarian licensing system for the operation of games of chance. Licences for the organisation of online gaming were reserved to operators running casinos in Hungary under a concession. So, like in *Gambelli*, access to the market for games of chance was reserved to operators situated on national territory.[326] The Hungarian licensing system was ruled discriminatory and thus incompatible with EU law.

E. The Regulatory Implications of the Case Law

i. *The Regulation of Gambling in the Internal Market: The Scope for Restrictive Measures*

To summarise the developments in the case law: the Court recognises that Member States enjoy broad discretion when regulating their gaming and betting markets, which in turn means that measures restricting gambling can in principle be justified in light of the various public interest considerations and that they will not be subjected to proportionality review in full force.

The Court's rationale behind the grant of a broad regulatory discretion to national authorities lies in the peculiar nature of the gambling sector. Gambling does not abide by market rules. Given the scale of earnings and potential winnings, it involves a high risk of fraud, money laundering and other criminal practices.[327] Furthermore, it incites consumers to spend, which may have damaging individual and social consequences. As a result of the controversy of the issues involved, legislation on gambling displays significant moral, religious and cultural differences between Member States. Yet a common

[324] *Gambelli* (n 281), para 74.

[325] Affd in *Ladbrokes* (n 297), paras 53–55. See also Case C-203/08 *Sporting Exchange & Others (Betfair)* EU:C:2010:307, [2010] ECR I-4695.

[326] Case C-3/17 *Sporting Odds* EU:C:2018:130 (CJEU, 28 February 2018), paras 36–44.

[327] *Läärä* (n 272), para 37; *Zenatti* (n 273), para 35.

regulatory response appears to restrict, or even prohibit, gambling activities in order to prevent them from being a source of private profit.

In light of the diversity of national regulatory approaches and in the absence of EU-wide harmonisation, the Court holds that it is for each Member State to determine, in accordance with its own scale of values as well as social and cultural features, what is required to protect the players and maintain order in society.[328] States can impose a complete or partial prohibition on gambling, create a system of non-exclusive licences, establish a monopoly on games of chance or opt for a combination of these measures. For instance, a Member State seeking to ensure a particularly high level of protection may take the view that the only way it can tackle the risks connected with the gambling sector effectively is by granting exclusive rights to a single entity controlled by the authorities.[329]

The Court has so far accepted most of the grounds of justification for restrictive measures, except for those of a purely economic, fiscal or protectionist nature.[330] The list of objectives deemed legitimate by the Court includes: the maintenance of the public order[331] and social order,[332] prevention of fraud, money laundering and other criminal activities,[333] prevention of incitement to squander money on gambling[334] and of the damaging individual and social consequences thereof,[335] protection of moral and cultural aspects of society,[336] and prevention of gambling from being a source of private profit.[337] Due to the substantive overlap between these various objectives, they are typically placed in one of the two categories – the protection of consumers or the maintenance of public order. However, all of the aforementioned objectives seem to serve the same purpose, that is, to protect consumers from gambling addiction and criminal and fraudulent practices.

To be justified in light of the legitimate public interest objectives, national measures must comply with the principle of non-discrimination and satisfy the requirement of proportionality.[338] An example of a discriminatory rule would be a requirement for the operators to have their seat in the Member State where services are provided.[339] The test of proportionality – in the way that it is applied in the context of gambling – mainly focuses on the suitability, or appropriateness, of the restrictive measures. National rules will be deemed suitable for ensuring the attainment of the objective pursued if they genuinely reflect a concern to attain it in a consistent and systematic manner.[340] The fact that games of chance are subject to different legal regimes – some being prohibited

[328] *Schindler* (n 266), para 61.
[329] *Stanleybet* (n 309), para 29.
[330] For examples of failed attempted justification grounds, see S Planzer, *Empirical Views on European Gambling Law and Addiction* (New York, Springer, 2014) 63–66.
[331] *Läärä* (n 272), para 31.
[332] *Schindler*, para 58.
[333] ibid, para 60; *Läärä*, para 32; *Zenatti* (n 273), para 30.
[334] *Stoss* (n 292), paras 20–22, 70; *Stanleybet*, paras 23, 29.
[335] *Schindler*, para 60; *Zenatti*, paras 30, 35.
[336] *Schindler*, para 60.
[337] *Placanica* (n 288), para 54.
[338] *Gambelli* (n 281), para 65.
[339] *Gambelli*, para 71.
[340] See, eg, *Gambelli*, para 67; *Liga Portuguesa* (n 320), paras 59–61; *Stanleybet*, para 27.

and some subject to a monopoly or licensing system – cannot in itself affect the consistency of the whole system because different games have different characteristics and so may require different forms of regulation.[341] However, if restrictions on the games that pose greater risk to consumers are milder than on other games, consistency may be jeopardised. It is not entirely clear whether the co-existence of different regulatory regimes among the constituents of a federal State undermines the consistency of the overall gambling policy. The answer may depend on the extent and temporal nature of the discrepancies between local regimes.[342] However, the judicial assessment in this case will be guided by the national identity clause, enshrined in Art 4(2) TEU, which protects regional and local self-government.

It has been suggested earlier that the same regulatory rules could be upheld in light of the objective of combatting crime but fail the consistency requirement in the context of consumer protection. However, when Member States invoke both objectives, the prevention of gambling addiction *and* the fight against fraud or crime, which they normally do, these objectives will be considered together. In this situation, national courts will have the task to determine whether public authorities have drawn a fair balance between demand for a controlled expansion of authorised games, in light of the objective of combatting fraud and crime, and the need to reduce as far as possible consumer addiction to such games.[343] In order for this balance to be struck, the marketing policy adopted by the authorities should be commensurate to the level of unauthorised gambling in the territory, and the advertising of games should be sensible and limited to what is necessary to channel the players' desire to gamble into activities that are lawful and regulated.[344]

Otherwise, the role of the necessity review is minimal. National authorities are not required to justify why they have chosen one regulatory model over another, perhaps a less restrictive one, because such choice falls within their margin of discretion. The proportionality of the system is assessed solely in the framework of the objectives and the level of protection pursued by public authorities. Accordingly, if the authorities decide to monopolise the sector, they need to make sure that, as pointed out above, they expand the supply of games of chance and advertise them insofar as is necessary to protect consumers from addiction and criminal behaviours on the part of the operators. If States opt for a licensing system, this system must comply with the procedural requirements of the principle of proportionality: it needs to be transparent[345] and based on objective, non-discriminatory criteria, capable of circumscribing administrative discretion.[346] For instance, if Member States exclude listed companies from the tendering process, such practice would be deemed disproportionate in light of the objective of combatting fraud.[347]

[341] Stoss (n 292), paras 94–96, recently affd in Case C-375/17 *Stanley International Betting Ltd* (CJEU, 19 December 2018), paras 49–53.
[342] *Digibet* (n 98), paras 34–36.
[343] *Ladbrokes* (n 297), para 32.
[344] ibid, paras 29–31, 34–35.
[345] See, eg, *Sporting Odds* (n 326), where the Court held that reserving the organisation of games of chance to operators that are considered 'trustworthy' fails the transparency criterion.
[346] *Stanleybet* (n 309), para 47.
[347] *Gambelli* (n 281), paras 71–74; *Sporting Odds*, paras 34–44.

ii. Implications for the Scope of National Regulatory Autonomy

The case law on gambling seems to be based on the premise that the specific nature of the gambling market makes its liberalisation undesirable and thus justifies regulatory intervention targeted at controlling the associated social risks. The position adopted by the Court, in turn, suggests that EU free movement law is capable of accommodating social and public policy concerns underlying national systems for the regulation of gambling. While in theory this position is welcome from the perspective of the protection of national regulatory autonomy, in practice it is prone to overlook domestic policies that are inconsistent with the objectives of consumer protection and may serve as a cover for protectionism.

a. The Rationale for National Margin of Discretion

At the core of the Court's approach, there lies the recognition that Member States have broad discretion when regulating their gaming and betting markets. The basis for this discretion seems to be two-fold: one, the religious and cultural aspects linked to gambling and, two, its socially and financially harmful consequences for the individual and society. In particular, the Court considers that the presence of undistorted competition in this very specific market would lead the operators to compete with each other in making their offers more attractive than their competitors and in that way would encourage consumers' expenditure on gaming and increase their risk of addiction.[348] Moreover, the free market would be incapable of preventing fraud, money laundering and other criminal practices conducted by the operators against consumers. The Court's language also appears to pass a moral judgment on gambling by describing it as a platform for 'squandering' money and one that should not be accepted as 'a source of private profit'.[349]

The conceptual basis for the Court's approach is not immune to challenge. As has been discussed in chapter two, academic literature advances a multitude of reasons for why Member States regulate gambling. The belief that market forces and general negligence laws are inadequate to protect consumers and society from the harmful effects associated with gambling is one of those reasons. However, a more plausible explanation suggests that the need to regulate gambling stems from the political sensitivity of the sector. From a purely economic point of view, governments have a significant financial interest in the profitability of the gambling sector because it generates significant revenues, derived from tax and State operation of games of chance.[350] However, culturally, gambling is widely perceived as dangerous and immoral, which makes the liberalisation of the gambling sector unpopular. In light of this, governments' interest in regulating gambling might stem not so much from a genuine concern about the social risks associated with gambling but rather from the need to counteract public perceptions about gambling in order to gain more widespread support for the industry among

[348] *Stanleybet* (n 309), para 45.
[349] The language referring to 'squandering money on gambling' was first used by the Court in *Gambelli* (n 281), para 67. For a detailed account of the morality aspect in the case law, see Planzer (n 330) 73–81.
[350] P Collins, *Gambling and the Public Interest* (Westport, Praeger Publishers, 2003) 66.

the general, non-gambling public.[351] Thus, by regulating, governments communicate to the public that this extremely profitable industry is, however, tightly controlled and socially responsible.[352]

In light of this, it could be suggested that in deferring to governments on the regulatory choices in the gambling market, the Court may be primarily protecting their financial interests vested in this industry rather than safeguarding the welfare of consumers and society.[353] This proposition seems highly plausible if one takes a closer look at the standard of judicial review employed by the Court in the gambling cases. It demonstrates an unusual tolerance towards regulatory frameworks which permit a policy of expansion in the gambling market whilst, at the same time, barring the entry to that market for foreign operators. This position is analysed in detail below.

b. The Scope of Discretion

The discretion accorded to national authorities manifests itself in various ways, but first and foremost, in choosing the specific regulatory model, from a complete prohibition of gambling activities to a non-exclusive licensing system. Member States' choices are, however, not unlimited. If the authorities decide to establish a monopoly on games of chance, they must exercise effective and strict controls over it. If, on the other hand, they opt for a more liberal model, such as a licensing system, they must ensure that it is transparent and non-discriminatory. In both cases, the requirements that public authorities must comply with are oriented towards the form, or procedure, rather than the content of national choices.

Accordingly, the proportionality review seems to be aimed primarily at counteracting protectionism rather than controlling the degree by which national rules restrict the free movement of companies operating in the European gambling market. This is evidenced by the minimal application of the test of necessity and a low standard of proof employed by the Court. As pointed out earlier, Member States are not required to show why an alternative, less restrictive regulatory model would not be feasible in the particular case, and the fact that systems of protection differ from one Member State to another is immaterial when assessing their proportionality.

The *Gambelli* and *Placanica* decisions seem to provide a narrow exception where the necessity test plays an important role. The conditions governing tender procedures for the grant of licences for the operation of games of chance cannot contain a blanket exclusion of companies quoted on the regulated markets. The authorities have to examine whether there are no other means of checking the accounts and activities of gaming operators for reliability. Apart from this specific circumstance, Member States are not required to trust the controls of other Member States or open up their markets to foreign operators just because they are subject to statutory regulation in their Member

[351] Collins (n 350) 66.

[352] ibid; Planzer (n 330) 73–81.

[353] In support of this view, see *Gambelli* (n 281), Opinion of AG Alber, para 126; V Yanchev, 'Between the Hammer and the Hard Place: European Gambling Regulation in the Post-Santa Casa Era' (2012) 23 *European Business Law Review* 213, 222.

States of establishment. The reason behind this view is, very generally, 'the difficulties liable to be encountered' by Member States when assessing the professional qualities and integrity of operators established in their territory.[354] As Yanchev points out, this approach seems to depart from the major part of the Court's case law on the freedom to provide services, where judicial inquiry focuses on eliminating situations that would make cross-border operators face a double regulatory burden.[355]

Moreover, the Court's reasoning seems to be incoherent, as it does not question the difficulties that may be encountered by State-controlled monopolies in regulating gambling, especially gambling on the Internet, which is deemed to be harder to control.[356] There is no compelling basis (at least the Court provides none) to assert that a public monopoly system will be more effective in this respect than a system allowing the participation in the market of certified private operators. To make that determination, the principle of necessity laid down in *Gambelli* would at least require that national authorities take into consideration the anti-fraud regulations applicable to the EU's licensed operators, keeping in mind that these regulations are aimed specifically at ensuring a high level of integrity of the operators and transparency and traceability over online gaming transactions.[357]

Finally, although the Court states that justifications invoked by Member States must be accompanied by an analysis of the proportionality of restrictive measures, the standard of proof required is low. The study conducted by Bogaert and Cuyvers concludes that the burden of proof almost appears to be reversed, with foreign operators having to prove that the system is not consistent instead of the other way around.[358] Indeed, the Court often endorses abstract, unsubstantiated government submissions, such as that online gambling market presents unique and greater dangers compared to other forms of gambling and other markets of the economy; that foreign gambling operators cannot effectively be supervised and controlled by their States of establishment; and that national measures can, in fact, achieve the objectives of consumer protection they set out to achieve.[359] Needless to say, there is little evidence to suggest that policies which involve active promotion of games of chance can realistically lead to a decrease in gambling addiction. Yet, the Court seems to take governments' claims at face value. It even gives explicit instructions to national courts that the absence of studies on the part of the authorities supporting the adoption of particular legislative measures is immaterial for the assessment of the proportionality of those measures.[360] The ultimate problem with the Court's approach seems to be that while some of the claims made by

[354] S Planzer, '*Liga Portuguesa* – the ECJ and its Mysterious Ways of Reasoning' (2009) 11 *European Law Reporter* 372.

[355] Yanchev (n 353) 223.

[356] See, eg, *Stoss* (n 292), paras 40, 84–87.

[357] On the standards and controls applicable to licensed gambling operators, see A Bujalski, 'ECJ Victory for Portuguese Gaming Monopoly' (2010) 16 *Computer and Telecommunications Law Review* 30; Yanchev (n 353) 224–29.

[358] S van den Bogaert and A Cuyvers, '"Money for Nothing": The Case Law of the EU Court of Justice on the Regulation of Gambling' (2011) 48 *CML Rev* 1175, 1191, 1204–06.

[359] Bogaert and Cuyvers (n 358) 1191, 1204–1206; *Liga Portuguesa* (n 320), paras 70–72; Planzer (n 354) 379–80.

[360] See, eg, *Stoss*, paras 70–72; *Pfleger* (n 301), para 51; *Sporting Odds* (n 326), para 63.

governments may well be true, they are rarely backed by empirical evidence, yet they often inform the Court's position on questions of law that decide the outcome of the case, such as the standard of proportionality review.

c. The Consistency Requirement and its Implications

The test of consistency, which underpins the case law, is, by definition, not meant to liberalise or dismantle national regulatory frameworks. Rather, it is targeted at identifying policies that are internally incoherent and may, therefore, be masking protectionism. However, because of the way it is interpreted by the Court, the consistency requirement may be inapt to achieve its very purpose.

The threshold for meeting this requirement seems to be low. One thing that is clear is that a policy that expands and actively promotes activities in the gambling sector cannot be reconciled with the objective of consumer protection. However, when in addition to consumer protection, States declare they are also aiming to reduce the scale of unauthorised gambling, the same policy of expansion will be tolerated despite its apparent conflict with the objective to protect players from spending and problem gambling. In this respect, public authorities will have to show that unlawful activity in their gambling market is significant and the measures adopted are designed to channel consumers' 'propensity' to gamble into activities that are lawful and regulated. Let us not forget that the standard of proof required to substantiate these claims is extremely low. Alternatively, the authorities may choose to refer exclusively to the objective of combatting crime, thus avoiding the limitations that consumer protection requirements impose on the marketing of games.[361] In this case, Member States will only have to demonstrate that the problem of clandestine gambling is real and serious enough to necessitate a more substantial expansion of the regulated gambling market.[362] It almost seems that the case law provides governments with guidelines on how to draft legislation in order to avoid it being struck down under EU law.

A restricted judicial approach at the EU level means that national courts are granted a lot of leeway when applying the Court's interpretations to the facts of the case. National courts are the ones to assess whether domestic legislation genuinely meets the consumer protection and public order concerns in light of the level of protection sought by the authorities. They are also the ones to determine whether national measures strike an appropriate balance between, on the one hand, the expansion of the sector, aimed at channelling gambling into controllable systems, and, on the other hand, the reduction of opportunities to gamble, aimed at preventing problem gambling. In this respect, Bogaert and Cuyvers observe that often the roles of the CJEU and national courts get reversed, with the CJEU duly following the observations and suggestions of the referring court.[363] In *Stoss*, for example, the Court endorsed the German court's suggestion that the system was inconsistent,[364] whereas in a factually similar situation in *Ladbrokes*,

[361] Cf *Placanica* (n 288) and *Stoss* (n 292).
[362] *Ladbrokes* (n 297), paras 29–30.
[363] Bogaert and Cuyvers (n 358) 1204. See also *Schindler* (n 266), paras 47–48; *Stanleybet* (n 309), para 13; *Pfleger* (n 301), para 49.
[364] *Stoss*, paras 20, 25, 39, 100, 106; Bogaert and Cuyvers (n 358) 1204.

it reached an opposite conclusion following the view of the Dutch court even though the consistency of the system was disputed by some of the parties.[365] Where the national court does not provide its assessment on the question of consistency, the Court either allows the restriction or refers the ultimate decision back to the national court.[366] It seems plausible that the Court's self-restraint is not isolated from political considerations. A more aggressive intervention might upset gambling arrangements in much of the EU and encourage further litigation, thus creating a risk of depriving Member States of a significant source of revenue.[367]

Institutional deference to national courts also suggests that the CJEU is prepared to accept discrepancies in the application of judicially developed rules in different jurisdictions. An empirical study conducted by the Swiss Institute of Comparative Law reveals that domestic courts in some Member States, including Germany, Italy, Sweden and the Netherlands, are more likely to dismiss government justifications for restrictive regimes where public gambling operators extensively advertise their services or regularly introduce new games. The Dutch and French courts, on the other hand, hold a position whereby an increase in the supply of games is not considered inconsistent with an otherwise restrictive gambling policy, as it serves as a countermeasure against illegal gambling.[368] As a result, essentially the same policy of gambling regulation may be considered legal in some Member States but not others.

Overall, the implications of EU free movement case law for national regulatory autonomy in the gambling sector seem to be relatively insignificant, especially if compared to implications for the healthcare, education and industrial relations systems. As a result of the broad regulatory discretion accorded to the Member States, even policies that are not entirely consistent with the objectives pursued by the governments can survive judicial scrutiny, especially if they are accompanied by a positive endorsement from the referring court. Whichever the decisive factor behind the Court's approach – the moral objections, real or perceived social risks associated with gambling, or the financial benefit to the public purse – the Court shows readiness to delegate the ultimate choices to national legislative, administrative and judicial authorities. Therefore, as long as a national regulatory system works adequately within its own frame of reference, virtually every rule will be considered as a lawful exception to the economic freedoms.

VI. The Implications of the Case Law for the Principles of Subsidiarity and Proportionality

The previous four sections examined case law developments in each of the areas under study, focusing on the implications of the case law for the regulatory autonomy

[365] *Ladbrokes* (n 297), paras 13, 38.
[366] See, eg, reasoning in *Pfleger* (n 301). See also Bogaert and Cuyvers (n 358) 1204–05.
[367] Bogaert and Cuyvers (n 358) 1209. See also Tridimas (n 43) 207; Yanchev (n 353) 227.
[368] Swiss Institute of Comparative Law, 'Study of Gambling Services in the Internal Market of the European Union' (Swiss Institute of Comparative Law 2006) 6 www.e-collection.isdc.ch/zoom/4362/view?page=6&p=separate&tool=info.

of the Member States. They demonstrated how the regulatory capacity associated with the judicial exercise of EU internal market competences, discussed in chapter one, manifests itself through the interpretation of free movement law. This section takes a comparative view of the case law and examines it in light of the principles of subsidiarity and proportionality. It demonstrates that the Court's observance of these principles has not been consistent across the four policy areas under study. Owing to a strict-scrutiny approach employed in relation to the areas of healthcare, education and labour law, but not gambling, the Court has reduced the scope of national regulatory autonomy in those areas to an extent incompatible with the principle of subsidiarity. In doing so, the Court has advanced the deregulatory element of the internal market to the point of undermining the social values whose protection falls within the scope of national regulatory autonomy, thus also departing from the principle of proportionality.

A. Subsidiarity

i. Subsidiarity in Judicial Reasoning

It was argued in section I that the exercise of EU internal market competences involves much more than simply the removal of obstacles to free movement or distortions of competition in the EU. Action taken by the EU under Art 114 TFEU and other functionally broad legal bases is often aimed at finding solutions to problems that lie at the heart of national regulatory policies, such as the protection of public health, consumer protection, worker protection and the maintenance of public security, amongst others. The principle of subsidiarity would require that the EU's capacity to solve these various problems effectively be weighed against the right of the Member States to address the issues concerned without external interference. In other words, the particular exercise of EU internal market competences has to be necessary in light of its potential impact on the scope of national regulatory autonomy in the area concerned.

It was further argued that the above considerations by and large apply to the *judicial* exercise of EU internal market competences in the form of the interpretation of EU free movement rules. The removal of obstacles to free movement through the judicial interpretation of the Treaties in reality means much more than just the advancement of free movement as such. Like EU legislation, the Court's judgments inevitably interfere with and shape domestic regulatory activity in a number of ways, as has been demonstrated through the analysis of the regulatory implications of the case law in the areas under study. The regulatory capacity associated with the case law should, therefore, be considered not as a mere externality of the judicial interpretation of free movement rules but, rather, an intended and integral part of the exercise by the Court of EU internal market competences. As such, it should be accounted for in light of the requirements of the principle of subsidiarity.

This does not mean that when interpreting the free movement rules, the Court should premeditate the various regulatory objectives that might be pursued by a particular interpretation of those rules in a given situation. Nor does it mean that the Court should weigh the potential costs and benefits of its interpretative choices in light of those objectives. This would entail making policy judgments that no court should be expected to make, at least not openly, when delivering a judicial interpretation of the law. However, the Court could, and should, be expected to pursue an interpretation of EU law that is sensitive to subsidiarity concerns. This would require that the Court advance the free movement law to a degree that is necessary in light of the impact of free movement law – or, specifically, the impact of the judicial interpretation of that law – on the scope of national regulatory autonomy. This can be achieved through adjusting the standard of judicial review employed to assess the validity of Member State justifications for restrictive measures.

The analysis of the case law under study demonstrates that the Court has systematically failed to take into account the requirements of subsidiarity in all but one of the areas under study. It has largely ignored government concerns about the effect of unrestricted free movement on national regulatory autonomy and pushed free movement law so far that tensions with subsidiarity have been created. The extent of the Court's respect for the principle of subsidiarity can be observed through comparing the standards of judicial review employed to assess the legality of national measures across the four areas. Notably, the Court accepts most of the reasons advanced by Member States as *in principle* capable of justifying a barrier to free movement. However, Member States are required to prove that a particular reason is valid in the circumstances of the case and that the restrictive measures taken are appropriate and necessary. It is exactly at this stage of judicial inquiry that major differences can be observed in cases concerning, on the one hand, healthcare, education and collective labour law and, on the other, gambling.

Whilst judgments concerning the first three areas under study display a close-scrutiny approach, the case law on gambling exemplifies a mild review, grounded in respect for the regulatory discretion of national authorities. The comparative inquiry suggests that the Court's reasoning in cases involving healthcare, education and collective labour law fails to consider the necessity of a particular judicial interpretation (and application) of the free movement rules in light of its impact on the scope of national regulatory autonomy. This indicates the Court's disregard of the requirements of subsidiarity.

ii. A Comparative Analysis of Judicial Compliance with Subsidiarity

a. Gambling

Virtually every judgment of the Court concerning gambling is premised on the recognition of the subsidiary nature of EU law and the role of the Court itself in supervising the regulatory choices of national authorities. The Court holds that each Member State is entitled to a margin of discretion to determine, in accordance with its own scale of values as well as social and cultural features, what is required in the regulation of gambling in order to protect consumers and maintain order in society:[369]

> [D]etermination of the scope of the protection which a Member State intends providing in its territory in relation to lotteries and other forms of gambling falls within the margin of appreciation which the Court, in paragraph 61 of *Schindler*, recognised as being enjoyed by the

[369] *Schindler* (n 266), paras 59–61.

> national authorities. It is for those authorities to consider whether, in the context of the aim pursued, it is necessary to prohibit activities of that kind, totally or partially, or only to restrict them and to lay down more or less rigorous procedures for controlling them.[370]

Due to the margin of appreciation accorded to national authorities, the proportionality review focuses on checking national rules for consistency rather than necessity. National authorities are not required to justify why they have chosen one regulatory model over another, perhaps less restrictive, model because such choice falls within their margin of discretion. The fact that one system of protection differs from a system adopted by other Member States has no bearing on the assessment of the need for, or proportionality of, the more restrictive system. The language of 'the least restrictive means' does not appear in the Court's reasoning.

A consistency-focused review means that the Court will not question the validity of each and every rule, or aspects of implementation thereof, as long as the regulatory system as a whole appears to be logically defensible. Accordingly, if the authorities decide to monopolise the gambling sector, they must exercise effective control over the monopoly, ensuring that the expansion of the gambling sector is commensurate to the scale of unauthorised gambling in the territory. This would be in line with the purpose of channelling consumers' 'propensity' to gamble into activities that are lawful and regulated. If, on the other hand, the authorities opt for a more liberal model, such as a licensing scheme, they must ensure the transparent and non-discriminatory character of the scheme.

An important aspect of the Court's review is that not only public authorities, but also national courts are granted considerable room for discretion when applying the Court's interpretative guidelines to the facts of the case. They are the ones to determine whether the regulatory system in question can be considered consistent in light of the objectives it pursues. To this end, national courts will evaluate whether national measures strike an appropriate balance between, on the one hand, the expansion of the sector, aimed at channelling gambling into controllable systems, and, on the other hand, the reduction of opportunities to gamble, aimed at preventing problem gambling. Case law analysis demonstrates that the CJEU will normally follow the observations and suggestions put forward by the referring courts on the question of consistency of domestic measures, and where those courts do not provide their view, the CJEU will either allow the restriction or refer the ultimate decision back to them.

Deference to both national authorities and national courts serves to ensure that final judgments adopted in the gambling cases are tailored to the specific social and cultural context of the Member State concerned. It also goes to show that the Court is prepared to tolerate a substantial degree of fragmentation of the internal market resulting from disparities in the regulation of the gambling sectors in different Member States. This, in turn, suggests two things: first, that the Court considers the systemic goals underlying national regulatory frameworks for gambling – namely, consumer protection and the preservation of order in society – to be more important than the individual economic freedoms of businesses operating in the EU's gambling market; second, that the regulatory diversity in the gambling sector, which is embraced in the name of subsidiarity,

[370] *Läärä* (n 272), para 35; *Zenatti* (n 273), para 33.

takes precedence over the goals of liberalisation pursued in the name of the internal market. This approach is exemplary of how the requirements of subsidiarity can be translated into context-sensitive judicial interpretation of free movement law.

b. Healthcare, Education and Collective Labour Law

The case law involving healthcare, education and collective labour law does not even remotely resemble the approach employed by the Court in judgments concerning gambling. Here, judicial review is focused on the necessity, as opposed to consistency, of domestic regulatory frameworks. Moreover, the Court usually takes an active role and provides detailed guidelines to national courts on how to apply the test of necessity in the circumstances of the case. It will not refrain from suggesting that there may be (hypothetical) less restrictive alternatives available in a given situation;[371] it will not hesitate to provide EU law definitions of key concepts which decide the lawfulness of Member State action, such as what constitutes a medically justifiable waiting time for hospital treatment;[372] and it will go on to instruct the courts on the standard of proof and the type of evidence that is admissible.[373] The guidelines provided by the Court often lead to only one conclusion, that is, that the national measures in question cannot be justified.

The Court's reasoning in all constitutionally sensitive areas under study – healthcare, education and collective labour law – seems to follow the same pattern. The Court will in principle accept the lawfulness of national measures restricting the free movement, thus implicitly recognising that Member States are entitled to a degree of national regulatory autonomy within the internal market. Yet, it will ultimately strike those measures down as unlawful after a detailed inquiry into their proportionality.

For example, the Court accepts that the requirement of prior authorisation for receiving inpatient medical treatment in other Member States is a reasonable and necessary measure, considering the need for planning and control of costs of hospital care. However, the Court will closely scrutinise the specific conditions attached to the grant of authorisation. Authorisation cannot be refused if equally effective treatment in the patient's home country is not available within a medically justifiable time. As previously discussed, the Court's interpretation of what constitutes a medically justifiable time focuses on the individual situation of the patient concerned. Therefore, a refusal to grant prior authorisation cannot be based merely on the existence of government-mandated waiting lists or predetermined clinical priorities. National authorities must take into account all the circumstances that help to determine the seriousness of the medical condition of the patient and the probable course of their illness. Where the waiting time for treatment appears to be excessive having regard, exclusively, to an objective medical assessment of the state of health and the clinical needs of the patient, virtually no consideration advanced by the government is capable of justifying the refusal to grant prior authorisation.

[371] See, eg, *Commission v Germany* (n 197), paras 53–56; *Commission v Austria* (n 130), para 61; *Bressol* (n 128), para 78, Opinion of AG Sharpston, para 105.

[372] *Smits and Peerbooms* (n 64), paras 94, 104; *Watts* (n 73), paras 62, 68, 119.

[373] See especially *Bressol*, paras 72–73, 76.

Proportionality review appears to be equally rigorous in the case law concerning cross-border access to education. On the one hand, the Court appears to be receptive to government concerns regarding the systemic problems associated with an uncontrollable influx of foreign students, namely, the impact on the quality of teaching and the system's capacity to produce a sufficient number of professionals ready to establish in the country. Yet concerns alone are not enough. They must be substantiated by specific and consistent evidence and accompanied by an analysis of the appropriateness and necessity of restrictive measures. Governments need to demonstrate, in the first place, that their concerns about the influx of foreign students are justified and, then, that the means employed to address those concerns are also justified. Accordingly, judicial review is heavily focused on scrutinising the evidence required to support the adoption of government policies. Furthermore, the Court takes the view that there might exist alternative, less restrictive measures capable of counteracting excessive demand for access to university programmes, which makes the task of proving the validity of the different measures chosen by the governments even more challenging.

Judgments concerning collective labour rights display a similar pattern of reasoning. The Court appears to accept, in principle, that in the achievement of social policy objectives, in particular, that of the protection of workers, Member States might legitimately restrict the freedom of movement of businesses operating in the internal market. However, in doing so, governments should choose the means that will have the least impact on the economic freedoms. In the context of collective labour relations, this means that strike action taken by trade unions will be unlawful unless invoked with the objective of securing employment conditions that are 'jeopardised or under serious threat' *and* there are no other, less restrictive means at the disposal of trade unions to convince the employer to enter into collective agreement on reasonable terms. Collective bargaining, on the other hand, is generally not considered as an appropriate or necessary method for regulating working conditions in transnational situations unless it produces universally or generally applicable collective agreements. A more flexible system of collective bargaining is viewed by the Court as insufficiently precise and accessible for businesses to be able to determine their obligations as employers. The language used by the Court suggests that the threshold for the exercise of collective labour rights to be justified in transnational situations is extremely high, if not insurmountable.

c. The Implications of the Standard of Judicial Review for Subsidiarity

One might question the relevance of the standard of judicial review as a means of measuring the Court's compliance with the principle of subsidiarity. In fact, the standard of review seems not only relevant but decisive. In order to understand why, we need to look into considerations that come into play when the Court performs a review focused on the necessity, as opposed to consistency, of national measures. The emphasis on a measure's necessity presupposes a type of inquiry that intrinsically prioritises individual interests over and often at the expense of the broader objectives of the system.[374] For

[374] For a thoughtful discussion of the problems arising from the judicial review of social policies, see G Davies, 'The Price of Letting Courts Value Solidarity: The Judicial Role in Liberalizing Welfare' in M Ross and Y Borgmann-Prebil, *Promoting Solidarity in the European Union* (Oxford, OUP, 2010) 106–22.

instance, in the context of the present analysis, the test of 'medical necessity' employed to assess whether treatment abroad should be covered by national governments sets aside social solidarity concerns as the predominant criterion in making decisions regarding the supply of public healthcare. The needs of an individual patient are thus prioritised over the objectives of the healthcare system as a whole. In a similar vein, a rigorous scrutiny of public decisions that limit the numbers of foreign students in national universities cuts to the heart of education policies based on the principles of open and free access to all citizens. Here, the rights of mobile students are prioritised over the systemic goals of national education policies. In order to maintain policies of open and free access, governments are forced to either sacrifice the level of quality of higher education or give financial injections into their systems. Finally, a case-by-case assessment of the necessity of trade union action in light of its impact on the free movement of businesses undermines the autonomy of collective bargaining, thus calling into question the very foundations underlying the operation of industrial relations systems. In this context, the commercial freedoms of businesses operating in the EU are prioritised over the collective interests of workers.

It could be argued, as a matter of policy or ideology, that a specific individual right or interest that is being advanced in the aforementioned situations should indeed override the objectives of the regulatory system as a whole. Yet those sorts of considerations have no role to play in the assessment of the judicial interpretation of free movement law in light of the principle of subsidiarity. The key consideration in this assessment is that the broader, systemic objectives, which are set aside in favour of the individual ones, will typically embody national regulatory prerogatives. As argued earlier, those prerogatives are exactly what the principle of subsidiarity is meant to protect through requiring that the implications for national regulatory autonomy be accounted for in the judicial interpretation of free movement rules. This requirement becomes of utmost importance in situations where the free movement law creeps upon the constitutionally sensitive areas of national policy. Consequently, when the standard of judicial review neglects or fails duly to consider the implications of unrestricted free movement for the scope of national regulatory autonomy, it also neglects the requirements embodied in the principle of subsidiarity. Conversely, when the standard of judicial review is construed to take into account the impact of free movement rules on the capacity of national governments to pursue their chosen regulatory objectives, as in the gambling sector, it will, by design, also preserve the requirements of subsidiarity.

The above analysis has explained the mechanism by which the standard of judicial review comes to determine the extent to which the Court observes the principle of subsidiarity in the free movement case law. It has demonstrated that a judicial review focused on the consistency of national restrictions of free movement can effectively accommodate the regulatory and policy choices of national governments. By doing so, it also preserves the diversity of the regulatory models existing in the EU. On the other hand, a judicial review focused on the test of necessity is prone to deprive Member States of a meaningful degree of regulatory autonomy in otherwise highly regulated areas of national policy. This approach subordinates the value of regulatory diversity to the goals of uniformity and effectiveness of EU law. The latter approach, which has been employed by the Court in the areas of healthcare, education and collective labour law, puts that case law at odds with the principle of subsidiarity, which requires taking into account the implications of the judicial interpretation of free movement law for the scope of national regulatory autonomy.

Moreover, the apparent contrasts between the standards of review employed in the gambling case law, on the one hand, and case law involving the rest of the areas under study, on the other, demonstrate that the Court is capable of accounting for the requirements of subsidiarity in the judicial interpretation of free movement law and has the means to do so by adjusting the intensity of judicial review. This brings into sharp relief the fact that the Court has systematically disregarded the principle of subsidiarity in the areas of healthcare, education and collective labour law.

B. Proportionality

i. Proportionality in Judicial Reasoning

Questions of proportionality are closely related to those concerning subsidiarity. As discussed earlier in this chapter, both principles protect national regulatory autonomy by ensuring that the EU regulatory intervention does not intrude disproportionately into the scope of national regulatory autonomy (subsidiarity) and the values protected within that scope of autonomy (proportionality). The following discussion argues that the case law under study departs from the requirements of proportionality because it establishes the sort of relationship between the economic and social values in EU law that is detrimental to the protection of the latter.

It was suggested in section I that the principle of proportionality in application to the judicial exercise of EU internal market competences requires that the Court take into consideration the impact of free movement rules – or the judicial interpretation thereof – on the non-market interests protected by national regulatory policies. It will be proposed in chapter five that judicial compliance with proportionality could be achieved by adopting a balancing approach, which would provide the Court with a methodological tool to limit EU-level judicial interference with the interests protected at the national level to what is necessary in light of the objectives of the internal market. The following analysis does not intend to look for the balancing approach in the case law under study. This is so because, arguably, there is no one formula that would determine the observance (or disregard) of the principle of proportionality in the judicial interpretation of EU law. The balancing approach is but one method to ensure the judicial compliance with this principle.

In light of the above, the purpose of the present discussion is to look for any elements in the Court's reasoning that would give an indication whether the Court has considered the impact of its interpretation of free movement rules on the protection of the various interests protected by national regulatory policies. There exist certain patterns of reasoning, which can be traced in the judicial review performed by the Court, that expose inconsistencies in the way that the Court treats public interests protected by domestic regulatory measures across the four areas under study. These inconsistencies suggest that the Court is aware of and considers the requirements of proportionality in its judgments, albeit it does so selectively.

ii. A Comparative Analysis of Judicial Compliance with Proportionality

a. Healthcare, Education and Collective Labour Law

As demonstrated earlier, the Court promotes an often-aggressive, deregulatory approach in the areas of healthcare, education and collective labour law, leaving little or no space for justification of national measures and thereby creating tensions with both subsidiarity and proportionality. As regards the observance of proportionality in particular, the aspect of judicial review that seems to expose the lack thereof most poignantly is the standard of proof required to justify restrictive measures. Together with the standard of review, the standard of proof employed by the Court determines the degree to which the Court advances the objectives of the internal market in relation to the various public and social interest considerations invoked by national governments.

If the standard of proof is low, governments will still have to give a plausible explanation as to why they believe their chosen regulatory goals and measures employed to achieve those goals justify a restriction on the freedom of movement. However, if the standard of proof is high, governments will in addition have to provide proof that every step taken in their decision-making process – from identifying the problem to choosing the regulatory means to address it – has, essentially, an undeniable justification. So, the difference between a low and a high standard of proof is that between a duty to provide a plausible explanation, on the one hand, and a duty to provide solid evidence supporting that explanation, on the other.

Not unexpectedly, the standard of proof appears to be particularly high in cases involving healthcare, education and collective labour law. In these cases, the Court requires that the government's case be supported by precise evidence.[375] The language that the Court uses in *Bressol* to assess the lawfulness of Belgian measures limiting foreign students' access to medical programmes offers a good illustration:

> The reasons invoked by a Member State by way of justification must thus be accompanied by an analysis of the appropriateness and proportionality of the measure adopted by that State and by specific evidence substantiating its arguments. […] Such an objective, detailed analysis, supported by figures, must be capable of demonstrating, with solid and consistent data, that there are genuine risks to public health.[376]

In particular, the data required by the Court needs to demonstrate that the future provision of healthcare in the territory of the Member State concerned is likely to suffer because of the diminished training capacity of health specialists. The analysis also has to account for the possibility that foreign students may decide to establish themselves in the State where they complete their studies, while some local students may choose to practise abroad. The standard of proof required seems to be extremely high considering that the link between education and the protection of public health is only indirect and depends on a variety of contingent and uncertain factors, as expressly recognised by the Court itself.[377]

[375] See, eg, *Commission v Luxembourg* (n 197), paras 51–53.
[376] *Bressol* (n 128), para 71. See also *Commission v Austria* (n 130), para 63.
[377] *Bressol*, para 69.

Specific evidence is also required to support the analysis of the appropriateness and necessity of a particular measure. For instance, Member States must provide various data and assessments showing that a limit on the number of non-resident students can really bring about an increase in the number of graduates ready to ensure the future availability of public health services within the territory. Furthermore, the Court tends to emphasise the existence of (often hypothetical) non-discriminatory alternatives that can help counteract the problems identified by governments, such as, in the case of education, an entry exam or a minimum grade requirement. Accordingly, Member States have to prove that their chosen measures are the least restrictive option capable of achieving the objectives pursued. The emphasis on the least restrictive option is also maintained in the case law involving the exercise of collective labour rights in transnational situations: a strike action will be lawful only if trade unions can prove that they have exhausted all other, less restrictive means to negotiate with the employer. This approach appears to show little, if any, consideration on behalf of the Court of potential disadvantages that unrestricted free movement may cause to the interests protected by national regulatory measures. Rather, it seems to suggest that in order to survive judicial scrutiny under EU law, those interests must be remoulded and tailored to fit the requirements of free movement.

b. Gambling

When faced with national regulatory rules on gambling, the Court accepts them insofar as they reflect a seemingly genuine concern on behalf of public authorities to protect consumers from gambling addiction and fraud. Member States are not required to prove that their chosen system of protection is the least regulatory one. Quite the contrary, the Court holds that

> [t]he mere fact that a Member State has chosen a system of protection different from that adopted by another Member State cannot affect the appraisal as to the need for and proportionality of the provisions adopted. They must be assessed solely in the light of the objectives pursued by the national authorities of the Member State concerned and of the level of protection which they seek to ensure.[378]

Remarkably, the standard of proof required to demonstrate that the regulatory system is internally consistent is extremely low. The Court often endorses abstract, unsubstantiated claims advanced by governments, such as that the online gambling market presents unique and greater dangers compared to other forms of gambling and other markets; that foreign gambling operators cannot effectively be supervised and controlled by their States of establishment; or that national measures will, in fact, achieve the objectives of consumer protection pursued by the government.[379] The Court even gives explicit instructions to national courts that the absence of studies on the part of the authorities supporting the adoption of particular legislative measures is immaterial for the

[378] *Läärä* (n 272), paras 36, 58; *Zenatti* (n 273), para 34.

[379] See, eg, *Liga Portuguesa* (n 320), paras 70–72. See also Planzer (n 354) 372; Bogaert and Cuyvers (n 358) 1191, 1204–1206.

assessment of the proportionality of those measures. The Court's ready acceptance of government claims is remarkable, considering that it will not hesitate to dismiss the same type of claims as unsubstantiated in cases involving other areas under study.

Let me illustrate this with a concrete example. The Court has consistently dismissed as unfounded governments' concerns about the quality of foreign healthcare provision. Since *Decker* and *Kohll*, it has taken a position that Member States cannot lawfully subject the purchase of medical goods and services from providers established in other Member States to a requirement of prior authorisation on the grounds that these goods and services do not afford the same quality standards as those provided at home. Governments are required to trust the quality standards applicable in other Member States. This is so because, as the Court points out, there exists an EU regulatory framework for the mutual recognition of professional qualifications, which covers the healthcare sector.[380] The existence of this framework means, according to the Court, that quality controls and professional guarantees applicable in the healthcare sector are 'equivalent' across the EU.[381] In that connection, it must be stressed that the EU's legal framework for the quality of healthcare rests solely on the mutual recognition of national standards and controls.[382] Apart from some guiding principles adopted by the Council, this framework contains neither a set of common quality standards applicable to healthcare providers established within the EU nor a mechanism for controlling the observance of the standards in force in the Member States.[383] Meanwhile, the Commission has officially recognised that there exist 'extensive national differences' in the quality of professional training and the medical skills and competencies of healthcare professionals.[384]

Now, against this background, consider the Court's approach towards similar concerns expressed by governments with regard to the regulation of the gambling sector. The Court holds that Member States are not required to open up access to their markets to foreign gambling operators just because these operators are subject to various standards and controls applicable in their Member States of establishment. The reason behind this view is, very generally, 'the difficulties liable to be encountered' by the Member States in assessing the professional qualities and integrity of operators established in their own territory. Accordingly, national authorities are justified in limiting or even barring foreign operators' access to their markets. The leeway that the Court is prepared to give to national authorities in this context is remarkable given that virtually every

[380] *Decker* (n 54), para 43; *Kohll* (n 55), para 48. See Council Directive 2013/55/EU amending Directive 2005/36/EC on the recognition of professional qualifications and Council Regulation (EU) 1024/2012 on administrative cooperation through the Internal Market Information System [2013] OJ L354/132.

[381] Case C-444/05 *Aikaterini Stamatelaki* EU:C:2007:231, [2007] ECR I-3185, para 37, referring to then applicable Council Directive 93/16/EEC to facilitate the free movement of doctors and the mutual recognition of their diplomas, certificates and other evidence of formal qualifications [1993] OJ 1993 L165/1.

[382] J Sylvest and C Adamsen, 'The Impact of the European Court of Justice Case Law on National Systems for Cross-Border Health Services Provision' (2007) Briefing Note, DG Internal Policies of the Union, 8 www.europarl.europa.eu/RegData/etudes/note/join/2007/382184/IPOL-IMCO_NT(2007)382184_EN.pdf.

[383] Council, 'Council Conclusions on Common values and principles in European Union Health Systems' [2006] OJ C146/1.

[384] Commission, 'Proposal for a Directive of the European Parliament and of the Council on the application of patients' rights in cross-border healthcare' COM (2008) 414 final, Explanatory Memorandum, 11. See also Commission, 'Communication from the Commission on effective, accessible and resilient health systems' COM (2014) 215 final.

single EU Member State has anti-fraud regulations applicable to licensed gambling operators. These regulations are aimed specifically at ensuring a high level of integrity of gambling operators and the transparency and traceability over online gaming transactions.[385] Needless to say, the Court's approach sits in marked contrast with that employed in relation to the regulation of healthcare. Yet there seems to be no apparent reason why Member States should place a high degree of trust in the effectiveness of foreign regulations in the healthcare sector but not the gambling sector.

c. The Nature of the Restrictive Measure

There is one more, final point to make. It could be argued that differences in the standard of judicial review and standard of proof observed in the case law across the areas under study may be explained by the nature of the contested measures. Specifically, judicial scrutiny might be more intense when the national rule in question is discriminatory as opposed to being merely restrictive, that is, indistinctly applicable. This could explain, for example, why the Court is particularly strict in the application of the proportionality test in cases concerning the mobility of patients and students. Authorisation schemes for medical treatment to be obtained in other Member States are specifically targeted at *foreign* healthcare provision. Measures limiting students' access to higher education are aimed at reducing the number of *foreign* students applying to local universities. Does this mean that the Court simply has low tolerance for discriminatory measures? The gambling case law seems to provide some support for this proposition. The Court is certainly more principled in the application of proportionality review to regulatory measures that mask blatant discrimination against foreign gambling operators, such as the requirement of having a company seat in the Member State concerned.[386] However, the judicial review of those measures still remains procedural and fairly deferential, unlike in cases concerning cross-border access to healthcare or education. It is grounded in the respect for national regulatory discretion and requires equal treatment *only if* the government decides to open up its market to foreign operators. If, on the other hand, it decides simply to exclude foreign operators from the market and instead organise gambling services through a system of exclusive licences, granted to specific national operators, it can legitimately do so. This suggests that whilst the discriminatory nature of the contested measure might have some role to play in determining the intensity of the proportionality review in the gambling sector, that role should not be overestimated.

Moreover, the nature of the contested measure cannot explain the high scrutiny approach employed by the Court in relation to the exercise of collective labour rights. The collective regulation of employment and working conditions, including in cross-border situations, can hardly be considered to have a discriminatory intent or effect. It is typically aimed at the protection of workers irrespective of their origin and is predominantly concerned with ensuring a consistent application of national labour standards in the territory of the Member State concerned. It targets all businesses, local and foreign. Notwithstanding this, the Court's review of collectively set conditions of labour and employment, and of trade union action as such, is extremely rigorous. This clearly

[385] Bujalski (n 357); Yanchev (n 353) 224–29.
[386] See, eg, *Gambelli* (n 281), paras 71, 73–74.

demonstrates that the nature of the contested measure, whether discriminatory or not, cannot account for differences in the standard of review across the areas under study.

C. Is Gambling More Special?

As is clear from the above analysis, the argument advanced in this chapter regarding the Court's compliance with the principles of subsidiarity and proportionality relies on exposing sharp discrepancies in the standard of judicial review and standard of proof employed in relation to the areas of healthcare, education and collective labour law, on the one hand, and gambling, on the other. This prompts an important question: does there exist a compelling reason that would allow the Court to distinguish gambling as a unique policy area which requires a more deferential judicial approach? Let us explore this possibility.

The Court's position in relation to gambling seems to be premised on the recognition that the gaming and betting market is too politically and socially sensitive to be subjected to the full force of free movement rules. Accordingly, judicial review is aimed at counteracting overt protectionism rather than controlling the degree to which national rules restrict the free movement of companies operating in the EU's gambling market. The judicial logic here seems to be reasonable and appropriate: the political and social sensitivities surrounding the gambling sector justify the exercise of judicial deference on behalf of the Court. It is, however, noteworthy that, as argued in section V, the Court often fails to counteract protectionism in this sector by exercising judicial deference even in cases where the evidence that would attest to the consistency of the regulatory framework in question is clearly lacking. This goes to show that a restricted judicial approach to the regulation of gambling is not immune to challenge.

What is, however, more significant and often overlooked by the Court is that the political and social sensitivities that underpin domestic regulatory action in the gambling sector equally pertain to the areas of healthcare, education and collective labour law. This chapter has firmly established this to be the case through a comparative analysis of the case law across the areas under study. The grounds that governments put forward to justify regulatory action in all of those areas are underpinned by considerations of social solidarity and the need to protect vulnerable groups. Moreover, as discussed in chapter two, the areas of healthcare, education and collective labour law also carry additional sensitivity for constitutional reasons: unlike gambling, they fall outside the EU's explicit legislative competence. Therefore, it appears that the case for judicial deference in relation to the areas of healthcare, education and collective labour law is stronger than in the case of gambling. In light of this, there seems to be no valid general reason why the Court would differentiate between the four policy areas by employing standards of review that are on the opposite ends of the spectrum of intensity.

In conclusion, the inconsistencies in the free movement case law involving the four areas under study suggest that the Court is aware of the implications of its judgments for national regulatory autonomy and the protection of the interests rooted in that autonomy. In other words, the Court is aware of the tensions with the principles of subsidiarity and proportionality that might arise from the judicial interpretation of the Treaties. The gambling case law suggests that the Court is capable and willing to avoid those tensions. The problem, however, is that the Court does so selectively and only in relation to certain policy areas which it considers as more sensitive than others, albeit with no solid basis – conceptual or constitutional – for such distinctions. This compels the conclusion that the free movement case law involving healthcare, education and collective labour law is inconsistent with the principles of subsidiarity and proportionality.

VII. Conclusion

This chapter evaluated the interpretation by the Court of free movement rules in the areas under study for compliance with the principles of subsidiarity and proportionality. It argued that the judicial exercise of EU internal market competences includes much more than simply the removal of obstacles to free movement or distortions of competition in the EU. Just like EU legislation, the Court's judgments inevitably interfere with and shape domestic regulatory choices in a number of policy areas, as has been demonstrated through the analysis of the regulatory implications of the case law in the areas under study. The regulatory capacity associated with the case law should, therefore, be considered not as a mere externality of the judicial interpretation of free movement rules but, rather, an intended and integral part of the exercise by the Court of EU internal market competences. As such, it should be accounted for in light of the requirements of the principles of subsidiarity and proportionality.

The chapter demonstrated that the observance (or a lack thereof) by the Court of the principles of subsidiarity and proportionality manifests itself at the stage of the judicial inquiry into the justification of national measures. The Court's reasoning at this stage is what determines the space left for Member State regulatory action in the situation concerned. It also reveals the extent to which the Court chooses to exercise EU internal market competences in relation to the areas that are constitutionally and/or politically sensitive. If the Court employs a high standard of review of national restrictions of free movement, the scope of national regulatory autonomy is significantly reduced. If it opts for a deferential review, the space for autonomous decision making at the Member State level is preserved.

The comparative case law analysis revealed inconsistencies in the way that the Court treats the four areas under study. It employs a strict-scrutiny approach, focused on the test of necessity, in relation to national measures in the areas of healthcare, education and labour law, thereby showing little, if any, consideration of government concerns about the effect of unrestricted free movement on national regulatory autonomy and the interests whose protection is rooted in the exercise of that autonomy. By contrast, when faced with national gambling regulations, the Court adopts a low standard of review, focused on examining the consistency of national measures and grounded in respect for the regulatory discretion of national authorities.

The judicial approach to the regulation of gambling suggests that the Court is aware of and considers the requirements of subsidiarity and proportionality in its judgments, albeit it does so selectively. The chapter argued that this selectivity has no conceptual basis and that the discrepancies in the standard of review employed by the Court across the areas under study cannot be justified by the peculiarity of the gambling sector. The political and social sensitivities surrounding the gambling sector are comparable to those pertaining to the areas of healthcare, education and collective labour law. Moreover, the latter areas require special consideration for constitutional reasons: unlike gambling, they fall outside the EU's explicit regulatory competence. Against this background, the chapter has concluded that the free movement case law involving healthcare, education and collective labour law is inconsistent with the principles of subsidiarity and proportionality.

4

The Horizontal Balance of Powers

The Implications of Free Movement Case Law for the Principle of Institutional Balance

Constitutional principles that govern the scope and exercise of EU competences and institutional powers are interconnected. At their core, they all protect the regulatory autonomy of the Member States, thereby providing key support for the EU's federal balance of competences.[1] As a consequence, a departure by the Court from one of these principles will have implications for the observance of the others. Similarly, an imbalance in the vertical division of competences in the EU created by the case law will inevitably have an impact on the horizontal balance of powers between the EU's governing branches, namely the legislature and judiciary.

It has been suggested in chapter two, concerning the principle of conferral, that by adopting an expansive interpretation of the scope of the provisions of the Treaties, the Court also expands the lawmaking competences of the EU, thus creating further tensions with the principle of conferral at the legislative level. Paradoxically, while doing so, the Court also narrows down the margin of legislative discretion available to the EU's legislative institutions. This chapter illustrates this pattern of interaction between the Court and the legislature through the analysis of concrete legislative developments that have taken place in light of the case law. Ultimately, it argues that the case law in the areas under study has upset the institutional balance of powers in the EU because it created an interinstitutional dynamic, described here as a 'judicial trap', which has deprived the legislature of its constitutional lawmaking prerogative.

The chapter follows in seven sections. Section I discusses the meaning and content of the principle of institutional balance in EU law and examines the requirements it imposes on the judicial interpretation of internal market law. Section II introduces the concept of a quasi-legislative judgment, which exposes the regulatory ambition of the case law and helps to understand how it shapes EU legislative activity. Section III discusses the difficulties surrounding EU legislative process in situations where the legislative solution sought involves a constitutionally sensitive area that has already been regulated through the case law. In light of this analysis, sections IV–VI demonstrate that

[1] See ch 1, s I for a discussion of the importance of the principles under study for the federal balance of competences in the EU.

the case law in the areas under study has created an interinstitutional dynamic that has distorted the institutional balance of powers between the EU legislature and judiciary. It has done so by trapping the legislature into the choice of legislative options inadequate to remedy the case law in any meaningful way and by neutralising the legal effects of existing legislative solutions. This dynamic is illustrated through a discussion of three distinct models of judiciary–legislature interaction that have developed in light of the case law. Section VII concludes.

I. The Principle of Institutional Balance in Application to the Court

The discussion below begins with the analysis of the meaning and normative content of the principle of institutional balance in EU law and then turns to examining the requirements that this principle imposes on the judicial interpretation of internal market law.

A. The Legal Parameters of the Principle of Institutional Balance

The principle of institutional balance requires that EU institutions act within the scope of the powers conferred upon them by the Treaties and not encroach on the powers assigned to other institutions. It thus includes a positive obligation, requiring institutions to stay within the scope of their powers, and a negative obligation, requiring not to encroach on the powers of other institutions. The principle of institutional balance is specific to the EU, but the concept itself has been inspired by the principle of separation of powers applicable in national legal orders.[2] However, contrary to the national system of the separation of powers, the requirement for powers to be distributed at the EU level is not as such aimed at the protection of individuals against the abuse of power by the governing institutions.[3] Rather, its specific and primary purpose is to ensure that the balance among the powers of EU institutions established in the Treaties is maintained.[4] In this regard, the EU's conception of separation of powers seems to resemble Waldron's theory of articulated governance, or the functional separation of powers. For Waldron, the value of separation of powers lies in preserving the integrity of the individual branches of government and ensuring that each performs the distinctive functions it is best placed and equipped to perform.[5] This theory appears to embody the efficiency rationale behind the principle of separation of powers, which emphasises the importance of a smooth running of the State and to that end requires that branches of

[2] J-P Jacqué, 'The Principle of Institutional Balance' (2004) 21 *CML Rev* 383, 384; G Conway, 'Recovering a Separation of Powers in the European Union' (2011) 17 *European Law Journal* 304.

[3] For the traditional rationale behind the separation of powers, see, eg, J Madison, 'No. 47' in J Madison, A Hamilton and J Jay, *The Federalist Papers* (I Kramnick ed, London, Penguin Books, 1987).

[4] Jacqué (n 2). See also Case C-282/90 *Industrie-en Handelsonderneming Vreugdenhil BV v Commission* EU:C:1992:124, [1992] ECR I-1937, paras 20–21. On the link between separation of powers and liberty, see especially Montesquieu, *The Spirit of the Laws* 157 (AM Cohler et al eds and trans, Cambridge, CUP, 1989).

[5] J Waldron, 'Separation of Powers in Thought and Practice' (2013) 54 *Boston College Law Review* 433.

government be matched to the functions they are best suited for.[6] The EU's separation of powers, expressed through the principle of institutional balance, may be appropriately grounded in this rationale.[7]

From a systemic point of view, the principle of institutional balance seems to mirror the concerns associated with the principle of conferral. If an EU institution acts in disregard of the constraints inherent in the principle of institutional balance, by definition, it exercises more power than the Treaties confer upon it. In reality, this often means that in addition to upsetting the balance of powers on the horizontal, EU level, the institution concerned also disturbs the vertical balance of competences between the EU and Member States by interfering without a legitimate basis with the affairs of the latter.[8] Moreover, an *ultra vires* action by an EU institution often implicates the EU as a whole, meaning that the EU, as an organisation, finds itself in *ultra vires* of its competences. The principle of institutional balance is designed to prevent a situation like that from arising by ensuring that each institution of the EU stays *intra vires*. Thus, in a real sense, it protects the terms of the principle of conferral but does so in relation to the specific powers of the EU's institutions rather than the competences of the EU as a whole.[9]

The principle of institutional balance has been enshrined in the Treaties since the creation of the EEC, whose Art 4(1) stipulated that the tasks entrusted to the Community shall be carried out by its institutions, which 'shall act within the limits of the powers conferred upon [them] by this Treaty'.[10] The current version of this provision, contained in Art 13(2) TEU, maintains wording almost identical to the original and adds that '[t]he institutions shall practise mutual sincere cooperation'.[11] The cooperation aspect can also be found in the national conceptions of the principle of separation of powers. It highlights the presence of interdependence among the governing branches, which, in turn, presupposes the need for cooperation among them. Essentially, it means that whilst each branch carries out its respective functions, all branches must take account of the role and responsibilities of the other branches because they must work together towards the broader objectives of good governance.[12]

It is remarkable that Art 13(2) TEU and its predecessors have so far been discussed in the case law of the CJEU and academic literature mainly in relation to the distribution of powers among the legislative organs of the EU, that is, the Commission, Council

[6] N Barber, 'Prelude to the Separation of Powers' (2001) 60 *Cambridge Law Journal* 59, discussing relevant accounts.

[7] To that end, see C-101/08 *Audiolux* EU:C:2009:626, [2009] ECR I-9823, Opinion of AG Trstenjak, para 104.

[8] As illustrated by Case C-70/88 *Parliament v Council* EU:C:1990:217, [1990] ECR I-2041 (*Chernobyl*), discussed below.

[9] For comparison, see, eg, BR Clark, 'Separation of Powers as a Safeguard of Federalism' (2001) 79 *Texas Law Review* 1321, discussing the role of horizontal separation of powers in safeguarding US federalism. See also Case C-425/13 *Commission v Council* EU:C:2015:483 (CJEU, 17 March 2015), paras 75, 95, and Opinion of Advocate General Wathelet, para 103, linking institutional balance with the principle of conferral.

[10] Treaty establishing the European Economic Community (adopted 25 March 1957, entered into force 1 January 1958) (EEC), Art 4(1).

[11] Consolidated version of the Treaty on European Union [2008] OJ C115/13 (TEU), Art 13(2).

[12] A Kavanagh, 'The Constitutional Separation of Powers' in D Dyzenhaus and M Thorburn (eds), *Philosophical Foundations of Constitutional Law* (Oxford, OUP, 2015) 228ff, analysing the role of interinstitutional cooperation in the national systems of separation of powers.

and Parliament.[13] The provision has not gained much attention, scholarly or judicial, in the context of the distribution of powers between the EU legislature and judiciary. The principle of institutional balance was first mentioned in the case law as early as in 1958 in the *Meroni* judgment,[14] where the Court was asked to decide to what extent EU institutions could delegate their tasks to regulatory agencies. The Court took this opportunity to pronounce on the meaning of institutional balance. It stipulated that the balance of powers, characteristic of the institutional structure of the Community, required of its institutions to pursue Community goals whilst acting 'within the limits of their respective powers'.[15] Accordingly, any delegation of powers could 'only relate to clearly defined executive powers, the use of which must be entirely subject to the supervision of the [delegating authority]'.[16] With this ruling, the Court made clear that the principle of institutional balance was not merely declaratory and, therefore, could be enforced through judicial means.

It was, however, not until the *Chernobyl* case that the Court fully fleshed out the content of the principle of institutional balance. The case concerned a challenge brought by the European Parliament against a Council Regulation which had been allegedly adopted using the wrong legal basis and thus had failed to involve the Parliament through the cooperation procedure. At that time, the Treaties did not contain a provision allowing the Parliament to bring an action for annulment in this situation. Regardless, the Court ruled:

> The Treaties set up a system for distributing powers among the different Community institutions, assigning to each institution its own role in the institutional structure of the Community and the accomplishment of the tasks entrusted to the Community. Observance of the institutional balance means that each of the institutions must exercise its powers with due regard for the powers of the other institutions. It also requires that it should be possible to penalize any breach of that rule which may occur.[17]

In light of this, the Court held that the Parliament had *locus standi* in order to defend its Treaty-assigned prerogatives in the adoption of Community legislation. The judgment thus secured the protection of the right of the Parliament, and of EU citizens through that parliament, to participate in EU political decision making.[18] But the role that the principle of institutional balance played in *Chrenobyl* was broader than that. By precluding a regulation that was adopted using the wrong legal basis, the principle of institutional balance also protected the regulatory autonomy of the Member States from an *ultra vires* encroachment by one of the EU institutions, the Council in this case.

[13] P Craig, 'Democracy and Rule-Making within the EC: An Empirical and Normative Assessment' (1997) 3 *European Law Journal* 105; Y Devuyst, 'The European Union's Institutional Balance after the Treaty of Lisbon: "Community Method" and "Democratic Deficit" Reassessed' (2008) 39 *Georgetown Journal of International Law* 249, 306–08; B Smulders and K Eisele, 'Reflections on the Institutional Balance, the Community Method and the Interplay between Jurisdictions after Lisbon' (2012) College of Europe, Department of European Legal Studies Research Paper 04/2012 aei.pitt.edu/39285.

[14] Case C-9/56 *Meroni* EU:C:1958:7, [1958] ECR 133.

[15] ibid, para 152.

[16] ibid.

[17] *Chernobyl* (n 8), paras 21–22, 26–27.

[18] On the participation of European peoples in EU decision making through the Parliament, see Case C-138/79 *Roquette Frères* EU:C:1980:249, [1980] ECR I-3333, para 33.

This demonstrates the importance of the principle of institutional balance in preserving the requirements of the principle of conferral at the horizontal, EU level.

B. The Principle of Institutional Balance as a Limit to Judicial Lawmaking

If institutional balance is meant to ensure that EU institutions do not exceed the scope of their powers, the question is: how does one determine the outer limit of the powers of the CJEU, in particular, in relation to the powers of the EU legislative institutions? As discussed in chapter one, the Court's remit under Art 19 TEU is formulated extremely broadly, which suggests that the Court is a relatively autonomous institution and, as such, enjoys a degree of discretion when performing its interpretative functions. But, crucially, how far does this discretion go? Where does it end?

These questions do not have clear-cut answers, as demonstrated by analysis of the Opinion of AG Trstenjak in the *Audiolux* case. In that case, the Court was asked to decide whether (then) Community law recognised the existence of a general principle of equal treatment of minority shareholders upon a transfer of control. This proposition was based on the fact that there existed Community legislation that laid down certain provisions relating to the protection of minority shareholders. In her Opinion, AG Trstenjak suggested, generally, that institutional balance required that judicial discretion be subject to the requirement to respect the rule-making role of the EU legislature. This proposition seems to reflect the Court's language in *Chernobyl*, whereby each of the institutions must exercise their powers with due regard for the powers of the other institutions. In the circumstances of *Audiolux*, this meant, according to AG Trstenjak, that the Court was required to exercise 'the necessary self-restraint in developing general principles of EU law which might possibly run counter to the legislature's aims'.[19] In other words, the Court was not supposed to 'assume the role of the Community legislature if a gap in the law [could] be filled by the Community legislature'.[20] The Court ruled that EU law did not contain a general principle of equal treatment of minority shareholders. However, it never endorsed the view of AG Trstenjak on the meaning of the principle of institutional balance as applied to the Court, and rightly so.

The restrictive approach suggested by AG Trstenjak does not seem to be suitable for defining the limits of judicial action at the EU level. Given the breadth of the Court's mandate under Art 19 TEU and the breadth of the legislative mandate under the functionally broad legal bases,[21] a degree of overlap between the powers of the two institutions is both inevitable and constitutionally justified. After all, the Court, as the interpreter of the Treaties, lays down the principles that guide the EU legislature in the

[19] *Audiolux* (n 7), Opinion of AG Trstenjak, para 107.

[20] ibid. See similar suggestions put forward in relation to areas already covered by EU legislation in P Craig, *EU Administrative Law* 2nd edn (Oxford, OUP, 2012) 519–20; P Syrpis, 'EU Secondary Legislation and Its Impact on Derogations' in P Koutrakos, N Shuibhne and P Syrpis (eds), *Exceptions from EU Free Movement Law* (Oxford, Hart Publishing, 2016) 287–92.

[21] For a discussion on the functionally broad legal bases, see ch 2, s I.

adoption of legislative acts.[22] For instance, the Court ruled in *Brasserie du Pêcheur* that the principle of institutional balance did not prevent it from recognising the existence in Community law of a general right of compensation for breaches of that law, even in the absence of Community legislation on the matter.[23] This goes to show that neither the Treaties nor the judicial interpretation thereof prioritise the role of one institution over another – that is, the legislature over the judiciary, or vice versa – in filling 'gaps' in EU law, to use the phrasing of AG Trstenjak.

The interaction between the EU legislature and judiciary and, specifically, the interference by the latter into the lawmaking function of the former, appears justified also as a matter of constitutional theory. On the one hand, the judicial interpretation of the Treaties provides orientation for the EU lawmaking process by clarifying the meaning and contours of EU law. This increases the efficiency of political decision making at the EU level and contributes to a smooth governance of the EU, in line with the efficiency rationale behind the principle of the separation of powers. On the other hand, the Court's interference into EU lawmaking allows it to perform a check on the EU's legislative branch, thus ensuring – typically through the means of judicial review – the compliance of EU legislation with the Treaties and general principles of EU law. This practice serves the 'checks and balances' function of the separation of powers, which is inherent in virtually all modern conceptions of this principle.[24]

If a degree of interference by the judiciary into the legislative function is both constitutionally justified and desirable from the point of view of efficiency and legitimacy of EU decision making, at what point does this interference become too great to be compatible with the principle of institutional balance? What is the limit that the principle of institutional balance imposes on the judicial interpretation of the Treaties? The task of determining that exact limit is a challenging one because the principle of institutional balance is not phrased as a hard rule. However, my understanding is that in order to determine how institutional balance constrains judicial lawmaking, one has to identify the point beyond which the judicial guidance provided by the Court to EU legislative institutions no longer serves the objectives of this principle, viewed in light of the precepts of the separation of powers described above.

In that respect, the theory of checks and balances would suggest that judicial guidance to the legislature cannot result in the usurpation by the judiciary of the core of the legislative function. Therefore, it would appear unacceptable if the Court were to extend judicial powers to the detriment of the legislative prerogative, that is, to an extent that would prevent any meaningful exercise of the legislative powers. Such practice would neither increase the efficiency nor legitimacy of EU lawmaking. Rather, it would create

[22] See, eg, D Sindbjerg Martinsen, *An Ever More Powerful Court? The Political Constraints of Legal Integration in the European Union* (Oxford, OUP, 2015) 67–71, analysing legislative developments in discrimination law following case C-43/75 *Defrenne* [1976] ECR 455.

[23] Joined Cases C-46/93 and C-48/93 *Brasserie du Pêcheur* EU:C:1996:79, [1996] ECR I-1029, paras 24–27; K Lenaerts and A Verhoeven, 'Institutional Balance as a Guarantee for Democracy in EU Governance' in C Joerges and R Dehousse (eds), *Good Governance in Europe's Integrated Market* (Oxford, OUP, 2002) 35, 46.

[24] On how the checks and balances fit within the concept of separation of powers, see, eg, G Marshall, *Constitutional Theory* (Oxford, Clarendon Press, 1971) 102–03; J Madison, 'No. 51' in J Madison, A Hamilton and J Jay, *The Federalist Papers* (C Rossiter ed, New York, Penguin Putnam, 1999) 276–93; Kavanagh (n 12) 233ff.

a legal situation that the principle of institutional balance exactly aims to prevent: where the actions of one institution undermine the prerogatives assigned by the Treaties to other institutions.[25]

In light of this, I would argue that Art 13(2) TEU should be read as preventing the type of exercise of judicial powers of interpretation which would nullify the legislative discretion accorded to EU legislative institutions. In the context of the present study, this means that the Court should refrain from construing the free movement rules in a way that would undermine the discretion that the legislature enjoys in the regulation of the internal market. In other words, the judicial interpretation of free movement law should not go so far as to place the Court in a position of a political decision maker with the consequence of de facto taking that power away from the EU legislature.[26]

It might be difficult to visualise at this point what it means to nullify legislative discretion and how the principle of institutional balance thus construed works in practice. That is the task for the remainder of this chapter, which applies the theoretical framework provided by the principle of institutional balance to examine the constitutional legitimacy of the free movement case law under study in light of its interaction with EU legislative activity.

II. The Process of Judicial Lawmaking: Quasi-Legislative Judgments

Chapter one argued that the structure of the EU endows the Court with a regulatory capacity characteristic of that possessed by bodies which exercise political authority on behalf of the State, in particular, legislative and executive institutions. One of the main ways in which the Court exercises this regulatory capacity is through the interpretation of EU internal market law. Chapter three demonstrated this by the analysis of the implications of the Court's free movement case law for national regulatory autonomy in four constitutionally and/or politically sensitive areas of national policy. In light of that analysis, the following discussion introduces the concept of a quasi-legislative judgment as a primary source of the regulatory implications of the case law. The concept of a quasi-legislative judgment also helps to understand the mechanism by which the case law comes to shape the institutional balance of powers between the EU legislature and judiciary.

The term 'quasi-legislative' is typically used to describe the rule-making authority granted to public administrative bodies in the exercise of their statutory powers.[27]

[25] To this effect, see Case C-149/85 *Wybot v Faure* EU:C:1986:310, [1986] ECR 2391, para 23, where the Court stipulates that 'the practice of [one institution] cannot deprive the other institutions of a prerogative granted to them by the treaties themselves'.

[26] In this connection, see Lenaerts and Verhoeven (n 23) 45–46, referring to cases in which the Court itself refuses to make judgments on issues falling within the ambit of political decision making: Case 109/75 R *National Carbonising Company Limited v Commission* EU:C:1975:133, [1975] ECR 1193, para 8; Case 415/85 *Commission v Ireland* EU:C:1988:320, [1988] ECR 3098, paras 8–9; Case C-249/96 *Grant v South-West Trains Ltd* EU:C:1998:63, [1998] ECR I-621, paras 35–36, 47–48.

[27] See, eg, T Volgy, 'The Role of the "Outsider" in Quasi-Legislative Systems: The Potential Utility of a Legislative Model' (1973) 27 *International Organization* 85; KW Saunders, 'Interpretative Rules with Legislative Effect: An Analysis and a Proposal for Public Participation' (1986) *Duke Law Journal* 346.

However, quasi-legislative functions are also inherent in judicial lawmaking. This is particularly true of supreme and constitutional courts, which are entrusted by law with the responsibility of interpreting the law rather than just applying it to the legal dispute at hand. The institutional position of supreme and constitutional courts endows these courts with a power to produce rules that create generally applicable rights and obligations.[28] In the context of EU law, the constitutional power, and responsibility, to interpret EU law is conferred upon the CJEU, whose task is to 'ensure that in the interpretation and application of the Treaties the law is observed'.[29] As discussed in chapter one, due to the broad framing of the Court's judicial mandate, the exercise of that mandate necessarily entails a degree of discretion.[30] The presence of that discretion makes it almost inevitable that the Court's judgments will vary to some extent in terms of their mode of reasoning, the standard of review employed and their normative scope. In that connection, Tridimas offers a classification of the Court's judgments according to the degree of specificity, sorting them into outcome, guidance and deference judgments.[31] The outcome judgments, he explains, give an answer so specific that they provide the referring court with a ready-made solution to the dispute; guidance judgments offer guidelines as to how to resolve the dispute; and deference judgments answer the question in such general terms that the decision is essentially left to be made by the referring court. Notably, in Tridimas' classification, the specificity of the ruling is not necessarily correlated to the standard of review employed by the Court. Although an outcome case would be naturally associated with a high standard of review,[32] it may equally be determined by a low standard of review.[33] Of course, the outcomes produced by these two types of review will be very different from one another in terms of the room left for autonomous decision making by national authorities.

But what makes a judgment deserve the label of quasi-legislative? Quasi-legislative judgments do not fit neatly into the categories of judgments offered by Tridimas. In my view, a judgment acquires a quasi-legislative character by virtue of its normative scope and regulatory ambition. Due to being predominantly of an interpretative nature, *all* of the Court's judgments tend to produce certain normative regulatory effects extending beyond the narrow scope of application to the circumstances of a particular case. However, quasi-legislative judgments do more than that. They tend to lay down rules that create rights and obligations applicable to a wide range of social situations. The regulatory effects produced by these judgments thus could be characterised as quasi-legislative effects.

[28] See ch 1, s III for a discussion on the institutional position of constitutional and supreme courts. This topic is also explored in AHY Chen and MP Maduro, 'The Judiciary and Constitutional Review' in M Tushnet, T Fleiner and C Saunders (eds), *Routledge Handbook of Constitutional Law* (Abingdon, Routledge, 2013) ch 8; A Gramper, 'Constitutional Courts and Judicial Law-Making: Why Democratic Legitimacy Matters' (2015) 4 *Constitutional Courts and Judicial Law-Making* 423.

[29] Art 19(1) TEU.

[30] K Lenaerts, 'The Court's Outer and Inner Selves: Exploring the External and Internal Legitimacy of the European Court of Justice' in M Adams et al (eds), *Judging Europe's Judges: The Legitimacy of the Case Law of the European Court of Justice* (Oxford, Hart Publishing, 2013) 13–18.

[31] T Tridimas, 'Constitutional Review of Member State Action: The Virtues and Vices of an Incomplete Jurisdiction' (2011) 9 *International Journal of Constitutional Law* 737.

[32] ibid 753, referring to Case C-144/04 *Mangold* EU:C:2005:709, [2005] ECR I-9981.

[33] Tridimas (n 31), referring to Case C-36/02 *Omega* EU:C:2004:614, [2004] ECR I-9609, to be discussed in ch 5, s II.

Quasi-legislative judgments can be distinguished by their peculiar rhetoric. Often, they are drafted in a manner that resembles more the language used in a legislative act than a judgment. In addition to deciding a particular point of law, they will lay down generally framed rules and principles of wider application.[34] The quasi-legislative character of a judgment may stem, on the one hand, from the specificity and prescriptive detail of judicial reasoning. The *Altmark* judgment serves as a prominent example of that type of judgment. The case concerned State subsidies for the provision of regional transport services. The judgment prescribed concrete criteria that Member States must comply with in order to ensure the compatibility with EU law of State subsidies granted to undertakings providing public services.[35] These criteria were later codified by the Commission.[36] On the other hand, a high level of detail in the judgment, like that in *Altmark*, does not always indicate quasi-legislative character. Rather, it may be a sign of an interpretation of the law that is carefully tailored to the particular facts of the case, such as in the *Liga Portuguesa* judgment, which examined the specifics of the Portuguese monopoly on Internet gambling.[37] Sometimes, a regulatory ambition lies exactly in the laconic style adopted and the abstraction of the judicial reasoning, especially where this type of reasoning masks a possible lack of consensus among the members of the Court with regard to the details of the principle that is being (newly) developed.[38] A good illustration of this type of judgment is offered by the *Zambrano* judgment, where the Court famously ruled that EU citizens must not be deprived of 'the genuine enjoyment of the substance of their rights as Union citizens' without elaborating on what this requirement specifically entails.[39] *Zambrano* encouraged more litigation, which resulted in the application of the principle laid down in it to a variety of circumstances. This goes to show that the specificity of the language alone is not enough to determine whether a particular judgment has a quasi-legislative character: quasi-legislative judgments may be drafted in a very specific manner, but equally may be very laconic and abstract. In the latter case, only subsequent litigation can fully reveal the regulatory ambition of the initial judgment.

[34] J Komarek, 'Reasoning with Previous Decisions: Beyond the Doctrine of Precedent' (2013) 61 *American Journal of Comparative Law* 149, discussing the 'legislative' method of reasoning in the CJEU and other constitutional courts of continental law tradition. See also M Bobek, 'The Court of Justice of the European Union' in D Chalmers and A Arnull (eds), *Oxford Handbook of European Union Law* (Oxford, OUP, 2015) 154. For an account describing features of 'legislated law', see J Gardner, 'Some Types of Law' in J Gardner, *Law as a Leap of Faith: Essays on Law in General* (Oxford, OUP, 2012) 54–65.

[35] Case C-280/00 *Altmark* EU:C:2003:415, [2003] ECR I-7747, paras 77–82, referred to in Tridimas (n 31) 754. For other prominent examples of quasi-legislative judgments, see, eg, C-6/90 and C-9/90 *Francovich* EU:C:1991:428, [1991] ECR I-5357, paras 30–46; *Brasserie du Pêcheur* (n 23), paras 20–58.

[36] Further discussed in s IV of this chapter.

[37] Case C-42/07 *Liga Portuguesa* EU:C:2009:519, [2009] ECR I-7633, discussed in ch 3, s V. Outside the confines of the present analysis, see, eg, Case C-456/02 *Trojani* EU:C:2004:488, [2004] ECR I-7573, paras 13–46, discussed in Komarek (n 34) 153. See also Tridimas (n 31) 750–51.

[38] For a discussion on how disagreements among the judges may influence the language of CJEU judgments, see Tridimas (n 31) 753–54; Bobek (n 34) 170–72; on the impact of differences in judges' legal culture, see FG Mancini and D Keeling, 'Language, Culture and Politics in the Life of the European Court of Justice' (1995) 1 *Columbia Journal of European Law* 397, 399–403.

[39] Case C-34/09 *Zambrano* EU:C:2011:124, [2011] ECR I-1177, paras 41–45, discussed in T Tridimas, 'The ECJ and the National Courts: Dialogue, Cooperation, and Instability' in Chalmers and Arnull (n 34) 409–10. For an example from the Court's early jurisprudence, see, eg, Case C-8/74 *Dassonville* EU:C:1974:82, [1974] ECR 837, paras 4–9.

Against this background, two other factors may assist in identifying the quasi-legislative character of a judgment: the standard of judicial review employed by the Court and the sensitivity of the legal issue concerned. Notably, these factors may not explain all of the Court's case law, but they seem to be highly relevant when the judgment concerns policy areas that fall outside of the EU's explicit regulatory competence.

The correlation between the standard of review and a quasi-legislative character of a judgment is almost self-explanatory: the closer national measures are scrutinised, the less space there is left for Member State action in the area, and the more likely that space will be occupied by the rules and principles developed by the Court. The spectrum of the Court's standard of review can range, at least in theory, from a complete deference to strict scrutiny. By and large, this spectrum is illustrated by the comparative analysis of the case law conducted in the preceding chapter. The analysis demonstrates how in judgments concerning healthcare, education and collective labour law judicial interpretation not only decides the outcome of the case, but also lays down what could be considered a generally applicable regulatory framework meant to govern the matter concerned – be it access to medical treatment abroad; conditions of admission of foreign students to universities; or the parameters of collective regulation of labour and employment in transnational situations. By contrast, the entire gambling case law is premised on the judicial recognition that national authorities are entitled to a margin of discretion when regulating the gambling sector, save for certain basic limits imposed by EU free movement law. The language of discretion sends a signal to national courts that they, too, should adopt a deferential approach in relation to decisions adopted by national authorities in the gambling sector. This line of case law thus effectively sanctions the right of the Member States to make autonomous decisions in the gambling sector as a matter of EU primary law. Accordingly, Member States remain free to choose to continue regulating their gambling markets on their own or to take a concerted action together with other Member States at the EU level.

The quasi-legislative effects associated with a high standard of judicial review are certainly going to be more pronounced if the issue at stake is a sensitive one, which typically is the case if the policy area involved falls outside the EU's explicit sector-specific legislative competence. Policy areas that are reserved by the Treaties to the competence of the Member States are usually highly regulated at the national level. It is, therefore, almost inevitable that a more aggressive application of EU internal market law in these areas is going to disrupt domestic regulatory frameworks. In this connection, it has been demonstrated in chapter three that a high standard of judicial review has had the effect of subjecting the policies of the Member States in the areas of healthcare, education and collective labour law to EU-wide deregulation and, in some cases, prompted specific reforms at the national level. Admittedly, even in these circumstances, Member States retain the possibility of re-regulating the areas concerned through legislative action at the EU level, using one of the functionally broad Treaty bases for that purpose. Yet the way in which this theoretical possibility plays out in practice is a different matter.

The following sections demonstrate how through generating quasi-legislative regulatory effects in constitutionally sensitive areas of national policy, the case law effectively comes to determine the scope of available EU-level legislative action. It creates a peculiar interinstitutional dynamic of power between the EU's judiciary and legislature, referred to here as a 'judicial trap', where the latter is either prevented from acting altogether or left with a limited choice of legislative options, essentially confined to those reaffirming and codifying the case law. Judicial trap effectively nullifies the discretion that the EU legislature would otherwise be entitled to when carrying out its functions, thus putting the Court in tension with the principle of institutional balance. To illustrate the described dynamic, this chapter considers three distinct models of judiciary-legislature interaction that have developed in light of the case law under study: (i) the Court predetermines the content of new legislation; (ii) the Court pre-empts novel legislative solutions; (iii) the Court prevents legislative overturn of the case law.[40]

III. The Legislative Process: Political Constitutional Constraints and the 'Judicial Trap'

In line with the logic underlying the relationship between negative and positive law, EU-level legislative action complements the judicial interpretation of the Treaties.[41] Legislative action can be taken in order to replace the disputed national standard with a European one, to clarify the Court's interpretation of the law or even correct it, provided that political consensus is achieved.[42] This logic does not, however, apply in situations where the case law involves matters which are constitutionally sensitive, such as those pertaining to the areas of healthcare, education and collective labour law under study here. Due to the political and constitutional constraints pertaining to the legislative process in this context, the range of legislative options available to the EU legislature will be, inevitably, inadequate to counteract the regulatory effects of the case law or remedy them in a meaningful way.

A. Regulatory Diversity

The inadequacy of legislative options is presupposed, in part, by the political sensitivity of the area in question and the resulting diversity of national regulatory approaches. This set of circumstances makes it extremely challenging to devise an EU-wide legislative framework or standard that would counteract or remedy the regulatory effects of the case law whilst also reflecting the concerns of all, or at least the majority, of the Member States of the EU. Just like the case law, a uniform legislative framework is likely to produce varying effects on national regulatory systems in terms of regulatory burdens and costs. The following discussion demonstrates that EU measures concerning matters that fall within the constitutionally sensitive areas of EU competence are likely to have the greatest impact on Member States with strong welfare systems as opposed to more liberal systems.

[40] For the origins of this idea, see V Velyvyte, 'A Power to Shape the Internal Market: Implications of CJEU Case Law for the Principle of Institutional Balance' (2016) 12 *Croatian Yearbook of European Law and Policy* 25.

[41] On the dynamic between positive and negative law, see ch 1, s III.

[42] See, eg, S Weatherill, 'Did Cassis de Dijon Make a Difference?' in A Albors-Llorens, C Barnard and B Leucht (eds), *Cassis de Dijon: 40 Years On* (Cambridge, CUP, 2021), discussing EU regulation of blackcurrant liqueur and crème de cassis.

Given the lack of explicit legislative competence on behalf of the EU to regulate matters of social policy, including those under study here, legislative action would have to be undertaken using Art 114 TFEU or other functionally broad legal bases.[43] However, since legislation adopted under those legal bases must have some sort of link with the functioning of the internal market or the free movement of persons, inevitably, it has to balance the achievement of social objectives with those of the internal market.[44] For that reason, much of EU social legislation can never be quintessentially social in character. In terms of legislative design, EU directives normally establish only minimum levels of social protection, in theory allowing Member States to go beyond those levels. However, in practice, Member States are prevented from going beyond the protections enshrined in the legislation if doing so would jeopardise the objectives of the internal market pursued by such legislation. As a result, a measure providing a floor of standards of social protection may in reality turn out to be one establishing a ceiling of such standards. This is exactly what happened with the infamous Posted Workers Directive in light of its interpretation by the Court.[45] Against this background, it appears highly likely that legislative action carried out on the basis of the functionally broad legal basis will have a deregulatory effect in the Member States with strong welfare models and high levels of social protection.

The example of collective labour rights offers a helpful illustration. Member States vary greatly in the ideological underpinning and institutional organisation of their industrial relations systems.[46] In countries with strong industrial relations models, such as Germany and the Scandinavian countries, an EU-wide legislative solution harmonising aspects of collective bargaining or the right to strike – even as modest in scope as the failed Monti II draft[47] – could bring about a major, systemic change because it would interfere with the power of the social partners to regulate the conditions of labour and employment autonomously. On the other hand, countries with weaker social structures or statutory regulation of employment, such as Lithuania or Poland, would not experience any substantial impact, apart from, possibly, a slight increase in the level of worker protection.[48]

[43] See Consolidated version of the Treaty on the Functioning of the European Union [2008] OJ C115/47 (TFEU), eg, Arts 50, 59, 114 and 352, discussed in ch 2, s I. For examples of measures adopted using functionally broad legal bases, see, eg: Council Regulation (EC) 883/2004 on the coordination of social security systems [2004] OJ L166/1 (Reg 883/2004), adopted on the basis of Arts 42 and 308 EC (now Arts 48 and 352 TFEU); Council Directive 96/71/EC concerning the posting of workers in the framework of the provision of services [1997] OJ L18/1 (Posted Workers Directive), adopted on the basis of Arts 57(2) and 66 of the EC Treaty (now Arts 53(1) and 62 TFEU), both discussed later in this chapter. Exceptions include matters which fall within the EU's explicit legislative competence, eg, Council Directive 89/391/EEC on the introduction of measures to encourage improvements in the safety and health of workers at work [1989] OJ L183/29.

[44] See, eg, the interpretation by the CJEU of Council Directive 23/2001/EC on the approximation of the laws of the Member States relating to the safeguarding of employees' rights in the event of transfers of undertakings, businesses or parts of undertakings or businesses [2001] OJ L82/16 (Acquired Rights Directive), adopted under what is now Art 115 TFEU, in Case C-426/11 *Alemo-Herron* EU:C:2013:521 (CJEU, 18 July 2013).

[45] To be discussed in detail later in this chapter.

[46] The Adoptive Parents, 'The Life of a Death Foretold: The Proposal for a Monti II Regulation' in M Freedland and J Prassl (eds), *EU Law in the Member States:* Viking, Laval *and Beyond* (Oxford, Hart Publishing, 2014) 95 ff.

[47] To be discussed later in this chapter.

[48] For a broader discussion, see D Schiek et al, 'EU Social and Labour Rights and EU Internal Market Law' (European Parliament DG for Internal Policies 2015) www.europarl.europa.eu/RegData/etudes/STUD/2015/563457/IPOL_STU(2015)563457_EN.pdf, analysing the varying impacts of the case law on national social models.

Variations in impacts might be even more pronounced in the education sector, if for different reasons. To date, the consequences of the Court's student mobility case law have been experienced by a relatively small number of Member States: those with open access, low-threshold education policies. This situation makes it difficult to envisage a common regulatory measure that would provide clear advantages for those countries, notably, Belgium and Austria, without at the same time imposing unnecessary or undesirable costs on the systems of the rest of the Member States.[49] More generally, when it comes to the provision of public services, education and healthcare being primary examples, the adoption of a uniform legislative standard at the EU level would risk creating excessive financial burdens on the poorer Member States in the Southern and Eastern Europe, especially the recent members (ie Bulgaria, Romania and Croatia).[50] This situation could be avoided if a uniform standard is based on the lowest common denominator. In fact, it is likely that this would be the case, given the need to achieve political consensus on the matter.[51] However, a standard based on the lowest common denominator would merely maintain the *status quo* rather than create an added value that comes with harmonised regulation.

Moreover, harmonisation as a legislative technique may not be suited to deal with problems created by the case law. For instance, as has been suggested in chapter three, what is necessary for patient mobility to be effective in practice is an EU budget for cross-border healthcare. A similar solution could be fitting in the case of cross-border education. However, as these types of legislative measures do not entail harmonisation of national laws, the appropriate legal bases to be used would be the sectoral ones, yet these explicitly exclude the adoption of measures that would create binding obligations on the Member States, such as those involving making financial contributions to an EU-wide budget for cross-border healthcare or education. Notably, innovative legislative solutions could be adopted on the basis of Art 352 TFEU, as it empowers the EU to take action in cases where no other Treaty provision provides the necessary powers. However, the conditions for relying on Art 352 are strict. The measures proposed need to receive unanimity in the Council, they must not entail harmonisation where it is excluded by the Treaties and they must not lead to the Union's competences being extended beyond those provided for by the Treaties.[52] And even where a competence can be shown to exist in principle, any meaningful initiative on behalf of the Commission can easily be trumped by a single veto. Unfortunately, the latter scenario is a likely one given the immense political and social sensitivity of the issues involved.

B. Voting Rules and the 'Judicial Trap'

As alluded to above, another set of constraints on legislative activity stems from the voting rules. In areas of high political sensitivity, achieving unanimity or even the

[49] For a comprehensive analysis of the impact of the student mobility case law on Austria and Belgium, see ch 3, s III.

[50] For illustration, see Case C-268/13 *Petru* EU:C:2014:2271 (CJEU, 9 October 2014), discussed in ch 3, s II.

[51] FW Scharpf, 'The Joint-Decision Trap. Lessons From German Federalism and European Integration' (1988) 66 *Public Administration* 239.

[52] See this provision discussed in the context of other legal bases in ch 2, s I.

required qualified majority in Council voting is a challenge. This problem has been identified by Scharpf as the 'joint decision trap'.[53] Scharpf's notion of a trap refers to the near impossibility of amending or abrogating existing legislation due to the difficulty in reaching a political agreement that is necessary in order to make a change in policy.[54] This situation, then, leads to the adoption of sub-optimal policy solutions or none at all. Essentially, what we see in Scharpf's 'joint decision trap' is national regulatory diversity manifesting itself through the voting process. Member States with more liberal regimes or smaller budgets can always gather enough votes to veto legislative initiatives that would impose more demanding social regulations than the current ones. Conversely, Member States with strong welfare models and larger budgets could in the same way block proposals that might threaten to dismantle their existing regulatory structures. The resistance on both sides is likely to be supported by national populations, which typically favour the continuation of existing systems of social protection and therefore tend to resist major structural changes. As Scharpf puts it, rather poetically:

> [v]oters in Britain simply could not accept the high levels of taxation that sustain the generous Swedish welfare state; Swedish families could not live with the low level of social and educational services provided in Germany; and German doctors and patients would unite in protest against any moves toward a British-style National Health Service.[55]

Now, imagine a situation where there is no pre-existing legislation that would 'trap' the decision-making process in the Council, thus preventing it from responding effectively to changed circumstances or national preferences. However, instead there exists a strand of case law that governs the matter in question across the EU and does so in a way that leaves little scope for regulatory discretion on the part of the Member States. Member States and other actors that take part in the EU's lawmaking process might not be satisfied with the rules developed in the case law, yet they find themselves unable to agree to change those rules due to the sensitivity of the questions concerned. This situation could be described as a 'judicial trap'. The greater the regulatory ambition of the Court's judgments, the more likely the judicial trap is to occur. Therefore, whenever the Court adopts a quasi-legislative interpretation of the Treaties, as in the areas under study here in the context of free movement law, the EU's legislature is likely to find itself trapped by the case law and unable to enact a meaningful legislative response to the rules developed by the judiciary.

However, unlike Scharpf's joint decision trap, the judicial trap does not necessarily frustrate the adoption of legislation. In fact, it encourages legislative action, albeit the type that leads to the adoption of measures that effectively codify the case law. Here, we see a model of interinstitutional interaction where the judiciary predetermines the content of the measures adopted by the legislature. This model is discussed in the next section.

[53] Scharpf (n 51); FW Scharpf, 'The Joint-Decision Trap Revisited' (2006) 44 *Journal of Common Market Studies* 845; FW Scharpf, 'Negative and Positive Integration in the Political Economy of European Welfare States' in G Marks et al (eds), *Governance in the European Union* (London, SAGE Publications, 1996); FW Scharpf, 'Community and Autonomy: Multi-Level Policy-Making in the European Union' (1994) 1 *Journal of European Public Policy* 219.

[54] Scharpf, 'Joint-Decision Trap' (n 51) 257–58, 265 ff; Scharpf, 'Joint-Decision Trap Revisited' (n 53) 848.

[55] FW Scharpf, 'The European Social Model: Coping with the Challenges of Diversity' (2002) 40 *Journal of Common Market Studies* 645, 651–52.

IV. Model of Interaction No 1: The Court Predetermines the Content of Legislation

This and the following two sections discuss the models of interaction that have developed between the Court and EU legislature in light of the case law under study. Each model uses concrete examples of legislative developments to illustrate the effects of the case law on EU legislative activity. The example of the Patients' Rights Directive (PRD) demonstrates that a legislative measure concerning the subject matter already regulated by the case law has the greatest likelihood of being successfully adopted if it essentially replicates that case law.

A. The Patients' Rights Directive

The adoption of the PRD has been seen by some as a significant step marking the EU's involvement in the domestic healthcare policies of the Member States.[56] The discussion below shows this is an overstatement. Adopted on the basis of Arts 114 and 168 TFEU, the Directive harmonises national rules on reimbursement of costs of cross-border healthcare. Its adoption was long anticipated and came five years after an unsuccessful attempt by the Commission to include healthcare services in the Services Directive.[57] Healthcare had been excluded from the Services Directive because the health policy stakeholders objected to the largely economic logic embedded in the Directive. It was argued that the country of origin principle enshrined in the Commission's initial proposal[58] was not an appropriate means to regulate the healthcare sector, which by its nature necessitated a high level of regulatory intervention and control by national governments.[59]

The legislative proposal dedicated specifically to cross-border healthcare was meant to provide a comprehensive legal framework on matters of cross-border healthcare, whilst also striking a balance between the economic and social dimensions pertaining to the sector.[60] Not incidentally, the Commission's proposal was ambitiously entitled a directive on 'Patients' Rights', suggesting the creation of EU-wide rights for patients –

[56] W Sauter, 'Harmonisation in Healthcare: the EU Patients' Rights Directive' (2011) TILEC Discussion Paper 2011-030 papers.ssrn.com/sol3/papers.cfm?abstract_id=1859251.

[57] Council Directive 2006/123/EC on services in the internal market [2006] OJ L376/36, Preamble, Recital 23, Art 2(2)(f).

[58] ibid, Art 16.

[59] 'Recommendations on Health Services and the Internal Market' (*European Health Policy Forum*, 26 May 2005) 15, ec.europa.eu/health/archive/ph_overview/health_forum/docs/recom_health_services.pdf. For an in-depth discussion, see W Gekiere, R Baeten and W Palm, 'Free Movement of Services in the EU and Health Care' in E Mossialos et al (eds), *Health Systems Governance in Europe: The Role of European Union Law and Policy* (Cambridge, CUP, 2010) 487–504.

[60] Commission, 'Proposal for a Directive of the European Parliament and of the Council on the application of patients' rights in cross-border healthcare' COM (2008) 414 final, Explanatory Memorandum, 2 (Proposal for PRD); Commission, 'Consultation regarding Community action on health services' (Communication) COM (2006) 1195/4; European Parliament, Committee on the Internal Market and Consumer Protection, 'Motion for a European Parliament Resolution on the impact and consequences of the exclusion of health services from the Directive on services in the internal market' 2006/2275(INI).

a concept much broader in scope than simply the reimbursement of the costs of cross-border medical treatment.[61] The ambition of the Directive is also evidenced by the reference in the preamble and Art 5 to the 'overarching values' common to the health systems across Europe: universality, access to good quality care, equity and solidarity. These values, which are based on the conclusions produced by the Council,[62] are to be observed by national authorities in providing cross-border treatment.[63]

Yet, despite an ambitious title and some aspirational value rhetoric, in reality the Directive does not do much more than codify the rules already developed in the case law, simply adding to the legal certainty of the current regulatory regime via the transparency of legislation, as opposed to the relative opacity of case law. The Directive does not create, and was not intended to create, any new rights for patients. The Explanatory Memorandum and the Preamble to the Directive both stipulate that the objective of the Directive is to provide sufficient clarity about the rights to be reimbursed for healthcare provided in other Member States in order to enable patients to exercise those rights in practice.[64] Recital 8 expressly states that the Directive intends 'to achieve a more general, and also effective, application of principles developed by the Court of Justice on a case-by-case basis'.[65] In line with this promise, a number of the provisions of the PRD are qualified by references to the case law of the CJEU, such as, 'in accordance with the principles established by the Court of Justice' or 'according to the constant case-law of the Court of Justice'.[66]

The provisions regarding the reimbursement of the healthcare costs incurred abroad replicate the rules developed by the Court, often even their exact wording. For example, Art 7 obliges the Member States of affiliation to cover the costs of cross-border healthcare up to the level of the costs that would have been assumed by the Member State of affiliation had this healthcare been provided in its territory, without exceeding the actual costs of healthcare received. Art 8 establishes the general validity of a prior authorisation requirement for inpatient care and lays down the procedural and substantive requirements applicable to prior authorisation, in accordance with the case law of the Court.

The so-called new elements introduced by the Directive – those going beyond the rules developed by the Court – mainly concern the procedural guarantees aimed at ensuring that the cross-border system works effectively in practice. The relevant rules include provisions on access to information, transparency of procedures, coordination of safety and quality of treatment, and information exchange through the national contact points and the E-Health system.[67] Accordingly, Member States are required to

[61] Sauter (n 56) 8–9.

[62] Council, 'Council Conclusions on Common values and principles in European Union Health Systems' [2006] OJ C146/1.

[63] Council Directive 2011/24/EU on the application of patients' rights in cross-border healthcare [2011] OJ L88/45 (Patients' Rights Directive), Recital 12, Art 5.

[64] Proposal for PRD (n 60), Explanatory Memorandum, 7; Patients' Rights Directive (n 63), Preamble, Recital 10, Art 1(1).

[65] Patients' Rights Directive (n 63), Preamble, Recital 8.

[66] ibid, Preamble, Recitals 10, 12, 27, 38, 40, 42, 44, 46, Art 1(1).

[67] Patients' Rights Directive (n 63), eg, Arts 4–5, 9(1) 6, 10, 14–15; Proposal for PRD (n 60), Explanatory Memorandum, 11–12, 17–20.

provide healthcare quality and safety standards; to ensure patients' access to the information necessary for making informed choices regarding their healthcare; to put in place a complaints procedure for seeking remedies, to respect patients' privacy when processing personal data; and other requirements. One could argue that these procedural guarantees are required anyway under the free movement law, but at least the Directive makes them concrete. Otherwise, the PRD does not seem to do much more than give a legislative expression to the rules that had already been in force for a while by virtue of the Court's case law.

B. The '*Altmark* Package'

Another example of a measure that has transposed the rules developed in the case law into an EU-wide measure comes from the area of competition law. It is the Commission's so-called '*Altmark* package', adopted in light of the Court's interpretation of EU State aid rules. The *Altmark* judgment set out a four-part test to determine whether the financial support provided to an undertaking performing a service of general economic interest (SGEI) constitutes compensation for performance of that service rather than State aid within the meaning of EU law. In response to this judgment, the Commission adopted a package of measures, which included a decision creating a generally applicable framework for compensation that did not meet all the *Altmark* criteria but would be considered as aid compatible with the internal market. Remarkably, the language of the Commission's Decision largely reiterates the *Altmark* judgment, omitting just one of the conditions out of the four-fold test laid down by the Court.[68] The *Altmark* package of measures has since governed the validity of financial compensations provided by national governments to undertakings running SGEIs.

Both examples – the Patients' Rights Directive and the *Altmark* package – illustrate the circumstances in which quasi-legislative rules developed in the case law end up being almost automatically transposed into EU-level legislation (in the *Altmark* example, also bypassing the Council and Parliament).[69] This happens because when the rules have already been laid down – even if through a judicial route – and are binding across the EU, their transposition into EU-wide legislation seems to be a relatively straightforward option. At the same time, the alternative of negotiating the matter on the political level with the view to finding better or otherwise preferable solutions may be seen as too cumbersome and time-consuming.

[68] Commission Decision on the application of Article 86(2) of the EC Treaty to state aid in the form of public service compensation granted to certain undertakings entrusted with the operation of services of general economic interest [2005] OJ L312/67, replaced by Commission Decision on the application of Article 106(2) of the Treaty on the Functioning of the European Union to State aid in the form of public service compensation granted to certain undertakings entrusted with the operation of services of general economic interest [2012] OJ L7/3.

[69] Notably, this situation also creates problems concerning the balance of powers among the legislative organs of the EU – the Commission, on the one hand, and the Council and Parliament, on the other.

V. Model of Interaction No 2: The Court Pre-empts Novel Legislative Solutions

Apart from predetermining the content of new legislation, quasi-legislative case law also pre-empts the adoption of *novel* legislative solutions. This happens when enough votes cannot be gathered to adopt a legislative response designed to remedy the judgments seen as problematic. In this situation, judicial trap manifests itself by freezing EU legislative action. The piece of legislation that best illustrates this interinstitutional dynamic is the draft Monti II Regulation.

Proposed on the basis of Art 352 TFEU, the draft Monti II Regulation was intended to provide a legislative response to the Court's interpretation of the relationship between the exercise of the fundamental freedoms and the right to strike.[70] Although the draft contained a provision explicitly stating that it was not reversing the case law of the Court, it did seem to endeavour to correct it by explicitly recognising the general equality between the fundamental rights and fundamental freedoms in EU law.[71] Specifically, the Proposal stated that 'the exercise of the freedom of establishment and the freedom to provide services enshrined in the Treaty shall respect the fundamental right to take collective action, including the right or freedom to strike, and conversely, the exercise of the fundamental right to take collective action, including the right or freedom to strike, shall respect these economic freedoms.'[72] The proposal also highlighted the need for the national courts to strike a 'fair balance' in the process of reconciliation of both legal values, referring to the language of the *Commission v Germany* judgment.[73] Monti II thus appeared to have established a double proportionality review as a means of striking an equitable balance between the exercise of the right to strike and the fundamental freedoms, thereby deviating from the sort of balance between the two values established by *Viking* and *Laval*.[74] Monti II was eventually officially withdrawn, following objections raised by national parliaments regarding a breach of subsidiarity and the lack of EU legislative competence to regulate collective labour rights. In fact, this was the first time that national parliaments triggered the 'yellow card' mechanism established by the Lisbon Treaty.[75]

The fate of Monti II shows that the case law may have the effect of pre-empting the adoption of any meaningful legislation at the EU level. The more controversial the case law, the more likely that is to be the case. Monti II sought to achieve a more equitable balance in the relationship between the economic freedoms and the right to strike, in this way departing from the position adopted by the Court. However, not surprisingly,

[70] Commission, 'Proposal for a Council Regulation on the exercise of the right to take collective action within the context of the freedom of establishment and the freedom to provide services' COM (2012) 130 final (Monti II). For a commentary on Monti II by its drafters, see The Adoptive Parents (n 46) 95 ff.

[71] Monti II (n 70), Arts 3.4.2, 3.4.4 and Explanatory Memorandum, 10 ec.europa.eu/social/BlobServlet?docId=7480&langId=en.

[72] Monti II (n 70), Art 2.

[73] Case C-271/08 *Commission v Germany* [2010] ECR I-7091, analysed in ch 3, s IV.

[74] This approach was proposed in *Commission v Germany* (n 73), Opinion of AG Trstenjak, paras 81, 84, 188–89, 215, discussed in more detail in ch 5, s III.

[75] M Goldoni, 'The Early Warning System and the Monti II Regulation: The Case for a Political Interpretation' (2014) 10 *European Constitutional Law Review* 90.

the proposal raised some controversial reactions from the stakeholders. The European Trade Union Confederation rejected the Proposal, claiming that it was too restrictive of the right to strike, while Business Europe, an association representing more than 20 million European companies, was against it for an opposite reason: Monti II was less favourable to employers than the case law. Similar divisions appeared between the old and new Member States, none of which saw quite what they wanted in the proposal. The reforms introduced by the Lisbon Treaty had granted national parliaments the right to raise formal objections to a legislative proposal and even challenge it before the Court if they suspected a breach of the principle of subsidiarity.[76] Protecting the national interests, national parliaments used this right to challenge Monti II, alleging both the breach of subsidiarity and an unlawful interference with national systems of industrial relations.[77]

Due to the objections raised by national parliaments, the Commission was required to review the Proposal and eventually withdrew it. However, the Proposal did not die because there were real concerns over subsidiarity – after all, the draft dealt with the interpretation of the free movement rules in cross-border situations. As the Commission admitted in a formal letter addressed to the national parliaments in response to the raised objections, Monti II was withdrawn because it was 'unlikely to gather the necessary political support' to enable its adoption.[78] This goes to show that the objections raised by national parliaments may manifest a general lack of agreement in the Council rather than a genuine concern about subsidiarity or competence more generally.

Ultimately, although the adoption of Monti II had been in theory enabled by Art 352, the lack of consensus between the stakeholders and the lack of political will to support the EU's interference in national industrial relations systems resulted in the eventual withdrawal of the Proposal. Ironically, the *Viking* and *Laval* rulings, which had attracted widespread criticism, thus triggering the legislative response, remained unchanged. They remain good law and continue to govern the exercise of collective labour rights in cross-border situations.

On the other hand, the heated debate over Monti II in a way was much ado about nothing. Even if adopted, the regulation could not in reality have replaced the Court's particular interpretation of the free movement rules. Judicial interpretation of primary law is superior to legislation, national or EU-wide, and remains intact as long as the Treaties remain unamended. In other words, the rules developed in *Viking* and *Laval* would have continued to apply, as a matter of law, even if Monti II had gained a unanimous vote. The only possible scenario where Monti II could have had real impact was if the Court was willing to temper its position as a sign of deference to the political consensus and perhaps also due to the grant of binding force to the Charter, which offers protection to both the right to collective bargaining and the right to strike. It is, however, difficult to estimate how likely this outcome would have been, especially considering that the Court has in the past gone against the express wishes of the legislature even

[76] Protocol No 2 to TFEU on the application of the principles of subsidiarity and proportionality [2008] OJ C115/206, Arts 6–8.

[77] For a detailed account, see, eg, I Cooper, 'A Yellow Card for the Striker: National Parliaments and the Defeat of EU Legislation on the Right to Strike' (2015) 22 *Journal of European Public Policy* 1406.

[78] ibid; The Adoptive Parents (n 46) 96, 99.

where the legislation in question had gained unanimous support in the Council. This issue is discussed below.

VI. Model of Interaction No 3: The Court Prevents Legislative Overturn

Let us assume, for the sake of argument, that a political agreement is reached to enable the adoption of a sophisticated legislative measure that could potentially address the issues raised by the case law. The aim of the following discussion is to demonstrate that even in those situations the effects of quasi-legislative judgments are unlikely to be corrected by any type of legislation.

Where the Court interprets EU primary law, a Treaty change will be necessary to reverse that interpretation. In the majority of cases, this will require a unanimous agreement among 27 (formerly 28) Member States and subsequent ratification in accordance with their national constitutional provisions.[79] Given the cumbersome nature of the amendment procedure and great uncertainty about its eventual success, this task may prove impossible to achieve in practice,[80] especially when the question concerns a sensitive area of national policy.

The core of the problem lies in that the Court's internal market case law for the most part constitutes an interpretation of EU primary law. As such, this case law can at any point override a legislative consensus on the matter. The case law is, however, unlikely to do so directly. The Court can offset or at least modify EU legislative choices by reading the provisions of existing secondary legislation in light of the Treaties, thus avoiding direct confrontation with the legislature. By doing so, the Court will elevate (its interpretation of) secondary law to the status of primary law, thus making it immune to legislative overturn. The Court has done so in the past on multiple occasions, as will be illustrated below by the analysis of EU legislation in three areas: students' rights to financial assistance for studies abroad; the exercise of collective labour rights in transnational situations; and patients' access to cross-border healthcare.

A. Directive 93/96 on the Right of Residence for Students

Before the adoption of the Citizens' Rights Directive, the access of students to financial assistance in other Member States was governed by Directive 93/96 on the right of residence for students. Art 1 of this directive stipulated that Member States shall recognise the right of residence for students who are nationals of other Member States provided that such students have a social security cover and 'sufficient resources to avoid becoming a burden on the social assistance system of the host Member State'. In the *Grzelczyk* judgment, delivered in 2001, the Court ruled that the principle of non-discrimination and the concept of EU citizenship required that Member States hosting foreign students

[79] Art 48 TEU.
[80] H de Waele, 'The Role of the European Court of Justice in the Integration Process: A Contemporary and Normative Assessment' (2010) 12 *Europarecht* 3, 15–16.

grant them the right to social assistance available to nationals of those States.[81] This interpretation appeared to be in conflict with the provisions of Directive 93/96, which conditioned foreign students' residence rights on the existence of sufficient financial resources. Seemingly to avoid this conflict, the Court observed that the Directive did not require foreign students to have resources of 'any specific amount' and otherwise contained no provisions that 'preclude[d] those to whom it applie[d] from receiving social security benefits'.[82]

The Court later extended the right of foreign students to financial assistance to cover student maintenance grants, albeit access to such grants was qualified by the requirement to demonstrate a certain degree of integration into the society of the host Member State.[83] Notably, Directive 93/96 explicitly excluded the possibility of students claiming maintenance grants from the Member State in which they studied.[84] However, in the Court's view, that provision did not preclude a student from relying directly on EU citizenship rules and the principle of non-discrimination, which had to be read as giving foreign students the right to maintenance assistance on the same basis as nationals of the host Member State.[85]

The above developments demonstrate how the Court can effectively set aside the provisions of EU legislation by reading them in light of the Treaty free movement rules. Where the dissonance between the language of the relevant legislative measure and the Court's interpretation thereof is too obvious, the Court will rely directly on the provisions of the Treaties, thereby making clear that a piece of legislation cannot preclude it from doing so.[86] The broader implication of the Court's position in *Grzelczyk*, as confirmed in subsequent case law, was that economically inactive persons – such as students, pensioners and people out of work – were in principle granted access to the welfare systems of the Member States in which they resided.[87] Remarkably, this went against express EU-level legislative consensus of that time, whereby economically inactive individuals residing in other Member States had no access to welfare benefits there. In fact, their right of residence itself was conditional on the possession of sufficient financial resources.[88]

Moreover, the Court's interpretation of the scope of free movement rights enjoyed by EU students has been, by and large, transposed into the Citizens' Rights Directive.[89]

[81] Case C-184/99 *Grzelczyk* EU:C:2001:458, [2001] ECR I-6193, paras 44–46, also discussed in ch 2, s III.

[82] ibid, paras 39–40.

[83] Case C-209/03 *Bidar* EU:C:2005:169, [2005] ECR I-2119, paras 57–59, discussed in ch 3, s III.

[84] Council Directive 93/96/EEC on the right of residence for students [1993] OJ L317/59 (Directive 93/96), Art 3.

[85] ibid, para 46.

[86] See also Case C-120/95 *Decker* EU:C:1998:167, [1998] ECR I-1831, paras 27–29 and Case C-158/96 *Kohll* EU:C:1998:171, [1998] ECR I-193, paras 25–27, where the Court avoids ruling on the validity of Council Regulation (EEC) 1408/71 on the application of social security schemes to employed persons and their families moving within the Community [1971] OJ L149/2 (Reg 1408/71) by resolving the dispute directly on the basis of the Treaty free movement rules. See ch 2, s II for a comprehensive discussion.

[87] See, eg, *Trojani* (n 37), para 43.

[88] Council Directive 90/364/EEC on the right of residence [1990] OJ L180/26, Preamble, Recital 4, Art 3; Council Directive 90/365/EEC on the right of residence for employees and self-employed persons who have ceased their occupational activity [1990] OJ L180/28, Preamble, Recital 4, Art 3; Directive 93/96 (n 84), Preamble, Recitals 10 and 11, Art 4.

[89] Council Directive 2004/38/EC on the right of citizens of the Union and their family members to move and reside freely within the territory of the Member States [2004] OJ L158/79 (Citizens' Rights Directive). See also Case C-333/13 *Dano* EU:C:2014:2358 (CJEU, 11 November 2014), suggesting that, at least on the issue of cross-border access to social security, the CJEU has become more cautious and attentive to the political mood.

The drafting history of the Directive suggests that this issue attracted heated political debate between, on the one hand, the Commission and Parliament, advocating for the interests of students, and, on the other hand, the Council, determined to protect the financial interests of the Member States.[90] This debate was won by the Commission, which, crucially, had made its case by relying on the case law. The Directive entitles students to the right to social assistance and maintenance support in the host Member States under the conditions laid down in *Grzelczyk* and subsequent judgments.[91] Thus, the reversal by the Court of the pre-existing political consensus in *Grzelczyk* ultimately became 'legitimised' through the legislative process. However, in reality, the EU legislature had no other option – or at least not a constitutionally sound one – but to follow the Court's interpretation of the Treaties. This, once again, showcases the power of the Court to predetermine, or at least heavily influence, the content of future legislation – as discussed earlier in relation to the adoption of the Patients' Rights Directive.

B. Legislation Governing the Exercise of Collective Labour Rights

The following discussion considers the Posted Workers Directive (PWD) and the Acquired Rights Directive (ARD), both of which have been interpreted by the Court in light of the goals of the internal market.

i. *The Posted Workers Directive*

The judicial interpretation of the Posted Workers Directive in light of free movement rules has been widely criticised for reducing to a significant extent the protection of posted workers. As demonstrated by the analysis of the *Laval* judgment in chapter three, the directive has been interpreted by the Court as a measure establishing maximum standards of protection as regards the employment and working conditions of posted workers whilst commonly having been perceived as a measure providing a floor of rights for those workers.[92] The terms of the directive itself place the protection of workers among its central aims. Recital 5 indicates that the adoption of the directive has been motivated by the need to create a climate of fair competition and guarantee respect for the rights of workers in the transnational provision of services. In line with that aim, Art 3(7) explicitly states that paras 1–6, which set out the core of the working conditions applicable to posted workers, 'shall not prevent application of terms and conditions that are more favourable to workers'.[93] Notwithstanding these stipulations, since *Laval*, the

[90] For a detailed overview of the drafting process, see F Wasserfallen, 'The Judiciary as Legislator? How the European Court of Justice Shapes Policy-Making in the European Union' (2010) 17 *Journal of European Law and Policy* 1128, 1139–43.

[91] Citizens' Rights Directive (n 89), Recitals 3, 10, Arts 14(3), 24. For a detailed discussion of the case law, see ch 3, s III.

[92] Case C-346/06 *Rüffert* EU:C:2008:189, [2008] ECR I-1989, Opinion of AG Bot, para 83; J Malmberg and T Sigeman, 'Industrial Actions and EU Economic Freedoms: The Autonomous Collective Bargaining Model Curtailed by the European Court of Justice' (2008) 45 *CML Rev* 1115, 1116; J Malmberg, 'The Impact of the ECJ Judgments in *Viking, Laval, Rüffert* and *Luxembourg* on the Practice of Collective Bargaining and the Effectiveness of Social Action' (2010) European Parliament Directorate General for Internal Policies, 3–5 ff.

[93] Posted Workers Directive (n 43), Art 3.

Court has taken a view that the directive had a dual purpose, which included both the protection of posted workers *and* the advancement of the free movement of services in the EU.[94] This construction of the purpose of the directive implied that its provisions on the protection of workers were subject to the Treaty free movement rules. In concrete terms, this meant that the level of protection to be guaranteed to posted workers was effectively limited to the nucleus of mandatory rules for minimum protection laid down in Art 3(1) PWD.[95]

In order to remedy the case law and its implications for the protection of workers, the PWD has been recently amended.[96] Effective from mid-2020, the Posted Workers Amendment Directive aims to strengthen the protection of posted workers by putting them on par with local workers in terms of remuneration and, in certain circumstances, other working conditions. The biggest achievement of the Amendment Directive is the introduction of the principle of equal pay between local and posted workers. Under the original directive of 1996, posted workers were only guaranteed a minimum rate of pay applicable in the host Member State. Now, they are entitled to the same remuneration as local workers for the same work at the same place.[97] This provision is designed to eliminate wage competition between the two categories of workers. As such, it is an example of the EU legislature having successfully navigated, at least as regards the terms of pay, around the Court's restrictive interpretation of Art 3(1) PWD.[98] The directive also improves the status of workers in long-term postings. After 12 months, a period which can be prolonged to 18 months upon a 'motivated notification' by the employer, posted workers are entitled to almost all mandatory working conditions of the host Member State.[99] Yet the impact of this provision should not be overestimated. Considering that the average duration of posting in Europe remains shorter than four months,[100] the majority of posted workers will not be able to avail themselves of the improved protections.

Notably, the Amendment Directive also broadens the use of collective agreements as a means for laying down pay obligations and other working conditions applicable to posted workers. The application of collective agreements, previously limited to the construction sector, is now extended to all sectors. However, that does not change the type of collective agreements that can be used for laying down the terms and conditions of employment. Collective agreements must be applicable to all similar undertakings in the geographical area and in the profession or industry concerned or concluded by the most representative worker and employer organisations and applied throughout

[94] Confirmed recently in Case C-620/18 *Hungary v Parliament and Council* EU:C:2020:1001 (CJEU, 8 December 2020), especially paras 50, 58–60.

[95] Case C-341/05 *Laval* EU:C:2007:809, [2007] ECR I-11767, para 81, discussed in ch 3, s IV.

[96] Council Directive (EU) 2018/957/EU amending Directive 96/71/EC concerning the posting of workers in the framework of the provision of services [2018] OJ L173/16 (Posted Workers Amendment Directive).

[97] ibid, Art 1(2)(a).

[98] To that effect, see *Hungary v Parliament and Council* (n 94), especially paras 121–129, affirming the validity of the Posted Workers Amendment Directive.

[99] Posted Workers Amendment Directive (n 96), Art 1(2)(b), making an exception for the rules regarding the conclusion and termination of the employment contract and the supplementary occupational retirement pension schemes.

[100] F De Wispelaere, L De Smedt and J Pacolet, 'Posting of Workers: Report on A1 Portable Documents issued in 2018' (European Commission Directorate-General for Employment, Social Affairs and Inclusion 2019) 11.

the territory.[101] This means that collective agreements which do not have universal or general applicability within the meaning of Art 3(8) PWD continue to be excluded from the permissible means of regulation of pay and working conditions of posted workers. The legislative position in relation to collective agreements is consistent with the judicial interpretation of the original directive in light of Art 56 TFEU, whereby collective bargaining which produces agreements other than those falling within the framework of Art 3(8) PWD is considered insufficiently 'precise and accessible' for businesses to be able to determine their pay obligations as employers.[102]

There is one more provision in the Amendment Directive that merits a mention. Art 1, entitled subject-matter and scope, introduces a paragraph stipulating that:

> This Directive shall not in any way affect the exercise of fundamental rights as recognised in the Member States and at Union level, including the right or freedom to strike or to take other action covered by the specific industrial relations systems in Member States, in accordance with national law and/or practice. Nor does it affect the right to negotiate, to conclude and enforce collective agreements, or to take collective action in accordance with national law and/or practice.

This paragraph clearly seeks to address the concern of trade unions and some of the Member States about the impact that the judicial interpretation of the original PWD has had on collective labour rights and industrial relations systems. In reality, however, it changes nothing. Whilst stipulating that the directive 'shall not in any way affect' the exercise of fundamental rights to collective bargaining and collective action, the same sentence qualifies this guarantee by referring to collective labour rights and their exercise 'as recognised … at Union level'. Certainly, the recognition of the right to collective bargaining and right to strike at Union level includes their judicial interpretation in light of free movement rules.[103] In that sense, the directive cannot be seen as a serious attempt to address the problematic relationship between collective labour rights and economic freedoms established by the case law.

Overall, whilst generally improving the status of posted workers, the amended version of the PWD in no way challenges EU case law on the exercise of collective labour rights in situations concerning the posting of workers. Neither does it challenge the judicial interpretation of the scope of the directive as a measure establishing the maximum levels of protection for posted workers and precluding Member States from imposing on foreign undertakings the conditions that go above or beyond those listed in Art 3(1) PWD. If anything, the amended PWD seems to solidify the position taken by the Court by stipulating that its objective is to balance the protection of the rights of posted workers with the freedom to provide services.[104] So, in reality, the Amendment Directive is far less ambitious than might appear at the outset. To a large extent, it follows and cements the rules developed in the case law, thus providing us with yet another example of the legislative legitimisation of the case law.

[101] Note that the amended Art 3(8) now allows generally applicable agreements to be used 'in addition' to those applicable universally as opposed to only 'in the absence' of a system for declaring collective agreements of universal application.

[102] *Laval* (n 95), paras 107–10, examined in this respect in ch 3, s IV.

[103] As confirmed in *Hungary v Parliament and Council* (n 94), para 168.

[104] To that effect, see Recital 4.

ii. The Acquired Rights Directive

Another legislative measure in the area of social policy whose judicial interpretation displays a market bias is the Acquired Rights Directive.[105] The Court for the first time delivered an interpretation of the directive in the infamous *Alemo-Herron* judgment, concerning the validity of the UK's transposition of this directive.[106] This judgment was analysed in detail in chapter three, but it deserves a brief mention here.[107] Before *Alemo-Herron*, the ARD had been widely interpreted as a measure providing the minimum worker protections in the event of transfer of undertakings.[108] However, the Court considered that the directive required a fair balancing of the interests of businesses, on the one hand, and workers, on the other. In practice, this balance meant prioritising the former over the latter. The Court concluded that the requirement that the transferee observe 'dynamic' contractual clauses permitting ongoing determination of contractual terms by reference to applicable collective agreements placed too much burden on the transferee undertaking, thus inhibiting its ability to adjust to changes resulting from the transfer.[109]

Remarkably, this interpretation of the ARD, in the Court's view, was supported by the Charter of Fundamental Rights. The Court's reading of the Charter also seemed to be biased towards the protection of business interests. It singled out the freedom to conduct a business protected under Art 16 CFR while completely disregarding the Charter's 'Solidarity' chapter,[110] which is dedicated almost in its entirety to the protection of workers.[111] By relying on the Charter, the Court elevated a commercial freedom to conduct a business to the level of a seemingly absolute fundamental right.[112] It almost seemed that the Court's reference to the Charter was made in a strategic way. It served the purpose of affirming the judicial understanding of the relationship between the freedom of contract and the right to collective bargaining whereby the former took priority over the latter. Notably, the *Alemo-Herron* decision now stands as an authoritative, Treaty-mandated interpretation of the ARD.

C. Regulation 1408/71 on the Coordination of Social Security Schemes

The final and perhaps most poignant example of the Court's capacity to override existing legislative consensus and thus simultaneously pre-empt legislative overturn of the

[105] Acquired Rights Directive (n 44).

[106] *Alemo-Herron* (n 44).

[107] See ch 3, s IV for a detailed analysis.

[108] To that effect, see Acquired Rights Directive (n 44), Preamble and Art 8. See also *Alemo-Herron*, Opinion of AG Cruz Villalón, para 20; J Prassl, 'Freedom of Contract as a General Principle of EU Law? Transfers of Undertakings and the Protection of Employer Rights in EU Labour Law: Case C-426/11 *Alemo-Herron and Others v Parkwood Leisure Ltd*' (2013) 42 *Industrial Law Journal* 434, 444–45; S Weatherill, 'Use and Abuse of the EU's Charter of Fundamental Rights: on the Improper Veneration of "Freedom of Contract". Judgment of the Court of 18 July 2013: Case C-426/11, *Mark Alemo-Herron and Others v Parkwood Leisure Ltd*' (2014) 10 *European Review of Contract Law* 167, 170.

[109] *Alemo-Herron*, paras 28–29.

[110] Charter of Fundamental Rights of the European Union [2000] OJ C364/1 (CFR), title IV 'Solidarity'.

[111] See, in particular, Art 27 CFR on the right to information and consultation and Art 28 on the right to collective bargaining.

[112] Weatherill (n 108) 177–80.

case law is Regulation 1408/71, whose judicial interpretation in light of free movement rules has produced dramatic results.

Regulation 1408/71 was adopted for the purposes of coordination of basic national rules in the field of social and healthcare benefits.[113] Art 22(2) of the Regulation allowed EU nationals to travel to another Member State for medical goods and services at the expense of their own healthcare system provided that the healthcare authorities at home had given express authorisation beforehand. The original wording of Art 22(2) accorded Member States a considerable margin of discretion in making decisions regarding the grant of authorisation for medical treatment abroad. Governments were free to refuse such authorisation unless the treatment in question could not be provided for the person concerned within the territory of their State of residence. This provision was unqualified by references to either the timing or effectiveness of the treatment. As such, it gave a lot of leeway to national healthcare authorities to assess whether, in principle, they were capable of providing the treatment in question.

The Court was given the opportunity to deliver an interpretation of Art 22(2) in the *Pierik* cases, concerning a Dutch national who went to Germany to receive hydrotherapy treatment.[114] The patient's request for reimbursement was refused because hydrotherapy was not among the types of treatment covered by the Dutch health insurance. The Court took the view that the intention of the Regulation was to give the medical requirements the decisive role in the decision of competent authorities to grant or refuse the authorisation for treatment abroad. Accordingly, authorisation could not be refused when the foreign treatment was considered 'necessary and effective', even if it was not offered in the health package of the State of insurance.[115] The Court's interpretation of Art 22 in the *Pierik* cases caused a political backlash at the EU level. Worried about the implications for their healthcare budgets, Member States 'corrected' the Court's interpretation of the said provision by adopting unanimously several important amendments to the Regulation.[116] Art 22 was amended to include a provision expressly stating that the authorisation could not be obtained for treatment that was not among the benefits provided for by the legislation of the patient's Member State of residence.[117] If this condition was fulfilled, the prior authorisation could not be refused where the patient could not be given adequate treatment in their State of affiliation within the time normally necessary for obtaining such treatment, taking account the patient's state of health and the probable course of the disease.[118] The latter condition in essence reiterated the requirements laid down by the Court in *Pierik II*.[119] In addition,

[113] Reg 1408/71 (n 86), Preamble, discussed in ch 2, s II.

[114] Case C-117/77 *Pierik* EU:C:1978:35, [1978] ECR 825 (*Pierik I*); Case C-182/78 *Pierik* EU:C:1979:142, [1979] ECR 1977 (*Pierik II*).

[115] *Pierik I* (n 114), para 26; *Pierik II* (n 114), paras 12–13.

[116] See Council Regulation (EEC) 2793/81 amending Regulation (EEC) 1408/71 on the application of social security schemes to employed persons and their families moving within the Community and Regulation (EEC) 574/72 fixing the procedure for implementing Regulation (EEC) 1408/71 [1982] OJ L122/14 (Reg 2793/81), Art 22(2), discussed in AP van der Mei, *Free Movement of Persons Within the European Community: Cross-Border Access to Public Benefits* (Oxford, Hart Publishing, 2003) 254–256; V Hatzopoulos, 'Actively Talking to Each Other: the Court and the Political Institutions' in B de Witte, E Muir and M Dawson (eds), *Judicial Activism at the European Court of Justice* (Cheltenham, Edward Elgar Publishing, 2013) 135.

[117] Reg 2793/81 (n 116), Preamble and Art 22(1).

[118] ibid.

[119] *Pierik II*, paras 9–12.

a new recital was introduced in the preamble of the Regulation, which, referring to the practical 'experience' of its implementation, emphasised the importance of extending 'the discretionary power of an institution of a Member State … in granting or refusing authorisation'. Evidently, the purpose of the overall amendments was to reinstate the control of national authorities over decision making in matters of public healthcare and curb the interference of the Court into questions concerning the financing of medical treatment received abroad.

In subsequent case law, the Court did not challenge the political agreement on the scope of treatment covered by Art 22. Nevertheless, it sustained an expansionist interpretation of this provision. It did so in two ways: first, by giving a Europeanised meaning to the terms that were key in defining the scope of the benefits package[120] and, second, by providing an extremely detailed interpretation of the 'medical necessity' criterion, focused solely on the individual circumstances of the patient in question.[121] In doing so, the Court narrowed down, once again, the margin of discretion bestowed upon the Member States by Regulation 1408/71. The Court justified this approach by reference to the purpose of Art 22, which, according to the Court, was to facilitate the free movement of insured persons and the cross-border provision of medical services.[122] Considering the judicial construction of the purpose of Art 22, it was not unexpected that the Court eventually arrived at the conclusion that there was 'no reason which seriously justifie[d] different interpretations' of 'undue delay' in waiting for medical treatment depending upon whether the context was Art 22 of Regulation 1408/71 or Art 49 EC.[123] By aligning the interpretation of Art 22 of the Regulation with that adopted under Art 49, the Court has effectively given its interpretation of Art 22 the status of EU primary law. Notably, this interpretation was later codified in Art 20 of Regulation 883/2004, which replaced Regulation 1408/71. Art 20(2) provides that the competent institutions must grant the authorisation for treatment abroad if a person cannot be given treatment in their home Member State 'within a time limit which is medically justifiable, taking into account his/her current state of health and the probable course of his/her illness'.[124] This almost word by word replicates the language employed by the Court in the case law.

The foregoing analysis goes to show that the power of judicial interpretation of EU law includes the power also to prevent legislative reversal of the case law. It demonstrates how the intentions of the drafters of Regulation 1408/71 have been shaped and moulded by the Court in order to fit the logic of free movement rules. In result, the Court has drastically changed the meaning of Art 22 of Regulation 1408/71, turning it into an EU-wide obligation, binding the Member States, to reimburse the costs of medical treatment received abroad to all patients whose condition is serious enough to necessitate treatment. Moreover, by basing this interpretation on the provisions of both

[120] Case C-157/99 *Smits and Peerbooms* EU:C:2001:404, [2001] ECR I-5473, para 94, discussed in ch 3, s II, asserting that the medical treatment considered as 'normal in professional circles', according to the Dutch legislation, had to be read as also including treatment 'sufficiently tried and tested by international medical science'.

[121] For a detailed discussion, see ch 3, s II.

[122] Case C-372/04 *Watts* EU:C:2006:325, [2006] ECR I-4325, paras 54, with further reference to Case C-56/01 *Inizan* EU:C:2003:578, [2003] ECR I-12403, para 21.

[123] ibid, para 60, referring to Art 49 of the Consolidated version of the Treaty Establishing the European Community [2002] OJ C325/33 (EC). Also discussed in ch 3, s II.

[124] Reg 883/2004 (n 43), Art 20(2).

the Regulation and the Treaties, the Court has effectively precluded the possibility of it being overturned by a legislative amendment.

It was pointed out above that the EU's legislative institutions had attempted, at least initially, to 'correct' the case law through the process of legislative amendment. The correction point is a noteworthy one. It is true that in theory, in situations where the political actors are dissatisfied with the developments in the case law, the EU legislature retains the right to enact a legislative reversal of the case law – something it attempted to do in the Monti II draft. Of course, in strictly legal terms, the constitutionality of such a reversal would be doubtful, given that the case law embodies an authoritative interpretation of the Treaties. However, from the political point of view, there remains a possibility that the Court would choose to defer to the legislature in the event of a legislative reversal of the case law, thereby showing respect to the legislative consensus and persisting political will.

Questions concerning judicial deference towards the legislature are not specific to the context of the EU – they have echoes in the practice of supreme and constitutional courts around the world. How to determine the proper reach of the judicial role always involves also looking at the political and legislative process. However, the EU's context is different, and more complex, because the role of the Court is shaped not only by the response of the EU legislative institutions but also by the claims of national governments via the principle of conferral. Considering this, the choice on behalf of the Court to defer the resolution of a particular matter to the EU legislature could also ease the tensions that arise between the EU and Member States due to the often strained judicial interpretation of EU legislation in light of the Treaties. At the same time, however, it could weaken the institutional position of the Court in the eyes of both the EU legislature and national governments, thereby potentially challenging the ability of the Court to protect the rule of law in the EU. Perhaps this explains why the extent to which the Court allows the passage of secondary legislation to affect its reading of primary law, as observed by Syrpis, generally varies from case to case and is, therefore, extremely hard to predict.[125] The lesson to be learned from the legislative history of Regulation 1408/71 is that the Court should not be expected to retract from previous rulings without a compelling reason and that a legislative reversal of the case law might not be enough of a reason in that respect.

D. Policy Solutions under the Open Method of Coordination

A final point that needs to be addressed in this discussion is the policy solutions that are available to the EU legislature under the Open Method of Coordination (OMC).

When judicial interpretation undermines legislative choices, Member States retain the option of resorting to soft law mechanisms, such as the OMC, which allows the adoption of a variety of measures that do not necessarily need to follow the Court's case law. The OMC is normally employed to deal with matters that are not dealt with (or meant to be dealt with) by binding measures, especially in situations where the imposition of

[125] In that connection, see P Syrpis, 'The Relationship between Primary and Secondary Law in the EU' (2015) 52 *CML Rev* 461, suggesting that the Court is not consistent in deferring to secondary legislation.

a uniform solution would be undesirable due to the diversity among domestic regulatory regimes.[126] The most prominent examples of areas governed by the OMC are the European Employment Strategy and the coordination of Member States' economic policies. In these areas, the OMC offers a tempting alternative to binding legislation because it does not require the same drafting precision and is an easier route by which to reach consensus. Sometimes it is even preferred to hard law because of its reflexive nature and the leeway in implementation it offers to the Member States.[127] The effectiveness of the OMC is, however, fairly limited in practice precisely because it is not meant to replace binding rules. For that reason, the OMC appears to be unsuitable for addressing the problems that arise from the judicial interpretation of the Treaties. At the end of the day, if binding measures are not capable of offsetting the quasi-legislative effects of the case law, the OMC, consisting predominantly of incentive measures, will be even less, if at all, capable of doing so.

VII. Conclusion

This chapter demonstrated how the Court's case law has shaped the institutional balance of powers in the EU. It introduced the concept of a quasi-legislative judgment, which explains the character of much of the case law under study here. In addition to deciding a particular point of law, quasi-legislative judgments lay down generally framed rules and principles that create rights and obligations of wider application. This quality makes the rules laid down in the case law easily transposable into EU-level legislation, which has a major impact on EU legislative activity in the areas that are constitutionally sensitive. Using concrete examples of legislation from the areas under study here, the chapter argued that the case law puts the legislature into the so-called judicial trap, leaving it with a limited choice of legislative options, neither of which can provide an adequate legislative response to the issues regulated by the case law. This happens due to a combination of several factors: the constitutional constraints on EU action, reflected in the limited availability of legislative bases, the diversity of national regulatory preferences, given high political and social sensitivity of the matters concerned, and the ensuing difficulty in achieving EU-wide political agreement. Constraints surrounding the legislative process typically lead to the development of certain models of interinstitutional interaction between the legislature and judiciary which undermine any meaningful exercise of legislative discretion, thus upsetting the horizontal balance of powers in the EU.

Model of Interaction No 1 described a situation where quasi-legislative rules laid down in the case law *predetermine the scope and content* of legislative action, as in the case of the Patients' Rights Directive and the Commission's *Altmark* Package. The legislature finds itself trapped in a position where a political agreement necessary to change the rules developed in the case law cannot be achieved and, therefore, the only feasible option left is to codify those rules. At times, especially in relation to more controversial issues, a political agreement cannot be reached to adopt any legislation at all. This is

[126] Craig (n 20) 198–203, 218.

[127] D Ashiagbor, 'Evaluating the Reflexive Turn in Labour Law' in A Bogg et al (eds) *The Autonomy of Labour Law* (Oxford, Hart Publishing, 2015).

captured by Model of Interaction No 2, whereby the case law serves de facto to *pre-empt the adoption* of any novel legislative solutions, as happened with the Monti II draft. In this scenario, the matters concerned continue to be regulated directly by the case law. Model of Interaction No 3 refers to circumstances where a legislative measure is already in place, but its judicial interpretation in light of the Treaties *overrides the existing legislative consensus*, thus rendering EU-wide political agreement devoid of practical force. By the same token, this new interpretation becomes immune from subsequent legislative amendment, thus *preventing legislative reversal* of the case law. The examples that best illustrate this dynamic are the Posted Workers Directive and Regulation 1408/71.

As a result, the EU legislative institutions are in these circumstances barred from any meaningful degree of autonomous action. Essentially, their role gets reduced to the legitimisation of judicial lawmaking through the legislative enactment of the rules developed by the Court. This interinstitutional dynamic is problematic from the point of view of both the horizontal balance of powers and the vertical division of competences in the EU because it makes the Court de facto the ultimate lawmaker in the policy areas which were supposed to stay within the prerogative of national legislative bodies.

The Court's practice also has broader implications for the EU's democratic legitimacy. On the one hand, it removes a number of highly sensitive matters from the ambit of democratic decision making at the level of the Member States and does so in the absence of a sophisticated constitutional mandate that would authorise the EU to regulate those matters.[128] On the other hand, it diminishes the role of democratic elements at the supranational, EU level. In particular, it deprives the EU legislature of the opportunity to address the matters concerned through a deliberative process, which would ensure that different interests are represented and debated.[129] At the end of the day, we are left with EU-wide rules, regardless of whether they are later transposed into EU legislation, that are borne out of litigation, made on an ad-hoc basis and by a body lacking the expertise to make highly sensitive, socio-economic policy choices.[130] This not only compromises the legitimacy of the Court itself, as a judicial institution, but also implicates the legitimacy of the EU as a whole.

[128] See also ch 1, s I for a discussion of the democratic consequences of the judicial interpretation of internal market law.

[129] See Arts 10–11 TEU on the role of participation and representation of interests in EU governance. See also *Roquette Frères* (n 18), para 33; Lenaerts and Verhoeven (n 23) 45–46. On the Court's relationship with the values of representative democracy in the EU, see T Horsley, *The Court of Justice of the European Union as an Institutional Actor: Judicial Lawmaking and its Limits* (Cambridge, CUP, 2018) 188–93.

[130] For academic commentary on these various aspects, see C Newdick, 'Citizenship, Free Movement, and Healthcare: Cementing Individual Rights by Corroding Social Solidarity' (2006) 43 *CML Rev* 1645; ACL Davies, 'One Step Forward, Two Steps Back? The *Viking* and *Laval* Cases in the ECJ' (2008) 37 *Industrial Law Journal* 126, 143; G Davies, 'The Price of Letting Courts Value Solidarity: The Judicial Role in Liberalizing Welfare' in M Ross and Y Borgmann-Prebil, *Promoting Solidarity in the European Union* (Oxford, OUP, 2010); Schiek et al (n 48) 89; J Zglinski, *Europe's Passive Virtues: Deference to National Authorities in EU Free Movement Law* (Oxford, OUP, 2020) 170 ff, discussing the issues of representation and expertise in CJEU lawmaking.

5

Rebalancing the Court, Rebalancing the EU

Building on the argument advanced in the previous chapters that the degree of the Court's interference with national regulatory autonomy through the interpretation of free movement rules is neither dictated nor justified by the reading of the Treaties and that the case law lacks firm conceptual constitutional and substantive grounds, this chapter proposes a solution aimed at restoring the balance of competences and powers within the EU and thus ameliorating the tensions that the case law has created. This solution involves reforming the Court's interpretative methodology, albeit moderately, while using as a framework the Court's wider case law in the area of the internal market. The suggested reform is in essence a call for coherence in the case law, to be achieved through reinforcing the principles which govern the allocation of competences and powers in the EU into the judicial interpretation of free movement law. In practice, it would require that the Court, given the room for interpretative manoeuvre it enjoys in the exercise of its powers,[1] relax the standard of judicial review in relation to national measures that in principle fall outside the EU's regulatory competence.

The chapter follows in five sections. Section I lays down the conceptual and legal basis for a relaxed judicial review, grounded in the reinforcement of the principles of subsidiarity and proportionality into EU judicial practice. Sections II–IV introduce three techniques of judicial interpretation that could be considered as particular expressions of the principles of subsidiarity and proportionality in the form of judicial reasoning and could thus be employed to lower the standard of judicial review in constitutionally sensitive areas of national policy. The techniques in question are the doctrine of margin of appreciation (section II), the fair balance approach (section III) and the exemption from the scope of EU law (section IV). Section V concludes.

I. The Conceptual and Legal Basis for a Relaxed Judicial Review

From a conceptual point of view, the proposition for a relaxed judicial review rests on the combination of the constitutional principles which govern the allocation of

[1] The question concerning the breadth of judicial discretion is discussed in detail in ch 1, s III.

competences and powers in the EU: conferral, subsidiarity, proportionality and institutional balance. As has been discussed in chapter one and demonstrated throughout this book, these principles are interconnected in their functions and share common theoretical underpinnings. Therefore, none of them on their own is decisive in determining the constitutional legitimacy of the judicial interpretation of free movement law and none is a rule rather than a principle.[2] For reasons of clarity and legal certainty, this chapter primarily focuses on subsidiarity and proportionality as the two principles to be reinforced into EU judicial practice. These two principles have been chosen as a legal basis for the proposed reform because they are capable of being effectively operationalised in judicial reasoning, as will be demonstrated in this chapter. However, the observance by the Court of the two principles would undoubtedly improve the legitimacy of the case law in light of the wider constraints on EU competence by ensuring respect for national regulatory autonomy in the judicial interpretation of the Treaties.

To achieve compliance with the principle of subsidiarity, the Court is invited to reflect more seriously on the subsidiary nature of EU law and, accordingly, advance the objectives of the internal market whilst taking into account the implications of its decisions for the scope of national regulatory autonomy in areas that are constitutionally sensitive from the EU law point of view. Apart from the policy areas studied in this book, this approach could be extended to the areas of crime prevention, culture and tourism, sport, civil protection, and tax. A subsidiarity-guided approach would require the Court to show more deference to domestic actors – legislative, administrative and judicial – by according them a margin of appreciation, or margin of discretion, in their actions (section II). The exact breadth of the margin of appreciation would depend on the peculiarities of the domestic context and should take into account the level of protection pursued by national regulatory policies. This would allow the Court to preserve the diversity of the regulatory models of the Member States. In certain cases, subsidiarity could justify an exemption of the matter from the purview of EU internal market law (section IV). Notably, the question whether a matter falls within the scope of EU law is a primary concern of the principle of conferral.[3] However, it can also be approached through the lens of subsidiarity, which determines not only the extent to which the EU should exercise competences conferred upon it, but also whether those competences should be exercised in the first place.[4]

In a similar vein, the principle of proportionality should ensure that the Court's interpretation of internal market law does not interfere excessively with non-market values protected at the national level. To that end, the Court would be expected to strike a fair balance in the reconciliation of the two sets of values. This could be achieved through conducting a two-fold inquiry into their relationship: in addition to the proportionality review employed to assess the lawfulness of restrictions on free movement, the Court

[2] For a discussion of the theoretical underpinnings of the principles under study, see ch 1, s I. See also RM Dworkin, 'The Model of Rules' (1967) 35 *University of Chicago Law Review* 14, describing principles as standards which must be taken into account, where relevant, as a consideration inclining in a certain direction, as opposed to rules, which apply in all-or-nothing fashion.

[3] For a comprehensive discussion, see ch 2.

[4] See ch 3, s I for a comprehensive analysis of the principles of subsidiarity and proportionality and their application to EU judicial practice.

would need to assess whether a particular interpretation (and application) of free movement rules is necessary for the achievement of the objectives of the internal market in light of the restrictive effect that such interpretation may have on the protection of legitimate interests advanced by Member States. This approach would thus put limitations on both the economic freedoms and the non-market interests protected at the national level, whilst at the same time ensuring that neither is sacrificed for the sake of protecting the other.

II. The Margin of Appreciation

As previously mentioned, judicial review performed by the Court can be relaxed by employing a set of techniques, or methods, of judicial interpretation, all of which are already to be found in EU internal market case law. This and the following two sections focus on three interpretative techniques that could be considered as particular expressions of the principles of subsidiarity and proportionality in the form of judicial reasoning. The techniques in question are the doctrine of margin of appreciation; the fair balance (or double proportionality) approach; and exemption from the application of EU law. Each of the three techniques represent a different point in the spectrum of intensity of judicial review, from complete deference (exemption), to a grant of more room for national manoeuvre (margin of appreciation), to an equitable weighing of competing legal interests (fair balance). Most significantly, all of them entail a review less intense than the Court normally performs in its free movement case law in relation to national regulatory measures in the areas of healthcare, education and collective labour law.

A. Margin of Appreciation as a Manifestation of Subsidiarity

The doctrine of margin of appreciation is one of the most commonly used doctrines of judicial deference in supranational jurisprudence. The grant of a margin of appreciation means that national authorities will be accorded some room for manoeuvre in fulfilling their international obligations. In the European context, this doctrine is renowned for its application in the case law of the ECtHR.[5] The ECtHR conceptualises the doctrine of margin of appreciation as a manifestation of the principle of subsidiarity in judicial reasoning. In that connection, it holds that the European Convention on Human Rights[6]

[5] See, eg, *The Belgian Linguistic case (No 2)* (1968) 1 EHRR 252, para 48; *Branko Tomašić v Croatia* App no 46598/06 (ECtHR, 15 January 2009), para 74. For academic discussion, see, eg, Y Shany, 'Toward a General Margin of Appreciation Doctrine in International Law?' (2006) 16 *European Journal of International Law* 907; Open Society Justice Initiative, 'Margin of Appreciation – An Overview of the Strasbourg Court's Margin of Appreciation Doctrine' (*Open Society Justice Initiative*, April 2012) www.opensocietyfoundations.org/sites/default/files/echr-reform-margin-of-appreciation.pdf; D Spielmann, 'Allowing the Right Margin: The European Court of Human Rights and the National Margin of Appreciation Doctrine: Waiver or Subsidiarity of European Review?' (2015) 14 *Cambridge Yearbook of European Legal Studies* 381.

[6] Convention on the Protection of Human Rights and Fundamental Freedoms (ECHR) (adopted 4 November 1950, entered into force 3 September 1953) ETS 5.

has only a subsidiary role in protecting human rights, whereas the primary responsibility lies with the national authorities of the member States. It is, therefore, inevitable that the Convention will be interpreted differently in different member States, given their divergent legal and cultural traditions.[7] Differences in interpretation are, however, tolerated because national authorities are considered to be better positioned than an international judge to assess the necessity and appropriateness of restrictions on the exercise of fundamental rights in the specific national context.

When determining the breadth of margin of appreciation, the ECtHR usually takes into account a number of factors that are relevant to the circumstances of the case, most prominently the nature of the protected right, the objective pursued by the contested measure, and the degree of European consensus regarding the regulation of the matter in question.[8] Naturally, the more fundamental the protected right, the smaller the margin for national authorities. Conversely, the margin will be wider when there is no consensus among the Contracting States 'either as to the relative importance of the interest at stake or as to the best means of protecting it, particularly where the case raises sensitive moral or ethical issues'.[9] The ECtHR will also be more lenient when national authorities are faced with a task of balancing between competing private and public interests or conflicting Convention rights.[10]

The doctrine of margin of appreciation is also well known in the case law of the CJEU. Frequently referred to as margin of discretion, it is employed in two main contexts: when performing judicial review of EU legislative acts;[11] and when assessing the compatibility of national regulatory frameworks with EU law, most notably internal market law. The discussion below focuses on the latter context. The Court does not seem to have a single theory as regards the set of circumstances in which the doctrine applies. Nor does it adopt the methodology of the ECtHR – at least not openly. Typically, the Court will invoke margin of appreciation in relation to issues and areas of national policy that are sensitive, whether constitutionally, politically, socially or culturally.[12] It considers as an important indication of the sensitivity of a particular issue the persisting divergence in regulatory approaches across the Member States. This suggests that,

[7] *The Belgian Linguistic case (No 2)* (n 5), para 10; *Handyside v UK* (1976) 1 EHRR 73, para 48; *Branko Tomašić v Croatia* (n 5), para 74; Open Society Justice Initiative (n 5). On this point, see also ch 1, s III.

[8] See, eg, *S and Marper v UK* App nos 30562/04 and 30566/04 (ECtHR, 4 December 2008), para 102, providing an overview of the relevant factors. For a comprehensive analysis of these factors, see J Gerards, 'Pluralism, Deference and the Margin of Appreciation Doctrine' (2011) 12 *European Law Journal* 80, advocating for a systematic use of a 'doctrine of deference' by EU courts on the basis of the ECtHR model. See also J Gerards, 'Margin of Appreciation and Incrementalism in the Case Law of the European Court of Human Rights' (2018) 18 *Human Rights Law Review* 495.

[9] *Evans v UK* (2007) 41 EHRR 21, para 77; *Schalk & Kopf v Austria* App no 30141/04 (ECtHR, 24 June 2010), para 98.

[10] ibid; *Chassagnou v France* (1999) 29 EHRR 615, para 113.

[11] On legislative discretion, see, eg, S Weatherill, 'The Limits of Legislative Harmonisation Ten Years after *Tobacco Advertising*: How the Court's Case Law Has Become a "Drafting Guide"' (2011) 12 *German Law Journal* 827.

[12] N Shuibhne, 'Margins of Appreciation: National Values, Fundamental Rights and EC Free Movement Law' (2009) 34 *European Law Review* 254; Gerards (n 8). For a comprehensive recent study of the circumstances in which margin of appreciation is invoked in EU free movement case law, see J Zglinski, *Europe's Passive Virtues: Deference to National Authorities in EU Free Movement Law* (Oxford, OUP, 2020) 68–96.

just like in the framework of the ECHR, the doctrine of margin of appreciation in EU law can be viewed as a concrete application of the principle of subsidiarity in judicial practice.

In light of the above, it is suggested that the Court should employ the doctrine of margin of appreciation in cases concerning the interpretation (and application) of free movement law in policy areas that are predominantly reserved by the Treaties to national competence, such as the areas under study. This would not entail any radical reform in the Court's methodology of legal reasoning. It would, however, help to achieve greater coherence in the case law, thereby increasing its overall constitutional legitimacy. Examples from the Court's existing case law in the context of the internal market demonstrate how, and in what circumstances, the doctrine of margin of appreciation can be extended to the areas of healthcare, education and collective labour law. The segments of the case law which will be used in the analysis concern the free movement of healthcare providers and the exercise of fundamental rights in transnational situations.

B. The Free Movement of Healthcare Providers

i. The Question of Persons versus Businesses

The discussion below proposes that the Court could use its case law concerning the free movement of healthcare providers as a model for extending the application of margin of appreciation to situations involving patients' access to cross-border healthcare.

The standard of judicial review that the Court employs in cases concerning the free movement of healthcare providers, discussed in detail in chapter three, is in principle equivalent to that employed in the context of free movement of gambling operators.[13] In both strands of case law, judicial review is premised on the recognition that the particular political and social sensitivity of the sector – be it healthcare or gambling – requires a broad margin of discretion to be granted to national authorities. The healthcare sector also requires additional sensitivity for constitutional reasons, as it is excluded from the explicit legislative competence of the EU. Accordingly, the Court recognises that national healthcare authorities have the prerogative to determine the 'level of protection' they wish to pursue through their regulatory policies and to choose the appropriate means to attain that level of protection.[14]

Owing to the margin of discretion enjoyed by national authorities, judicial inquiry into national measures that restrict healthcare provision by foreign operators focuses on the suitability, or appropriateness, of respective measures, reducing the test of necessity to a minimum.[15] National rules will be deemed suitable for ensuring the attainment of

[13] See ch 3, ss II and V, respectively.

[14] See, eg, Case C-169/07 *Hartlauer* EU:C:2009:141, [2009] ECR I-1721, paras 29–30; Joined cases C-570/07 and C-571/07 *Pérez and Gómez* EU:C:2010:300, [2010] ECR I-4629, para 44.

[15] On necessity, see, eg, Case C-496/01 *Commission v France* EU:C:2004:137, [2004] ECR I-2351, paras 68–70; Case C-140/03 *Commission v Greece* EU:C:2005:242, [2005] ECR I-3177, paras 34–35, discussed in ch 3, s II.

the objective pursued if they 'genuinely' reflect a concern to attain it in a 'consistent and systematic' manner. On the procedural side, national regulatory frameworks must be designed in a way that adequately circumscribes the exercise of administrative discretion, in order to prevent arbitrary decision making.[16] This requirement would not be met if, for instance, the system in question conditions the entry to the market of new healthcare providers on a discretionary assessment of the needs of that particular market.[17]

The above approach stands in sharp contrast to the Court's approach in cases concerning patients' access to cross-border healthcare. As discussed at length in chapter three, the judicial review of restrictions on access to healthcare provided in other Member States focuses on the necessity of national authorisation schemes. As a consequence, governments are obliged to cover the costs incurred by their nationals for medical care obtained abroad unless they can prove that an equally effective treatment was available at home without delay.[18] The assessment of what constitutes a timely and effective treatment has to be performed in light of the criterion of 'medical necessity' as defined in the case law. Judicial review in these cases is significantly more intense than in cases concerning the free movement of healthcare operators. Yet the regulatory context seems to be broadly the same. It concerns a sector that is constitutionally sensitive from the EU law point of view and politically and socially sensitive from a national point of view. The Court appears to recognise this and in both strands of case law it emphasises the prerogative of Member States to organise and manage their social security systems, in particular, health services and medical care. What, then, explains the divergence in judicial review?

One possible explanation stems from the relative constitutional importance attached to the different types of free movement within the framework of EU law. An argument could be made that the right of patients to access healthcare, forming part of the free movement of persons, is more important than a purely economic right of healthcare providers to access foreign markets. This circumstance would, then, explain why free movement is protected to a greater degree in situations concerning the mobility of patients as opposed to businesses providing healthcare. Indeed, the Court has declared on multiple occasions that the right of EU nationals to move and reside in other Member States constitutes the 'very essence' of the principle of freedom of movement guaranteed by the Treaty.[19] Accordingly, any limitations of this right can only be accepted in exceptional circumstances.[20] This approach seems to be driven by a desire to ensure an effective protection of the rights of EU citizens, in this context, to access public services. That rationale can also clearly be seen playing a key role in the case law concerning student access to higher education in other Member States.[21]

However, I would argue that the free movement case law under study, by and large, falls short of achieving an effective protection of EU citizens. By focusing narrowly

[16] *Hartlauer* (n 14), paras 55, 57–71.

[17] ibid.

[18] See, eg, Case C-372/04 *Watts* EU:C:2006:325, [2006] ECR I-4325, para 75, discussed in ch 3, s II.

[19] See, eg, Case C-147/03 *Commission v Austria* EU:C:2005:427, [2005] ECR I-5969, para 70; Case C-73/08 *Bressol* EU:C:2010:181, [2010] ECR I-2735, para 79.

[20] ibid.

[21] To that effect, see case law analysis in ch 3, s III.

on the perceived individual benefits of unrestricted access to public services across borders, be it healthcare or education, it neglects the broader implications of such free movement for national systems of social protection. Proper functioning of a public healthcare system is essential for ensuring the protection of the rights of *all* citizens, not just mobile ones. Judicial interference with the functioning of that system puts at risk the most vulnerable groups of patients, who might be deprived of necessary treatment in favour of patients with less urgent medical needs but with the resources to travel abroad.[22] Although the consequences may be less dramatic in the context of access to education, they are similar in nature. The judicial endorsement of the rights of mobile students threatens the financial sustainability of education systems based on free and open access, thereby putting at a disadvantage local students who are unable due to financial or family circumstances, or simply unwilling, to pursue studies abroad. In both contexts, a systemic perspective that would lower the Court's standard of review of domestic regulatory measures seems to be overall better suited to protect the rights of EU citizens. It should thus be taken into account in cases involving the free movement of patients and persons more generally.

Finally, the distinctive treatment of persons in comparison to businesses maintained by the Court loses some of its plausibility when viewed in light of the wider EU free movement case law. Case law on collective labour rights provides a powerful illustration in that respect. The Court has consistently employed a strict-scrutiny approach in the review of trade union actions that came into conflict with the cross-border provision of services. One might speculate that in this way the Court has been, in fact, implicitly promoting the free movement of workers across the EU through increasing opportunities for employment abroad. This would be in line with the Court's emphasis on the fundamental importance of the free movement of individuals in the EU. Yet, as appealing as this explanation might be, not least because it gives a sense of coherence to the case law, it is unconvincing. The Court has not once considered any of the *Viking* and *Laval* line of cases in light of the Treaty provisions concerning the free movement of workers.[23] In fact, the Court's approach to collective labour rights seems to have little to do with the empowerment of the working individual. Quite the contrary, this approach has empowered businesses operating across borders; it has done so expressly and often at the expense of the protection of workers' rights.[24] Therefore, it would seem that the Court's primary concern has always been, and remains, the advancement of *free movement as such*, regardless of who the beneficiaries of that free movement may be.

The above analysis goes to show that there is little justification left for maintaining marked differences in the standard of judicial review in cases concerning the free movement of patients, on the one hand, and healthcare providers, on the other. Viewing both types of free movement from a systemic perspective would allow the Court to adopt a coherent standard of review: one that is guided by the principle of subsidiarity and thus

[22] For a comprehensive analysis, see ch 3, s II.

[23] Case C-438/05 *Viking* EU:C:2007:772, [2007] ECR I-10779; Case C-341/05 *Laval* EU:C:2007:809, [2007] ECR I-11767.

[24] See ch 3, s IV for a comprehensive discussion of the Court's reasoning and implications thereof for the protection of workers.

premised on the recognition of national margin of appreciation in the organisation and management of the healthcare sector.

Accordingly, I would propose that in future cases concerning patients' access to cross-border healthcare, the Court adopt an approach whereby restrictions on access to healthcare stemming from government-mandated waiting lists and general clinical priorities will be justified provided that: (a) the criteria that determine the waiting time for treatment are fair, objective and transparent; (b) the available treatment is sufficiently effective; and (c) the procedures for granting authorisation to receive treatment abroad comply with the procedural requirements of the principle of proportionality.[25] The test of medical necessity, which shifts the focus towards the circumstances of the individual and away from the healthcare system as a whole, should be done away with as it is incompatible with the principle of subsidiarity.[26]

ii. Healthcare Services under Competition Law

Before concluding this discussion, mention should also be made of EU competition case law in the healthcare sector, which offers some valuable insights into the Court's wider understanding of the contours of the internal market. Competition case law suggests that EU internal market law is well suited to accommodate national regulatory choices in the healthcare sector.

As pointed out in chapter two in the context of the principle of conferral, EU competition rules apply only to those aspects of national healthcare systems which are not covered by the principle of solidarity.[27] Solidarity, first of all, informs the classification of an activity as economic. In that connection, the Court held in *FENIN*, concerning the Spanish national health system, that the provision of healthcare free of charge and financed through social security contributions is not subject to competition law.[28] The same logic applies to the management and funding of healthcare through the operation of health insurance schemes. Insurance schemes that pursue a social function and are organised on the basis of financial solidarity fall outside the scope of competition law.[29]

[25] To this effect, cf Case C-157/99 *Smits Peerbooms* EU:C:2001:404, [2001] ECR I-5473, para 90 and *Hartlauer* (n 14), para 64.

[26] On this point, see ch 3, s VI.

[27] On the meaning of the concept of solidarity in competition case law, see, eg, T Hervey, '"Social Solidarity": A Buttress Against Internal Market Law?' in J Shaw (ed), *Social Law and Policy in an Evolving European Union* (London, Hart Publishing, 2005); J Baquero Cruz, 'Beyond Competition: Services of General Interest and European Community Law' in G de Búrca (ed), *EU Law and the Welfare State. In Search of Solidarity* (Oxford, OUP, 2005); T Prosser, 'EU Competition Law and Public Services' in E Mossialos et al (eds), *Health Systems Governance in Europe: The Role of European Union Law and Policy* (Cambridge, CUP, 2010); D Gallo, 'Functional Approach and Economic Activity in EU Competition Law, Today: The Case of Social Security and Healthcare' (2020) 26 *European Public Law* 569.

[28] Case C-205/03 *FENIN* EU:C:2006:453, [2006] ECR I-6295, para 26 and Opinion of AG Maduro, para 13. See also Case C-475/99 *Glöckner* EU:C:2001:577, [2001] ECR I-8089, para 20 and Opinion of AG Jacobs, para 67.

[29] For a landmark judgment in the context of social insurance, see Case C-159/91 and C-160/91 *Poucet and Pistre* EU:C:1993:63, [1993] ECR I-637, paras 19–21. In the context of health insurance, see, eg, Joined Cases C-264/01, C-301/01, C-354/01 and C-355/01 *AOK* EU:C:1993:63, [2004] ECR I-2493, paras 35–36, 51–55; most recently, Cases C-262/18 P and C-271/18 P *European Commission and Slovak Republic v Dôvera* EU:C:2020:450 (CJEU, 11 June 2020) (*DZP/UZP*), para 30.

Notably, the Court recognises that in the process of performing social functions, health insurance funds may engage in a degree of competition with one another and also seek to make profit. These seemingly economic activities will not, however, compromise the overall social character of the insurance scheme as long as they help to preserve the viability and proper functioning of the scheme in question.[30] This approach accords space for national authorities to experiment with different methods of management and financing of healthcare in order to increase the efficiency of the overall system.

In situations where the activities of healthcare operators are found to be economic in nature, they may nevertheless be exempted from the application of competition law. This will be the case where the operator in question is entrusted with the provision of a service of general economic interest (SGEI).[31] The judicial review of national measures governing the provision of SGEIs is fairly deferential. It is premised on respect for the prerogative of the Member States to organise and manage the provision of public services, including healthcare.[32] Accordingly, the Court holds that restrictions on competition resulting from the grant of exclusive rights or financial support to undertakings providing SGEIs do not have to be minimised to what is strictly necessary for the provision of the service in question.[33] The provision of SGEIs should be 'economically viable', and the assessment of the viability of the service must take into account the importance of maintaining its quality, reliability and affordability.[34] Therefore, the scope of exclusive rights granted to undertakings providing SGEIs, such as public hospitals, can be legitimately extended to also cover services that are profitable and could in principle be provided under market conditions.[35] This approach ensures that governments have considerable flexibility when making choices about the type of service they want to provide.

Competition case law in the healthcare sector suggests that the Court acknowledges the right of national governments to organise and manage their healthcare systems without excessive interference by the EU and shows awareness of the financial challenges associated with the provision of public healthcare. This demonstrates a judicially sensitive approach to the collision between competition law, as an exclusive area of EU competence, and healthcare, which is a politically sensitive area and one that is reserved by the Treaties to the prerogative of the Member States. This approach stands in contrast to that employed by the Court in the free movement case law concerning cross-border access to healthcare. The scope of this book does not allow to go into the detail of competition case law, but it seems worthwhile briefly to examine the reasons behind a more deferential judicial approach in this context.

[30] *AOK* (n 29), para 56; *DZP/UZP* (n 29), paras 34, 62.

[31] For a definition of the concept of an SGEI, see Commission, 'A quality framework for services of general interest in Europe' (Communication) COM (2011) 900 final, 3.

[32] See, eg, Case T-289/03 *BUPA* EU:T:2008:29, [2008] ECR II-81, paras 166–67.

[33] *Glöckner* (n 28), para 57. In the context of State aids, see *BUPA* (n 32), paras 222, 266, 268–69, stipulating that governments are allowed to provide compensation to undertakings providing SGEIs for the additional costs incurred as a result of running a public service as long as such compensation is not 'manifestly inappropriate'.

[34] *Glöckner*, paras 58–61. In the context of health insurance, see Case C-437/09 *AG2R* EU:C:2011:112, [2011] ECR I-973, para 77.

[35] On that point, see *Glöckner*, where the Court ruled that a monopoly over the provision of all ambulance services granted to several non-profit organisations was compatible with EU competition law because it

The Court's softer stance in applying competition rules to healthcare services, and public services more generally, might be explained by differences relating to the normative scope of free movement law, on the one hand, and competition law, on the other. Whilst the free movement law is meant to govern State action, competition rules are primarily designed to control the conduct of private operators. For that reason, they are worded as precisely defined prohibitions, which allow only limited exceptions, and are accompanied by an elaborate mechanism of enforcement. Unlike the free movement rules, they do not offer an open-ended list of grounds for justification of restrictive measures. The very design of competition rules implies that, if applied to the public sector in full force, they are likely to disrupt national regulatory structures to a greater degree than the free movement rules – risking dismantling national models of social protection and provision of public services.[36] This might explain why the Court takes a relatively cautious approach to the application of competition rules in the healthcare sector.

That said, a strict distinction between public and private, which characterises the personal scopes of free movement and competition law, no longer seems to hold true. In the last two decades, free movement law has been increasingly applied to horizontal and quasi-horizontal situations, as exemplified by *Bosman*[37] and the *Viking* and *Laval* judgments.[38] Therefore, it cannot be plausibly maintained that free movement law governs exclusively State action. Essentially, it covers all practices, public or private, that produce regulatory effects on the economic freedoms.[39] At the same time, free movement law should not be *a priori* presumed to have a lesser impact on national regulatory systems than competition law. Some areas of free movement case law display a judicial tendency to narrow down the scope of justifications available to national governments (and other regulatory actors) in relation to measures restrictive of free movement. A high-scrutiny approach to justifications considerably reduces the scope of national regulatory autonomy, especially when employed in relation to the provision of essential public services, such as healthcare and education.[40] These developments suggest that the free movement and competition rules both affect public and private sectors and that those effects may be in important ways comparable.[41] This, in turn, calls for greater coherence in the judicial interpretation of the two sets of rules.

It was also pointed out above that the available scope for justifications in competition law is generally narrower. Competition law does not contain a category equivalent to 'overriding reasons of public interest', or 'mandatory requirements',[42] apart from

enabled the obligations associated with the provision of ambulance services to be carried out in economically viable conditions, which might have been impossible if the scope of the monopoly rights were narrower.

[36] See D Damjanovic, 'The EU Market Rules as Social Market Rules: Why the EU Can Be a Social Market Economy' (2013) 50 *CML Rev* 1685, 1703, illustrating this problem by the example of liberalisation of public utilities at the EU level, further discussed in G Monti, *EC Competition Law* (Cambridge, CUP, 2007) 440–52.

[37] Case C-415/93 *Bosman* EU:C:1995:463, [1995] ECR I-4921.

[38] The horizontal effect of Art 56 TFEU in the context of *Viking* and *Laval* is discussed in ch 2, s IV.

[39] See, eg, *Viking* (n 23), para 33.

[40] To this effect, see the *Watts* (n 18) and *Bressol* (n 19) judgments, analysed in ch 3, ss II and III, respectively.

[41] For a comprehensive account discussing trends of convergence between free movement and competition law, see J Baquero Cruz, *Between Competition and Free Movement: The Economic Constitutional Law of the European Community* (Oxford, Hart Publishing, 2002) chs 6–8.

[42] First applied in Case C-120/78 *Cassis de Dijon* EU:C:1979:42, [1979] ECR 649, para 8.

the specific considerations of public interest included in the concept of an SGEI.[43] This could explain why the Court tends to define the scope of economic activity more narrowly in competition law[44] and shows deference to national governments when reviewing restrictions on competition arising from the provision of SGEIs. There are, however, signs indicating that the Court's approach to derogations in competition law is changing. Some of the Court's judgments suggest that the Court already allows general derogations from competition law justified by non-economic factors, at least in certain circumstances.

Wouters concerned the compatibility with Art 101 TFEU of a decision taken by the Dutch Bar Association to ban multidisciplinary partnerships between accountants and lawyers.[45] The Court held that the decision in question was not contrary to the cartel prohibition laid down in Art 101 because it was 'necessary in order to ensure the proper practice of the legal profession'.[46] *Meca-Medina* concerned the lawfulness of anti-doping rules issued by sports associations. In its judgment, the Court made a general observation that agreements restrictive of competition had to be assessed in light of their objectives. Accordingly, it had to be considered whether the effects restrictive of competition were inherent in the pursuit of those objectives and were proportionate to them.[47] The Court held that anti-doping rules at issue were justified in light of the objective of combatting doping in order for competitive sport to be conducted fairly.[48] So, the anti-doping rules were assessed not only for anti-competitive effect but also for contributing to the integrity of the sport. The judgments in *Wouters* and *Meca-Medina* suggest that the Court is prepared to assess practices restrictive of competition in their broader context.[49] This, in turn, allows a softened approach to the normal assumptions of competition law where other values are at stake. The latter approach seems to be functionally aligned to the category of public interest objectives in free movement law.[50] As such, it throws into sharp relief the Court's approach to free movement in the areas under study, which demonstrates insufficient consideration of the broader context behind domestic regulatory measures that govern access to essential public services or regulate employment and working conditions.

The point of the above analysis is not to suggest that competition law and free movement law are the same in their detailed scope, nor that the legal interests at stake should be interpreted in exactly the same way. However, both competition rules and free movement rules are dedicated to the protection of the internal market. This means that the broad foundational principles underlying these rules and their interpretation should

[43] See also L Hancher and W Sauter, 'One Step Beyond? From Sodemare to DocMorris: The EU's Freedom of Establishment Case Law Concerning Health Care' (2010) 47 *CML Rev* 117, 129–30.

[44] See ch 2 for a comprehensive analysis of the scope of free movement law in relation to the areas under study.

[45] See Consolidated version of the Treaty on the Functioning of the European Union [2008] OJ C115/47 (TFEU), Art 101, prohibiting cartels.

[46] Case C-309/99 *Wouters* EU:C:2002:98, [2002] ECR I-1577, paras 97–110.

[47] Case C-519/04 P *Meca-Medina* EU:C:2006:492, [2006] ECR I-6991, para 42.

[48] ibid, paras 42–45, 47.

[49] To that effect, see S Weatherill, *Principles and Practice in EU Sports Law* (Oxford, OUP, 2017) ch 7, suggesting that judicial approach in *Meca-Medina* represents a sporting margin of appreciation, giving deference to the choices of the sport's governing body as the rule-maker.

[50] S Weatherill, *The Internal Market as a Legal Concept* (Oxford, OUP, 2017) 107–09.

be the same. In that respect, competition case law demonstrates that the Court has a choice to interpret and apply the rules of the internal market in a way that would allow it to preserve the goals of that market without thereby undermining national regulatory choices in areas that are sensitive from a constitutional and/or political point of view.

C. Fundamental Rights versus Labour Rights

There are also lessons to be learned from the Court's fundamental rights case law. The starting point of judicial review in cases concerning conflicts between the free movement rules and the exercise of fundamental rights seems to be the recognition that Member States have a wide margin of discretion when choosing the level of protection to be accorded to fundamental rights and later balancing that protection against the exercise of economic freedoms. Proportionality review is thus mainly focused on assessing the suitability and reasonableness of the decisions adopted by national authorities.[51] This body of case law offers a powerful example of the way in which the Court should treat collective labour rights in the context of free movement.

i. Omega: *The Protection of a Fundamental Right as a Self-Standing Objective*

The landmark case concerning the application of margin of appreciation in relation to fundamental rights is *Omega*, in which the Court delivered one of the most important judgments in the history of its case law. The case is well known. It concerned a German order prohibiting the operation of games that involved simulated killing. The government argued that such games constituted an affront to human dignity, the protection of which was guaranteed in Art 1(1) of the German Constitution. The Court was asked to determine to what extent the exercise of the right to human dignity could justify derogation from free movement rules.

The Court held that the protection of fundamental rights fell within the 'public policy' ground of justification, which, in line with settled case law, had to be interpreted strictly and thus relied on only if there was a genuine and sufficiently serious threat to a fundamental interest of society.[52] Moreover, measures restricting the free movement of services could be considered as justified 'only insofar as those objectives [could not] be attained by less restrictive measures'.[53] Notably, up to this point, the Court's reasoning resembles that employed in *Commission v Luxembourg*, which concerned the exception for public policy provided in Art 3(10) of the Posted Workers Directive (PWD).[54] But then it changes.

[51] For an explicit use of the term 'reasonable', see Case C-112/00 *Schmidberger* EU:C:2003:333, [2003] ECR I-5659, para 93.

[52] Case C-36/02 *Omega* [2004] ECR I-9609, para 30.

[53] ibid, para 36.

[54] Case C-319/06 *Commission v Luxembourg* EU:C:2004:614, [2008] ECR I-4323, paras 30–31, 50, discussed in ch 3, s IV.

The Court notes that since 'the specific circumstances' for recourse to the concept of public policy could vary 'from one country to another and from one era to another', national authorities have to be allowed a margin of discretion within the limits imposed by the Treaties.[55] Making a reference to its gambling case law, the Court emphasises that the need for, and proportionality of, national measures are not put into question merely because one Member State has chosen a system of protection different from that adopted by another Member State.[56] The German rules correspond to the level of protection of human dignity which the national constitution seeks to guarantee and thus have to be regarded as justified and necessary in the circumstances of the case.[57]

This approach seems to be remarkably different from that adopted in relation to collective labour rights. Judicial review in the latter context focuses on whether the exercise of collective bargaining and right to strike is necessary considering its capacity to restrict the free movement of businesses. Collective labour rights are seen by the Court merely as a means for achieving the objectives of worker protection rather than legitimate objectives in and of themselves, whose protection could justify the restrictive effect on the fundamental freedoms. As a means to an end, they are placed under a rigorous proportionality review. By contrast, in the fundamental rights cases, as illustrated by but not confined to *Omega*, fundamental rights are treated as self-standing objectives, whose level of protection – to be determined by national authorities – dictates the level of intensity of judicial review.[58]

The sharp contrast in the respective standards of review can only be explained by the fact that socio-economic rights in the judicial understanding of EU human rights law occupy an inferior status compared to civil and political rights.[59] The difference in treatment cannot, however, be justified in light of the Court's recognition that both collective bargaining and the right to strike form part of the general principles of EU law together with other fundamental rights.[60] Moreover, both of these rights are protected under the Charter, which, crucially, does not differentiate between civil and political rights and those of a social nature in terms of either their legal status or the level of protection that they warrant.[61] This suggests that the standard of judicial review in cases where free movement intersects with the exercise of the right to strike or the right to collective bargaining should be, in principle, the same as the standard of review employed in relation to the exercise of civil and political rights.

[55] *Omega* (n 52), para 31. See also Case C-41/74 *Yvonne van Duyn v Home Office* EU:C:1974:133, [1974] ECR 1337, para 18, where margin of appreciation is applied for the first time in the context of public policy derogation from free movement law.

[56] *Omega*, paras 37–38, with further references to, inter alia: Case C-124/97 *Läärä* EU:C:1999:435, [1999] ECR I-6067, para 36; Case C-67/98 *Zenatti* EU:C:1999:514, [1999] ECR I-7289, para 34, discussed in ch 3, s V.

[57] *Omega*, para 39.

[58] See, eg, Case C-244/06 *Dynamic Medien* EU:C:2008:85, [2008] ECR I-505, paras 44, 49; *Schmidberger* (n 51).

[59] For an in-depth analysis, see V Velyvyte, 'The Right to Strike in the European Union after Accession to the European Convention on Human Rights: Identifying Conflict and Achieving Coherence' (2015) 15 *Human Rights Law Review* 73, 87–90.

[60] *Viking* (n 23), paras 43–46; *Laval* (n 23), para 91.

[61] Charter of Fundamental Rights of the European Union [2000] OJ C364/1, Art 28. For academic discussion, see, eg, C Semmelmann, 'The European Union's Economic Constitution under the Lisbon Treaty: Soul-Searching among Lawyers Shifts the Focus to Procedure' (2010) 35 *EL Rev* 516, 524–28.

ii. Sayn-Wittgenstein: *The Protection of National Identities*

Another fundamental rights case, *Sayn-Wittgenstein*, demonstrates the capacity of the national identity clause enshrined in Art 4(2) TEU to strengthen national claims to margin of appreciation.[62] The case concerned Austrian law on the abolition of the nobility, prohibiting the acquisition, possession and use of a title of nobility. The claimant in the case argued that this law was incompatible with the freedom of movement guaranteed to the citizens of the EU under Art 21 TFEU, whereas the government maintained that the said law implemented the constitutional principle of equality of all Austrian citizens.

In line with the reasoning in *Omega*, the Court held that although derogations from the free movement should be interpreted strictly, Member States were to be granted a margin of appreciation when defining the scope of public policy, which meant that they were entitled to choose a system of protection which differed from other Member States.[63] Moreover, the Court emphasised that, in accordance with Art 4(2) TEU, the EU was obliged to respect the national identities of the Member States, 'inherent in their fundamental structures, political and constitutional'.[64] In the context of Austrian constitutional history, this identity included the status of the State as a Republic, expressed in the law on the abolition of the nobility. Austria's identity as a Republic thus had to be taken into consideration when striking a balance between the legitimate interests pursued by the Austrian government and the right of free movement of persons in EU law.[65] In light of this, the Court concluded that the prohibition of the use of titles of nobility was a proportionate measure. Austrian constitutional identity, expressed through the principle of equality, acted as a buffer against a more aggressive application of the proportionality review.

Another interesting example comes from EU gambling case law. The *Digibet* case concerned the German regulatory framework for gambling which was characterised by the co-existence of different regional regulatory regimes.[66] Essentially, the Court found that the consistency of the German regulatory framework for gambling was not affected by differences in the regional regimes within the country because the division of competences between the German *Länder* was protected under Art 4(2) TEU.[67] The judgment thus made clear that Art 4(2) TEU could be used to protect a State's choice to regulate in a decentralised manner.

Both *Sayn-Wittgenstein* and *Digibet* demonstrate that national identity clause informs the breadth of national margin of appreciation and can thus be used to lower the standard of proportionality review. The potential of Art 4(2) should not, however, be overestimated, as it can only be invoked in relation to a 'fundamental' aspect of a national

[62] Consolidated version of the Treaty on European Union [2008] OJ C115/13 (TEU), Art 4(2). See ch 1, s II for a discussion of Art 4(2) in the context of the reforms brought about by the Lisbon Treaty.

[63] Case C-208/09 *Sayn-Wittgenstein* EU:C:2010:806, [2010] ECR I-13693, paras 86–87, 91–92. See also *Dynamic Medien* (n 58), paras 81–82.

[64] Art 4(2) TEU.

[65] *Sayn-Wittgenstein* (n 63), paras 83, 92.

[66] Case C-156/13 *Digibet* EU:C:2014:1756 (CJEU, 2 June 2014), discussed in ch 3, s V.

[67] See also Case C-51/15 *Remondis v Region Hannover* EU:C:2016:985 (CJEU, 21 December 2016), concerning re-organisation of competences of public authorities in the context of Art 4(2) TEU.

identity, the assessment of which is subject to supervision by the Court.[68] As pointed out in chapter one, the Court has not yet provided a comprehensive definition of the scope of Art 4(2) and thus far taken a case-by-case approach to its interpretation. In *Sayn-Wittgenstein*, it recognised as a fundamental aspect of the Austrian national identity the constitutional principle of equality and the status of the Austrian State as a Republic; in *Digibet*, it did so in relation to the federal division of competences between the German *Länder*. In the well-known *Runevič-Vardyn* case, it held that Art 4(2) applied to national linguistic identity protected by the Lithuanian constitution.[69] This raises an important question: what other aspects could be considered as fundamental for the purposes of Art 4(2)? How broadly should this clause be interpreted? Would regulatory policies that are rooted in national social identities qualify for protection?

Although there is a disagreement in the literature about how broad the scope of Art 4(2) should be, there seems to be a firm consensus that an aspect of national identity which has a constitutional basis would be considered 'fundamental' and protected by this clause.[70] This would suggest that Art 4(2) could, for example, offer protection to collective labour rights in the Member States, such as Sweden and Germany, in which these rights enjoy constitutional recognition. Thus construed, Art 4(2) should in principle protect the choice of at least some governments to delegate the regulation of employment and working conditions to trade unions. But what about Member States which do not accord constitutional protection to collective labour rights? And what about other aspects of social policy that might have only a vague expression in national constitutions, such as through some declaratory principles, or none at all? For instance, could the specific features of a national education system be protected as part of that State's national identity? In particular, could reliance on Art 4(2) change the way in which the Court treats concerns about the impact of the influx of foreign students on education systems that are based on free and open access? Potentially, yes.

The language of Art 4(2) does not confine this clause to the protection of, exclusively, national constitutional identities. It simply refers to national identities, as expressed through fundamental political and constitutional structures. This concept seems to encompass those features of a State (or nation) that define its very character. Constitutions may embed the basis of such character, but they are not the sole means of expressing it. In that respect, Cloots rightly points out that the notion of *constitutional* identity is unable to account for *non-constitutional* fundamental structures that give expression to national identity. Cloots gives the example of the system of norms concerning the Belgian federal structure and language regime, neither of which have

[68] Case C-62/14 *Gauweiler* EU:C:2015:400 (CJEU, 16 June 2015), Opinion of AG Cruz Villalón, paras 59–61. See also N Shuibhne, 'Primary Laws: Judging Free Movement Restrictions after Lisbon' in P Koutrakos, N Shuibhne and P Syrpis (eds), *Exceptions from EU Free Movement Law* (Oxford, Hart Publishing, 2016) 312–18.

[69] Case C-391/09 *Runevič-Vardyn* EU:C:2011:291, [2011] ECR I-3787.

[70] For an interpretation of Art 4(2) as dedicated to the protection of national *constitutional* identities, see, eg, LFM Besselink, 'National and Constitutional Identity before and after Lisbon' (2010) 6 *Utrecht Law Review* 36, 44; A von Bogdandy and S Schill, 'Overcoming Absolute Privacy: The Respect for National Identity under the Lisbon Treaty' (2011) 48 *CML Rev* 1417, 1430–40.

been anchored in the Belgian Constitution but arguably form part of Belgian national identity.[71]

It certainly seems right from the conceptual point of view not to equate the notion of national identity with that of national constitutional identity, but the practical challenge is then to determine what aspects of national identity are to be regarded as 'fundamental' to merit protection under Art 4(2). I do not have an ambition to offer a universal definition of the scope of this concept, but I would argue that the assessment of what is fundamental should also take into account the treatment of a particular national interest in EU law, as opposed to only domestic law.[72] What I mean, specifically, is that if an interest falls within a policy area that is recognised as constitutionally sensitive by the Treaties, this should be considered as an indication of the fundamental importance of that interest to the Member State invoking Art 4(2).

In light of the above, I would suggest that Art 4(2) could be construed as designed to accommodate interests that Member States consider to be part of their national social identities if those interests enjoy constitutional protection in domestic legal systems *or* if they fall within the areas of EU competence whose constitutional sensitivity is explicitly recognised by the Treaties, such as the areas under study here.[73] This implies a potentially broad interpretation of Art 4(2), but such interpretation is supported by the wider constitutional framework of the EU, which includes, most notably, the EU's commitment to the principles of conferral, subsidiarity and proportionality, requiring that the exercise of EU competences, including their judicial exercise, take due account of national regulatory autonomy and the interests protected within the exercise of that autonomy.[74] Moreover, the requirement for the protected interest to have a constitutional recognition either through national or EU law would ensure that the aspects of national identities that would warrant protection under the suggested interpretation would indeed be of a fundamental nature, in accordance with Art 4(2) TEU.

D. Conclusion

The above analysis demonstrated how the doctrine of margin of appreciation can be applied in different legal contexts. The application of this doctrine in the patient mobility case law would ensure judicial compliance with the principle of subsidiarity consistently across EU internal market case law in the healthcare sector. Similarly, the extension of margin of appreciation to cases involving the exercise of collective labour

[71] E Cloots, *National Identity in EU Law* (Oxford, OUP, 2015) 166. To that effect, see Case C-202/11 *Las* EU:C:2013:239 (CJEU, 16 April 2013), in which the Belgian linguistic identity was protected as part of Belgian national identity rather than constitutional identity.

[72] See *Runevič-Vardyn* (n 69), para 86 and *Las* (n 71), para 26, suggesting that the Court is already doing so indirectly at least in cases concerning cultural identities.

[73] In this connection, see B Guestaferro, 'Beyond the Exceptionalism of Constitutional Conflicts: The Ordinary Function of the Identity Clause' (2012) 31 *Yearbook of European Law* 263, 286, demonstrating that the drafting history of Art 4(2) reveals that it was originally meant to protect the areas of competence whose sensitivity was later recognised through the introduction into the Treaties of a list of the EU's complementary competences.

[74] See chs 1, 2 and 3 for a comprehensive analysis of these principles.

rights would bring coherence into the Court's wider approach to fundamental rights as general principles of EU law. Finally, national claims to margin of appreciation in either of the areas under study could be strengthened through reliance on Art 4(2) TEU where the invoked public interest forms part of the national identity of the Member State concerned.

III. Fair Balance

As a technique of judicial reasoning, the act of balancing is well known in the jurisprudence of national constitutional and international human rights courts. Its key function lies in resolving conflicts between competing legal interests.[75] This technique is not unfamiliar to the EU legal system. It has been employed in the case law of the CJEU, the opinions of Advocates General, and EU legislative initiatives. It is not uncommon for the fair balance approach to be employed together with the doctrine of margin of appreciation: where a margin of appreciation is granted, national administrative and judicial authorities are delegated the right to perform the balancing exercise between the competing interests involved.

The following discussion will demonstrate that the technique of balancing is particularly suited to ensure the observance of the constitutional principle of proportionality in the exercise of EU judicial authority because it limits EU-level judicial interference with the interests protected at the national level to what is necessary in the pursuit of the objectives of the internal market.

A. Fair Balance in *Schmidberger* and *Commission v Germany*

In order to understand the detail and scope of the fair balance approach, the *Schmidberger* case deserves a particular mention. *Schmidberger* was the first case in the history of the Court where the protection of fundamental rights, namely the freedoms of expression and of assembly, was invoked as a justification for restricting EU economic freedoms. The case concerned a permission granted by the Austrian government to close a national motorway in order to allow a demonstration against the levels of pollution caused by heavy traffic. The Court ruled that economic freedoms and fundamental rights were values of equal importance in EU law and could both be subject to restrictions, and that the task for the national authorities was therefore to strike a fair balance between the two values.[76] Moreover, national authorities

[75] SA de Vries, 'Balancing Fundamental Rights with Economic Freedoms According to the European Court of Justice' (2013) 9 *Utrecht Law Review* 169, with a further reference to S Gardbaum, 'Limiting Constitutional Rights' (2007) 54 *UCLA Law Review* 789. For an account of this practice in the German Constitutional Court, see especially T Marauhn and N Ruppel, 'Balancing Conflicting Human Rights: Konrad Hesse's Notion of "Praktische Konkordanz" and the German Federal Constitutional Court' in E Brems (ed), *Conflicts Between Fundamental Rights* (Cambridge, Intersentia-Hart, 2008) 273.

[76] *Schmidberger* (n 51), paras 77–81.

were to enjoy a 'wide margin of discretion in the balancing exercise', which suggests that the two approaches go hand in hand.[77]

In *Schmidberger*, the balancing exercise required that in addition to assessing the lawfulness of national measures in light of the free movement of goods, the Court assess the effect of the free movement on the exercise of the fundamental rights in question. The Court noted that the freedom of expression and freedom of assembly could be subject to certain limitations justified by objectives in the public interest as long as those limitations were in accordance with the law, motivated by legitimate aims and necessary in a democratic society, and proportionate to the legitimate aim pursued.[78] However, interference with those fundamental rights could not go as far as to impair their very substance.[79] For that reason, the Court rejected the proposition of the referring court that the freedom of assembly could have been exercised in a manner less restrictive on free movement, for example, by holding the demonstration next to the motorway or limiting its duration. It explained that, first, the choice of appropriate means fell within the 'wide margin of discretion' accorded to the Member States and, second, the imposition of stricter conditions on the exercise of the rights concerned could have deprived the environmental action of a substantial part of its scope.[80]

The Court's reasoning in *Schmidberger* stands in contrast to that employed in relation to collective labour rights, in particular the right to strike. Notably, in *Schmidberger*, the Court was particularly concerned with protecting the effectiveness of the environmental action, whilst in *Viking* and *Laval*, it seemed to have found the strike actions in question disproportionate precisely because of their effectiveness. Moreover, in *Viking* and *Laval*, the Court performed the necessity review in relation, directly, to the actions of trade unions rather than governments, thus denying trade unions the autonomy they enjoy as bodies governed by private law. The apparent paradox of that situation was that trade unions, despite their status as private actors, were treated like States in terms of their regulatory role and responsibility in complying with EU free movement rules,[81] yet, in contrast to governments in *Schmidberger*, *Omega* and other human rights cases, they were given no margin of discretion in their actions.[82]

As already pointed out earlier, considering that collective labour rights are recognised as fundamental rights in EU law and protected under the Charter, the Court would be expected to treat them in the same way it treats civil and political rights. This, accordingly, means that collective labour rights should benefit from the fair balance approach. This proposition is not new to the Court. In fact, it has been advanced by AG Trstenjak in her Opinion in *Commission v Germany*[83] and in the failed Monti II draft proposed by

[77] *Schmidberger* (n 51), paras 82–89.
[78] ibid, para 79.
[79] ibid, paras 80, 89–90.
[80] ibid, paras 90–91, 93.
[81] *Viking* (n 23), paras 34–37, 64–65; *Laval* (n 23), para 98.
[82] J Malmberg and T Sigeman, 'Industrial Actions and EU Economic Freedoms: The Autonomous Collective Bargaining Model Curtailed by the European Court of Justice' (2008) 45 *CML Rev* 1115, 1130–31; L Azoulai, 'The Court of Justice and the Social Market Economy: The Emergence of an Ideal and the Conditions for its Realisation' (2008) 45 *CML Rev* 1335, 1343–46, 1350–51.
[83] Case C-271/08 *Commission v Germany* EU:C:2010:426, [2010] ECR I-7091, discussed in ch 3, s IV.

the Commission,[84] which was in part based on the Opinion of AG Trstenjak. Referring to *Schmidberger*, AG Trstenjak highlighted the need to adopt a symmetrical approach to the reconciliation of economic freedoms and fundamental social rights: '[i]n the case of a conflict between a fundamental right and a fundamental freedom, both legal positions must be presumed to have equal status' and a 'fair balance' between them must be sought.[85] The exact boundary between the two legal values is to be drawn by conducting a double proportionality review:[86]

> it must be determined whether, having regard to all the circumstances of the case, fundamental freedoms may justify a restriction on the fundamental right to bargain collectively … or, conversely, whether those fundamental rights demand that the scope of those fundamental freedoms and the secondary law based thereupon must be limited.[87]

Despite a promising rhetoric, the conclusions reached by AG Trstenjak did not reflect a symmetrical application of the proportionality review. Trstenjak concluded that the right to collective bargaining was not capable of justifying the restriction on Arts 49 and 56 of the TFEU because it was 'possible to conceive of [a less restrictive] alternative scheme compliant with Community law' to achieve the social objectives pursued.[88]

Arguably influenced by the Opinion of AG Trstenjak, the Court, for the first time in its case law on collective labour rights, also emphasised the importance of striking a *fair* balance between social and economic interests at stake. Enhancement of the level of retirement pensions for workers had to be fairly balanced against the attainment of business freedoms to pursue cross-border activities.[89] The balancing process adopted by the Court was, however, asymmetrical and favoured commercial interests over collective labour rights. Following AG Trstenjak's Opinion, the Court concluded that it was possible for Germany to accommodate its social policy objectives without completely disregarding the framework of EU public procurement rules.[90]

A proper application of the balancing test would require a genuine two-fold enquiry into the relationship between economic freedoms and collective labour rights. So, for instance, in the case of the right to strike, Barnard proposes that the proportionality review currently employed by the Court would need to have an additional dimension whereby the Court would assess whether the exercise of the freedom of establishment or freedom to provide services – for example, in the form of asking for an injunction to restrain strike action – is appropriate and necessary for the achievement of the economic

[84] Commission, 'Proposal for a Council Regulation on the exercise of the right to take collective action within the context of the freedom of establishment and the freedom to provide services' COM (2012) 130 final, discussed in ch 4, s V.

[85] *Commission v Germany* (n 83), Opinion of AG Trstenjak, paras 81, 188, 192–95.

[86] ibid, para 189.

[87] ibid, para 84. The origins of this balancing technique seem to lie in the German constitutional practice, see above Marauhn and Ruppel (n 75). The term 'balancing' (konkordanz) is associated with German constitutionalist Konrad Hesse: K Hesse, *Grundzüge des Verfassungsrechts der Bundesrepublik Deutschland*, 20th edn (Heidelberg, CF Müller, 1995).

[88] *Commission v Germany*, Opinion of AG Trstenjak, para 215.

[89] *Commission v Germany*, para 52.

[90] ibid, paras 53–56.

objectives of the Union in light of the impact on the right to strike.[91] Similarly, I would add, the Court should assess whether an exercise of economic freedoms that disregards the terms of collective agreements applicable in the Member State concerned is justified in light of its impact on the right to collective bargaining.

Thus applied, a fair balance approach would ensure the observance by the Court of the principle of proportionality, which requires taking into account the impact of the judicial interpretation of internal market rules on the non-market interests protected through the exercise of national regulatory autonomy.[92] As Barnard puts it, this approach would limit both economic freedoms and collective labour rights, but only insofar as each could be optimised without undermining the essence of the other.[93] Applied in combination with the doctrine of margin of appreciation, this approach would also require that the act of balancing itself be primarily performed by the national authorities and supervised by national courts, with guidance by the CJEU.[94] The increased role of national administrative and judicial authorities would not only ensure that the constitutional limits of EU action are respected, but would also guarantee that decisions affecting the most sensitive areas of national policy are adopted by actors that are most familiar with the context and implications of those decisions.

B. *Santos Palhota*: The Role of the Lisbon Reforms

The idea of relaxing the Court's standard of review in cases concerning the protection of social rights and interests more generally has been gaining increasing support in light of the reforms brought about by the Treaty of Lisbon. A special mention must be made of the Opinion of AG Villalón delivered in *Santos Palhota* just weeks after the Opinion of AG Trstenjak in *Commission v Germany*.[95] *Santos Palhota* did not concern either collective bargaining or collective action, but the judgment is notable for cementing the judicial logic that domestic labour regulations can, and should, be designed in a way that would cause minimum interference with the exercise of the economic freedoms.

The measure under challenge was a Belgian law that required companies posting workers to its territory to submit a prior declaration of posting, including, inter alia, information about the terms and conditions of employment applicable to posted workers. The declaration was registered by the Belgian authorities, thereby authorising the posting of workers. The Court held that the requirement of registration, by virtue of which the declaration in question assumed the nature of an administrative authorisation procedure, went beyond what was necessary in order to ensure the protection of

[91] C Barnard, 'A Proportionate Response to Proportionality in the Field of Collective Action' (2012) 37 *European Law Review* 117, 124. See also P Syrpis, 'Reconciling Economic Freedoms and Social Rights – The Potential of *Commission v Germany* (Case C-271/08, Judgment of 15 July 2010)' (2011) 40 *Industrial Law Journal* 222, 226.

[92] See ch 3, s I for a comprehensive analysis of the principle of proportionality in application to EU judicial practice.

[93] Barnard (n 91) 122–24.

[94] For a comprehensive analysis of what margin of appreciation entails for the distribution of tasks between the CJEU and national courts, see Zglinski (n 12) 97–124.

[95] Case C-515/08 *Santos Palhota* EU:C:2010:589, [2010] ECR I-9133.

posted workers.[96] A prior declaration alone, without its subsequent registration and notification, was, in the Court's view, sufficient to enable the monitoring by the authorities of foreign employers' compliance with the national welfare and wages legislation during the posting.

The judgment sits in marked contrast to the Opinion of AG Cruz Villalón, who advised the Court that the Belgian measures were compatible with the freedom to provide services. The starting point in AG Villalón's Opinion was that the freedom to provide services had to be interpreted 'in the light of the social provisions' introduced by the Treaty of Lisbon.[97] Among the relevant provisions, Villalón highlighted Art 9 TFEU, which constituted a 'cross-cutting' social protection clause obliging the EU 'to take into account requirements linked to the promotion of a high level of employment, the guarantee of adequate social protection, the fight against social exclusion and a high level of education, training and protection of human health'.[98] Art 9 TFEU was to be read as a more detailed expression of the EU's objective to strive for a *social* market economy, laid down in Art 3(3) TEU. Villalón also made a reference to Art 31 of the Charter, which provided 'a minimum framework for the protection of workers' by guaranteeing to every worker the right to the working conditions that respect his or her health, safety and dignity.[99]

Having taken the view that fundamental freedoms had to be interpreted in light of the Lisbon reforms, AG Villalón advocated for a relaxed proportionality review of national legal interests that were protected under the Treaties:

> To the extent that the new primary law framework provides for a mandatory high level of social protection, it authorises the Member States, for the purpose of safeguarding a certain level of social protection, to restrict a freedom, and to do so without European Union law's regarding it as something exceptional and, therefore, as warranting a strict interpretation. That view, which is founded on the new provisions of the Treaties cited above, is expressed in practical terms by applying the principle of proportionality.[100]

This paragraph seems to reflect the spirit of the propositions advanced in this chapter. Effectively, AG Villalón suggests that non-market interests which have a legal expression in the Treaties stand on par with the fundamental freedoms. This, in turn, requires the Court to make the necessary adjustments to its proportionality review so that to accommodate the protection of those interests. This chapter argues that such accommodation can be achieved through a wider application of the doctrine of margin of appreciation and the fair balance approach.

Notably, AG Villalón places a strong emphasis on the reforms brought about by the Treaty of Lisbon as the legal basis for a change in the Court's approach to social rights. I would agree with AG Villalón that the Lisbon reforms should certainly be seen as an incentive for the Court to re-evaluate its long-standing position relating to the protection of social values in free movement law. However, the Lisbon reforms should not

[96] *Santos Palhota* (n 95), para 52.
[97] ibid, para 51. On this point, see also discussion in ch 1, s II.
[98] *Santos Palhota*, Opinion of AG Cruz Villalón, para 51.
[99] ibid, para 52.
[100] ibid, para 53.

be regarded as the legal basis or, more specifically, the sole legal basis justifying the reversal of the Court's case law. Crucially, the primary basis for such a reversal lies in the constitutional sensitivity of the policy areas which throughout the years have been shaped by EU internal market law in the absence of a sophisticated mandate conferred upon the EU, let alone the Court. Moreover, as has been demonstrated in chapter one, historically the framework of the Treaties has always included both an economic and a social dimension, requiring, as recognised by the Court itself, that economic freedoms under EU free movement rules be balanced against the social policy objectives.[101] In that respect, the Lisbon Treaty does not introduce anything substantially novel; rather, it seems only to make more express the need to protect the non-market values in EU law.[102]

C. Conclusion

This section introduced the fair balance approach as a way to achieve judicial compliance with the principle of proportionality in the interpretation of free movement law. This approach would ensure that the Court duly takes into account the protection of social interests when they come into conflict with the economic freedoms. By doing so, it would bring the case law on collective labour rights in line with the value system enshrined in the Treaties, in which the economic and social dimensions of EU law are accorded equal importance.

IV. Exemption

Exemption from the application of EU law is the last of the three interpretative techniques proposed in this chapter. It could be considered as the strongest form of expression of the principle of subsidiarity as it protects national regulatory autonomy to the highest degree by removing certain matters from the purview of internal market law.[103]

The idea of exemption builds on the Court's judgment in the *Albany* case, briefly discussed in chapter two. *Albany* concerned the validity of a collective agreement which established an occupational pension scheme for the textile sector in the Netherlands. The affiliation to the scheme was made compulsory for the entire sector by a ministerial order. The collective agreement was challenged under Art 85 EEC (Art 101 TFEU),

[101] *Viking* (n 23), paras 78–79; *Laval* (n 23), paras 104–05. For a comprehensive discussion of the relationship between the economic and social dimensions of EU law, see ch 1, s II.

[102] On this point, see S Weatherill, 'Justification, Proportionality and Consumer Protection' in Koutrakos, Shuibhne and Syrpis (n 68) 253–57, and Shuibhne (n 68) 307–10, both showing how the Court already 'mainstreams' non-economic considerations in some of its pre-Lisbon free movement case law.

[103] See also the conception of judicial subsidiarity in T Horsley, 'Subsidiarity and the European Court of Justice: Missing Pieces in the Subsidiarity Jigsaw?' (2012) 50 *Journal of Common Market Studies* 267.

prohibiting, inter alia, agreements that distort competition in the internal market through price-fixing. The Court held that:

> It is beyond question that certain restrictions of competition are inherent in collective agreements between organisations representing employers and workers. However, the social policy objectives pursued by such agreements would be seriously undermined if management and labour were subject to Article 85(1) of the Treaty when seeking jointly to adopt measures to improve conditions of work and employment.[104]

As the purpose of the collective agreement in question was to guarantee a certain level of pension for all workers in the sector, in this way contributing to improving one of their working conditions, namely remuneration, the agreement was considered to fall outside the scope of Art 85.[105] The *Albany* judgment thus established an exemption from EU competition rules for collective agreements. To be excluded from the scope of Art 101 TFEU, a collective agreement must satisfy two conditions: it must be concluded in the framework of collective negotiations and with a view to improving conditions of work and employment.[106]

Although the exemption for collective agreements established by *Albany* is a narrow one, it could potentially be extended to cover, more broadly, domestic practices that appear to be in inherent conflict with the deregulatory aspect of EU internal market law. This proposition draws on the submissions made to the Court by trade unions and a number of Member States in *Viking*, *Laval* and *Commission v Germany*. In those cases, it was argued that the rights to collective bargaining and collective action should be excluded from the application of Arts 49 and 56 TFEU by analogy with the *Albany* case. The Court, however, refused to do so. It explained that, unlike in the relationship between collective bargaining and competition law, it was not inherent in the very exercise of trade union rights that EU fundamental freedoms would be prejudiced.[107] At the same time, the free movement rules did not affect the essence of trade union rights in a manner equivalent to competition rules.[108]

The position taken by the Court demonstrates a highly formalistic judicial understanding of what constitutes an inherent conflict between the exercise of collective labour rights and fundamental freedoms. The assumption that there is no inherent conflict between the two legal interests does not seem accurate or convincing when viewed in light of the Court's own case law. Certainly, the exercise of the right to collective bargaining or collective action does not in itself 'prejudice' the transnational

[104] Case C-67/96 *Albany* EU:C:1999:430, [1999] ECR I-5751, paras 59–60.

[105] ibid, paras 63–64.

[106] Affd in Joined Cases C-115/97, C-116/97 and C-117/97 *Brentjens' Handelsonderneming BV* EU:C:1999:434, [1999] ECR I-6025, para 57; Case C-219/97 *Drijvende Bokken BV v Stichting Pensioenfonds* EU:C:1999:514, [1999] ECR I-6121, para 47; Joined Cases C-180/98 and C-184/98 *Pavlov* EU:C:2000:428, [2000] ECR I-6451, para 67; Case C-222/98 *Hendrik van der Woude* EU:C:2000:475, [2000] ECR I-7111, para 22; *AG2R* (n 34), paras 29–39. See also Case C-413/13 *FNV Kunsten Informatie en Media* EU:C:2014:2411 (CJEU, 4 December 2014), extending the *Albany* exemption to agreements covering the self-employed whose de facto status is comparable to that of employees.

[107] *Viking* (n 23), para 52. See also *Laval* (n 23), para 86; *Commission v Germany* (n 83), paras 45–47, discussed in this respect in ch 2, s IV.

[108] *Commission v Germany*, paras 47, 49.

provision of services. However, the Court's definition of a restriction of free movement is extremely broad and encompasses any measure or practice liable to make the free movement 'less attractive'. Accordingly, as pointed out in chapter two, as long as an undertaking wishes to provide services in a Member State offering a higher level of worker protection than the undertaking's home Member State, the legal environment of the host State will always be less attractive, as it takes away the undertaking's competitive advantage of using a cheaper labour force. Viewed from that perspective, the exercise of the right to collective bargaining or right to strike by trade unions in the host State will inevitably prejudice the exercise of the economic freedoms. Ironically, the conflict between collective labour rights and economic freedoms is created by the Court itself by broadly defining the category of restrictions. Yet this does not change the outcome of the situation, which is that the two competing interests appear to be, by (the Court's) definition, in an inherent conflict.

By the same token, it seems to be inherent in the exercise of the economic freedoms that whenever there is a collision between them and collective labour rights, the social policy objectives pursued via the exercise of collective labour rights will be undermined. This situation is predetermined by the Court's rigorous application of the proportionality review. *Commission v Germany* offers a useful illustration. In that case, the Court held that, unlike the obligation to comply with competition rules, obligation to designate pension providers in compliance with EU free movement rules did not affect the essence of the right to collective bargaining or undermine the objectives pursued by the social partners.[109] It was so because public procurement directives did not preclude a local authority employer from specifying in the call for tenders the conditions to be complied with by tenderers so that to prevent the selection of workers for insurance on the basis of their state of health.[110] This line of reasoning is technically correct. Certainly, public authorities always had the option of selecting insurance funds by themselves rather than delegating this choice to the social partners. Taken to its logical conclusion, this argument would equally suggest that in the circumstances like those in *Albany* the objective of providing the desired insurance cover for the workers in question could have been successfully achieved by the State acting alone, without the inevitable distortion of competition arising from the conclusion of an anticompetitive agreement by the social partners. Yet in *Albany*, the Court chose not to follow that line of logic. Rather, it took the view that doing so would have undermined the prerogative of trade unions to regulate work and employment conditions through the process of collective bargaining. Remarkably, the Court did not show the same level of sensitivity to trade union prerogatives in *Commission v Germany*. Without elaborating much, it concluded that EU rules on public procurement precluded the use of collective agreements as a method of regulating questions of worker protection.

The above analysis goes to show that the interpretation of an 'inherent conflict' adopted by the Court is incoherent across the contexts of competition law and free

[109] *Commission v Germany* (n 83), para 49.
[110] ibid, paras 57–58, discussed in more detail in ch 3, s IV.

movement law. At the same time, however, if the existence of an inherent conflict between internal market rules and domestic interests were determined on the basis of how the Court interprets the concept of a restriction or the test of proportionality, the category of measures and practices that would be inherently in conflict with internal market rules would be virtually limitless. If all those measures and practices were accordingly exempted from the scope of internal market law, this would frustrate the goals of the internal market and compromise its integrity.

In light of this, it seems that in order for the exemption from EU law to become a workable technique of judicial interpretation, the Court needs to clarify its exact contours, but in a way qualitatively different from its attempt to do so in *Commission v Germany*. Admittedly, it is far from certain whether this task is possible to accomplish in practice given the ad-hoc, reactive nature of judicial lawmaking. This does not, however, detract from the fact that in the current state of the law, the principle formulated in *Albany* and somewhat refined in *Commission v Germany* is not capable of offering to certain types of national practices a reliable general exemption from the scope of internal market rules. The *Albany* exemption may well remain confined to very specific, exceptional circumstances arising in the context of, exclusively, competition law.

Against this background, it would seem that the interpretative techniques of margin of appreciation and fair balance both offer more attractive alternatives to the *Albany* exemption for protecting national regulatory practices from the deregulatory effects of free movement law.

V. Conclusion

This chapter has demonstrated that the Court possesses a rich arsenal of tools, or interpretative techniques, in its case law that can be employed in order to achieve compliance with EU competence constraints which, as this book has argued, govern the exercise of EU judicial authority. Such compliance can, and should, be achieved consistently throughout the free movement case law and across the range of policy areas of comparable constitutional and political sensitivity.

The concrete propositions advanced in this chapter were based on operationalising the principles of subsidiarity and proportionality in judicial practice through the employment of three techniques of judicial interpretation: the doctrine of margin of appreciation; fair balance approach; and exemption from the scope of EU law. The choice of one technique over another is a matter of judicial discretion. All of them serve the same function of relaxing the standard of judicial review, if in different degrees, and all of them protect the principles of subsidiarity and proportionality through reducing the extent of judicial interference with national regulatory autonomy and interests protected within the exercise of that autonomy.

The grant of a margin of appreciation would generally allow more leeway to the Member States in making decisions about the organisation and management of national systems for social protection and provision of public services. The fair balance technique, which often goes together with the grant of margin of appreciation, appears particularly suited to protect collective labour rights from the deregulatory effects of unrestricted free movement. This technique would also bring the Court's case law on collective labour rights in line with the value system enshrined in the Treaties, in which the economic and social dimensions of EU law are accorded equal importance. Finally, the exemption from the scope of application of EU law could apply to domestic regulatory practices that are found to be in inherent contradiction with the deregulatory dimension of the internal market. Yet in order for the exemption to become a viable defence against the reach of EU internal market law, its scope needs to be clarified. Apart from the policy areas under study here, the described techniques of judicial interpretation would be suited to apply *mutatis mutandis* to any other constitutionally sensitive area of EU law and policy, such as crime prevention, culture and tourism, sport, civil protection, and tax.

A relaxed judicial review would also alter the institutional balance of powers between the EU's judiciary and legislature. By showing deference to national regulatory choices, the Court would give more space for the EU legislature to address the issues concerned under the functionally broad legal bases. At the same time, however, in the absence of detailed regulatory guidelines on behalf of the judiciary, legislative intervention would become less likely, as there would be no pressing need to remedy or, as often is the case, codify the case law in order to enhance the clarity and transparency of the regulatory framework. Problems that are politically sensitive but require common solutions could also be addressed by EU-level soft-law initiatives or by taking intergovernmental action, thus maintaining an appropriate degree of respect for autonomous decision making at Member State level.[111]

Bringing the judicial interpretation of free movement law in line with the principles of subsidiarity and proportionality would inevitably entail a reversal of some of the Court's case law. The Court would have to minimise the use of the test of necessity in its review of national regulatory frameworks and move towards a review focused on examining the consistency of such measures. This is not, however, a radical proposition. The Court has in the past revised, and departed from, its earlier judgments or even line of case law.[112] It is authorised to do so under Art 19 TEU, which allows for an ample degree of discretion in the exercise of EU judicial powers. The Court's reasons for deviating from its previous decisions might be political as much as they are legal. As argued in chapter one, the Court is not isolated from the political institutional context in which it operates. It might choose to change the direction of its case law as a result of a major change in the political climate that would show decreasing tolerance on behalf of

[111] For examples of such measures taken in the gambling sector, see Council of Europe Convention on the Manipulation of Sports Competitions (adopted 18 November 2014) CETS 215; Commission, 'Towards a comprehensive European framework on online gambling' (Communication) COM (2012) 596 final; Commission Recommendation 2014/478/EU on principles for the protection of consumers and players of online gambling services and for the prevention of minors from gambling online [2014] OJ L214/38.

[112] See, eg, Joined cases C-267/91 and C-268/91 *Keck and Mithouard* EU:C:1993:905, [1993] ECR I-6097; Case C-333/13 *Dano* EU:C:2014:2358 (CJEU, 11 November 2014); Case C-42/17 *Criminal proceedings against M.A.S. and M.B.* EU:C:2017:936 (CJEU, 5 December 2017) (*Taricco II*). Also cf *Commission v Luxembourg* (n 52) and *Omega* (n 52), offering contrasting interpretations of the public policy exception.

the Member States to the judicial transgressions into national regulatory autonomy.[113] Equally, it might do so in the spirit of respect for and cooperation with the EU's legislative institutions, especially if the position of the legislature is backed by wider shifts in the political mood across the region.[114] The bottom line is that as long as the reversal of the case law can be justified as a matter of constitutional principle, as it is in this case, it is both legitimate and desirable.

[113] See especially *Dano* (n 112).
[114] On this point, see ch 4, s VI.

Conclusion

This book examined the role of the European Court of Justice in the regulation of the internal market from a competence perspective. However, rather than focusing on the Court's role in enforcing the limits of EU competence in the EU's political decision making, it tackled a related, albeit largely understudied, question: to what extent does the Court observe the limits of EU competences and institutional powers in the interpretation of EU internal market law laid down in the Treaties? The answer to this question was sought through a two-fold inquiry: a comparative analysis of EU free movement case law involving the areas of national policy of comparable political and social sensitivity, namely, healthcare, education, collective labour law and gambling; and the assessment of the legitimacy of that case law in light of the constitutional principles that govern the allocation of competences and powers in the EU.

Whilst the free movement case law, and the judicial exercise of EU internal market competences more generally, have been subject to academic criticism before, this book represents the first comprehensive study that assessed that case law from a competence point of view. By doing so, it exposed the scale of the problem of the EU's creeping competence, showing that this extends way beyond the EU's legislative domain, and demonstrated that the judicial interpretation of free movement rules is a major, and often the dominant, source of that problem.

Having demonstrated that the Court is endowed by the Treaties with a regulatory and policy making capacity, the book argued that the Court often exercises that capacity – through the interpretation of free movement law – in a way that is not consistent with the constitutional principles that govern the allocation of competences and powers in the EU. In particular, it found that the Court's interpretation of free movement rules in cases involving the areas of healthcare, education and collective labour law, but not gambling, has overstretched the principles of conferral, subsidiarity and proportionality. By doing so, it has undermined the regulatory autonomy of the Member States protected by the vertical division of competences in the EU and has upset the institutional balance of powers between the EU legislature and judiciary, depriving the former of the core of its constitutional prerogatives. In light of these findings, the book proposed certain interpretative solutions on the part of the Court which could rectify inconsistencies in the case law and the constitutional and institutional imbalances which have resulted therefrom.

Argument

Chapter one examined the importance of the principles governing the allocation of competences and powers in the EU for the EU's legal order and reasons why these principles should bind the judicial interpretation of the Treaties. It demonstrated that the four principles – conferral, subsidiarity, proportionality and institutional balance – are the pillars underlying the federal nature of the EU's legal order. They maintain the balance between, on the one hand, the need for supranationalism and uniformity of EU law and, on the other hand, respect for the autonomy and diversity of the Member States. As the EU's constitutional judiciary, the Court has a duty to uphold this balance both in the decision making of the EU's political institutions and in the judicial interpretation of the Treaties. It is, therefore, bound to observe the four constitutional principles in the interpretation of EU internal market rules laid down in the Treaties.

Yet, according to the conventional perception, the principles of conferral, subsidiarity and proportionality are not meant to apply to the Court – they exclusively govern the EU's legislative and administrative practices. The chapter challenged this perception. It offered a systemic explanation for why these principles should govern the exercise of EU judicial authority. It argued that the structure of the EU endows the Court with a regulatory capacity characteristic of that possessed by bodies which exercise political authority on behalf of the State, namely legislative and executive institutions. This regulatory capacity is presupposed by a set of legal constitutional and political institutional circumstances: the broad scope of the EU's judicial mandate; the equally broad framing of the substantive rules of the Treaties, most notably the rules of the internal market, whose interpretation lies in the hands of the judiciary; and, lastly, the procedural weaknesses and democratic deficiencies pertaining to the EU's political decision making, which indirectly strengthen the role of the judiciary as a guardian of the rule of law in the EU. The regulatory capacity associated with the exercise of EU judicial authority is what makes a situation where the Court is exempt from constraints on competence that apply to the rest of the EU's institutions constitutionally unacceptable.

Chapter two examined the legitimacy of the interpretation by the Court of EU free movement law in light of the principle of conferral. It argued that while the principle of conferral does not preclude judicial interference into the constitutionally sensitive areas of EU competence, it sets a limit to such interference. In the context of the internal market, that limit lies in the conditions that trigger the application of free movement law: the economic nature of the activity; the presence of a restriction of free movement; and, as regards the prohibition of discrimination on grounds of nationality, the connection of the situation concerned with a substantive rule of EU law. When interpreting and applying those conditions in the circumstances of a given case, the Court is expected to adopt a systemic approach, contextualising them in the constitutional requirements of the principle of conferral. This means that when approaching the question whether the situation in question falls within the scope of free movement, concerns about the protection of national competence and regulatory autonomy in the areas of national policy that are constitutionally sensitive from EU law point of view should be taken into account.

The analysis demonstrated that the Court has systematically failed to engage in any meaningful reflection of competence concerns in the interpretation of the scope of free movement rules in the areas under study. It has also failed to achieve a satisfactory level of coherence in its reasoning in light of the broader framework of the Treaties, whether this meant giving consideration to its wider internal market case law or taking a balanced view of the reforms introduced by the Treaty of Maastricht, which, whilst having expanded the competences of the EU into new areas, also made explicit the principles limiting the scope and exercise of those competences. The neglect of the requirements of conferral in the judicial interpretation of free movement law has had consequences for the effectiveness of the legislative dimension of this principle. It opened up the possibility for matters that had been reserved to the regulatory prerogative of the Member States to be addressed at the EU's legislative level through the functionally broad legal bases. This meant that the prohibitions contained in sectoral legal bases excluding interference by the EU in constitutionally and politically sensitive areas could now be legitimately circumvented, thus further diminishing the practical significance of the principle of conferral.

Chapter three evaluated the free movement case law under study in light of the principles of subsidiarity and proportionality. It argued that the judicial exercise of EU internal market competences includes much more than simply the removal of obstacles to free movement or distortions of competition in the EU. Just like EU legislation, the Court's judgments inevitably interfere with and shape domestic regulatory activity in a number of ways, as demonstrated through the analysis of the regulatory implications of the case law in the areas under study. The regulatory capacity associated with the case law should, therefore, be considered not as a mere externality of the judicial interpretation of free movement rules but rather as an intended and integral part of the exercise by the Court of EU internal market competences. As such, it should be accounted for in light of the requirements of the principles of subsidiarity and proportionality. This would require that the Court advance the free movement law to a degree that is necessary in light of the impact of that law – or, specifically, the impact of the judicial interpretation of that law – on the scope of national regulatory autonomy (subsidiarity) and the legal interests protected via the exercise of that autonomy (proportionality).

In order to determine the extent to which the Court has complied with these requirements in the case law, the chapter examined the standard of judicial review employed by the Court to assess the lawfulness of national derogations from the free movement rules. The inquiry found that the observance by the Court of the principles of subsidiarity and proportionality has not been consistent across the areas under study. Owing to a strict-scrutiny review, focused on the test of necessity, the Court has advanced the free movement in the areas of healthcare, education and collective labour law at the expense of the broader, systemic objectives pursued by national regulatory policies. Doing so has had serious implications for both the scope of national regulatory autonomy and the social interests protected through its exercise. By contrast, in the gambling case law, the Court has employed a deferential review, focused on assessing the consistency of national measures and grounded in respect for national regulatory prerogatives in the gambling sector.

The chapter argued that discrepancies in the standard of judicial review employed in relation to the areas under study could not be justified considering the comparable political and social sensitivity of those areas. Those discrepancies, therefore, demonstrate that the Court has failed duly to consider the requirements of the principles of subsidiarity and proportionality in the judicial interpretation of free movement law in the areas of healthcare, education and collective labour law.

Chapter four demonstrated how the Court's case law has shaped the horizontal balance of powers between the EU legislature and judiciary. The chapter introduced the concept of a quasi-legislative judgment in order to explain the regulatory ambition of the case law and how it affects EU legislative activity. Using concrete examples of legislation from the areas under study, it argued that the case law puts the legislature into a so-called 'judicial trap', leaving it with a limited choice of legislative options, none of which can provide an adequate legislative response to the issues regulated by the case law.

The chapter identified three models of judiciary–legislature interaction that have developed in light of the case law. Model of Interaction No 1 described a scenario where quasi-legislative rules laid down in the case law predetermine the scope and content of legislative action, as in the case of the Patients' Rights Directive[1] and the Commission's *Altmark* package.[2] The legislature finds itself trapped in a position where a political agreement necessary to change the rules developed in the case law cannot be achieved and, therefore, the only feasible option left is to codify those rules. At times, especially in relation to more controversial issues, a political agreement cannot be reached to adopt any legislation at all. This is captured by Model of Interaction No 2, whereby the case law serves de facto to pre-empt the adoption of any novel legislative solutions, as happened with the Monti II draft.[3] In this scenario, the matters concerned continue to be regulated directly by the case law. Model of Interaction No 3 refers to circumstances where a legislative measure is already in place, but its judicial interpretation in light of the Treaties overrides existing legislative consensus, thus rendering EU-wide political agreement devoid of practical force. By the same token, this new interpretation becomes immune from subsequent legislative amendment, thus preventing legislative reversal of the case law. The examples that best illustrate this dynamic are the Posted Workers Directive[4] and Regulation 1408/71.[5]

The EU legislative institutions are in the above circumstances barred from any meaningful degree of autonomous action. Essentially, their role gets reduced to the legitimisation of judicial lawmaking through the legislative enactment of the rules developed by the Court. This undermines the legislative prerogative conferred by the Treaties upon EU legislative institutions, thereby suggesting that the judicial interpretation of free movement law upsets the horizontal balance of powers enshrined in the Treaties and protected by the principle of institutional balance.

[1] Council Directive 2011/24/EU on the application of patients' rights in cross-border healthcare [2011] OJ L88/45.

[2] Commission Decision on the application of Article 86(2) of the EC Treaty to state aid in the form of public service compensation granted to certain undertakings entrusted with the operation of services of general economic interest [2005] OJ L312/67, replaced by Commission Decision on the application of Article 106(2) of the Treaty on the Functioning of the European Union to State aid in the form of public service compensation granted to certain undertakings entrusted with the operation of services of general economic interest [2012] OJ L7/3.

[3] Commission, 'Proposal for a Council Regulation on the exercise of the right to take collective action within the context of the freedom of establishment and the freedom to provide services' COM (2012) 130 final.

[4] Council Directive 96/71/EC concerning the posting of workers in the framework of the provision of services [1997] OJ L18/1, replaced by Council Directive (EU) 2018/957/EU amending Directive 96/71/EC concerning the posting of workers in the framework of the provision of services [2018] OJ L173/16.

[5] Council Regulation (EEC) 1408/71 on the application of social security schemes to employed persons and their families moving within the Community [1971] OJ L149/2, replaced by Council Directive 2004/38/EC on the right of citizens of the Union and their family members to move and reside freely within the territory of the Member States [2004] OJ L158/79.

Building on the argument advanced in the previous chapters that the degree of the Court's interference with national regulatory autonomy through the interpretation of free movement rules is neither dictated nor justified by the reading of the Treaties, chapter five proposed a solution aimed at restoring the balance of competences and powers within the EU and thus easing the tensions created by the case law. The concrete propositions advanced in this chapter were based on operationalising the principles of subsidiarity and proportionality in judicial practice through the employment of certain techniques of judicial interpretation that could be considered as particular expressions of the two principles in the form of judicial reasoning. These techniques, which are already used in the Court's wider case law, are the margin of appreciation, the fair balance approach and the exemption from the scope of EU law. Apart from the policy areas studied in this book, they are suited to apply *mutatis mutandis* to any other constitutionally sensitive area of EU law and policy, such as crime prevention, culture and tourism, sport, civil protection, and tax.

Bringing the judicial interpretation of free movement law in line with the principles of subsidiarity and proportionality would inevitably entail a reversal of some of the Court's case law. The Court would have to minimise the use of the test of necessity in the review of national regulatory measures and move towards a review focused on examining the consistency of such measures. This is not, however, a radical proposition. The Court has in the past revised, and departed from, its earlier judgments or even a line of case law.[6] The Court's reasons for doing so might be political as much as they are legal. The Court might choose to change the direction of its case law as a result of a major change in the political climate that would show decreasing tolerance on behalf of the Member States to the judicial transgressions into national autonomy.[7] Equally, it might do so in the spirit of respect for and cooperation with the EU's legislative institutions, especially if the position of the legislature is backed by wider shifts in the political mood across the region. The bottom line is that as long as the reversal of the case law can be justified as a matter of constitutional principle, as it is in this case, it is both legitimate and desirable.

Future Research

The competence questions explored in this book arise not only in the context of EU free movement law but also competition law, as another major component of EU internal market law. Whilst the scope of this book did not allow the discussion to go into the detail of competition case law, chapter five examined certain aspects of the Court's approach concerning the reach of competition law in constitutionally and politically sensitive contexts. A cursory analysis seemed to suggest that the Court interprets EU competition rules, unlike the free movement rules, in a way that preserves the goals of the internal market without thereby undermining national regulatory choices in the areas that are sensitive from a constitutional and/or political point of view. These broad observations suggest that an inquiry into the judicial interpretation of EU internal

[6] See, eg, Joined cases C-267/91 and C-268/91 *Keck and Mithouard* EU:C:1993:905, [1993] ECR I-6097; Case C-333/13 *Dano* EU:C:2014:2358 (CJEU, 11 November 2014) Case C-42/17 *Criminal proceedings against M.A.S. and M.B.* EU:C:2017:936 (CJEU, 5 December 2017) (*Taricco II*).

[7] See especially *Dano* (n 6).

market rules from a competence perspective could benefit from exploring the Court's approach in competition law more fully.

Significance

This book has showcased the constitutional implications of EU judicial authority in the interpretation of internal market law. Having placed the Court at the centre of supranational decision making involving questions of particular political and social sensitivity, this authority has allowed the Court to shape the federal balance of competences in the EU. In other words, it has allowed the Court to determine the extent to which EU supranationalism could legitimately interfere with the autonomy of the Member States. The inquiry conducted in this book demonstrated that the Court has exercised its interpretative authority in a way that is inconsistent with the constitutional principles that govern the limits of EU competence and its exercise – conferral, subsidiarity and proportionality. Doing so has created constitutional imbalances both in the vertical division of competences and horizontal distribution of powers in the EU. This practice undermines the Court's credibility as a guardian of the rule of law in the EU and risks compromising its legitimacy as a judicial institution. More fundamentally, it threatens to destabilise the very foundations of the EU's legal order. This has consequences for the whole of the EU.

First, there are democratic consequences. An unwarranted judicial interference with national regulatory autonomy undermines democratic decision making in the Member States. By overstretching the limits of EU competence, the Court has placed itself in a position which allows it to influence – at times, even determine – government decisions on highly sensitive, socio-economic issues at the core of national public policy, such as decisions relating to the financing of public healthcare, policies concerning access to higher education, or choices regarding the role of the social partners in the regulation of labour and employment, all discussed in the context of this study. This practice creates problems for democracy not only at the level of the Member States but also at the level of the EU. It deprives the EU legislature of the opportunity to address these issues through the EU's political decision-making process. While this process may not be perfectly democratic, it nonetheless ensures that different interests will be represented and deliberated in the Council and Parliament. By foreclosing opportunities for political deliberation both at the EU and Member State levels, the Court threatens to compromise the already fragile democratic legitimacy of the EU.

Second, the failure on behalf of the Court to preserve the limits of EU competence – in fact, even a perception of such failure – threatens the supremacy and integrity of EU law. The past several decades have witnessed a growing tendency among national constitutional and supreme courts to question the authority of EU law and specifically of the Court as the institution responsible for the interpretation of that law. From *Melloni*[8] to *Taricco*[9] to *Weiss*[10] – national highest courts are sending a clear signal to the CJEU

[8] Spanish Constitutional Court, Order of 9 June 2011, ATC 86/2011.
[9] Corte Costituzionale, Order 24/2017, 26 January 2017.
[10] BVerfG, Judgment of 5 May 2020, 2 BvR 859/15.

that they are prepared to disobey both its rulings and the rules of EU law which, in their view, overstep the limits of EU competence.[11] This undermines the authority of the CJEU as the exclusive interpreter of EU law. Furthermore, it challenges the supremacy of EU law, which relies on national courts' acceptance of that law as interpreted by the CJEU. Without this acceptance, both the supremacy and integrity of the EU legal order risk being jeopardised.

On the political level, the EU's competence problem, exacerbated by the Court's practice, fuels populist, Eurosceptic narratives, which might endanger the future of European integration. Recent years have seen the rise of political movements that demonstrate open defiance to the authority of the EU and its core values, such as democracy and the rule of law. Populist parties have gained election victories or significant increases in the share of votes in a number of Member States, including the original members. The calls to leave the EU have been gaining traction, backed by emotionally charged slogans to 'take back control' from the unaccountable bureaucrats of the EU. Whilst the described developments cannot be attributed solely to concerns about the reach of EU competence, those concerns have undoubtedly been exploited by populist movements and used as a tool to incite anti-European nationalist sentiments.[12] The current political climate threatens, in the long run, to compromise the success of European integration and puts into question the future of the European project as such.

In light of these developments, it is of utmost importance that the Court, as the EU's highest judicial institution charged with the responsibility to ensure that the rule of law prevails in the interpretation and application of the Treaties, is seen as duly observing and enforcing the limits of EU competence and limits of its own institutional powers in the exercise of EU judicial authority. This could not be more poignant considering the role that the Court plays in the regulation of the internal market through the interpretation of the rules of the internal market enshrined in the Treaties. The observance by the Court of the limits of EU competence is key to preserving the integrity of the EU legal order and maintaining its legitimacy in the eyes of the Member States. It is key to ensuring that the success of European integration continues.

[11] See also BVerfG, judgment of 14 January 2014, 2 BvR 2728/13 (*OMT*); Danish Supreme Court, Case no. 15/2014 'Dansk Industri (DI) acting for Ajos A/S v The estate of A', Judgment of 6 December 2016, which was a response to the Court's judgment in Case C-441/14 *Danske Industri*, Judgment of 19 April 2016. Most recently, see Polish Constitutional Tribunal, Decision No. K 3/21, 7 October 2021.

[12] For an analysis of the reasons behind these various political developments, see P Sandrin, 'The Rise of Right-Wing Populism in Europe: A Psychoanalytical Contribution' in B De Souza Guilherme et al (eds), *Financial Crisis Management and Democracy: Lessons from Europe and Latin America* (New York, Springer, 2021) 227–28.

BIBLIOGRAPHY

'Statement of Retired Judges of the Polish Constitutional Tribunal' (*VerfBlog*, 11 October 2021).

Alter K, *The European Court's Political Power: Selected Essays* (Oxford, OUP, 2010).

Arnull A, 'The European Court and Judicial Objectivity: A Reply to Professor Hartley' (1996) 112 *Law Quarterly Review* 411.

Arnull A, *The European Union and its Court of Justice*, 2nd edn (Oxford, OUP, 2006).

Ashiagbor D, 'Evaluating the Reflexive Turn in Labour Law' in Bogg A et al (eds) *The Autonomy of Labour Law* (Oxford, Hart Publishing, 2015) 123–48.

Ashiagbor D, 'Unravelling the Embedded Liberal Bargain: Labour and Social Welfare Law in the Context of EU Market Integration' (2013) 19 *European Law Journal* 303.

Avbelj M, 'Can the New European Constitution Remedy the EU "Democratic Deficit"' (*Open Society Institute*, 2009).

Azoulai L, 'The Court of Justice and the Social Market Economy: The Emergence of an Ideal and the Conditions for its Realisation' (2008) 45 *CML Rev* 1350.

Azoulai L, '"Retained Powers" Formula in the Case Law of the European Court of Justice: EU Law as Total Law?' (2011) 4 *European Journal of Legal Studies* 192.

Azoulai L, 'Introduction' in Azoulai L (ed), *The Question of Competence in the European Union* (Oxford, OUP, 2014) 1–16.

Banks J, 'Online Gambling and Crime: A Sure Bet?' (2012) *The Ethicomp Journal*.

Banks J, *Online Gambling and Crime: Causes, Controls and Controversies* (Farnham, Ashgate Publishing Ltd, 2014).

Baquero Cruz J, *Between Competition and Free Movement: The Economic Constitutional Law of the European Community* (Oxford, Hart Publishing, 2002).

Baquero Cruz J, 'Beyond Competition: Services of General Interest and European Community Law' in De Búrca G (ed), *EU Law and the Welfare State. In Search of Solidarity* (Oxford, OUP, 2005) 170–211.

Baquero Cruz J, 'The Socioeconomic Model of the European Union: Stuck with the Status Quo' in Amato G et al (eds), *Génèse et Destinée de la Constitution Européenne – Genesis and Destiny of the European Constitution* (Brussels, Bruylant, 2007) 1105–28.

Barber N, 'Prelude to the Separation of Powers' (2001) 60 *Cambridge Law Journal* 59.

Barnard C, 'The Economic Objectives of Art 119' in Hervey T and O'Keeffe D (eds), *Sex Equality Law in the European Union* (New Jersey, Wiley, 1996) 321–34.

Barnard C, 'A Proportionate Response to Proportionality in the Field of Collective Action' (2012) 37 *European Law Review* 117.

Bassini M, 'ECJ Case Law on Gambling: How Technology Thwarts Regulatory Barriers' (*Media Laws*, 14 December 2014).

Bellamy R, '"An Ever Closer Union Among the Peoples of Europe": Republican Intergovernmentalism and Demoicratic Representation within the EU' (2013) 35 *Journal of European Integration* 499.

Benjamin A, 'La Belgique Instaure des Quotas D'Étudiants Étrangers en Médecine et Dentaire' *Le Monde* (Paris, 2012 June 29).

Bermann GA, 'Taking Subsidiarity Seriously: Federalism in the European Community and the United States' (1994) 94 *Columbia Law Review* 331.

Besselink LFM, 'National and Constitutional Identity before and after Lisbon' (2010) 6 *Utrecht Law Review* 36.

Betten L, 'The EU Charter of Fundamental Rights: A Trojan Horse or a Mouse?' (2001) 17 *International Journal of Comparative Labour Law & Industrial Relations* 151.

Bieber R et al, 'Back to the Future: Policy, Strategy and Tactics of the White Paper on the Creation of a Single European Market' in Bieber R et al (eds), *1992: One European Market?* (Baden, Nomos Verlagsgesellschaft, 1998) 18–20.

Bilchitz S, 'South Africa: Right to Health and Access to HIV/AIDS Drug Treatment' (2003) 1 *International Journal of Constitutional Law* 524.
Blauberger M, 'With *Luxembourg* in Mind … The Remaking of National Policies in the Face of ECJ Jurisprudence' (2012) 19 *Journal of European Public Policy* 109.
Bobek M, 'The Court of Justice of the European Union' in Chalmers D and Arnull A (eds), *Oxford Handbook of European Union Law* (Oxford, OUP, 2015) 154–76.
Box U, 'The European Parliament: Historical Background' (*European Parliament website*, January 2021).
Brewer-Carías A, *Constitutional Courts as Positive Legislators. A Comparative Law Study* (Cambridge, CUP, 2017).
Bücker A and Warneck W (eds), '*Viking – Laval – Rüffert*: Consequences and Policy Perspectives' (2010) European Trade Union Institute Report 111.
Bujalski A, 'ECJ Victory for Portuguese Gaming Monopoly' (2010) 16 *Computer and Telecommunications Law Review* 30.
Burley A-M and Mattli W, 'Europe before the Court: A Political Theory of Legal Integration' (1993) 47 *International Organization* 41.
Bzdera A, 'Comparative Analysis of Federal High Courts: A Political Theory of Judicial Review' (1993) 26 *Canadian Journal of Political Science* 3.
Calado F and Griffiths MD, 'Problem Gambling Worldwide: An Update and Systematic Review of Empirical Research (2000–2015)' (2016) 5 *Journal of Behavioral Addictions* 592.
Cambien N, 'Student Mobility in the European Union: Facing New Hurdles?' (2009) 11 *Revista Universitaria Europea* 77.
Cappelletti M, 'The Law-Making Power of the Judge and Its Limits: A Comparative Analysis' (1981) 8 *Monash University Law Review* 15.
Cappelletti M, 'Is the European Court of Justice "Running Wild"?' (1987) 12 *European Law Review* 3.
Cass Z, 'The Word That Saved Maastricht? The Principle of Subsidiarity and the Division of Powers within the European Community' (1992) 29 *CML Rev* 1107.
Cassese S, 'Ruling Indirectly: Judicial Subsidiarity in the ECtHR' (Seminar 'Subsidiarity: A Double Sided Coin?', Strasbourg, 30 January 2015).
Chen AHY and Maduro MP, 'The Judiciary and Constitutional Review' in Tushnet M, Fleiner T and Saunders C (eds), *Routledge Handbook of Constitutional Law* (Oxford, Routledge, 2013) 97–109.
Chevalier C and Gerard M, 'Financing Higher Education and Student Mobility across Europe' (2008) ARPEGE Research Paper.
Claes M and De Visser M, 'The Court of Justice as a Federal Constitutional Court: A Comparative Perspective' in Cloots E, De Baere G and Sottiaux S (eds), *Federalism in the European Union* (Oxford, Hart Publishing, 2012) 83–109.
Claes M and Reestman J-H, 'The Protection of National Constitutional Identity and the Limits of European Integration at the Occasion of the *Gauweiler* Case' (2015) 16 *German Law Journal* 917.
Claus LP and Kay RS, 'Constitutional Courts as "Positive Legislators" in the United States' (2010) 58 *American Journal of Comparative Law* 479.
Clark B, 'Separation of Powers as a Safeguard of Federalism' (2001) 79 *Texas Law Review* 1321.
Cloots E, *National Identity in EU Law* (Oxford, OUP, 2015).
Collins P, *Gambling and the Public Interest* (Westport, Praeger Publishers, 2003).
Constantinesco V, 'Who's Afraid of Subsidiarity?' (1991) 11 *Yearbook of European Law* 33.
Conway G, 'Recovering a Separation of Powers in the European Union' (2011) 17 *European Law Journal* 304.
Conway G, *Limits of Legal Reasoning* (Cambridge, CUP, 2012).
Cooper I, 'The Watchdogs of Subsidiarity: National Parliaments and the Logic of Arguing in the EU' (2006) 44 *Journal of Common Market Studies* 281.
Cooper I, 'A Yellow Card for the Striker: How National Parliaments Defeated EU Strikes Regulation' (2015) 2 *Journal of European Public Policy* 1406.
Coppel A and O'Neill J, 'The European Court of Justice: Taking Rights Seriously' (1992) 29 *Common Market Law Review* 669.
Cort P, 'The EC Discourse on Vocational Training: How a "Common Vocational Training Policy" Turned into a Lifelong Learning Strategy' (2009) 2 *Vocations and Learning* 87.
Corwin ES, 'The Passing of Dual Federalism' (1950) 36 *Virginia Law Review* 1.
Craig P, 'Democracy and Rule-making within the EC: An Empirical and Normative Assessment' (1997) 3 *European Law Journal* 105.

Craig P, '"Competence": Clarity, Conferral, Containment and Consideration' (2004) 29 *European Law Review* 323.

Craig P, 'Competence and Member State Autonomy: Causality, Consequence and Legitimacy' in Micklitz HW and De Witte B (eds), *The European Court of Justice and the Autonomy of the Member States* (Cambridge, Intersentia, 2012) 9–34.

Craig P, *EU Administrative Law*, 2nd edn (Oxford, OUP, 2012).

Craig P and De Búrca G, *EU Law: Text, Cases, and Materials*, 6th edn (Oxford, OUP, 2015).

Damjanovic D, 'The EU Market Rules as Social Market Rules: Why the EU Can Be a Social Market Economy' (2013) 50 *CML Rev* 1685.

Daniele L, 'Non-Discriminatory Restrictions to the Free Movement of Persons' (1997) 22 *European Law Review* 191.

Davies ACL, 'Should the EU Have the Power to Set Minimum Standards for Collective Labour Rights in the Member States?' in Alston P (ed), *Labour Rights as Human Rights* (Oxford, OUP, 2005) 177–213.

Davies ACL, 'One Step Forward, Two Steps Back? The *Viking* and *Laval* Cases in the ECJ' (2008) 37 *Industrial Law Journal* 126.

Davies G, 'Subsidiarity: The Wrong Idea, in the Wrong Place, at the Wrong Time' (2006) 43 *CML Rev* 6.

Davies G, 'The Process and Side-Effects of Harmonisation of European Welfare States' (2006) NYU Jean Monnet Program Working Paper 2/2006.

Davies G, 'The Price of Letting Courts Value Solidarity: The Judicial Role in Liberalizing Welfare' in Ross M and Borgmann-Prebil Y (eds), *Promoting Solidarity in the European Union* (Oxford, OUP, 2010) 107–17.

Davies G, 'The Competence to Create an Internal Market: Conceptual Poverty and Unbalanced Interests' in Garben S and Govaere I (eds), *The Division of Competences between the EU and the Member States: Reflections on the Past, the Present and the Future* (Oxford, Hart Publishing, 2017) 74–89.

Davies P, 'The Emergence of European Labour Law' in McCarthy W (ed), *Legal Intervention in Industrial Relations: Gains and Losses* (Hoboken, Blackwell, 1993) 313–59.

De Búrca G, 'The Principle of Proportionality and its Application in EC Law' (1993) 13 *Yearbook of European Law* 13.

De Búrca G, 'The Principle of Subsidiarity and the Court of Justice as an Institutional Actor' (1998) 36 *Journal of Common Market Studies* 217.

De Búrca G and Weiler J, *The European Court's Political Power* (Oxford, OUP, 2001).

De Vries SA, 'Balancing Fundamental Rights with Economic Freedoms According to the European Court of Justice' (2013) 9 *Utrecht Law Review* 169.

De Waele H, 'The Role of the European Court of Justice in the Integration Process: A Contemporary and Normative Assessment' (2010) 12 *Europarecht* 3.

De Waele H and Van der Vleuten A, 'Judicial Activism in the European Court of Justice – the Case of LGBT Rights' (2011) 19 *Michigan State International Law Review* 639.

De Wispelaere F, De Smedt L and Pacolet J, 'Posting of Workers: Report on A1 Portable Documents issued in 2018' (European Commission Directorate-General for Employment, Social Affairs and Inclusion 2019).

De Witte B, 'A Competence to Protect: The Pursuit of Non-Market Aims through Internal Market Legislation' in P Syrpis (ed), *The Judiciary, the Legislature and the EU Internal Market* (Cambridge, CUP, 2011) 25–46.

De Witte F, 'The Constitutional Quality of the Free Movement Provisions: Looking for Context in the Case Law on Article 56 TFEU' (2017) 42 *European Law Review* 313.

Deakin S, 'Regulatory Competition after Laval' (2008) 10 *Cambridge Yearbook of European Legal Studies* 581.

Devuyst Y, 'The European Union's Institutional Balance after the Treaty of Lisbon: "Community Method" and "Democratic Deficit" Reassessed' (2008) *Georgetown Journal of International Law* 249.

Dobbs M, 'Sovereignty, Article 4(2) TEU and the Respect of National Identities: Swinging the Balance of Power in Favour of the Member States?' (2014) 33 *Yearbook of European Law* 298.

Donahue JD, *Disunited States* (New York, Basic Books, 1997).

Dougan M, 'Fees, Grants, Loans and Dole Cheques: Who Covers The Costs Of Migrant Education Within The EU?' (2007) 1 *Journal of Contemporary European Research* 4.

Dworkin RM, 'The Model of Rules' (1967) *35 University of Chicago Law Review* 14.

Easson A, 'Legal Approaches to European Integration: The Role of Court and Legislator in the Completion of the European Common Market' (1989) 12 *Journal of European Integration* 101.

Editorial, 'The Guardian View on NHS Waiting Lists: Blame Cuts as well as Covid' *The Guardian* (London, 7 October 2021).

Elazar D, *The American Partnership: Intergovernmental Co-operation in the Nineteenth-Century United States* (Chicago, University of Chicago Press, 1962).
Elazar D, *Exploring Federalism* (Tuscaloosa, University of Alabama Press, 1987).
Emiliou N, *The Principle of Proportionality in European Law: A Comparative Study* (London, Kluwer Law International, 1996).
Ervin Jr SJ, 'Separation of Powers: Judicial Independence' (1970) 35 *Law Contemporary Problems* 108.
ETUC, Press release: '*Rüffert* case: ETUC Warns that ECJ's Judgment Is Destructive and Damaging' (*ETUC*, 3 April 2008).
EuroEducation, 'Belgium (Flemish Community) Higher Education System' (*euroeducation.net*).
European Commission, 'A guide to the rights of mobile students in the European Union' (Staff Working Document) COM (2010) 477 final.
European Commission, 'Progress towards the common European objectives in education and training (2010/2011): Indicators and benchmarks' (Staff Working Document) COM (2011) 526 final.
European Commission, 'Free movement of students: Commission closes infringement case against Austria' (Press release) (European Commission, 17 May 2017).
European Gaming & Betting Association, 'European Online Gambling Key Figures 2020 Edition' (2020).
European Health Policy Forum, 'Recommendations on Health Services and the Internal Market' (*European Health Policy Forum*, 26 May 2005).
European Parliament, DG Internal Policies of the Union, 'The ECJ Case Law on Cross-Border Aspects of Health Services' (Briefing note) [2006] IP/A/IMCO/FWC/2006-167/C3/SC1.
European Parliament, 'Online Gambling, Focusing on Integrity and a Code of Conduct for Gambling' (Policy Department Economic and Scientific Policy 2008).
Eurostat, 'Learning Mobility Statistics' (*Eurostat*, October 2020).
Ewing KD and Hendy J, 'The Dramatic Implications of *Demir and Baykara*' (2010) 39 *Industrial Law Journal* 2.
Fabbrini F, 'The Margin of Appreciation and the Principle of Subsidiarity: A Comparison' (2015) iCourts Working Paper Series 15/2015.
Fichera M, 'Constitutional Courts / Supreme Courts as Positive Legislators', *Max Planck Encyclopedia of Comparative Constitutional Law* (2020).
Flynn T, 'Constitutional Pluralism and Loyal Opposition' (2021) 19 *International Journal of Constitutional Law* 241.
Follesdal A and Hix S, 'Why There is a Democratic Deficit in the EU: A Response to Majone and Moravcsik' (2006) 44 *Journal of Common Market Studies* 533.
Freedland M and Prassl J (eds), *EU Law in the Member States:* Viking, Laval *and Beyond* (Oxford, Hart Publishing, 2014).
Fric K, 'Statutory Minimum Wages in the EU 2016' (*Eurofond*, 29 January 2016).
Gaeta M et al, 'An Overview of Different Health Indicators used in the European Health Systems' (2017) 58 *Journal of Preventive Medicine and Hygiene* 114.
Gallo D, 'Functional Approach and Economic Activity in EU Competition Law, Today: The Case of Social Security and Healthcare' (2020) 26 *European Public Law* 569.
Garben S, 'The Belgian/Austrian Education Saga' (2008) Harvard European Law Working Paper 1/2008.
Garben S, 'The Bologna Process: From a European Law Perspective' (2010) 16 *European Law Journal* 186.
Garben S, 'The Future of Higher Education in Europe: The Case for a Stronger Base in EU Law' (2012) LSE 'Europe in Question' Discussion Paper 50/2012.
Garben S, 'Competence Creep Revisited' (2019) 57 *Journal of Common Market Studies* 205.
Gardbaum S, 'Limiting Constitutional Rights' (2007) 54 *UCLA Law Review* 789.
Gardner J, 'Some Types of Law' in Gardner J, *Law as a Leap of Faith: Essays on Law in General* (Oxford, OUP, 2012) 55–88.
Gardner T and Fraser C, 'Elective Care: How Has Covid-19 Affected the Waiting List?' (*The Health Foundation*, 27 September 2021).
Garlicki L, 'Constitutional Courts versus Supreme Courts' (2007) 5 *International Journal of Constitutional Law* 44.
Gekiere W, Baeten R and Palm W, 'Free Movement of Services in the EU and Health Care' in Mossialos E et al (eds), *Health Systems Governance in Europe: The Role of European Union Law and Policy* (Cambridge, CUP, 2010) 461–508.
Gerards J, 'Pluralism, Deference and the Margin of Appreciation Doctrine' (2011) 12 *European Law Journal* 80.

Gerards J, 'Margin of Appreciation and Incrementalism in the Case Law of the European Court of Human Rights' (2018) 18 *Human Rights Law Review* 495.
Gillet K, 'Romania's Underfunded Health System Creaks under the Pressure of the Pandemic' *The New York Times* (New York, 3 March 2021).
Goldoni M, 'The Early Warning System and the Monti II Regulation: The Case for a Political Interpretation' (2014) 10 *European Constitutional Law Review* 90.
Gormley L, 'Free Movement of Goods and EU Legislation in the Court of Justice' in Syrpis P (ed), *The Judiciary, the Legislature and the EU Internal Market* (Cambridge, CUP, 2012) 49–61.
Grabher A et al, 'Student Mobility in the EHEA: Underrepresentation in Student Credit Mobility and Imbalances in Degree Mobility' (Research Report, Institute for Advanced Studies, Vienna, January 2014).
Gramper A, 'Constitutional Courts and Judicial Law-Making: Why Democratic Legitimacy Matters' (2015) 4 *CJICL* 423.
Greer SL, 'Power Struggle: The Politics and Policy Consequences of Patient Mobility in Europe' (Observatoire Social Européen Policy Paper 2/2008).
Griffiths M, 'Crime and Gambling: A Brief Overview of Gambling Fraud on the Internet' (2010) *Internet Journal of Criminology*.
Grimm D, 'The Democratic Costs of Constitutionalisation: The European Case' (2015) 21 *European Law Journal* 460.
Grinols EI, 'The Hidden Social Costs of Gambling' (Center for Christian Ethics at Baylor University 2011).
Guestaferro B, 'Beyond the Exceptionalism of Constitutional Conflicts: The Ordinary Function of the Identity Clause' (2012) 31 *Yearbook of European Law* 263.
Hancher L and Sauter W, 'One Step Beyond? From *Sodemare* to *DocMorris*: The EU's Freedom of Establishment Case Law Concerning Health Care' (2010) 47 *CML Rev* 117.
Harbo T-I, 'The Function of the Proportionality Principle in EU Law' (2010) 16 *European Law Journal* 158.
Harley T, 'The European Court, Judicial Objectivity and the Constitution of the European Union' (1996) 12 *Law Quarterly Review* 95.
Hatzopoulos V, 'Actively Talking to Each Other: the Court and the Political Institutions' in De Witte B, Muir E and Dawson M (eds), *Judicial Activism at the European Court of Justice* (Cheltenham, Edward Elgar Publishing, 2013) 102–41.
Health and Consumer Protection Directorate-General, European Commission, Summary report of the responses to the consultation regarding 'Community action on health services' SEC (2006) 1195/4.
Hervey T, '"Social Solidarity": A Buttress Against Internal Market Law?' in Shaw J (ed), *Social Law and Policy in an Evolving European Union* (London, Hart Publishing, 2005) 31–48.
Hesse K, *Grundzüge des Verfassungsrechts der Bundesrepublik Deutschland*, 20th edn (Heidelberg, CF Müller, 1995).
Hirschl R, 'The Judicialization of Mega-Politics and the Rise of Political Courts' (2008) 11 *Annual Review of Political Science* 98.
Hoogenboom A, 'Mobility of Students and the Financial Sustainability of Higher Education Systems in the EU: a Union of Harmony or Irreconcilable Differences?' (2013) 9 *Croatian Yearbook of European Law and Policy* 15.
Höpner M, 'Proportionality and Karlsruhe's Ultra Vires Verdict: Ways out of Constitutional Pluralism?' (2021) MPIfG Discussion Paper 21/1.
Hörnle J, 'Social Policy and Regulatory Models' in Hörnle J and Zammit B, *Cross-Border Online Gambling Law and Policy* (Cheltenham, Edward Elgar Publishing, 2010) 10–77.
Horsley T, 'Subsidiarity and the European Court of Justice: Missing Pieces in the Subsidiarity Jigsaw?' (2012) 50 *Journal of Common Market Studies* 267.
Horsley T, *The Court of Justice of the European Union as an Institutional Actor: Judicial Lawmaking and its Limits* (Cambridge, CUP, 2018).
Hös N, 'The Principle of Proportionality in the *Viking* and *Laval* Cases: An Appropriate Standard of Judicial Review?' (2009) EUI Department of Law Working Paper 2009/06.
Hutchinson AC, 'A "Hard Core" Case against Judicial Review' (2008) 121 *Harvard Law Review Forum* 57.
International Labour Organization, Group of Experts, 'Social Aspects of European Economic Co-operation' (1956) 74 *International Labour Review* 99 (Ohlin Report).
Jacobs FG, 'Citizenship of the European Union – A Legal Analysis' (2007) 13 *European Law Journal* 591.
Jacqué J-P, 'The Principle of Institutional Balance' (2004) 21 *CML Rev* 383.

Joerges C and Rödl F, 'Informal Politics, Formalised Law and the 'Social Deficit' of European Integration: Reflections after the Judgments of the ECJ in *Viking* and *Laval*' (2009) 15 *European Law Journal* 1.
Johnson CH, 'The Dubious Enumerated Power Doctrine' (2005) 22 *Constitutional Commentary* 25.
Kaczorowska A, 'A Review of the Creation by the European Court of Justice of the Right to Effective and Speedy Medical Treatment and its Outcomes' (2006) 12 *European Law Journal* 345.
Kavanagh A, 'The Constitutional Separation of Powers' in Dyzenhaus D and Thorburn M (eds), *Philosophical Foundations of Constitutional Law* (Oxford, OUP, 2016) 224–40.
Kearney MS, 'The Economic Winners and Losers of Legalized Gambling' (2005) 58 *National Tax Journal* 281.
Kelsen H, 'La Garantie Juridictionnelle de la Constitution' (1928) 45 *Revue de Droit Public* 197.
Kenner J, *EU Employment Law: From Rome to Amsterdam and Beyond* (Oxford, Hart Publishing, 2003).
Kiiver P, *The Early Warning System for the Principle of Subsidiarity: Constitutional Theory and Empirical Reality* (London, Routledge, 2012).
Komarek J, 'Reasoning with Previous Decisions: Beyond the Doctrine of Precedent' (2013) 61 *The American Journal of Comparative Law* 149.
Konstadinides T, 'Drawing the Line between Circumvention and Gap-Filling: An Exploration of the Conceptual Limits of the Treaty's Flexibility Clause' (2012) 31 *Yearbook of European Law* 227.
Konstadinides T, 'Dealing with Parallel Universes: Antinomies of Sovereignty and the Protection of National Identity in European Judicial Discourse' (2015) 34 *Yearbook of European Law* 127.
Kosta V, 'The Principle of Proportionality in EU Law: An Interest-Based Taxonomy' in Mendes J, *EU Executive Discretion and the Limits of Law* (Oxford, OUP, 2019) 198–219.
Kumm M, 'Constitutionalising Subsidiarity in Integrated Markets: The Case of Tobacco Regulation in the European Union' (2006) 12 *European Law Journal* 503.
Larsen SR, *The Constitutional Theory of the Federation and the European Union* (Oxford, OUP, 2021).
Lenaerts K, 'Constitutionalism and the Many Faces of Federalism' (1990) 38 *The American Journal of Comparative Law* 205.
Lenaerts K, 'Some Thoughts About the Interaction Between Judges and Politicians in the European Community' (1992) 12 *Yearbook of European Law* 1.
Lenaerts K, 'The European Court of Justice and Process-Oriented Review' (2012) 31 *Yearbook of European Law* 3.
Lenaerts K, 'The Court's Outer and Inner Selves: Exploring the External and Internal Legitimacy of the European Court of Justice' in Adams M et al (eds), *Judging Europe's Judges: The Legitimacy of the Case Law of the European Court of Justice* (Oxford, Hart Publishing, 2013) 13–60.
Lenaerts K and Verhoeven A, 'Institutional Balance as a Guarantee for Democracy in EU Governance' in Joerges C and Dehousse R (eds), *Good Governance in Europe's Integrated Market* (Cambridge, OUP, 2002) 35–88.
Madison J, 'No. 47' in Madison J, Hamilton A and Jay J (eds), *The Federalist Papers* (I Kramnick (ed), London, Penguin Books, 1987) 216–21.
Madison J, 'No. 51' in Madison J, Hamilton A and Jay J, *The Federalist Papers* (C Rossiter (ed), New York, Penguin Putnam, 1999) 276–93.
Maduro M, *We the Court: The European Court of Justice and the European Economic Constitution* (Oxford, Hart Publishing, 1998).
Majone G, 'Europe's "Democratic Deficit": The Question of Standards' (1998) 4 *European Law Journal* 5.
Malmberg J, 'The Impact of the ECJ Judgments in *Viking*, *Laval*, *Rüffert* and *Luxembourg* on the Practice of Collective Bargaining and the Effectiveness of Social Action' (2010) European Parliament Directorate General for Internal Policies 7.
Malmberg J and Sigeman T, 'Industrial Actions and EU Economic Freedoms: The Autonomous Collective Bargaining Model Curtailed by the European Court of Justice' (2008) 45 *CML Rev* 1115.
Mancini FG, 'The Making of a Constitution for Europe' (1989) 26 *CML Rev* 595.
Mancini FG and Keeling D, 'Language, Culture and Politics in the Life of the European Court of Justice' (1995) 1 *Columbia Journal of European Law* 397.
Marauhn T and Ruppel N, 'Balancing Conflicting Human Rights: Konrad Hesse's Notion of "Praktische Konkordanz" and the German Federal Constitutional Court' in Brems E (ed), *Conflicts Between Fundamental Rights* (Cambridge, Intersentia-Hart, 2008) 273–96.
Marshall G, *Constitutional Theory* (Oxford, Clarendon Press, 1971).

Martinico G and Pollicino O, 'Use and Abuse of a Promising Concept: What Has Happened to National Constitutional Identity?' (2020) 39 *Yearbook of European Law* 228.
Mc Govern M, 'Vienna Aims to Halt Influx of German Students' (*Presseurop*, 28 May 2013).
Micklitz HW and De Witte B (eds), *The European Court of Justice and the Autonomy of the Member States* (Cambridge, Intersentia, 2012).
Miedema D, 'Government – Gambling's Biggest Addict. Profligate Spending Feeds Government Gambling Addiction' (*Institute of Marriage and Family Canada*, March 2012).
Montesquieu, *The Spirit of the Laws* 157 (AM Cohler et al, eds and trans, Cambridge, CUP, 1989).
Monti G, *EC Competition Law* (Cambridge, CUP, 2007).
Moravcsik A, 'The Myth of the European Democratic Deficit' (2003) 10 *Raisons Politiques* 87.
Mossialos E et al, 'Health Systems Governance in Europe: The Role of European Union Law and Policy' in Mossialos E et al (eds), *Health Systems Governance in Europe: The Role of European Union Law and Policy* (Cambridge, CUP, 2010) 1–83.
Mulder J, *Social Legitimacy in the Internal Market: A Dialogue of Mutual Responsiveness* (Oxford, Hart Publishing, 2018).
Myklebus JP, 'Facing a Rising Imbalance of Mobile Students' (*University World News*, 31 January 2014).
Nair A, 'Online Gambling: Gambling with Regulation' (2012) 3 *European Journal of Law and Technology*.
Neill P, *The European Court of Justice: A Case Study in Judicial Activism* (European Policy Forum, 1995).
Newdick C, 'Citizenship, Free Movement, and Healthcare: Cementing Individual Rights by Corroding Social Solidarity' (2006) 43 *CML Rev* 1645.
Nolte G, 'General Principles of German and European Administrative Law: A Comparison in Historical Perspective' (1994) 57 *Modern Law Review* 191.
Novitz T and Germanotta P, 'Globalisation and the Right to Strike: The Case for European-Level Protection of Secondary Action' (2002) 18 *International Journal of Comparative Labour Law* 67.
Novitz T and Syrpis P, 'The United Kingdom' in Freedland M and Adams-Prassl J, *Viking, Laval and Beyond* (London, Hart Publishing, 2014) 261–76.
Öberg J, *Limits to EU Powers: A Case Study of EU Regulatory Criminal Law* (Oxford, Hart Publishing, 2017).
Öberg J, 'Subsidiarity as a Limit to the Exercise of EU Competences' (2017) 36 *Yearbook of European Law* 391.
OECD, *Waiting Times for Health Services: Next in Line* (OECD Health Policy Studies, OECD Publishing, Paris 2020).
OECD/European Union, *Supporting Entrepreneurship and Innovation in Higher Education in Austria* (OECD Skills Studies, OECD Publishing, Paris 2019).
Open Society Justice Initiative, 'Margin of Appreciation – An Overview of the Strasbourg Court's Margin of Appreciation Doctrine' (*Open Society Justice Initiative*, April 2012).
Osaghae EE, 'A Reassessment of Federalism as a Degree of Decentralization' (1990) 20 *Publius: The Journal of Federalism* 83.
Pescatore P, 'Foreword' in Sandalow T and Stein E (eds), *Courts and Free Markets: Perspectives from the United States and Europe*, Vol I (Oxford, Clarendon Press, 1982).
Pinder J, 'Positive Integration and Negative Integration: Some Problems of Economic Union in the EEC' (1968) 24 *The World Today* 88.
Planzer S, '*Liga Portuguesa* – the ECJ and its Mysterious Ways of Reasoning' (2009) 11 *European Law Reporter* 372.
Planzer S, *Empirical Views on European Gambling Law and Addiction* (New York, Springer, 2014).
Pliakos A and Anagnostaras G, 'Fundamental Rights and the New Battle over Legal and Judicial Supremacy: Lessons from Melloni' (2015) 34 *Yearbook of European Law* 97.
Pollack M, 'Creeping Competence: The Expanding Agenda of the European Community' (1994) 14 *Journal of Public Policy* 95.
Prassl J, 'Freedom of Contract as a General Principle of EU Law? Transfers of Undertakings and the Protection of Employer Rights in EU Labour Law: Case C-426/11 *Alemo-Herron and Others v Parkwood Leisure Ltd*' (2013) 42 *Industrial Law Journal* 434.
Prechal S, 'Competence Creep and General Principles of Law' (2010) 3 *Review of European Administrative Law* 5.
Prosser T, 'EU Competition Law and Public Services' in Mossialos E et al (eds), *Health Systems Governance in Europe: The Role of European Union Law and Policy* (Cambridge, CUP, 2010) 315–36.

Rasmussen H, *On Law and Policy in the European Court of Justice. A Comparative Study in Judicial Policymaking* (Leiden, Martinus Nijhoff Publishers, 1986).
Rasmussen H, 'Towards A Normative Theory of Interpretation of Community Law' (1992) *University of Chicago Legal Forum* 135.
Reynolds S, 'Explaining the Constitutional Drivers behind a Perceived Judicial Preference for Free Movement over Fundamental Rights' (2016) 53 *CML Rev* 643.
Rich RF and Merrick KR, 'Cross Border Health Care in the European Union: Challenges and Opportunities' (2006) 23 *Journal of Contemporary Health Law and Policy* 64.
Rieder C, 'Case C-147/03, *Commission of the European Communities v. Republic of Austria*, Judgment of the Court (Second Chamber) 7 July 2005' (2006) 43 *CML Rev* 1711.
Runner P, 'EU Parliament Opposes Creation of Online Gambling Market' (*EUobserver*, 10 March 2009).
Ryan B, 'The Charter and Collective Labour Law' in Hervey TK and Kenner J (eds), *Economic and Social Rights Under the EU Charter of Fundamental Rights – A Legal Perspective* (Oxford, Hart Publishing, 2003) 67–90.
Šadl U and Mair S, 'Mutual Disempowerment: Case C-441/14 *Dansk Industri, acting on behalf of Ajos A/S v Estate of Karsten Eigil Rasmussen and Case no. 15/2014 Dansk Industri (DI) acting for Ajos A/S v The estate left by A*' (2017) 13 *European Constitutional Law Review* 347.
Sandrin P, 'The Rise of Right-Wing Populism in Europe: A Psychoanalytical Contribution' in De Souza Guilherme B et al (eds), *Financial Crisis Management and Democracy: Lessons from Europe and Latin America* (New York, Springer, 2021) 227–50.
Saunders KW, 'Interpretative Rules with Legislative Effect: An Analysis and a Proposal for Public Participation' (1986) 35 *Duke Law Journal* 346.
Sauter W, 'Harmonisation in Healthcare: the EU Patients' Rights Directive' (2011) TILEC Discussion Paper 2011–030.
Sauter W, 'Proportionality in EU Law: A Balancing Act?' (2013) 15 *Cambridge Yearbook of European Legal Studies* 439.
Scharpf FW, 'Community and Autonomy: Multi-Level Policy-Making in the European Union' (1994) 1 *Journal of European Public Policy* 219.
Scharpf FW, 'Negative and Positive Integration in the Political Economy of European Welfare States' in Marks G et al (eds), *Governance in the European Union* (London, SAGE Publications, 1996) 15–39.
Scharpf FW, 'The Joint-Decision Trap. Lessons From German Federalism and European Integration' (1988) 66 *Public Administration* 239.
Scharpf FW, 'The European Social Model: Coping with the Challenges of Diversity' (2002) 40 *Journal of Common Market Studies* 645.
Scharpf FW, 'The Joint-Decision Trap Revisited' (2006) 44 *Journal of Common Market Studies* 845.
Scharpf FW, 'Legitimacy in the Multilevel European Polity' (2009) 1 *European Political Science Review* 173.
Scharpf FW, 'The Asymmetry of European Integration, or Why the EU Cannot Be a "Social Market Economy"' (2010) 8 *Socio-Economic Review* 211.
Schiek D, 'The EU Constitution of Social Governance in an Economic Crisis: in Defence of a Transnational Dimension to Social Europe' (2013) 20 *Maastricht Journal of European and Comparative Law* 195.
Schiek D, 'A Constitution of Social Governance for the European Union' in Kostakopoulou D and Ferreira N (eds), *The Human Face of the European Union: Are EU Law and Policy Humane Enough?* (Cambridge, CUP, 2016) 17–47.
Schiek D et al, 'EU Social and Labour Rights and EU Internal Market Law' (European Parliament DG for Internal Policies 2015).
Schilling T, 'A New Dimension of Subsidiarity: Subsidiarity as a Rule and a Principle' (1994) 14 *Yearbook of European Law* 203.
Schmidt SK, 'Governing by Judicial Fiat? Over-Constitutionalisation and its Constraints on EU Legislation' (EUSA international Biennial Conference, Denver, May 2019).
Schütze R, *From Dual to Cooperative Federalism: The Changing Structure of European Law* (Oxford, OUP, 2009).
Schütze R, 'Subsidiarity after Lisbon: Reinforcing the Safeguards of Federalism?' (2009) 68 *Cambridge Law Journal* 525.
Schütze R, 'EU Competences: Existence and Exercise' in Chalmers D and Arnull A (eds), *Oxford Handbook of European Union Law* (Oxford, OUP, 2015) 75–102.

Schwartz H, *The Struggle for Constitutional Justice in Post-Communist Europe* (Chicago, The University of Chicago Press, 2000).
Semmelmann C, 'The European Union's Economic Constitution under the Lisbon Treaty: Soul-Searching among Lawyers Shifts the Focus to Procedure' (2010) 35 *European Law Review* 516.
Shany Y, 'Toward a General Margin of Appreciation Doctrine in International Law?' (2006) 16 *European Journal of International Law* 907.
Shetreet S and Forsyth C (eds), *The Culture of Judicial Independence: Conceptual Foundations and Practical Challenges* (Leiden, Martinus Nijhoff Publishers, 2012).
Shuibhne N, 'Margins of Appreciation: National Values, Fundamental Rights and EC Free Movement Law' (2009) 34 *European Law Review* 254.
Shuibhne N, 'Primary Laws: Judging Free Movement Restrictions after Lisbon' in Koutrakos P, Shuibhne N and Syrpis P (eds), *Exceptions from EU Free Movement Law* (Oxford, Hart Publishing, 2016) 297–318.
Sindbjerg Martinsen D, *An Ever More Powerful Court? The Political Constraints of Legal Integration in the European Union* (Oxford, OUP, 2015).
Smulders B and Eisele K, 'Reflections on the Institutional Balance, the Community Method and the Interplay between Jurisdictions after Lisbon' (2012) College of Europe, Department of European Legal Studies Research Paper 04/2012.
Snell J, 'Who's Got the Power? Free Movement and Allocation of Competences in EC Law' (2003) 22 *Yearbook of European Law* 323.
Spaak PH, *Rapport des chefs de delegation aux Ministres des Affaires Etrangères* (1956 Intergovernmental Committee on European Integration).
Spielmann D, 'Allowing the Right Margin: The European Court of Human Rights and the National Margin of Appreciation Doctrine: Waiver or Subsidiarity of European Review?' (2015) 14 *Cambridge Yearbook of European Legal Studies* 381.
Stein E, 'Lawyers, Judges and the Making of a Transnational Constitution' (1981) 75 *The American Journal of International Law* 1.
Stone Sweet A, *Governing with Judges: Constitutional Politics in Europe* (Oxford, OUP, 2000).
Stone Sweet A, *The Judicial Construction of Europe* (Oxford, OUP, 2004).
Stone Sweet A, 'The Politics of Constitutional Review in France and Europe' (2007) 5 *International Journal of Constitutional Law* 79.
Stone Sweet A, 'The European Court of Justice' in Craig P and De Búrca G (eds), *Evolution of EU Law*, 2nd edn (Oxford, OUP, 2011) 121–54.
Stone Sweet A and Caporaso JA, 'From Free Trade to Supranational Polity: The European Court and Integration' in Sandholtz W and Stone Sweet A, *European Integration and Supranational Governance* (Oxford, OUP, 1998) 59–91.
Stuart M, 'Problems of the European Community: Transatlantic Parallels' (1987) 36 *The International and Comparative Law Quarterly* 183.
Swaine ET, 'Subsidiarity and Self-Interest: Federalism at the European Court of Justice' (2000) 41 *Harvard International Law Journal* 58.
Swiss Institute of Comparative Law, 'Study of Gambling Services in the Internal Market of the European Union' (Swiss Institute of Comparative Law 2006).
Sylvest J and Adamsen C, 'The Impact of the European Court of Justice Case Law on National Systems for Cross-Border Health Services Provision' (2007) Briefing Note, DG Internal Policies of the Union.
Syrpis P, 'Reconciling Economic Freedoms and Social Rights – The Potential of *Commission v Germany* (Case C-271/08, Judgment of 15 July 2010)' (2011) 40 *Industrial Law Journal* 222.
Syrpis P, 'The Relationship between Primary and Secondary Law in the EU' (2015) 52 *CML Rev* 461.
Syrpis P, 'EU Secondary Legislation and Its Impact on Derogations' in Koutrakos P, Shuibhne N and Syrpis P (eds), *Exceptions from EU Free Movement Law* (Oxford, Hart Publishing, 2016) 27–296.
Syrpis P and Novitz T, 'Economic and Social Rights in Conflict: Political and Judicial Approaches to their Reconciliation' (2008) 33 *European Law Review* 411.
Talmadge PA, 'Understanding the Limits of Power: Judicial Restraint in General Jurisdiction Court Systems' (1999) 22 *Seattle University Law Review* 695.
Taylor G, 'Germany: The Subsidiarity Principle' (2006) 4 *International Journal of Constitutional Law* 115.
Temple Lang J, 'Has the European Court of Justice Been Involved in "Judicial Legislation"?' (2011) 96 *SvJT* 299.

The Adoptive Parents, 'The Life of a Death Foretold: The Proposal for a Monti II Regulation' in Freedland M and Prassl J (eds), *EU Law in the Member States:* Viking, Laval *and Beyond* (Oxford, Hart Publishing, 2014) 95–110.
Tinbergen J, *International Economic Integration* (Amsterdam, Brussels, Elsevier, 1954).
Tridimas T, 'The Court of Justice and Judicial Activism' (1996) 21 *European Law Review* 199.
Tridimas T, 'The Principle of Proportionality in Community Law: from the Rule of Law to Market Integration' (1996) 31 *Irish Jurist* 83.
Tridimas T, *The General Principles of EU Law*, 2nd edn (Oxford, OUP, 2007).
Tridimas T, 'Constitutional Review of Member State Action: The Virtues and Vices of an Incomplete Jurisdiction' (2011) 9 *International Journal of Constitutional Law* 737.
Tridimas T, 'The ECJ and the National Courts: Dialogue, Cooperation, and Instability' in Chalmers D and Arnull A (eds), *Oxford Handbook of European Union Law* (Oxford, OUP, 2015) 409–10.
Van den Bogaert S and Cuyvers A, '"Money for Nothing": The Case Law of the EU Court of Justice on the Regulation of Gambling' (2011) 48 *CML Rev* 1175.
Van der Mei AP, *Free Movement of Persons Within the European Community: Cross-Border Access to Public Benefits* (Oxford, Hart Publishing, 2003).
Van der Mei AP, 'Free Movement of Students and the Protection of National Educational Interests: Reflections on *Bressol and Chaverot*' (2011) 13 *European Journal of Migration and Law* 123.
Van der Schyff G, 'Exploring Member State and European Union Constitutional Identity' (2016) 22 *European Public Law* 227.
Van Empel M, 'The 1992 Programme: Interaction between Legislator and Judiciary' (1992) 19 *Legal Issues of European Integration* 1.
Vanguard Healthcare Solutions, 'How Do Our Waiting Times Compare?' (*Vanguard Healthcare Solutions*, 27 April 2021).
Velyvyte V, 'The Right to Strike in the European Union after Accession to the European Convention on Human Rights: Identifying Conflict and Achieving Coherence' (2015) 15 *Human Rights Law Review* 73.
Velyvyte V, 'A Power to Shape the Internal Market: Implications of CJEU Case Law for the Principle of Institutional Balance' (2016) 12 *Croatian Yearbook of European Law and Policy* 25.
Volgy T, 'The Role of the "Outsider" in Quasi-Legislative Systems: The Potential Utility of a Legislative Model' (1973) 27 *International Organization* 85.
Von Bogdandy A, 'Founding Principles' in Von Bogdandy A and Bast J (eds), *Principles of European Constitutional Law*, 2nd edn (Oxford, Hart Publishing, 2009) 11–54.
Von Bogdandy A and Schill S, 'Overcoming Absolute Privacy: The Respect for National Identity under the Lisbon Treaty' (2011) 48 *CML Rev* 1417.
Waldron J, 'The Core of the Case Against Judicial Review' (2006) 115 *Yale Law Journal* 1346.
Waldron J, 'Separation of Powers in Thought and Practice' (2013) 54 *Boston College Law Review* 433.
Walker DM and Barnett AH, 'Social Costs of Gambling: An Economic Perspective' (1999) 15 *Journal of Gambling Studies* 181.
Walker N, 'The Philosophy of European Union Law' in Chalmers D and Arnull A (eds), *Oxford Handbook of European Union Law* (Oxford, OUP, 2015) 21–22.
Wasserfallen F, 'The Judiciary as Legislator? How the European Court of Justice Shapes Policy-Making in the European Union' (2010) 17 *Journal of European Law and Policy* 1128.
Weatherill S, 'The Function and Limits of Legislative Harmonization in Making the Internal Market' in Schütze R and Tridimas T (eds), *Oxford Principles of European Law: Volume II* (forthcoming, Oxford, OUP).
Weatherill S, 'Activism and Restraint in the European Court of Justice' in Capps P, Evans M and Konstadinidis S (eds), *Asserting Jurisdiction: International and European Legal Perspectives* (Oxford, Hart Publishing, 2003) 255–82.
Weatherill S, 'Competence Creep and Competence Control' (2004) 23 *Yearbook of European Law* 1.
Weatherill S, 'The Limits of Legislative Harmonisation Ten Years after *Tobacco Advertising*: How the Court's Case Law Has Become a "Drafting Guide"' (2011) 12 *German Law Journal* 827.
Weatherill S, 'The Consumer Rights Directive: How and Why a Quest for "Coherence" Has (Largely) Failed' (2012) 49 *CML Rev* 1279.
Weatherill S, 'Use and Abuse of the EU's Charter of Fundamental Rights: on the Improper Veneration of "Freedom of Contract". Judgment of the Court of 18 July 2013: Case C-426/11, *Mark Alemo-Herron and Others v Parkwood Leisure Ltd*' (2014) 10 *European Review of Contract Law* 167.

Weatherill S, 'Justification, Proportionality and Consumer Protection' in Koutrakos P, Shuibhne N and Syrpis P (eds), *Exceptions from EU Free Movement Law* (Oxford, Hart Publishing, 2016) 240–64.
Weatherill S, *Law and Values in the European Union* (Oxford, OUP, 2016).
Weatherill S, *Principles and Practice in EU Sports Law* (Oxford, OUP, 2017).
Weatherill S, *The Internal Market as a Legal Concept* (Oxford, OUP, 2017).
Weatherill S, 'Did Cassis de Dijon Make a Difference?' in Albors-Llorens A, Barnard C and Leucht B (eds), *Cassis de Dijon: 40 Years On* (Cambridge, CUP, 2021) 119–38.
Weiler J, 'The Dual Character of Supranationalism' (1981) 1 *Yearbook of European Law* 267.
Weiler J, 'The Court of Justice on Trial – A Review of Hjalte Rasmussen: On Law and Policy in the European Court of Justice' (1987) 24 *CML Rev* 555.
Weiler J, 'The Transformation of Europe' (1991) 100 *Yale Law Journal* 2403.
Wendel M, 'Lisbon before the Courts: Comparative Perspectives' (2011) 7 *European Constitutional Law Review* 96.
Winter JA, 'Direct Applicability and Direct Effect Two Distinct and Different Concepts in Community Law' (1972) 9 *CML Rev* 425.
Wyatt D, 'Subsidiarity: Is It Too Vague to Be Effective as a Legal Principle?' in Nicolaidis K and Weatherill S (eds), *Whose Europe? National Models and the Constitution of the European Union* (Oxford, European Studies at Oxford, 2003) 86–97.
Wyatt D, 'Could a "Yellow Card" for National Parliaments Strengthen Judicial as well as Political Policing of Subsidiarity?' (2006) 2 *Croatian Yearbook of European Law and Policy* 1.
Wyatt D, 'Community Competence to Regulate the Internal Market' in Dougan M and Currie S, *Fifty Years of the European Treaties: Looking Back and Thinking Forward* (Oxford, Hart Publishing, 2009) 93–136.
Wyatt D, 'If the Court of Justice Ignores the Principle of Conferral Simply Because It Can, How Do We Fix the Problem?' (14th Jean Monnet Seminar in EU Law, Dubrovnik, 17–23 April 2016).
Wynne HJ and Shaffer HJ, 'The Socioeconomic Impact of Gambling: The Whistler Symposium' (2003) 10 *Journal Gambling Studies* 111.
Yanchev V, 'Between the Hammer and the Hard Place: European Gambling Regulation in the Post-Santa Casa Era' (2012) 23 *European Business Law Review* 213.
Zglinski J, *Europe's Passive Virtues: Deference to National Authorities in EU Free Movement Law* (Oxford, OUP, 2020).
Zibold F, 'Online Gambling in the EU' (*Library Briefing, Library of the European Parliament*, 2013).

INDEX

www.ingramcontent.com/pod-product-compliance
Ingram Content Group UK Ltd.
Pitfield, Milton Keynes, MK11 3LW, UK
UKHW020243290926
15470UKWH00002B/718

9 781509 938995